D1594474

Women and Comedy

# Women and Comedy

*Rewriting the British Theatrical Tradition*

Susan Carlson

*Ann Arbor*
THE UNIVERSITY OF MICHIGAN PRESS

Library of Congress Cataloging-in-Publication Data

Carlson, Susan.
    Women and comedy : rewriting the British theatrical tradition /
Susan Carlson.
        p.      cm.
    Includes bibliographical references (p.   ) and index.
    ISBN 0–472–10187–0 (cloth : alk.)
    1. English drama (Comedy)—History and criticism.    2. Women and
literature—Great Britain.    I. Title.
    PR635.W6C37   1991
    822'.052309352042—dc20                                    90–26640
                                                                   CIP

*for Michael*

# Acknowledgments

In the writing of this book, I have had the support and encouragement of several communities, both here and abroad. Without all of them, *Women and Comedy* would not have been realized.

Many professional colleagues have been instrumental in my completion of this long-term project. Mary DeShazer accompanied me to both theatrical productions and conferences in my pursuit of comedy; over an Italian meal in Glasgow she gave me the inspiration for the organization of the book. Jenny Spencer shares my passion for the contemporary British theater, and to her I am thankful for both theatrical companionship and energetic, enlightening discussions. To Miriam Gilbert I am indebted not only for the theatrical occasions we shared, but also for her gracious hospitality in Stratford-upon-Avon and her scholarly assistance. With Barbara Hodgdon I have engaged in many detailed discussions of contemporary production; I am also grateful for her reading of several portions of the manuscript. She provides me with a model from which I am always learning. Jane Smiley has surrounded me with creative ideas: her energies and conversations provide me with a new way of looking at things. I thank Faye Whitaker for accompanying me through some difficult critical ground. And at several points in my theoretical investigation, Anita Helle has provided invaluable direction. All of these women have helped me understand the strengths and weaknesses of my research. In addition, I thank Elin Diamond, Lee Poague, and Rosanne Potter for their comments on portions of the manuscript. Finally, I found the detailed comments from Janelle Reinelt and Helene Keyssor, University of Michigan Press reviewers, full of insight and guidance. LeAnn Fields of the University of Michigan Press has been both patient and enthusiastic; I am thankful to her both for reasonable deadlines and for unwavering support.

My study of the contemporary theater would not have been possible without the generosity of the many people I interviewed during my 1986 residence in London. My thanks to Sandy Bailey, Jane Boston, Colin Chambers, Jane Dawson, Sue Dunderdale, Nell Dunn, Pam Gems, Catherine Hayes, Carole Hayman, Ann Jellicoe, Debby Klein, Bryony Lavery, Deborah Levy, Sue Long, Hazel Maycock, Jacqui Neave, Katina Noble, Louise Page, Philip Palmer, Karen Parker, Sue Parrish, Mary Remnant, Sue Townsend, Michelene Wandor, and

Timberlake Wertenbaker. These theater practitioners made time for me in their busy lives, and I am grateful that they have allowed me to share their observations on the contemporary stage. I owe a special thanks to Lou Wakefield, Lyn Gardner, Jude Alderson, and Julia Pascal, each of whom shared her expertise, time, and hospitality with me on several occasions. Juliet Stevenson could not meet with me, but has responded warmly to my letters. For my comfortable and affordable accommodations during my months in London, I also extend my appreciation to the staff of the William Goodenough House, and especially Warden J. C. Morrogh. I found expert assistance from the librarians at the British Theatre Association Library. In addition, I am grateful to Connie Johnson and Douglas Carlson for their efforts to secure research materials for me.

Several segments of this book have appeared in other publications. I am grateful to the following publishers and editors for their support of my work as well as their permission to reprint. An abbreviated version of chapter 1 appeared as "Women in Comedy: Problem, Promise, Paradox," in *Themes in Drama*, vol. 7, published by Cambridge University Press, 1985. A version of chapter 2 appeared in *Essays in Literature*, published by Western Illinois University, 1987. A segment of chapter 7 appeared in *New Theatre Quarterly*, published by Cambridge University Press, 1987. An early version of chapter 10 appeared in *Journal of Dramatic Theory and Criticism*, published by the University of Kansas, 1989. Portions of chapter 11 appeared in *Theatre Research International*, published by Oxford University Press, 1988.

I am thankful to The Society of Authors on behalf of the Bernard Shaw Estate for permission to quote from Bernard Shaw's *The Philanderer;* to AP Watt Limited on behalf of the Royal Literary Fund for permission to quote from Somerset Maugham's *The Constant Wife;* to Methuen London for permission to quote from *Masterpieces,* © 1984 by Sarah Daniels, and *Byrthrite,* © 1987 by Sarah Daniels; and to Faber and Faber Ltd. for permission to quote from Alan Ayckbourn's *Woman in Mind,* © 1986 by Redburn Productions (Overseas) Ltd. Sections of Congreve's play are reprinted from *The Way of the World* by William Congreve, edited by Kathleen Lynch, by permission of the University of Nebraska Press, © 1965 by the University of Nebraska Press.

My community here at home in Ames has provided me with the foundation for my work. To Iowa State University, the College of Liberal Arts and Sciences, the Graduate College, the Department of English, and my chair, Frank Haggard, I am indebted for support and acknowledgment. My months in London were made possible by a generous faculty improvement leave from Iowa State; the university, college, and department have offered me continual support for my writing and research. The English Department women's reading group has proved a comfortable environment for exploring feminist ideas. I have had careful typing and proofing from Linda Verrips and Norma Michalski, and timely assistance from Carol Palmquist and Sheryl Kamps. I owe Linda Boyle great and special thanks for her loving care of my two small sons. And for Michael Mendelson, my husband, I reserve my greatest debt and most loving thanks. He has offered me unflagging encouragement and has helped me eke out invaluable work time. His several readings of the manuscript and his meticulous editing have helped me sharpen my argument and negotiate its nuances.

This book owes its existence to my professional community, my London community, my publishing community, and my Ames community. All errors, omissions, and mistakes remain mine. While I dedicate this book to my most loyal fan, I offer it to all of those who have helped me. I hope that in it they will find the joy they have helped me reconstruct.

# Contents

# Introduction

I'm not a cheerful person, Marlene. I just laugh a lot.
— Nijo, in Caryl Churchill's *Top Girls* (8)

In Olwen Wymark's *Best Friends* (1981), comedy is a means both to limit and to liberate women. On the one hand, comedy offers Baba, the play's main character, an independence that is illusive. Baba rejects traditional female behavior, but her unorthodoxy is allowed because it can be contained. By making her departures from convention comic, those around her limit her freedom. Baba explains: "If I got serious about anything then it had to be funny. Barbara and her laughable little hobby. Women are supposed to be serious about the housekeeping and the cooking and scrubbing out the toilet!" (15). On the other hand, comedy is also used *by* Baba and her best friend Nelly to create an environment they regulate. When the two women share intimate thoughts, they seal the moment "convulsed" with laughter (18). The laughter that the women themselves control signals the strength of their friendship as well as their command of the moment. As Baba's experience indicates, comedy can be used against women to restrict behavior as well as by women to express their triumphs. These contradictory connections between women and comedy are the subject of my book.

My study of women in British stage comedy has brought me to a divided conclusion. I began my investigations—as I begin this book—by analyzing the treacherous freedom women characters find in comedy: i.e., I began by detailing the limitations that routinely circumscribe the power of women in the genre. Yet as I moved from the comic tradition to the study of contemporary British comedy and women playwrights, I discovered that when women write drama, comedy is one of their primary vehicles for expressing triumph. Paradoxically, then, I have found, like Baba, that comedy is for women both an alluring encumbrance and a regenerative force. In studying both the problems and the possibilities comedy offers women, my overriding concern has been to examine the way in which comic drama discourages, accommodates, and/or promotes change.

Part 1 of this book, "Women *in* Comedy," is about the tradition of British stage comedy from Shakespeare's time to the present. It is about male writers (mostly) and the women characters who have been central to these comedies. As a whole, part 1 is a warning that comedy has not been as good to its women as the critical community has been accustomed to thinking. While it is true that the women characters of British comedy have amassed a freedom, grace, and power unmatched in other dramatic genres, there are limits to the magnitude and beneficence of the women's presence. There is much to praise in the portraiture of Shakespeare's Rosalind, Congreve's Millamant, Shaw's Julia, and Ayckbourn's Susan. These women have been created with understanding and sensitivity. The approbation for such women must, however, be qualified. For even when comic heroines have been created by women, the result is rarely an easy confluence of women and power.

Chapter 1 introduces the methodologies and issues involved in my study of the British comic tradition in part 1. The approach I outline is fairly simple: I highlight comedy's inversion and its ending—the two generic structures that have had the greatest effect on women—to show how women's liberation in comedy's middle is qualified and women's joy in marriage at comedy's end is forced. My survey of criticism suggests how this focus on inversion and ending offers a new angle from which to study women's role in comedy. To demonstrate the overpowering presence of the two structures for comic women, I then turn to W. S. Maugham's *The Constant Wife*. Both this analysis of Maugham's play and my survey of comic criticism point to focal issues in the study of women and comedy: i.e., the importance of theatrical and social contexts and the possibilities for personal, political, and generic change.

In chapters 2 to 5 I apply the focus on inversion and ending to four comedies representative of the comic genre. Shakespeare's *As You Like It* (chap. 2) attests to the way comic structures allow women the power of language and friendship, though only by limiting both. Congreve's *The Way of the World* (chap. 3) celebrates comedy's strong woman, but with a qualified joy. Millamant fights to maintain her autonomy as she heads always toward a marriage into which she must "dwindle." In *The Philanderer* (chap. 4), Shaw's mocking portrait of unmanly men and unwomanly women concludes with a recognition both of the need for relational reform and the inadequacy of female empowerment in comedy. And in Ayckbourn's *Woman in Mind* (chap. 5), the heroine is crushed in a skewed comedy during which comic inversion and happiness are nightmarishly conveyed as fantasies. Chapters 1 to 5 substantiate my position that for several hundred years, comedy's welcoming of women has been compromised by the genre's structural checks against women's power. The paradoxes of comic treatment of women appear in a more encouraging light in the final chapter of part 1. In chapter 6, as I turn to the work of a seventeenth-century *female* playwright, Aphra Behn, I suggest that while the structural parameters of inversion and ending restrict her women, Behn also incorporates nontraditional actions and attitudes that make her work a prototype for the countertradition of comedy I outline in part 2. Most significant, she makes her Julia a heroine whose sexuality gives her power as a subject.

As a part of my analysis in chapters 2 to 6, I consider recent productions of the plays. For a genre as sensitive to its social context as is comedy, such analysis allows me to balance my discounting of comedy against inventive theatrical attempts to free these plays from their traditional restrictions. A 1985 production of *As You Like It*, for example, highlighted the play's enduring status quo by requiring certain actors to draw attention to their doubled roles: Dukes Senior and Frederick were played by one man and other actors likewise played attendants to both Dukes. Such staging increased awareness of the pervasive and unchanging institutional factors working against the heroine Rosalind, although the audience's awareness of the doubling could not, ultimately, enhance her power. A 1984 production of Behn's *The Lucky Chance* likewise cautioned that conclusions about a play's traditional comic structure must be relative. The production announced its feminism in the expanded use of the heroine's bed as a soapbox; and this staging device transformed the character's call for women's rights into a manifesto with a distinctly contemporary ring. While in the main my study in part 1 is focused on a textual analysis of dramatic structure, my attention to production is part of a flexible approach that any critic must bring to the dynamics of theatrical study. I am not claiming that the structure of comedy is monolithic or entirely predictable; and through consideration of contemporary production I have pointed to the ways in which the genre absorbs and reflects various ages and ideologies. Comedy has changed from century to century as it still changes from production to production; however, women's place as characters in comedy has remained notably consistent. Part 1 is about the nuances within this consistency.

The transition from part 1, "Women *in* Comedy," to part 2, "Women *Writing* Comedy," is an abrupt one. Yet I see the two halves of the book as complements, both in their methodologies and in their conclusions. Part 1 is a study of a generic tradition; the contours of this tradition are generally familiar to critics. My feminist reading of individual plays brings such familiarity into question, however, by posing questions feminist critics have brought to canonical works for some time: How is the status quo inscribed? In what ways are women contained and empowered? What is the relationship of the literary ending to the society it reflects? In pursuing such questions, I have necessarily studied how linguistic, social, and ideological systems have pressured the genre and its characters. For example, in chapter 2 I note that while language is the primary index of Rosalind's power, its control is never truly in her grasp. Of both Congreve's and Ayckbourn's heroines, I point out that their desires for autonomous selves are thwarted; their subjectivity is fractured by both literary and social forces. In sum, in part 1 I extend the critical debate about comedy with a textual analysis broad enough to acknowledge how its contained women bear the pressure of linguistic, theatrical, and social contexts. While part 2 is also a study of genre, its subject is a comedy in flux. Consequently, both my methodologies and conclusions change radically. In this second part, I focus on contemporary women playwrights and their revision of comic structure, character, and production. The result of their efforts is a genre still most profitably analyzed as the product of its environment. It is a comedy made possible by radical politics and inhibited by conservative ones; it is a comedy projecting whole women and often producing tentative selves; it is a comedy born in alternative theater but maturing in a range of theatrical venues; it is a comedy valorizing women though not always protecting them; it is a comedy idealizing women's community but still learning to integrate its participants effectively; and, most important, it is a comedy relentlessly pointed toward joy. My study in part 2 combines a look at texts—their structures, their characters, and their ideas—with a study of the complex world, theatrical and otherwise, molding those texts.

The six chapters of part 2 demonstrate how in the hands of contemporary women writers, comedy is an exploration of women characters and of fundamental social change. Both are long-standing subjects in comedy. Yet women writers have endowed their comic women with a power that comedy has traditionally counteracted, and as a result the women superintend increased possibilities for change. Traditional comedy remains recognizable in many of the plays women are currently writing. There are, for example, reversals of fortune and happy endings. There are many other plays, however, that accommodate comedy's good feelings in unconventional, unrecognizable ways. Chapters 7 through 12 offer a schema for understanding and identifying the connections between these newer plays and a long comic tradition.

Chapter 7 is a companion to chapter 1; it introduces part 2 and its methodological braiding of several approaches to theater by supplying information about women's engagement in fringe theater, by differentiating portraits of male and female comedians on the contemporary stage, and by reviewing feminist critical appraisals of women and comedy. Chapters 8 and 9 complete the scrutiny of comic structures begun in part 1 as I outline—through a sampling of the diverse architecture of women's plays—the playwrights' departures from traditional inversion and ending. Suggesting that the anarchy of Greek Old Comedy offers contemporary playwrights a precedent for their diverse, wide-ranging texturing of comedy, I detail new patterns in action and character, departures from realism, frequent casting against gender and number, and the incorporation of music and cabaret. I conclude, as chapter 9 ends, that novel strategies of narration, character, and performance have enabled women to generate comic endings that celebrate transformation and change. In chapters 10 and 11, my analysis of women-authored comedy narrows to two key components of comedy—sex and community. Chapter 10 draws on recent feminist rereadings of psychoanalytic thinking to argue that women's comedy reflects complicated and often difficult connections of self and sexuality. In practice, women playwrights are finding issues of subjectivity complicated by the institutionalization of gender, sex, and language. As women are rewriting comedy's foundation in sex, so too are they revamping its reliance on community. In my study of community in women's contemporary theater (chap. 11), I note how both on the fringe and in more established venues women are coming together in unprecedented ways, producing—simultaneously—camaraderie and division. I close, in chapter 12, with a consideration of several extratextual dimensions of women's comedy: I consider women playwrights' restructuring of the audience; the gender-sensitive reviewing of women's plays; and the mixed feelings with which women in theater look to their future. As a whole, part 2 of *Women and Comedy* demonstrates that contemporary comedy is not as recalcitrant for women as my part 1 study seems to imply. The comedy that women are now writing is not without its divisions and biases, but it points to a comic tradition revitalized.

This is an exciting time for those of us doing feminist analysis of theater and drama. Early waves of feminist criticism paid little attention to theater, in large part because the involvement of women in theater has been—until very recently—compromised. Before the last half of this century, there has been but a scattering of women playwrights and directors; and the many women who have contributed to theater through their acting have struggled to transcend their objectification. All of that is changing, however; women have begun writing dramas and assuming other leadership roles in theater organizations. At the same time, the last decade has given rise to increasingly sophisticated critical methods for bringing together feminist critical frameworks with both dramatic texts and theatrical production. Michelene Wandor is almost single-handedly responsible for chronicling the history of contemporary British theater by women; her contextual study of the sexual politics of theater has offered me a model for my own *(Carry On)*. Wandor's focus on the British theater is complemented by the work of several American theater critics who have been studying British, American, and continental theater. Sue-Ellen Case, Elin Diamond, Jill Dolan, Jeanie Forte, Helen Keyssar, and Janelle Reinelt have been the key players in shaping feminist approaches to theater. My study is informed and shaped by the evolving practices of this feminist criticism, a criticism of necessity plural, drawing on several ideological systems for various needs.

In brief, I join the feminist critical investigation of theater by studying comedy as a literary construct. Comic dramas are the products of literary, ideological, and social systems, products that change with the age and the theatrical production. In studying the comic tradition in part 1, one of my primary goals is to show how the seemingly free and autonomous comic heroine is, in fact, both constrained by comic structures and fractured by social and cultural processes encoded in the plays. Traditional attitudes to comedy have, in fact, presumed a subjectivity the genre itself makes impossible. In my study of the contemporary theater in part 2, this attention to the various forces that shape drama leads to still broader concerns. Through my use of interviews, reviews, and my own viewing of productions, I have been able to demonstrate how the female self in comedy can be a construct women control; how the exigencies of production can be manipulated to women's benefit; and how the genre of comedy can provide women with workable patterns of change and growth, however relative they may be.

I have restricted this study in two ways. First, I have taken only British drama as my arena. While many of my conclusions would be applicable to the drama and theater of other cultures, the specific power of the argument derives from the development of an artistic tradition rooted in its culture. American drama, especially, shares much with British drama, but its lack of a lengthy textual tradition and its different financial and cultural components set it apart. Second, I have not taken humor as my subject. There has been and continues to be significant work on the relationship between women and humor, most recently in Nancy Walker's *A Very Serious Thing*. I will discuss humor briefly in chapter 9 when I consider the conflation that now often brings women's cabaret and women's theater together, but in the main my study concerns scripted stage comedy.

When I began thinking about this project seven years ago, I set out to show that comedy written by women is different because women are different. But like many other feminists, I have learned that far too much intervenes between selves and society to base a critique of the status quo only on the basis of sex. Thus I offer this study of women and comedy because feminists engaged in the critical task need to understand how the genre has influenced both male and female writers and because only such knowledge can enable broader discussion of the connections between literature and social change. It offers me great hope to have found that as the world changes, so too can comedy.

I began this introduction with a quotation from Caryl Churchill's character Nijo; in her oxymoronic comment, Nijo epitomizes the complicated relationship women have had with comedy. Let me conclude by responding to a comment from my interview with playwright Sue Townsend. In looking for a way to describe the centrality of comedy to women and to the world at large, she finds that comedy is no less than a basic need of the human body, like the need for food and shelter. I share this vision, which sees comedy as a fundamental human response to a

changing, stressful environment. In the chapters that follow, I have de-
lineated the special hopes and despairs that women can find or may
express in comedy.

*Part 1*

# Women *in* Comedy

*Chapter 1*

# Women in British Comedy:
# The Limits of Freedom

Contrary to received critical opinion, comic heroines in the tradition of British theater have almost never been awarded unqualified freedom and power. From Shakespeare's Portia to Shaw's Barbara to Stoppard's Annie, the women of British comedy have exercised their wit and wisdom while checked by comedy's institutionalized limitations on their autonomy: sexual objectification, isolation, and marriage. These controls on the freedom of women characters are, in fact, as traditional in British comedy as the much fabled freedom of comedy itself. This study is about both the limitations on and the possibilities for women in British comedy. Many before me have paused over the intriguing vibrations between the words *gender* and *genre,* one against the other. As I join them to demonstrate the ambiguous and mutable relationship between comedy and women, I will outline the way comedy and its women depend on one another. Ultimately I will suggest how comedy has and has not changed to accommodate its women.

The long and rich tradition of studying comedy has been a labyrinthine search for definitions. Three of the most recent studies of the genre by Harry Levin, Alice Rayner, and Scott Shershow provide abundant evidence that comedy continues to be analyzed in a critical tradition that has come to highlight paradox and contradiction. As Shershow puts it, comedy is the "slippery" eel of literary definition (*Laughing Matters,* 3). While such intensive study has brought criticism of comedy to a high level of sophistication, women's connection to comedy has been studied all too rarely. In the twelve chapters of this book, I will study two primary connections between the genre and the gender in British literature by turning both to women characters in comedy and to women

comic playwrights. Paradox is inescapable even in my study, however;
for the limits on women in traditional comedy can indeed help to explain
the success of the women playwrights now revitalizing the genre. This
chapter provides a critical foundation for my two-pronged analysis in
the five chapters to follow. After reviewing the inadequate treatment of
women in comic theory, I will propose a concentrated study of comic
inversion and comic ending as a methodology for more appropriately
understanding women's connections to comedy. I turn then to an extended analysis of such structural qualities in W. S. Maugham's comedy
*The Constant Wife*. The play serves as a representative example of the
tensions under which women and comedy come together. I conclude the
chapter by broadening the investigation in two ways: first, by stressing
the importance of context in a study of comedy; second, by introducing
the possibilities of change for comedy and its women.

## The Critical Tradition

Women have played two oppositional roles in the developments of
comic theory. As comedy itself both valorizes and degrades women, so
has comic criticism exalted women on the one hand and ignored them
on the other. Both the exaltation and the avoidance are equally invidious
contributors to the confusion that continues to surround discussion of
women in comedy.

George Meredith's proclamation that comedy depends on and promotes sexual equality has been responsible for over one hundred years
of criticism that insists, with Meredith, that "the comic muse is one of
their [cultivated women's] best friends" ("Essay on Comedy," 32). Perhaps because of the tempting half-truth of this aphorism, Meredith's
chivalrous compliment to comedy has rarely been challenged. On the
contrary, his assertion that comedy can be equated with sexual equality
has inspired others. John Palmer made the praise of Restoration comic
heroines fashionable in 1913, and some of the best Restoration studies
to follow his—Norman Holland's, Thomas Fujimura's, and Virginia
Birdsall's—have offered an itemized accounting of Restoration heroines
and their power. Not surprisingly, the greatest attention to the comic
heroine has been lavished on Shakespeare's women. In the tradition of
H. B. Charlton, such critics as Linda Bamber, Ruth Nevo, and Marilyn
French have proclaimed Shakespeare's heroines the crowning achievement of his comedies. It has become so reflexive for critics and theorists

to equate comedy and women that in recent studies of comedy by Robert Heilman, George McFadden, and Harry Levin the authors consider it sufficient merely to pause over the presence of women in comedy. Even in the age of feminism, critics have appropriated Meredith's conclusion that for women comedy means power. Robert Polhemus has recently concluded that "in the culture of male supremacy, comedy, relatively speaking, has a built-in feminist bias" (*Comic Faith*, 19). He is joined by feminist critics who have also marked comedy as valuable territory for the empowering of women characters. Regina Barreca, in her important collection of essays on women and comedy, *Last Laughs*, collects several analyses of the power that accrues to women experiencing and writing comedy. I will turn in part 2 to the feminist criticism that takes issue with this connection of comedy and female power, but here I want to note that the few nonfeminist critics who have rejected Meredith's idea of sexual equality—Ian Donaldson (*World Upside-Down*, 10–14) and Allardyce Nicoll (*Theory of Drama*, 288) in particular—are guided more by oversight than insight.

This Meredithian elevation of women in comedy, while broadly influential, has been less powerful than the critical tendency to avoid the issue either fully or partially. Northrop Frye, whose contribution to comic definition cannot be overrated, locates the issue of women's place in comedy outside the comic realm by redefining strong women as the province of romance (*Anatomy*, 173). Maurice Charney appears to confront the issue, but as he attempts to explain how comedy can both offer women a clandestine power and then rob them of it, he gets tangled up in linguistic knots. He concludes of women in comedy, "On the question of women in comedy, we have to face the fact that social ends and comic endings may not coincide. Comedy is not, after all, social propaganda, *and* the women are consistently wittier and more intelligent than the men, especially in the domain of love and sex" (*Comedy High and Low*, 91, my emphasis). Charney's connective "and" is tellingly lame: he uses it to link two nearly opposite conclusions. Levin's more recent study provides further evidence that in a world now fully attuned to women's issues, the critical stance on women and comedy has not changed in substantive ways. Levin, like Charney, directly addresses the issue of women and comedy several times in *Playboys and Killjoys*. But he avoids conclusions about their treatment in the genre. The reticence that marks Charney's and Levin's studies is even more intense in the work of other comic theorists—for instance, Henri Bergson ("Laughter"), Walter Kerr

(*Tragedy and Comedy*), Eric Bentley (*The Life of the Drama*), J. L. Styan (*Dark Comedy*), and Wylie Sypher (*Comedy*)—who fail to identify women as an issue in comedy.

The silence of such writers is problematic, but the more distressing attitude to women in comedy comes from critics who consciously choose to ignore the comic heroine. William McCollom, for example, notes of the comic hero that "'he' is more often a woman than a man" (*Divine Average*, 82); and after making this proclamation, McCollom never again refers to one of those women. Also studying the comic hero, Robert Torrance justifies the exclusion of women from his book by explaining that while the future most certainly will produce strong comic heroines, those of the past can be devalued because of their anemic behavior: "Only in desperate renunciation or bittersweet retrospect could a rare Lysistrata or Wife of Bath flout the standards of conduct prescribed for her sex with some degree of impunity; most comic hero-ines were constrained, like those of Shakespeare, to adopt gentler forms of remonstrance within clearly acceptable limits" *(Comic Hero, ix)*. When Torrance later turns to *As You Like It,* he is then forced to conclude that the play has no hero (112–14).[1] The particular responses of Frye, Char-ney, Levin, McCollom, and Torrance are representative of the minor presence women characters have been accorded in comic criticism.

The co-existence of these two contradictory readings of women in comedy is explained in part by the larger context of comic theory. In describing the relationship between comedy and society, comic theory vacillates between two extremes. On the one hand, theorists highlight the opportunity comedy offers, through its inversions and social criti-cisms, for new, changing, even revolutionary roles. Rayner describes the possibilities for revolution fairly moderately:

> The deeper subversiveness of comedy, and perhaps of art forms in general, is that they open new possibilities for thought and behav-ior—they create an apparently new space for thought by rupturing the "fabric of the mind." . . . The danger of a new thought or a new form is that it does change the world: it adds to the vocabulary of potential that then redefines the actual. (*Comic Persuasion,* 114)

James Feibelman accelerates the claim for revolution, insisting that change is a direct effect of comedy: "For comedy, and consequently the role of the comedian, is essential to change; it can on occasion render

services to the forces of reaction by ridiculing the novel aspects of anything new and valuable, yet it is indispensable to progress" (*In Praise of
Comedy*, 269).[2] On the other hand, critics emphasize the temporary
nature of comedy's misrule and document how such inversion readies
an audience both for comedy's happy ending and its affirmation of the
status quo. Albert Cook states the case for comedy's conservatism most
bluntly: "But basically comedy is approval, not disapproval, of present
society; it is conservative, not liberal" (*Dark Voyage*, 49). A. N. Kaul
echoes this predictability, concluding that comedy "is not interested in
social conflict, in the necessity or even the possibility of social change"
(*Action of English Comedy*, 22). While they favor one critical extreme or
the other, the majority of theorists negotiate the middle ground, claiming for comedy both revolutionary and reactionary tendencies. Northrop
Frye, for example, has recently concluded that comedy is driven by the
tension between these two social possibilities.[3]

I do not assume that all of those who have lauded the place of
women in comedy believe in comedy's powers to change or that those
avoiding or ignoring comedy's women think of comedy as conservative.
There is a connection, however, between the two levels of contradiction
in comic theory. Clearly, comedy presents the theorist with tendencies
that defy unification. And just as clearly, this unresolvable tension leaves
the theorist with a series of choices to make about the issues on which
to focus. Consequently, in the face of the elusiveness of comedy itself,
critics have consistently made the choices that discount the women of
the genre. Both the critics who applaud comedy's women and those who
look past them rarely, if ever, have studied the connections between the
women and the assumptions by which critics define comedy.

## Extending the Critical Tradition

It is theoretically inadequate to accept either the simple praise or the
studious avoidance of an issue as central to a comprehensive criticism as
is the role of women in comedy. In extending the critical discussion
summarized above, I would like to consolidate the bifurcated consideration of comedy's women. In response to those who have found little to
say about comic women, I assert that women do exist, in a major way,
in comedy. But I hasten to add, in response to those who find traditional
comedy a haven for women, that the genre does more to reduce than to
enlarge female power. This second assertion is of primary concern in the

paragraphs to follow, especially in the sections on comic inversion and comic endings.

Before I consider the powerful role of comic inversion and comic endings in the shaping of comedy's women, however, I need to turn briefly to the notion of a comic sensibility that so consistently informs the range of attitudes to comedy. Women's place in the genre is heavily influenced by both comedy's traditional sense of joy and its twentieth-century accommodation of despair.

In spite of the disparity among critics trying to define dramatic comedy, the assumption behind almost every study is that a literary convention called comedy exists.[4] Material conditions influencing authorship, theatrical production, and audience mean, of course, that the identity of the genre will vary with the age and the society. Yet critics persist in identifying the norms of the genre, traditionally by pointing to its sanguine nature. L. J. Potts (*Comedy*) finds comedy "a mode of thought." Meredith ("Essay on Comedy") invents "the Comic Spirit," placing it angelically, unreachably above. And Susanne Langer describes the intangible in more glowing, earthy terms: "Because comedy abstracts, and reincarnates for our perceptions, the motion and rhythm of living, it enhances our vital feeling" ("Comic Rhythm," 124). This celebratory aura informs some comedies more than others; Shakespeare comes to mind but Wycherley does not. Shaw does; Jonson does not. Yet in most of the plays critics discuss as comic, even those of Wycherley and Jonson, the comic essence acts as an insurance that the dangers invoked and studied are temporary. The fact that an audience (rightly) assumes a comic ending is coming allows it to relax in these good feelings. Helen Gardner, lobbying for the retention of a belief in the happy ending even in a troubled, late twentieth-century world, sums up the persistent human (and critical) desire for comic joy:

> I hope the present sourness will not prove me wrong, and that we
> shall not much longer continue to doubt the possibility of happiness,
> and regard the absurd as cause for a metaphysical shudder rather
> than as an occasion for laughter. ("Happy Endings," 51)

The identification of comedy primarily by this sense of well-being, by the assurance that difficulties can be surmounted, is the foundation of traditional accounts of the genre.

Yet in this century, Gardner's optimism has come to represent a minority view of comedy. Playwrights and critics alike now join one another in despair at finding hope, joy, and happiness in a fragmented, polluted world, soiled by human atrocities like the Nazi death camps and swayed by fear of nuclear destruction. The despondency that has colored comic theory in the last eighty years has intensified in the recent work of critics like Wolfgang Iser, Herbert Blau, and Mathew Winston. Making Beckett his standard of contemporary comedy, Iser reads the comic process as the decomposing of the individual ("Art of Failure," 142). Similarly, Blau finds that what remains of comedy is no more than a self-conscious disintegration; "the laugh laughing at the laugh" ("Comedy since the Absurd," 561). And Winston concurs that "contemporary comedy posits no fixity to existence and no core to human identity" ("Incoherent Self," 388–89); he erases the sanguine world claimed by so many comic writers in announcing that there is no self, no joy, no norms in the "comedy" of a "disjunctive and chaotic world" (399). For the women in comedy, either extreme of definition—comedy as the celebration of joy or as the expression of metaphysical disintegration—means limitations. When comedy points to joyousness, women must marry; when comedy represents chaos, women rarely appear. In chapter 12, I will return to this comic tangle of joy and despair to outline some of the different directions male- and female-authored plays have taken in pursuit of what comedy may be. I will argue that, drawing on different backgrounds and traditions, women playwrights in this century have retained much of comedy's joy while many male writers have lost it.

Within a literary structure that can be seen to accommodate a quality called "comic" in such radically different ways, the treatment of women has been surprisingly consistent. In the vast range of dramatic comedy, which includes satire, romance, comedy of manners, farce, and festival, women do not always appear or take on substantial roles. But in the comic plays populated by women, two features proscribe what comedy's women can be: a basic inversion and a generally happy ending. To understand these two aspects of comic structure is to understand the limitations of comic women. Women are allowed their brilliance, freedom, and power in comedy only because the genre has built-in safeguards against such behavior.

In most comedies, the status quo is disrupted, and in the upheaval of role reversals the women characters acquire an uncharacteristic dominance. Women in power, or a group of women in power, are funny because they are so out of the ordinary. An audience is invited to accept and consider the novelty cushioned by the distancing techniques of comic convention. To make his strong women believable, for example, Shakespeare sends them and their men off to worlds of near fantasy. (When he does not turn to other worlds, as in *All's Well That Ends Well*, his strong woman is suddenly problematic.) Shaw invites an audience to respond to comic role reversals from the safe distance of near farce, and Maugham, following the precedent set by the manners playwrights before him, fashions a fragile, rarefied social atmosphere where women can rule. When women gain power in comedy, the world is somehow extraordinary. Edith Kern decisively notes the obligatory link between fantasy and women's rule in what she calls the "absolute comic":

> Their [women's] triumph is fleeting and nonmimetic. It is the fantasy triumph of the meek and powerless over those in authority. The morality prevailing in these tales and farces is that of the oppressed, not the rulers, and their liberating laughter belongs to the realm of the imaginary. (*Absolute Comic*, 43)

Several feminist critics have noted this connection of comic women to the unorthodox middle of comedy.[5]

The power accorded to women in comedy's inversion has undeniably explosive possibilities. However, the power is, as Kern and others hint, conditioned in complicated ways that are best explained in the work of Mikhail Bakhtin, Natalie Davis, and Victor Turner. To provide a framework for his study of Rabelais, Bakhtin studies the revolutionary potential of medieval and Renaissance carnival, noting that on such occasions ordinary people were offered access to "the utopian realm of community, freedom, equality, and abundance" (*Rabelais*, 9). Such liberation from the ordinary, he adds, exists in a perpetual tension with the established order. Thus, for Bakhtin, a basic "ambivalence" defines the nature of carnival humor and rebellion, making carnival at once revolutionary and reactionary (12). Michael Bristol (*Carnival and Theatre*) extends Bakhtin's concept by identifying this tension between the reinforcement of order and the rebellion against it in British Renaissance theater. Joining several new historicist critics of Renaissance drama, he finds the theater an unstable literary site, ripe for the disorderly possibilities of Bakhtin's carnival. Bristol echoes Bakhtin in finding the Renaissance theater, ultimately, a place where rebellion can always be appropriated; yet as Bristol highlights the phenomenal, temporal nature of the theater, he privileges carnival's revolutionary tendencies. Neither Bakhtin nor Bristol connects his study to the specific liberation women gain in carnival and in the reversals of comedy. Both Mary Russo ("Female Grotesques") and Wayne Booth ("Freedom of Interpretation") do forge such connections, each drawing on Bakhtin's valorization of carnival's grotesque body to comment specifically on comedy's obsession with women's bodies. What they implicitly conclude in bringing the triad of Bakhtin, comedy, and women together I would like to make explicit: Women in comedy are granted freedom of expression, command over selves and others, and corporality, but such expansion of traditional female roles is *part of* the same system that represses such conditions in normal times. While Bakhtin, Bristol, Booth, and Russo all acknowledge the great potential in an inverted order, they see carnival liberation as a part of the status quo.

In the broader social context that Natalie Davis and Victor Turner have explored, inversion has similarly been found to be qualified. Using literary in addition to historical examples, Davis (*Society and Culture*) provides a powerful compendium of "women on top" in her study of early modern France. In this survey of women in power, she acknowledges that such inversions of the status quo usually affirmed that status quo in some major way. Yet she persists in her opinion that moments of inversion, especially literary ones, were potent models for real women (131). She concludes, for example, that literary tales of women who changed roles or took on disguises could, in a limited way, serve as models for real women:

> By showing the good that could be done by the woman out of her place, they [literary tales of exceptional women] had the potential to inspire a few females to exceptional action and feminists to reflection about the capacities of women (we will see later whether the potential was realized), but they are unlikely symbols for moving masses of people to resistance. (133)

She would concur with Russo that some limited potential for women lies in the alternative worlds created in both literature and carnival.

Like other scholars troubling over the ramifications of inversion in both literary and social structures, anthropologist Victor Turner finds a tension between cultural reinforcement and systemic challenge. His work is the most compelling analysis of inversion as it involves theater.

What I am positing as the basic movement of a comic drama—a journey from established order through an inverted, upside-down world and back to the status quo—is paralleled by the basic movements Turner has identified as the "social dramas" of cultural ritual. Studying both primitive and advanced cultures, Turner has described two kinds of inversion in which he can, at least partially, separate the revolutionary and the reactionary potentials of inversion. Drawing from the work of Arnold van Gennep, Turner uses "liminal" to describe ritual movements of inversion-induced release that do not threaten the cultural order and that are ultimately reinforcements of the status quo. He uses "liminoid" to label moments of release during which the inversions that occur may actually threaten the system. The appropriateness of the labels "liminal" and "liminoid" for dramatic events, he contends, depends on a culture's complexity, with the more complex society offering more possibilities for the more disruptive liminoid *(From Ritual)*. In his writing, Turner displays a predilection for theatrical metaphors, but more important, he has also directly considered the "ritual" of theater. He finds that the stage, in fact, is a significant location for potent inversion (*From Ritual*, 18). The "heat of performance," he argues, contributes to the power of inversion and allows for "new paradigms and models which invert or subvert the old" (*Process*, 101). In its complexity, Turner's work suggests that the revolutionary and the reactionary strains of inversion, even theatrical inversion, are determined by context. With his concept of the liminal, he acknowledges the limitations of reversal; with his concept of the liminoid, he provides an explosive alternative. Taken together, the two concepts provide a theoretical path for arguing that while the inversion of traditional comic structures *could* be revolutionary, it will not necessarily become so. Only inversions of a very particular kind, in a particular environment, can result in modification of the status quo. Turner offers, then, a conceptualization of ritual structure that provides for both the reality *and* the rarity of change.[6]

My conclusion about what happens to women in the reversals of comedy parallels the qualifications offered by Bakhtin, Davis, Turner, and others. Like many feminists, I am attracted to the possibilities for women that comedy alone offers; and I will argue in part 2 that these possibilities are magnified in the work of women playwrights. Yet I find the tradition of British comedy consistent in imposing limitations on the liberty it allows. In other words, comedy has divided loyalties to the disenfranchised in general and to women in particular.

As powerful as inversion is in the shaping of women characters in comedy, comedy's ending has still greater impact. And as inversion works as part of comedy's extensive network of paradox, so too has the happy ending been both a boost and a boon for women. However, it seems far more certain with comic endings than with comic reversals that comedy's women are systematically disadvantaged. While women's dominance in the genre is temporary, their final positions are meant to reverberate far into the future. Almost every critic attending to the women of comedy and their ebullient power has downplayed the connection between women's comic reign and the resolutions that follow. Yet when comedy ends, the role reversals are *reversed,* the misrule is curtailed, and any social rebellion is tempered by the good feelings presumably attached to the reestablishment of order. For comedy's freewheeling women, the ending usually marks their retreat to more conventional activities. In an overwhelming percentage of cases, the comic ending, for women, is marriage. And while marriage has been represented as a happy ending, even the highest reward, the comic heroine usually finds love and happiness only at the price of freedom and power.[7] Comedy is, as Lee Edwards finds, an "insufficient" vehicle for female heroism (*Psyche as Hero,* 102). As I will demonstrate in the next section of this chapter with the example of W. S. Maugham's *The Constant Wife,* many comedies offer internal evidence of the trade-off a heroine makes in moving from comic "liberation" to comic "happiness."

Traditionally, the comic ending has been equated with happiness and joy. Ruth Nevo, for example, finds that the joy of Shakespeare's comic endings allows for a transcendent experience:

> They [Shakespeare's comedies] set out to remedy disorder, tension and deficiency by individual hazard, individual inventiveness and creativity. And so if they are "romantic" it is not only because they deal with lovers, but because they represent a dazzling, if brief, adventure in the discovery and exploration of what is humanly possible. (*Comic Transformations,* 224–25)

She suggests that comedy's paradoxical inclinations can ultimately be softened in the overriding power of its ending. Paeans like Nevo's decorate the criticism of those who laud comedy's revolutionary nature as well as those comforted by its predictability. A eucatastrophe does, in many ways, solve comedy's paradoxes. Even those critics who have made comedy a home for twentieth-century angst locate their despair not in comedy's ending (which they read as especially ironic) but in its arbitrary nature. Yet because most of these writers do not address the place of women in comedy, they have not considered the special burden such endings place on women. The arbitrariness and the predictability of the comic ending work in a demonstrably different way for women than for men. In essence, when a dialogue between the sexes is the subject of comedy (as it almost always is when strong women characters appear), the ending works against women.[8]

Diana Trilling clarifies why, in the traditional comic ending, women always lose. Audiences laugh at the foibles of both women and men in comedy. But, says Trilling, while a comic ending restores men to their power in the social hierarchy, it restores women to powerlessness.

> The defeated hero in literature always remains a commanding figure, deserving of our regard. . . . The defeated heroine is the object of our pity or of our loving ridicule. In being brought down, she is put in her place. ("Liberated Heroine," 506)

As long as men's destiny defines the comic world, this distinction will persist. Nancy Miller explains further why such divisive conclusions have an enormous impact on comic heroines. Writing of eighteenth-century French and English novels, Miller concludes that endings have a disproportionate bearing on all that precedes them: "Endings, however conventional, overdetermine narrative logic, and in this sense might be thought of as a taxonomy of telos" (*The Heroine's Text,* xi). In the genre of comedy, this means that the influence of the comic ending reaches both beyond and before its emphatic final position. For comedy's women, such omnipresence means that their comic power—however potent and extended it appears—can and usually is read as a disorder that will not persist. An audience knows, all along, that women's final role will be, as Trilling suggests, second-class. Thus, to experience the vigorous moments of female comic power is to know, simultaneously, their temporary nature.

Let me anticipate two objections that will be raised against my focus on comedy's conclusion. First, some will rightly note that many comedies do not end with marriage, the promise of marriage, or the resumption of marriage.[9] Some comedies end with feasts, for example, and some with avoided weddings. Some offer a sense of closure through community or a bright mood. Yet those comedies in which women take on a central role almost always move toward an ending in which men and women are joined. Even in Shaw's *Getting Married,* the playlong critique of marriage still leads to marriage.[10] Second, some will argue that a heavy dose of irony tempers the seemingly absolute resolution of much comedy. But irony, while always part of comedy's feast of self-consciousness, does not cancel the comic triumph of marriage. A comedy like *The Beggar's Opera* turns back on itself as it ends, challenging its audience to retain its sense of well-being. My point is that the audience almost always does exactly that. For all Eric Bentley's telling us that "happy endings are always ironical" *(The Life of the Drama,* 301) or Nevo's assurance that irony eclipses sentiment (*Comic Transformations,* 224), those responding to the irony do so in the context of the impending comic ending. As I will show, irony is a favorite weapon of comic heroines, but women are frequently its main target.

Women in comedy, then, are constrained primarily by comedy's inversion and ending. The collective portrait of women in comedy is conditioned by many additional factors: the number of women characters, their age and class, and their language—not to mention factors outside of the play, perhaps the most important of which is the playwright's sex. But even in the comedies most favorable to women, *even in those written by women,* comic structure has an inordinate influence on women characters.

## Maugham's *The Constant Wife*

Comic plays themselves provide the most convincing evidence of the paradoxical and strained connection between women and comedy. In chapters 2, 3, 4, and 5, I will consider some of the most important male British playwrights and their most powerful women to specify both the controlling and controlled presence of women in British comedy. I begin the analysis of texts, however, with a thorough account of W. S. Maugham's *The Constant Wife,* a little-known play that is *extraordinary* since it takes as its subject the *ordinary* role of women in comedy. In this extremely self-conscious play, Maugham takes on the subject matter of all comedy—social codes and manners, stereotypes of women and men, and socially affirmative endings like marriage—and shows how comedy's revolutionary mode is held in check by its reactionary mode. As the main character, Constance Middleton, somewhat jadedly questions her marriage to her husband, John, Maugham questions the marriage of playwrights and comedy. He even poses questions that extend to the current courtship of comedy by women. In particular, Maugham's scrutiny of comic inversion and comic ending makes his play fruitful for my examination of women and comedy. Inversion in *The Constant Wife* is primarily recognizable in the privileged and articulate position of the play's heroine, Constance. The ending of *The Constant Wife* is notably conditioned by the considerations of marriage that are present throughout the play's three acts. As Maugham manipulates these two basics of comic composition in this play, his self-conscious attention to the effect of such structures on women highlights the tensions under which women and comedy come together.

Maugham's early stage comedies—*Lady Frederick, Smith, Penelope,* and *Mrs. Dot*—attest to his facility with comic forms, and especially to his ability to bring comedy's joy to an audience. Although he has been charged with misogyny and some of his plays (especially the farces) corroborate the charges, he does show in these early plays that he understands women's strangely privileged position in comedy. However, his sensitivity to women's social and generic roles is most pronounced in his later comedies—*Our Betters, The Circle,* and *The Constant Wife.* At first glance, *The Constant Wife,* written in 1926, may appear a peculiar candidate for investigation since several aspects of the play's own history might counsel against my use of it in this pivotal position. Openings both in London and the United States, for example, were disasters. The American production recovered from Ethel Barrymore's poor preparation to run for several years in Cleveland, New York, and on the road; but the London production's doom was foretold by poor house management on the opening night. More pertinent to my study, however, are the reviewers, on both sides of the Atlantic, who remarked on the play's "old model" and "old-fashioned, artificial way" (Mander and Mitchenson, *Theatrical Companion to Maugham,* 202–3). Yet the recognizable, if traditional, comic patterns in the play are exactly what make it so appropriate for this study. I am not suggesting that *The Constant Wife* is a great play; I am suggesting that it is, in essence, an exemplar that foregrounds some of the principal connections of women and comedy.

The opening segments of the play provide a study of the four women who surround Constance Middleton, the title's "constant wife." After an opening exchange between Martha and Mrs. Culver (Constance's sister and mother, respectively) affirms a comic mood, the play settles into a typical exposition of comic character and situation. While Martha, Mrs. Culver, and Constance's friend Barbara categorize their acquaintances by type—respectable women, unfaithful husbands, and faithful wives—the playwright introduces three easily identifiable comic types. During the process, the three women are established as additional, familiar female types. To compensate for becoming what she would label an old maid (she is thirty-two and unmarried), Constance's sister Martha has adopted the role of truth seeker. Her abrasive sincerity alternately burdens and overwhelms the others. Barbara, Constance's single friend who owns a decorating business, is the "independent" woman who remains self-effacing enough to acquiesce to social rules and who skillfully dons social masks. With comments like "I hate giving a straight answer to a straight question" (97), she and her pseudo-assertiveness fade comfortably into the background. It is left to Mrs. Culver, Constance's mother, to preserve the social order such types grow out of. So sure of her sex's innate inferiority, she is even ready to do battle for a double standard that protects women from themselves:

> I am unable to attach any great importance to the philanderings of men. I think it's their nature. . . . We ascribe a great deal of merit to ourselves because we're faithful to our husbands. I don't believe we deserve it for a minute. We're naturally faithful creatures and we're faithful because we have no particular inclination to be anything else. (100)

Mrs. Culver is typical of women who defend a male-controlled system at any cost. A fourth woman, Marie-Louise, takes part in the opening all-female council only as its subject. As the beautiful, selfish, flighty, and brainless woman who doubles as Constance's best friend and Constance's husband John's mistress, Marie-Louise is another familiar, laughable type. The main subject of conversation before Constance enters in act 1 is how the three women should respond to Constance's ignorance of her husband's philandering with Marie-Louise. As the women wrangle, Maugham establishes his comic mood. Most important, with his all-female drawing-room world, Maugham establishes comedy's alternative power structure, one run by women. The comedy seems at this point predictable.

Constance is also a type: the comic heroine who has it all. She is intelligent, witty, beautiful, sensitive, buoyant, happily married, comfortably rich, and fit for mothering. From the moment she first appears, she marshalls the play's actions and the other characters' thoughts, always with grace. Shuttling between light repartee and serious thought, she gaily directs act 1. Constance does have her weaknesses, but they only serve to make her human and sympathetic. As the other women have made clear, Constance, for all her insight, remains ignorant of her husband's love affair with Marie-Louise. Thus, the audience is put in the position of worrying about her along with the other women. Constance's refusal to make waves also makes her particularly easy to deal with. This powerful woman is content to fit into her society as expected. She explains, for example, that she married John instead of her more passionate suitor Bernard because, aspiring to be a demure woman, she didn't want a husband she could walk all over (114). She politely but firmly refuses Barbara's offer of employment because of a similarly accepted social role: wives don't embarrass their husbands by undercutting their roles as breadwinners.

Yet Constance is something of a paradox as act 1 ends. As is usual in the inversion of comedy, she has a mastery of social intercourse in a man's world. But she also has a surprising blind spot regarding her husband's affair and an atypical self-effacing accommodation to expected roles. Her ignorance and her accommodation belie the freedom comedy should have and even seems to have conferred on her. This discrepancy is a central part of what makes this comedy extraordinary.

In act 2 a very different Constance appears. Her social acquiescence vanishes along with Maugham's comic complaisance. And both the limits and the cost of Constance's control and charm are revealed. Early in the second act, while the implicit subject is still "what to do about Constance," she continues to flourish in her self-confidence, wishing to spread her contented comic worldview everywhere. Her old lover, Bernard (the one she turned down for John) is back in town to woo her, and her advice to him as to the others is to maintain the healthy distance of a comic perspective:

> Bernard:    *(Good humouredly.)* I have a notion that you're laughing at me.
> Constance:  In the hope of teaching you to laugh at yourself. (131)

Such jolly companionship is, however, short-lived. This second act climaxes when Mortimer Durham, Marie-Louise's cuckolded husband, invades the fragile Middleton drawing room to tell Constance: "I thought you might like to know that your husband is my wife's lover" (139). He has not gained, nor asked for, a private audience, so his abrupt truth is revealed not only to Constance, but also to the others present— the two lovers, John and Marie-Louise; Mrs. Culver; Martha; and Bernard. In Constance's cool, calculated reaction to Mortimer's revelation she reveals that she has known all along about her husband's affair and has *chosen* to ignore it. Her reasons for this feigned ignorance are the crux of the play. They embody Maugham's commentary on women in comedy as well as Constance's own social indictment.

Constance's immediate reaction is to protect the lovers from Mortimer's wrath by lying. She is successful in this as in other orchestrations of social response, and before she sees him safely out of the soiled drawing room she even has him apologizing to his wife. On his departure, Constance's stupified, admiring audience of husband, family, and friends learns that these protective actions have not stemmed from goodwill, but rather complete a months-long deception on her part. She shocks them by revealing that "Mortimer told me nothing I didn't know before" (144). Then, as she settles into her explanation, her unfaltering self-possession seems not only unfeeling, but perverse. The irony is oppressive at this point because, by all rights, John and Marie-Louise, not Constance, should be doing the explaining.

Constance's first subject is marriage; her message is that it is outdated. She rehearses for John the stages of their fifteen-year-old marriage, warmly remembering that it was a union founded on shared love, a love that lasted five years. But for the last ten years the marriage has been comfortably, mutually loveless: "Because we ceased loving one another at the very same moment we never had to put up with quarrels and reproaches," she contends (153). As I outlined above, others have, like Constance, balked at the ideal of marriage as a happy-ever-after. L. J. Potts *(Comedy)*, William Gruber ("Polarization of Tragedy and Comedy"), Francis Cornford *(Attic Comedy)*, and Walter Kerr *(Tragedy and Comedy)* are among those who have specified the way marriage—as comedy's symbol of reconciliation—may be only a by-product of comedy's necessarily arbitrary ending. While Cornford and Gruber attribute arbitrary marriage to the ritual origins of the comic genre, Kerr equates it with an exposure of comedy's supposed joy: "Within comedy there is always despair, a despair of ever finding a right ending except by artifice and magic" *(Tragedy and Comedy, 79)*. Their quarrels are with marriage

as a literary ending. Joining hosts of feminist critics who have identified
the double standard marriage institutionalizes for women, Constance
also exposes marriage as a never-ending process of deceit. Undeniably,
as Constance puts her marriage on the line, she challenges the institution
of marriage and Maugham endangers his chances for a traditional comic
reconciliation.

Having put an end to the notion of marriage as an axiomatic happy
ending, Constance goes on to outline the difficult position her loveless
marriage has left her in. Very simply, a "modern wife" is "a prostitute
who doesn't deliver the goods" (157):

> My dear Bernard, have you ever considered what marriage is
> among well-to-do people? In the working classes a woman cooks
> her husband's dinner, washes for him and darns his socks. She looks
> after the children and makes their clothes. She gives good value for
> the money she costs. But what is a wife in our class? Her house is
> managed by servants, nurses look after her children, if she has re-
> signed herself to having any, and as soon as they are old enough she
> packs them off to school. Let us face it, she is no more than the
> mistress of a man of whose desire she has taken advantage to insist
> on a legal ceremony that will prevent him from discarding her when
> his desire has ceased. (160)

As Maugham has shown in act 1, the comic world is one where people
use masks, games, concessions, and compromise to survive together.
But although the act also encourages its own kind of social criticism as
a ballast, this comedy falters under the direct challenge Constance presents. It falters on at least two levels. First, the characters are discomfitted by Constance's directness. And second, an audience depending
on comic conventions is likewise discomfitted by the rupture in comedy's predictability.

Maugham studies the nervousness brought on by Constance's actions as he shows how those around her keep trying to fit her back into
the act 1 mold they understand and know how to respond to. Throughout Constance's explanations in act 2, the others try to make sense of her
heresy by searching for conventional answers to explain away their discomfort. Sister Martha, for example, wants Constance to play a role
easily understood—that of the outraged wife—by divorcing John to pun-
ish him. Mrs. Culver's response is just as predictable. She expects Con-

stance to be the forgiving, forever accommodating wife who will silently carry her pain for the appropriate length of time before welcoming her husband back to heart and home:

> In my day when a young wife discovered that her husband had been deceiving her, she burst into a flood of tears and went to stay with her mother for three weeks, not returning to her husband till he had been brought to a proper state of abjection and repentance. (154)

John clearly wants Constance to blame him for his indiscretion and make him feel just enough guilt to cleanse him of his sin. Even Bernard offers Constance a recognizable course of revenge by proposing a love affair between them, and he is surprised by her refusal: "I should despise myself entirely if I were unfaithful to John so long as I am entirely dependent on him" (162). The other characters do everything they can to rein Constance back within established social bounds, not so much to save her as to save the only world, the only conventions, they know how to operate in and by. Her insistence on breaking new social ground threatens the well-being of all of them.

Although one would be hard pressed to convince the other characters of this, Constance has behaved as they would wish, for as long as she could. As she explains, she played by the rules until Mortimer's revelation prohibited her from continuing to do so:

> You see, so long as I was able to pretend a blissful ignorance of your goings-on we could all be perfectly happy. You were enjoying yourself and I received a lot of sympathy as the outraged wife. But now I do see that the position is very difficult. You have put me in a position that is neither elegant nor dignified. (156)

In act 1, Constance was a predictable comic heroine. In act 2 she leaves no doubt that she has conformed for all the *wrong* reasons. Constance has played by the rules not because they codify her beliefs, but because without them she has no guidance on how to live her life. She has had to twist those rules to hide behind them, as a mask, and in doing so has—as the others fear—perverted all they stand for.

Constance resembles many other comic heroines, not only in her control, wit, and intelligence, but also in her need to engage in such subversive, indirect, and usually unconscious means of gaining her power. The tradition of the British comedy of manners especially has developed around heroines using their knowledge of social games to erect for themselves a makeshift equality in a world where they are faced with double standards rendering them, effectively, unequal. Many comedies are mainly about the ingenuity of their heroines in surviving and controlling through masks, disguises, and indirection. Only recently have critics begun to examine the ugly backside of the comic heroine's bright masks of power. Clara Claiborne Park, for example, has shown how the long-extolled disguises of Shakespeare's heroines are only another way to check women's power: "Male dress transforms what otherwise could be experienced as aggression into simple high spirits" ("As We Like It," 108). Shakespeare's Rosalind, in other words, is allowed all sorts of freedom, in part because her disguise as Ganymede assures the temporary nature of her power. As feminist critics have confirmed the great ingenuity of literary heroines, they have documented, again and again, the subversion that accompanies the heroine's triumph. Depending on such tactics as concealment, parody, madness, masks, pretense, and impersonation, the comic heroine is trapped by her indirection.[11] In Constance's case, the result of her negotiations between concealment and openness is a limited power. The power she gains by operating clandestinely is typical in both its temporary nature and its explosive effect. But more to the point, when she presumes to ignore the standard restrictions on her power by *talking about them,* the entire basis of her power is questioned.

As Constance investigates both the stated and unstated aspects of her position in comic inversion, Maugham offers her as a test case for studying the relationship between the comic heroine and comic convention. The bright creature that Constance is in act 1 epitomizes the traditional comic heroine, but for unconventional reasons. In act 2, Constance places herself in limbo, between what she is supposed to be and what she feels she is, and as a result, she threatens her family and friends. Yet even to this point, the development of Constance's position approximates convention. Only in act 3 does Maugham move his investigation of women and comedy to the extraordinary level. In this final act, Constance attempts to become a new kind of comic heroine, one not empowered by inversions *or* subversions. Her attempts place her beyond comic conventions and outside of social ones, so she spends her time attempting to map out new directions for herself and her world. Act 3 is about the joys and dangers of Constance's journey into new comic territory. But it is also about the power of the genre to bring her back within its bounds. That is, the dialectic of freedom and restriction that is at the heart of comedy and is the center of the heroine's dilemma is here articulated with clarity.

Constance's attempt to educate those around her about the inner workings of society's conventions is a monumental task. Act 3 opens one year after the events of acts 1 and 2. Constance is still faced with the refusal of husband, family, and friends to give up what they know for the surmises Constance offers about the unknown. And the subject is still marriage as Constance explains her reasons for the great change she is planning. She is tired of implicit power. As she tells John, she wants explicit power to make her own choices, to transcend convention:

> I am naturally a lazy woman. So long as appearances were saved I was prepared to take all I could get and give nothing in return. I was a parasite, but I knew it. But when we reached a situation where only your politeness or your lack of intelligence prevented you from throwing the fact in my teeth, I changed my mind. I thought that I should very much like to be in a position where, if I felt inclined to, I could tell you, with calm and courtesy, but with determination— to go to hell. (180)

John persists in trying to wish her back into familiar roles—"I would sooner you had made me scenes for a month on end like any ordinary woman and nagged my life out than that you should harbour this cold rancour against me" (181). But after she informs him that she's off on a holiday with Bernard, his defenses finally crack. In his first response he still clings to the conventional: "Of course I am not so silly as to think that because a man and a woman go away together it is necessary to believe the worst about them, but you can't deny that it is rather unconventional" (182).[12] But when his recourse to the old proves fruitless he fashions, ever so timidly, a new role for himself as an open-minded man of brave self-restraint:

> I flatter myself I'm a sensible man. I'm not going to fly into a passion. Many men would stamp and rave or break the furniture. I have no intention of being melodramatic, but you must allow me to say that what you've just told me is very surprising. (183)

   Moments later, he retreats to the familiar assurance of the double standard: "it's different for a man than for a woman" (184). And yet, for the first time, he has seemed educable, even if only briefly. When Mrs. Culver reappears late in the act to rave once again about men's natural polygamy and women's natural monogamy, her once laughable attitude now—in light of John's possible transformation—seems not only wrong, but dangerous as well. Through this concatenation of events, Maugham forces not only John but also the audience to accept some of Constance's new norms. Constance's new world remains sketchily defined but includes, as John has begun to see, the abolishment of the double standard and of any structures—like marriage—dependent on that standard. Just as important, Constance's interaction with John demonstrates her knowledge that the construction of her paradigms is a communal process.

   But despite her sincere call for a new social order and all her talk of trailblazing, Constance finally effects little change and ultimately returns to the conventional. Her new paradigms remain hypothetical. Most obviously, she retains her need for some old-fashioned romance, which only Bernard can offer—"I want to feel about me the arms of a man who adores the ground I walk on" (195). On the one hand, she concedes that Bernard is "a little conventional" (190); and on the other, she takes advantage of it. At the last possible moment, she brings her revolution in bounds. Although she echoes Ibsen's Nora by exiting at the end, "slamming the door behind her" (198), she has promised to remain John's "constant" (197) wife. For all of its revolution, challenging of conventions, and consideration of new paradigms, this comedy still ends with marriage. It is as if only marriage can signal that everything will be all right, despite this play's vile portrait of it and Constance's vigorous protest against it.

   With Constance's promised return to John, Maugham's play remains a comedy, but a comedy uncomfortably stretched past its normal boundaries. Basically, Maugham attempts to have it both ways in his use of Constance. She has been his mouthpiece of social criticism, as she has also been his insurance that the conventional marital ending will satisfy. Maugham, like Constance, flirts with the idea of abandoning a restrictive system. Maugham, like Constance, cannot. The result is that Maugham shows explicitly and self-consciously that comedy, like the society it imitates, can promote revolution and change only to a point. Constance may encourage hope for change, but hers is a hope perpetually undercut by the social structures that the comedy finally affirms.

Women's equality to men is not, as Meredith would have it, comedy's essential ingredient. Exactly the opposite is true. The fact that comedy's women are *never* quite equal is the key to its traditional definitions of joy, continuity, and hope. At the end of *The Constant Wife*, both Maugham and Constance become part of the attempt to satisfy what a Maugham character elsewhere calls "the human craving for a happy ending" (*The Unattainable*, 188).

Constance's final retrenchment does not nullify her complaints; but her eventual retreat, of which the conventions of the form are proleptic, affects any response to her revolt. Constance's hope for change is encased—effectively entombed—in the conventional order she rejoins. Leo Salingar conjectures that Shakespeare found the same incompatibility of comedy's liberation and measurable social change over three hundred years before Maugham (*Shakespeare and the Traditions of Comedy*, 322–23). As I will elaborate further, the dilemma Constance epitomizes is not restricted to a single play, a single age, or a single type of comedy.

## Comedy and Its Context

Maugham, in the writing of *The Constant Wife*, is particularly sensitive to the way in which British comedy has accommodated women. In chapters 2 to 5 I will study four generally more well-known plays in which comedy's celebration of women is similarly qualified. Both to anticipate my approach to these other plays and to conclude my concentration on Maugham, I turn now to a consideration of how theatrical contexts factor into an understanding of women's position in comedy.

It will have become clear in my reading of Maugham's Constance that a study of generic structures is not fully separable from an awareness of social ones. The exigencies of day-to-day life may be recognized apart from the patterns of a society's literature. Yet as Bakhtin *(Rabelais)*, Davis *(Society and Culture)*, and Turner *(From Ritual to Theatre)* argue, there are also parallels too significant to ignore between what we read and/or watch and how we live. The increasingly wide range of feminist literary and theater criticism (now embracing such fields as history, sociology, psychology, medicine, and anthropology) further urges that a feminist critique cannot overlook the intersections of art and its context.

The connection of theatrical texts to society is particularly complicated given the ephemeral nature of performance. New historicist critics of English Renaissance drama have demonstrated in the last decade how the relationship between the text and the context of performance is both dynamic and elusive. The work of Stephen Greenblatt, Jonathan Dollimore, Stephen Mullaney, Louis Montrose, and others has been powerful and influential. Study of Renaissance drama is now fully conditioned by attention not only to the subversive potential of performance but also to the influence on drama of various nontheatrical and nonliterary structures of power. Yet the feminist critique of such work by Carol Thomas Neely and Lisa Jardine, among others, has underscored the consistent way such contextual analyses overlook the place of women in both the literary texts and the larger social contexts. As these two women summarize, the new historicist enterprise is in danger of becoming but a new way to marginalize women. Neely explains:

> In spite of all that the new theoretical discourses seem to have in common with feminist criticism, in spite of their appropriation of some of its claims, their effect—not necessarily a deliberate or inevitable one—has been to oppress women, repress sexuality, and subordinate gender issues. . . . women continue to be marginalized, erased, displaced, allegorized, and their language and silence continue to serve the newly dominant ideology. The new approaches are not new enough. ("Constructing the Subject," 7)

New historicist studies have opened up the study of Renaissance drama to a recognition of contexts and to a consideration of forces, documents, and events not directly attached to "high" culture. Yet ironically, these new studies tend to focus on issues of power and class in ways that either exclude women or indicate their powerlessness. As Neely puts it, the criticism "erases" women in the same way many Renaissance literary texts have ("Constructing the Subject," 10). For the women reading such criticism as well as for the women inscribed in these texts, not much has changed.

Both Neely and Jardine have offered strategies for counteracting such neglect. Neely proposes "over-reading" as a strategy that can move feminist critics beyond the constrictions of a male-directed discourse to context; and to explain how one "over-reads" she offers a menu of possible critical activities, including the search for gendered (especially female) subjectivity, identity, and agency, and, in addition, the search for women's real-life resistance or even subversion ("Constructing the Subject," 15). In other words, Neely invites the intensification of feminist critics' exploration of the literary, theatrical, social, and political contexts that condition a text. Jardine similarly suggests that since the "vectors" located in Renaissance texts always place agency with men, women need to locate new points of intervention for their study of texts. She suggests strategies that are textual, intertextual, and extratextual (MLA paper). As Neely and Jardine urge, any feminist critic of theater must now not only be aware of the complicated forces that constitute drama but also be attentive to the particular pressures of these forces on women.[13]

My specific concern in this study is to broaden the feminist context for studying women in comedy with a new attention both to comic structures, predominantly inversion and ending, and to the performance of specific comedies. A contextual approach is, as students of Renaissance drama have indicated, urgently necessary in the study of theater where the text is frequently not only the basis but also the result of a public occasion. In developing a theater criticism that is both feminist and materialist, Sue-Ellen Case *(Feminism and Theatre)* and Jill Dolan *(The Feminist Spectator as Critic)* have offered examples of an approach that augments knowledge of the critical context with an analysis of performance and other extratextual concerns. In my study of plays and playwrights, I will not be able to attend to all of the contexts out of which the comic genre or even any one play has grown. My necessarily limited objective is to be particularly sensitive to the context provided by generic convention and by actual performance and to set my findings against the backdrop of existing criticism of comedy—both feminist and nonfeminist, both performance-centered and text-centered.

In analyzing Maugham, I have argued for an interpretation of the play that stems from my feminist re-investigation of comedy's structures. I do not pretend to have discovered Maugham's intentions in writing the play, but rather to suggest how it serves this reader, in 1991, in explaining a pattern. I would like to end my comments on the play, however, by turning briefly to its performance context. Maugham's own remarks on *The Constant Wife* and its theatrical context provide a final gloss to my comments on *The Constant Wife* as an exemplar of its genre.

In his introduction to volume 2 of his collected plays, the volume in which *The Constant Wife* appears along with five other plays, Maugham concludes by noting that *The Constant Wife* "was a failure in London." With some irony, he adds that it was "a great success" in America, other foreign countries, and even provincial English towns. He explains such discrepancies by noting that since "a play consists of the words, the production and the audience," the evaluation of a play can be highly variable (xix). In other words, the production of the drama plays a great role in determining or perhaps predicting its reception. Maugham does not speak directly to the issue of the women in his play; but in his commentary on the preferences, class, and temporality of theatrical audiences, he offers reasons for the variable readings. First he suggests that drama is and should be a popular entertainment; of *Home and Beauty* in particular he is proud to point out that "it was intended to amuse" (ix). He amplifies the point later in his introduction by suggesting proudly that his plays are "commercial." In part, he is responding to charges that his plays are too commercial to be valuable. Second, he displays a keen awareness of the broad class composition of his audience. Although Constance, her family, and her friends exist in the higher reaches of the social scale, Maugham contends that the drama "must address itself equally to the working man in the gallery and to the gilded youth in the stalls" (x). He goes on to argue that since the "audience is as much part of the play as the words and their interpreters" (x), this far-from-homogeneous group fashions its own play. This leads Maugham into his third point, which is perhaps the most important as it affects a consideration of *The Constant Wife*. In summarizing about the audience's response to a play, he notes that the response is collective and emotional rather than intellectual, and thus sensitive to particular conditions of time and place. He elaborates:

> It [the audience] has a moral code which, according to the time, may be stricter or more lax than that of the individual. At the present moment, in England at all events, it is shocked by things that would not shock the individual, though under the reign of Charles II, when probably the general morality was little different from what it is now, it accepted conduct which would have outraged him. It is emotional, but at the same time has more common-sense than the individual. It has its own theories of life which do not always coincide with life as known by the individual. (xi–xii)

Maugham's pronouncements about his theatrical audience are not novel; but they touch on subjects that influence and explain the variable responses to his play. It is ironic, for example, that in writing of plays exclusively about the upper-middle classes, Maugham (in the first two points cited in the preceding paragraph) is insistent about the much broader class makeup of his audience. By writing what he is proud to call "popular" or "commercial" drama, Maugham sees himself creating work widely accessible. This suggests that the particular, class-bound social norms he writes of are not the only ones by which his work will be judged. In his third point, he then details how such popular work, *because* of its diverse audience, gathers its many different responses. Crucially, he accepts here a relativity that attaches to the moral and aesthetic reception of a play. It is Maugham's acknowledgment of this variable moral response that is most closely connected to his portrait of women in *The Constant Wife.*

My depiction of *The Constant Wife* dwells on the constant tension that exists between its revolt against and certification of the status quo. As I read it, some parts of the play privilege rebellion and other parts ensure continuity. Maugham's reflections on the reception of his plays focus similarly on multifaceted audience responses; some audiences panned *The Constant Wife,* and some embraced it. The specific response to Constance attached to these different overall evaluations is difficult to meter: it is not clear, for example, if London audiences rejected the play because of or in spite of Constance or if other audiences welcomed the play in support or in defiance of her rebellion. What is clear is that her liberties and her limitations elicited different judgments at different times and in different places. For some audiences the play constituted a threatening rebellion. For others it offered social portraits supportive of the status quo. My point about the context of this play, then, is that structural analysis of Maugham's play, even when qualified by a consideration of its original performance context, points to paradox; i.e., the heroine in *The Constant Wife* does and does not find liberty.

My argument in this book depends on many of Maugham's assumptions, particularly the belief in the significance of context and in the possibilities for change. I have used his play primarily to suggest that there are certain limits to the power women gain in comedy; but I will also be depending on his example (especially his attention to theatrical context) throughout my study to recognize where and when changes are possible for women in comedy.

## Women, Comedy, and Change

I have repeatedly urged, in my reading of Maugham, that even the mutable and malleable genre of comedy has an enduring history of presenting women in restricted ways. Yet as I have also noted repeatedly, my goals in this book are twofold: not only to point out the limitations of the genre but also to consider possible changes in it. Thus, as final background for these dual goals, I want to end this chapter with a consideration of the possibilities for change in the conventions of the comic genre.

Playwrights themselves seem wary of labeling their own work within such formidable dramatic traditions as tragedy and comedy. Yet in practice, both writers and readers respond to literature largely through generic conventions that they know. Particular assumptions attach to particular genres; and as I noted earlier in this chapter, many students of comedy have found the genre averse to change. As Frye puts it, comedy "has been remarkably tenacious of its structural principles and character types" (*Anatomy*, 163). Yet recent developments in critical theory have been helpful in uncovering the possibilities for change, even deviation, in a literature dependent on convention. Feminist critics especially have been dedicated to tracing the possibilities for and the history of change in literary convention. Drawing on her feminist interpretation of reader response theory, Jean Kennard ("Convention Coverage") concludes of literary convention first that readers respond to literature according to the conventions they know at a specific time, and second that readers may or may not choose to use the conventions they know. In this second point lies the basis of her argument for the existence of "conventional" change. The set of conventions readers read by—and the structures such conventions project onto a text—are not fixed, she argues. Indeed, given changing sensibilities, changes in both convention and genre are inevitable. And when critics make explicit the reading strategies of readers, these critics discover the path to change *within* a study of convention (83). Kennard proposes, then, that when a literary community sees a convention as dishonest or inappropriate, that convention is, in fact, replaced: "When experience cannot be expressed in the available literary conventions, new conventions appear to develop" (83–84). This argument for change is basic also to Nancy Armstrong's two recent and incisive essays on literature as women's history. In introducing several other writers' essays on generic change, Armstrong establishes the theoretical background for many kinds of literary change. She cautions, for example, that gender is differently constituted in different ages ("Introduction: I," 359). More central for my work is her contention that many feminist critics are dramatically altering the critical landscape by exploding generic boundaries (355). At a fundamental level, my two-part study analyzes both the influence of comic conventions *and* their openness to change. My point is not that the genre of comedy is unchangeable, but that those aspects of the genre that are most closely tied to women have been resistant to change.

Armstrong's arguments also raise questions about the relationship between a writer's sex and his or her approach to literature. This relationship is a major issue in the portrayal of comedy's women as well as in the connection between comedy and change. I will be arguing in the chapters to come that while both men and women display sensitivity to the women of comedy, experimentation with new relations between women and comedy is more common among women playwrights. In the context of the eighteenth-century novel, Nancy Miller has explored a similar relationship between literary convention and the portrayal of women. The heroines in the largely male tradition of the novel, she argues, are images of the "female in the male imagination" that result from men writing "to and of each other" (*The Heroine's Text,* 153). Women writers, she argues elsewhere, have been more likely to produce heroines outside of the mold and the conventions ("Emphasis Added"). In the realm of comic drama, I too have found a correlation between the portrayal of women and the writer's sex. But to fully understand the operation of the conventions that account for such correlations, factors besides an author's sex must be noted. Armstrong makes the convincing case that the study of literature through a divided notion of gender both overlooks the range of factors that affect literature and is in danger of perpetuating distinctions of power based on gender. She simultaneously notes that gender-conscious studies remain necessary ways of uncovering a complete map of the literary terrain ("Introduction: I" and "Introduction: II").

I will address the issue of conventional change in both parts of this book. In the chapters to follow in part 1, I will establish further the promising, but inevitably limited, portraits of women in traditional British comedy. The possibilities for the comic heroine are explored in the work of male writers such as Shakespeare, Congreve, Shaw, and Ayckbourn (chapters 2 to 5). But in their plays, as in the plays of their earliest female challenger, Aphra Behn (chapter 6), these heroines face generic and social obstacles beyond such heroines' ingenuity. The possibilities for conventional change and thus for female liberation and freedom seem ever beyond the grasp of the heroine, her author, and most of her producers.

In part 2 of this book I will more insistently focus on this notion of changing generic conventions. For I have found that the contemporary British theater has for the first time seen the development of a comedy that offers women a change neither isolated nor illusory. The increased number of women writing for the theater has been primarily responsible for the appearance of comedies that conjoin women, freedom, and power in original, meaningful ways. The women-authored plays that are my subject in part 2 are not, however, directly analogous to the plays that have determined the traditional outlines of the genre. The organization of this second half of the book is, thus, substantially unlike that of part 1. In chapters 2 through 6, I focus on just five comedies to deliver a detailed account of the generic patterns that women characters traditionally encounter. Each of these plays is representative of the literary and theatrical situations that have typified British comedy in various eras. In part 2, however, my consideration of scores of plays establishes the broad nature of the change that women playwrights are bringing to comedy. In chapter 7, I introduce part 2 by outlining the political, generic, and critical contexts that have shaped the comic plays women are now writing. And in the remainder of part 2, I offer various strategies for understanding the differences of this comedy. In chapters 8 and 9, for example, I consider the structural qualities of these new comedies, showing their increasingly radical departures from the inversion and endings that have for so long trapped the female potential in comedy. Having established the basic differences in structure between this new comedy and its tradition, I then, in the final three chapters (10, 11, and 12), turn to a concentrated analysis of qualities besides the structural that distinguish this new work. In chapter 10 I consider the coterminous portraits of self and sexuality in contemporary women's comedy. While the body has always been a basic ingredient in comedy, these new comedies make the female body, for the first time, the site of a self and thus of power. In chapter 11 I consider another basic ingredient of comedy, community, again to point to fundamental alterations in the makeup of the genre. Through communities of women both on stage and off, these contemporary comedies by women establish groups of women as common, for the first time, in British comedy. In this chapter as in the final one (12), substantial extratextual analysis underscores the changing response of all parts of the theater community—writers, actors, directors, reviewers—to women's comedy. In fact, throughout part 2, structural considerations of the comic heroine are joined to such extratextual factors. In the final chapter, I consider the future of British comedy primarily through the lens of performance, for it is finally in production that the women of comedy—the heroine and the playwright alike—will succeed or fail in bringing new meanings to an old genre. Throughout the second half of this book, I consider plays not obviously "comic" or, more precisely, not comic in a traditional way. My point is that the comic work by recent women writers takes many shapes, not one. Through their transformations of comedy, contemporary female playwrights have not only offered heroines who find freedom and power; they have also offered a comedy that, through its alterations, also alters an entire theatrical context.

In both my review of comic criticism and my analysis of *The Constant Wife,* I have argued in this chapter that comedy is a relatively secure genre that, nevertheless, promotes instability and creates the climate for change. What this situation means for women varies; it varies with the playwright, with the playwright's era, and with the audience. It even varies with the individual production, as Maugham cautions. But among such variables, possibilities for change in the genre persist. As Catherine Belsey persuasively argues, the fluidity and plurality encouraged by comedy have the potential to disrupt whole systems ("Disrupting Sexual Difference"). Since such potential is sometimes realized and sometimes not, comedy both is and is not the province of women.

## Chapter 2

# Shakespeare's Rosalind:
# The Strong Woman in the
# Comic Tradition

Women in British comedy have often been illusory, weak, or—to the feminist, at least—simply objectionable. In Shakespeare's *The Taming of the Shrew,* Kate's seeming capitulation plagues feminist critics who defend Shakespeare's women and creates problems for contemporary theater directors. In Jonson's plays, women either have minor roles *(Volpone)* or are most palatable when they are actually men in disguise *(Epicoene).* In Wycherley's cynical world, the women are present as either pure virtue or despicable weakness. And in the philosophical world of Stoppard's *Jumpers,* women are alternately romping acrobats or concupiscent wives. But my concern in the rest of part 1 is not plays in which women are either objectified or vilified. It is instead the many plays in which women are strong and central, in which comic inversion gives rise to vocal, active women. In other words, the focus of my study is the comic plays that have the most to offer women; for it is in such plays that the tension between powerful comic heroines and restrictive comic structures is most fully on display.

Thus in this and the three chapters to follow, I turn first to plays by three of the most dominant figures in the tradition of English comedy—Shakespeare, Congreve, and Shaw—and then to a fourth play by the influential contemporary playwright Alan Ayckbourn. When taken together, these plays provide a representative picture of women's paradoxical place during the several hundred years of British comic tradition. In choosing these four writers, I have focused my study on the male writers almost exclusively responsible for shaping the English comic tradition. However, in chapter 6, I will turn to the work of a female

playwright, Aphra Behn, to suggest the parallel existence of a countertradition in comedy, a tradition that allows for more heretical though
still largely orthodox portrayals of women. Both the powerful male
playwrights and their almost invisible, infrequent female companions
(like Behn) have influenced the contemporary comedy that is the subject
matter of part 2. I begin with Shakespeare, the earliest British comic
playwright to recognize and exploit the power comedy can offer
women. In *As You Like It,* he creates a heroine, Rosalind, who sets the
standard for the strong woman in comedy.

At the end of *As You Like It,* when Hymen teases Phebe with the
notion that she cannot love Ganymede—"You to his [Silvius's] love
must accord, / Or have a woman to your Lord" (5.4.127–28)—he recalls
the comic advantage Shakespeare has found in Rosalind's disguise as
Ganymede. Less obvious, however, is his implicit reference to the most
steady love of the play, that between two women, Celia and Rosalind.
His mockery of such love and the uncharacteristic silence of the women
that accompanies it are two act 5 indications of the way women are
represented in the play. *As You Like It* has been acclaimed as a play about
the expansiveness of love, the graciousness of fate, and the inevitability
of human foible. But it is also a play about women in the comic world.[1]
And while Shakespeare's women claim control and voice in the play's
long-celebrated inversion, they fail to transcend the limits a traditional
comic ending imposes on them.

As noted in chapter 1, Shakespeare's plays have elicited the most
thorough critical analysis of women in British comedy. Such analysis
offers an exemplary display of the paradoxes that accompany critical
discussion of women in comedy. On the one hand, Charlton
*(Shakespearian Comedy),* Nevo *(Comic Transformations),* Bamber *(Comic
Women, Tragic Men),* and French *(Shakespeare's Division of Experience)*
focus on the festive liberation of the plays to find that comic women
benefit from their mid-play freedom. On the other hand, Park ("As We
Like It"), Garner ("A Midsummer Night's Dream"), Parten ("Re-establishing Sexual Order"), Erickson ("Sexual Politics"), and Neely *(Broken
Nuptials)* emphasize the power of the comic ending to defuse, even reverse, sexual revolution. Yet as Karen Newman has demonstrated, these
opposing responses to Shakespeare's comic women are not strictly incompatible. In studying *The Merchant of Venice,* Newman argues that
inversion is not always "simply a safety mechanism." On the contrary,
she asserts, it can be an efficient intrusion on male "structures of ex-

change" ("Portia's Ring," 29). Thus Newman acknowledges the limitations of inversion but maintains that even a restricted inversion can establish irrevocable transformations. I sympathize with this attempt to hold the two accounts of comic inversion in critical tension. Yet with *As You Like It,* as with the plays I will explore in the following chapters of part 1, I find even the most productive rebellion finally negated by comedy's multiple options for accommodation.

I can best explain the complicated position of this play's women by considering separately the play's status quo, its inversion of that standard order, and its return to order. What is important about the status quo in *As You Like It*'s duration is the fact that it never disappears. While the forest of Arden most obviously represents a rejection of the status quo, both the play's dependence on symmetry and its flirtation with androgyny prove strong indications of an uninterrupted status quo based on sexual double standards. In turn, this pervasive status quo affects the celebrated inversion that Arden represents. Thus my discussion of the play's inversion is focused on women's language and friendships, two areas in which the women's supposed liberation proves to be as qualified as it is empowering. My study of the play's conclusion, then, is a look at how the ending saturated with marriage completes this play's paradoxical foregrounding of women. A final section on contemporary production of the play takes note of recent attempts to secure the power this play offers women, but even these attempts to capitalize on Rosalind's strength prove the durability of comic structures that qualify comedy's women.

## The Status Quo

The establishment of a status quo world is a routine feature in Shakespearean comedy. In *As You Like It,* the court of Duke Frederick is a predictable world governed by civil laws and stable mores. It is also standard in Shakespearean comedy, however, that the status quo world, when it proves hostile to changing conditions, is challenged by an alternate world—usually a different place (Arden)—where the norms are relaxed, even reversed. Ultimately *As You Like It,* like other Shakespearean comedies, ends with a return to the status quo, a return acceptable because of the modifications that have, supposedly, been negotiated in the alternate location. While critics disagree on the effects of this cycle—is there or is there not a new (or better or different) world at play's end?—they generally agree on its presence.

The special effect such circular motions have on the women of *As You Like It* has been most thoroughly studied by Peter Erickson. To reach his conclusion that *"As You Like It* is primarily a defensive action against female power rather than a celebration of it,"* Erickson compiles an extensive list of the signs of patriarchy present throughout the play ("Sexual Politics," 82). Most important, he shows that the altered world of Arden is only superficially a release from everyday, patriarchal norms, and that as a temporary *reversal* of the norms Arden is never a threat to them. Although Erickson never makes the connection explicitly, he bases this reading of *As You Like It's* persistent everyday world on the presence of a sexual double standard. This double standard in Shakespeare's status quo world is not significant simply because it grants women less freedom and power than it does men. Rather, it is important because in the middle world of the play, when norms are reversed, the power and freedom women *do* gain is *still* based on the double standard. In other words, the middle world does not revoke the double standard, but only invokes a temporary criticism of it. While the social criticism of *As You Like It* is not negated by the play's cycle, it is continually undercut by the omnipresence of the play's double standard.

In my examination of *As You Like It's* middle, I will study how the temporary nature of the play's reversal limits its rebellions. Rosalind's powerful language and close female friendships that flourish in Arden are, for example, muted by the influence of patriarchal norms. Her male dress, symbolically, preserves the male as dominant. As a continuation of my argument that mid-play challenges to order are qualified, my examination of the ending will point to Rosalind's inability *not* to choose marriage. I introduce these considerations of inversion and ending, however, with a closer look at ways in which the status quo and its sexual double standards establish (and ultimately qualify) the play's portraits of women. Both the play's general manifestations of equality and its specific connections with androgyny are undermined by enduring norms and their reflection of the status quo.

Equality informs language and structure alike. While the words "equal" and "equally" each occur only once in the course of the play, they are notations of a pattern present throughout the play. Celia and Rosalind, in 1.2, offer equality as a desirable goal and a standard of judgment, first when Celia finds that the ideal bestowal of Fortune's gifts must be an equal one—"Let us sit and mock the good housewife Fortune from her wheel, that her gifts may henceforth be bestowed equally"

(1.2.29–31)—and later when she counsels Orlando to "a more equal enterprise" (1.2.161) than Charles the Wrestler appears to be. The construction of the play stands as the most striking example of the persistent valorization of symmetry and balance these comments hint at. For example, a standard of symmetry balances one action against another when a conversation on the killing of deer (2.1) is matched by the actual hunting of deer (4.2); when Rosalind's first wooing of Orlando (3.2) is mated to a second (4.1); when Orlando's triumphant dialogue with Jaques (3.2) is repeated in Rosalind's similar victory over the cynic (4.1). The significance of characters is likewise refined when they are considered in pairs—Jaques's cynicism is tempered by Touchstone's loving parody, Silvius's idealism is braced by Corin's realism, one bad brother (Oliver, Duke Frederick) is paired with one good one (Orlando, Duke Senior), and one unrequited love (Phebe's) is upstaged by another one, less vain (Silvius's).

Rosalind is the ultimate incarnation of all such equations, symmetries, and balances. For not only does she act as a matchmaker for others, but she is at the same time self-conscious of her own vacillations between the realistic and the idealistic. By the end of the play, when Silvius offers his litany of love in 5.2 and when Hymen and Jaques parcel out their verbal gifts of love in 5.4, the play's four marriages seem to be natural extensions of a play full of equations and balances. In the play's final scene, Celia's word "equal" has become "even"; first when Rosalind disappears "to make these doubts all even" (5.4.25) and second when Hymen elevates her "even" by rhyming it with heaven: "Then is there mirth in heaven / When earthly things made even / Atone together" (5.4.102–4). "Even," like the "equal" of 1.2, is meant to indicate that by the end of the play life is orderly and balanced.

While it has been common to link the play's balances to an idea of sexual equality, these formal and linguistic symmetries are better seen as reflections of the play's dependence on the status quo than as a guarantee of equitable relations between the sexes. In fact, the androgyny that critics have praised as the pinnacle of the play's many equalities is not a signpost of sexual liberation; instead, it is another signal of the play's foundation on inequitable norms.

In his study of the androgyny of the play, Erickson points out that a leveling of sexual differences is not possible, even in this play's measured world, because the basis for both of *As You Like It*'s worlds is patriarchy ("Sexual Politics," 77).[2] In the end, this limitation makes androgyny more meaningful to the men returning to power at the play's end than to the women about to give it up:

> However, the conservative counter-movement built into comic strategy applies exclusively to Rosalind. Her possession of the male costume and the power it symbolizes is only temporary. But Orlando does not have to give up the emotional enlargement he has experienced in the forest. Discussions of androgyny in *As You Like It* usually focus on Rosalind, whereas in fact it is the men rather than the women who are the lasting beneficiaries of androgyny. ("Sexual Politics," 77)

Androgyny is not a reality for the women in *As You Like It* in the same way it is for the men because the women are never equal to the men; the most that they gain is a reversal of an inequitable situation during the middle of the play. This temporary reversal ensures that while men learn their weaknesses and women their powers in the inversion of the play's middle world, norms do not change.[3] The status quo of male dominance that Duke Frederick's court represents thus remains present throughout the play. For the women of Shakespeare's comedy, then, the status quo conditions their extraordinary liberation as well as their ordinary endings.

## The Inverted World of Arden

The play's inequitable status quo is tested by its free, leveling middle, though little altered by it. Nevertheless, the play's inverted world calls for careful scrutiny, scrutiny that seeks to identify not only the play's retention of standard norms but also its fierce battles against convention. In Shakespeare, as in Maugham, the position of women in the inverted world is marked by a tension between unconventional power and conventional standards. By first examining women's language and then their friendships, I can detail both where freedom manifests itself and how it is restricted.

Rosalind commands the rich linguistic world at the center of *As You Like It,* yet her mastery of language varies. Her language is, in other words, a clear indication of the power she alternately does and does not have in the play. In 1.2, Shakespeare establishes the contradictions of the women's linguistic patterns in the realm of the status quo by contrasting their verbal acuity with their acquiescence. In 1.3 also, as Rosalind confronts the censure of Duke Frederick, she displays her verbal skill, but learns that women's language skills carry little weight in the Duke's court. Only when Rosalind and Celia move to Arden—i.e., to a world where Rosalind herself establishes the limits on her own language—does she realize her full linguistic range. Inversion, in short, sets her linguistically free.

In 3.2, Rosalind blossoms as literary critic, witty conversationalist, and lover. She is clear-headed enough to recognize the inadequacies of Orlando's verbal celebrations of her, telling Celia of his verses, "some of them had in them more feet than the verses would bear" (159–60). She can then banter with Celia over the concrete image of "feet" she calls up. She further displays her versatility by matching witty analogies to nature with Touchstone (111–15) and by making more learned allusions at her leisure—calling up Pythagoras, for example (168). But her power and control are most obvious in her first conversation with Orlando. From the exit of Jaques in line 281 to Rosalind and Orlando's joint exit at the scene's end, a simple measure of her command of this conversation is the number of lines both characters speak: Rosalind has ninety-eight lines to Orlando's thirty. But even such lopsided numbers only begin to suggest her mastery of their interaction. Orlando, on the one hand, takes a passive role and feeds lines and questions to Rosalind. In addition, Orlando has brief speeches devoid of imagination or wit. Rosalind, on the other hand, is represented by a hearty prose in which the melodies of the language are the melodies of her love. Act 3, scene 2 is evidence that only in Arden does Rosalind use her masterful prose for both power and pleasure.

There continue to be moments later in the play when Rosalind's wit and verbal acuity command attention, as she chides Phebe in 3.4 or directs the others in the recitations of 5.2. But the depth and range of her linguistic skills are clearest when her heart is in them, in 3.2 and 4.1 especially. Rosalind reaches the height of her powers in 4.1. Here the gymnastic playfulness of 3.2 is transformed into heartfelt pronouncements on love and marriage. When Rosalind plays the realist in denying to Orlando that one could die from lack of love, the great love she feels for him softens her harsh statement and gives it its graceful rhythms:

The poor world is almost six thousand years old, and in all this time there was not any man died in his own person, videlicet, in a love cause. Troilus had his brains dashed out with a Grecian club; yet he did what he could to die before, and he is one of the patterns of love. Leander, he would have lived many a fair year though Hero had turned nun, if it had not been for a hot midsummer night; for good youth, he went but forth to wash him in the Hellespont, and being taken with the cramp, was drowned; and the foolish chroniclers of that age found it was 'Hero of Sestos.' But these are all lies. Men have died from time to time, and worms have eaten them, but not for love. (4.1.85–98)

When Rosalind gives up her language along with her disguise and is silent at the play's end, a gaping hole is left in the play. As ritual takes prominence in the play's final scene, the language of all the characters is diminished. But the loss is greatest for Rosalind. As the emotions and powers of Rosalind's language give way to the comparative shallowness of song and dance, Rosalind takes her silent place in the marriage ritual. Even the epilogue, in awarding the last words to Rosalind, does not make up for her silence in the last scene. Erickson points out that the epilogue, in fact, subverts the woman's world of this play by recalling the boy Rosalind-Ganymede and not the woman who has been the linguistic heart of the play ("Sexual Politics," 79–80). I would suggest, in addition, that Rosalind's return as an actor (whether male *or* female) reinforces the signal present all along that her power comes only from a suspension of the play's—and the world's—reality. The fact that she still must enact her last moment of power while in her male disguise only increases my suspicion that the Rosalind of the play's middle disappears because her linguistic command is as dangerous as it is endearing.

The epilogue and the silence that precede it are, in fact, only the last indications of the way the women's linguistic powers remain attached throughout the play to assumptions that undercut them. In considering the variations in Rosalind's linguistic command, two conclusions are unavoidable. First, Rosalind's verbal control increases in scope and power when she enters the play's inverted territory of Arden. Second, her linguistic power is always conditioned (even in her grandest moments) by the patriarchal assumptions encouraged by comic structures. In other words, Rosalind's language is never quite her own. A second look at her language in the play will corroborate that her command is always accompanied by a discrediting of women's linguistic power. The discrediting comes predominantly from Rosalind herself, although it has corollaries in the language and behavior of all the play's women.

In 1.3, Duke Frederick warns Celia of the deception in Rosalind's language:

> She is too subtile for thee; and the smoothness,
> Her very silence and her patience,
> Speak to the people, and they pity her.
>
> (1.3.73–75)

His warning is dismissible since his character is suspect; yet Rosalind elsewhere voices similar reservations herself. For example, she prefaces her talk with Orlando in 3.2 by asking Celia the self-deprecating question, "Do you know I am a woman? When I think, I must speak" (3.2.237–38). She reconfirms her diagnosis of logorrhea by lacing the pyrotechnics of 4.1 with similar undercuttings of her skill. Here she warns her future husband Orlando that "certainly a woman's thought runs before her actions" (4.1.127–28) and counsels him, further, to be wary of his wife's wayward wit:

> Make the doors upon a woman's wit, and it will out at the casement; shut that, and 'twill out at the keyhold; stop that, 'twill fly with the smoke out at the chimney. (4.1.148–51)

Rosalind's comments are all tongue-in-cheek, but they cannot simply be dismissed as comic. Simply put, the direct discrediting of female language in these statements is of a piece with other subversive tactics that women have adopted.

Rosalind is responsible for the greatest share of such subversion and the self-deprecation it is linked to. Even as Ganymede, she accepts limiting stereotypes. One might speculate that Rosalind adopts her deferential behavior to preserve her male disguise. Yet she is similarly deferential in 1.2, before she adopts the guise of Ganymede. Of the disguise itself, Rosalind suggests in 1.3 that it will help her hide in her heart "what hidden woman's fear there will" (1.3.115). Later, while collapsing at the end of the journey into Arden, she blames the weak female in her: "I could find in my heart to disgrace my man's apparel and to cry like a woman; but I must comfort the weaker vessel, as doublet and hose ought to show itself courageous to petticoat" (2.4.4–7). She disdains the woman in herself at the same time that she feels an obligation to comfort Celia-Aliena. Even in 3.2, a scene enriched by her confidence and control, Rosalind's doubts about her female self loom large. She tells Celia that she retains the impatience of a woman (3.2.185–89). And later, after teasing Orlando with a catalogue of women's faults—"All like one another as halfpence are, every one fault seeming monstrous till his fellow-fault came to match it" (3.2.334–36)—she paints a giddy picture of the female lover:

> At which time would I, being but a moonish youth, grieve, be effeminate, changeable, longing and liking, proud, fantastical, apish, shallow, inconstant, full of tears, full of smiles; for every passion truly anything, as boys and women are for the most part cattle of this color; would now like him, now loathe him; then entertain him, then forswear him; now weep for him, then spit at him; that I drove my suitor from his mad humor of love to a living humor of madness, which was, to forswear the full stream of the world and to live in a nook merely monastic. (3.2.384–94)

Rosalind's self-conscious mockery means that such comments are always devalued; yet I am inclined to agree with Celia in her charge to Rosalind, "You have simply misused our sex in your loveprate" (4.1.185–86).

What Celia cannot realize, however, is how much the action in the play validates Rosalind's comments. Indeed, the subversion Rosalind vocalizes characterizes the behavior of all the play's women. For example, Rosalind, Celia, Phebe, and Audrey do become giddy and rash when in love, just as Rosalind has foretold. Rosalind herself presents the most severe case when, in 4.1, she demands a wedding ceremony one moment and warns of cuckolds the next. More numerically overwhelming are the many indirect actions of the women in the play. In her disguise, Rosalind gains strength and control, but her indirect expressions of love pale next to Orlando's direct confessions of being "love-shaked" (3.2.346). By the end of the play Rosalind has never once told Orlando she loves him. Phebe's description of her love for Ganymede similarly revolves around negations and contradictions:

> Think not I love him, though I ask for him;
> 'Tis but a peevish boy; yet he talks well.
> But what care I for words? Yet words do well
> When he that speaks them pleases those that hear.

It is a pretty youth; not very pretty;
But sure he's proud; and yet his pride becomes him.
. . . . . . . . . . . . . . . . . . . . . . . . . . . . . . . . . . . . . .
There be some women, Silvius, had they marked him
In parcels as I did, would have gone near
To fall in love with him; but, for my part,
I love him not nor hate him not; and yet
I have more cause to hate him than to love him;

(3.5.108–13, 123–27)

Audrey's nearly nonverbal reactions operate on the same principles. Her gross lack of understanding is only a less practiced indirection than the responses of the other women. Celia's love for and relationship with Oliver may be an exception to these female patterns of indirection; but since Oliver and Celia rarely interact, speculation about how she may have avoided indirection is useless.

In studying the consequences of such indirection, linguistic and otherwise, Madelon Gohlke and Coppélia Kahn have found the language of such comic heroines as Rosalind to be the reflection of a patriarchal order. Though Gohlke's work is primarily on the language of tragedy, she connects the linguistic freedoms of comic heroines to the threat of infidelity the women pose for their mates. Arguing that the indirections of the women's language connote infidelity for the men, she identifies the darkest threat implied in free female language such as Rosalind's:

> Whereas "honesty" in relations among men may be perceived primarily as a matter of keeping one's word, in relations with women, it is clearly a sexual concern. For a woman to lie is to be unfaithful. For this reason the attribution of complex speech to female characters in the comedies in the form of lies, riddles, puns and statements made in the context of disguise, often involves sexual matters generally or specifically the threat of infidelity. ("'All That Is Spoke,'" 167–68)

While such sexual betrayal remains latent in most comedies, the threat is so real that the linguistic freedom women gain in the play's middle is suspended by the play's end. Touchstone's prolonged digression on lies in 5.4 (which appropriately coincides with Rosalind's silence) is symbolic of the male recapturing of playful language at the end of *As You Like It*. Discussing *The Taming of the Shrew*, Kahn uncovers similar conse-

quences in the indirection of a comic heroine's language. She notes that
language is Kate's only way of asserting herself and Shakespeare's only
device for calling his male order into question. Even so, and despite her
ironic reading of Kate's final speech, Kahn ultimately finds such language to be but one more measure of patriarchal control: "But on the
deepest level, because the play depicts its heroine as outwardly compliant
but inwardly independent, it represents possibly the most cherished male
fantasy of all—that woman remain *un*tamed, even in her subjection"
*(Man's Estate,* 117). I believe, with Gohlke and Kahn, that the language
of the women in the play does double duty, acting both as a conduit for
female power and as an automatic check on it. Through her language
Rosalind creates a strong counteruniverse in the inverted world of *As
You Like It,* and yet her power is as temporary as her stay in Arden.

Few playwrights can match Shakespeare in his linguistic richness;
therefore, I will not repeat this concentration on women's language in
my analyses of Congreve, Shaw, and Ayckbourn. Yet my argument
based on the language of *As You Like It*—that the play's inversion but
deceptively empowers women—is transferable (though less applicable)
to other plays. The more important subsequent point, which I will argue
in chapter 10, is that women's language has become a major concern and
tool in the comic world of contemporary women playwrights. But even
in the theater of the last twenty years, language for the women of comedy remains simultaneously powerful and restrictive.

While Rosalind's most obvious source of power in the inverted
world of the play is language, a second expression of her strength—as
well as the limit to that strength—is her friendship with Celia. Not
surprisingly, the friendship between the two women is as much affected
by the cyclical patterns of the comedy as is the language.[4]

Initially, the court world of *As You Like It* seems hospitable to
female attachments. Although Celia and Rosalind's bond is introduced
in the hostile environment of 1.1, bone-breaker Charles softens while
describing what is, even to him, a beautiful, strong, enviable attachment:

> The Duke's daughter her cousin so loves her, being ever from their
> cradles bred together, that she would have followed her exile, or
> have died to stay behind her. She is at the court, and no less beloved
> of her uncle than his own daughter, and never two ladies loved as
> they do. (1.1.100–105)

When Celia and Rosalind appear in 1.2, the love, trust, and intimacy of their woman's world mark a distinct difference from the combative male world of 1.1. In the second scene, another man—this time Le Beau—reveals the depth of the women's love for one another: "[Their] loves /Are dearer than the natural bond of sisters" (1.2.256–57). But more important, their love glows in the intimate word games that open the scene; here familiarity produces a conversation with two wits in league against the world, not in combat with one another. Such teamwork characterizes the women's verbal games with Touchstone, Le Beau, and even Orlando. Their pleas to Orlando to abstain from wrestling are best described as choric:

> Rosalind: The little strength that I have, I would it were with you.
> Celia: And mine to eke out hers.
> Rosalind: Fare you well. Pray heaven I be deceived in you!
> Celia: Your heart's desires be with you!
> . . . . . . . . . . . . . . . . . . . . . . . . . . . . . . . . .
> Rosalind: Now Hercules be thy speed, young man!
> Celia: I would I were invisible, to catch the strong fellow by the leg.
>
> Wrestle.
>
> Rosalind: O Excellent young man!
> Celia: If I had a thunderbolt in mine eye, I can tell who should down.
> (1.2.177–82; 192–97)

The third scene stands as the climax of the play's celebration of women's love. Significantly, it is Celia, not Rosalind, who gives voice to this celebration.[5] The two tributes she makes to their love become the touchstones by which the cousins' relationship in the rest of the play must be considered. First Celia pleads with her father to respect the women's mutual love:

> If she be a traitor,
> Why, so am I. We still have slept together,
> Rose at an instant, learned, played, eat together;
> And whereso'e'er we went, like Juno's swans,
> Still we went coupled and inseparable.
> (1.3.68–72)

That he cannot understand or respect their love is predictable. That Celia must repeat the same plea to Rosalind suggests less the depth of their bond than its precariousness:

Rosalind lacks then the love
Which teacheth thee that thou and I am one.
Shall we be sund'red, shall we part, sweet girl?
No, let my father seek another heir.

(1.3.92–95)

The disguises the two women subsequently put on—one the garb of a man, one the skirts of a country woman—are obvious manifestations of the rift developing between them. This female-female couple must now become a female-male team to survive. The two can no longer appear (literally) "as one." Thus when Celia and Rosalind set off "to liberty," they set off without the full strength of the love that has previously sustained them. In the next four acts, a charting of their actions shows them moving progressively further apart. They never regain the closeness of act 1.

The forces that separate the two women include the subversion and self-deprecation I noted in my study of language, but most detrimental to their friendship is the assumption in the play that the natural, inevitable pairing is that of woman to man. In 2.2, for example, Duke Frederick assumes either that Celia and Rosalind must have run off with a man in their entourage or that a man is the cause of their running off. Yet as wrong as he is in assuming that they are chasing Orlando, he is only making the same assumption they have made in preparing their disguises—i.e., that two women could not take off on their own. The rest of act 2 reinforces such assumptions. Rosalind, dressed as a man, assumes a protective male role as she transacts the women's business with Corin in 2.4. Jaques, in his "seven ages of man" speech, does women the courtesy of inclusion when he speaks of "the men and women merely players," yet he mentions women again only as supernumeraries—nurses and mistresses. Although Celia and Rosalind temporarily gain power in Arden, they have only entered a different sort of man's world than the one they have left at the court, a world that forces one of them into dress as a man and prods both of them to marriage.

In the rich discussions of acts 3 and 4, further impositions on the women's friendship accumulate. In 3.2, the first scene in which the women are happily settled in Arden, Celia teases Rosalind with her (Celia's) knowledge of Orlando's presence in the forest. In a stressful moment, the two are refreshed and comforted by their well-known patterns of banter. Yet as soon as Rosalind begins to woo Orlando, Celia is silent. Her silence can be partially accounted for by the dynamics of the situation—it is Rosalind and Orlando who are in love, after all, not Celia. But Celia's presence as silent chaperon serves also as a strong visual reminder that her friendship with Rosalind is no longer Rosalind's primary concern. In 3.4, with the two women once again alone together, familiar patterns of conversation return. Celia provides the support Rosalind needs by echoing agreement to each outrageous statement Rosalind makes (3.4.1–23). She matches her praise for praise, complaint for complaint. But while Rosalind gets the support she needs, she can make no thankful acknowledgment of it. Her mind is all on Orlando, not Celia.

The two women continue to appear together in 3.5, 4.1, and 4.3. Yet there is no more linguistic evidence of the comfort and support the two women can provide for one another. While Celia participates in these scenes as a silent partner, Rosalind acts more and more on her own. In 3.5, for example, Rosalind handles Phebe and Silvius without a single word from Celia. In 4.1, at the height of Rosalind's linguistic control, Celia has only six short speeches. And finally, 4.3 is evidence that the two women, even in Arden, have come to face the world separately. The most convincing proof of Celia's sudden love for Oliver is the revival of her language in 4.3, the scene in which Oliver first appears in Arden. Earlier, in her six short speeches of 4.1, Celia had demonstrated a playful distaste for Rosalind's actions, charging her with the misuse of "our sex" (4.1.185), dismissing Rosalind's affections for Orlando as "bottomless" (4.1.193), and responding to Rosalind's announcement of her vigil for Orlando with an atypical lack of concern: "And I'll sleep" (4.1.202). So by 4.3 Celia is ready to focus her energy and concern elsewhere. In the early parts of that scene, she has only two short speeches; once Oliver enters, however, she explodes into speech, and it is Rosalind's turn to be the bystander. In addition, 4.3 marks the first time Celia pays primary attention to someone other than Rosalind. Celia and Rosalind's exit with Oliver at the end of the scene also marks the last time the two women make their motions in tandem. When Rosalind re-enters in 5.2, she is without Celia for the first time in the play. When Celia next appears, at the opening of 5.4, she is similarly without Rosalind, who enters shortly after with Phebe and Silvius. By the end of the play, the dominant pairing for the women is not each other but Celia with her love Oliver and Rosalind with her love Orlando. Hymen's amusement at the coupling of women in his comment to

Phebe adds a final, godly consent to the separation of the cousins (5.4.127–28).

Although Rosalind and Celia are the heart of the joyous woman's world, they are only half of the female population in the play. While the cousins are inseparable until the end of the play, Audrey and Phebe live isolated existences throughout. Their separate presences further accentuate the slimness of the possibilities for female community in this world. It is no accident that immediately after Rosalind's first show of power in 3.2 Audrey appears as an unforgettable reminder that few of the world's women are like Rosalind. Audrey is effectively speechless in response to Touchstone's verbal battering (3.3). And she is outnumbered three to one by men telling her what to do. Though she has been seen as a healthy reminder of sexuality in the play, by 5.1 she is no more than Touchstone's sexual possession. The choice of Audrey and Touchstone as the representatives of a lover and his lass in 5.3 is also revealing; instead of celebrating headstrong Rosalind and her lover, the two pages celebrate a more conventional couple, Audrey and her love. Finally, Audrey's fulfillment of expectations about conventional stereotypes of women is certified by her isolation. The only time she appears on stage with any other women is in 5.4, by which time the business of marriage assures she will be part of a married, heterosexual community, not a female one.

Phebe's journey through the inverted world of Rosalind's rule surpasses Audrey's in showing the play's restrictions on female community. Phebe appears first in 3.5 when Rosalind, Celia, and Corin are spying on her conversation with Silvius. For the first time, three women stand together on stage; and a potential expansion develops in that female community as Phebe is attracted to Rosalind-Ganymede. But Rosalind entertains Phebe's affection only as sport, and her decision ensures that Phebe's infatuation is cause for laughter—not for alarm or love. One might speculate, on the basis of her love for Celia, that Rosalind would show sympathy for Phebe. Instead, Rosalind shows disdain for her in 3.5 and belittles her love whenever possible throughout the rest of the play. In 4.3, for example, when Silvius carries Phebe's letter to Ganymede, Rosalind-Ganymede puts Phebe's love in the harshest terms, telling Silvius, "Wilt thou love such a woman? What, to make thee an instrument, and play false strains upon thee?" (4.3.68–69). And in 5.2, when Phebe tells Ganymede of her love, Phebe's desires become the comic link in Rosalind's love chain. In payment for her silly infatuation,

Phebe is suitably embarrassed in the couplings of the final scene and must find her refuge in the man who has picked her. While both Phebe and Silvius are silly in their poses, Silvius, through his doggish sincerity, earns a redemption Phebe cannot. There is no place in the play's final order for Phebe's attachment to Ganymede-Rosalind.

Audrey and Phebe serve double duty in the play. First they expose the isolation of the women in the play as Rosalind and Celia—with their long-standing love—cannot. In this way they defuse the threat of women that Shirley Nelson Garner finds responsible for similar isolations in *A Midsummer Night's Dream;* as Garner puts it, "the male characters think they can keep their women only if they divide and conquer them" (*"A Midsummer Night's Dream,"* 61). Second, Audrey and Phebe serve as a multipurpose counterpoint to Rosalind and Celia. The power, language, and love of Rosalind and Celia are undercut through the simplistic presences of Phebe and Audrey. What happens to Audrey and Phebe is especially important because they are women *only* of Arden. They, and not Rosalind and Celia, are the true representatives of Arden's inverted world. Most crucially, then, the presence of Phebe and Audrey assures that Rosalind and Celia are not the rule, that women can be separated, even in Arden. Or perhaps as a result of the underlying patriarchy, women are separated *especially* in Arden. In the end, the women in *As You Like It* are both without numbers (there are only four women in a cast of at least seventeen men) and without any effective claim to power and order.[6]

I have limited hope for the women of the play, partly because—as I have shown—the play limits female language and community and partly—and more basically—because in doing so it precludes change, especially a change for the women. While the inversion of the play allows the women primacy and control, that difference of status points not to change but to the return of convention. Individual change does occur in the play; the most obvious and important comes in Rosalind herself, who matures from a sharp and witty young woman into a loving, wise woman ready for the compromises of marriage. The giddy woman speculating about love in 1.2 becomes the magician of 5.4 and appears content to subordinate her own concerns to those she may share with Orlando. These personal changes, however, make no difference for the communal end of the play and may, in fact, simply allow for the group to take precedence. Rosalind has transformed herself, but the world of Arden (and, more important, the court world she is about to return to) remain firmly patriarchal and able to absorb her personal brilliance. The world emerging at the end of the comedy is marked by four new couples, yet they have been accepted as representatives of a familiar ritual indoctrination. The corrupt rule of Duke Frederick will be replaced by the predictable, benign rule of Duke Senior, Oliver, and Orlando. And as the actions and cycles of the play have made clear, part of that predictability includes the necessity of traditional sexual stereotypes and a naturalization of the double standard. The characters' final acceptance of each other is an acceptance of the limits that the play has enforced, namely, limits on women's words, friendships, and power. To put it more precisely, the kinds of change possible for *As You Like It*'s women are as restricted as are their language and their friendships. In a play headed irrevocably toward marriage, which *As You Like It* is as soon as it begins, women, their changes, and their choices are from the first circumscribed by the overriding authority of men. There is no lasting change in women's status; there is no lasting challenge to the comic genre.

Based on her considerations of the comic genre, Bamber comes to a nearly opposite conclusion from mine: she finds that the dictates of comedy are so flexible that choice prevails, or more precisely, that the liberation of this world makes choice unnecessary (*Comic Women, Tragic Men,* 117–29). Catherine Belsey's Saussurian reading of Shakespearean comedy and Renaissance society also suggests a more optimistic possibility for the instabilities allowed in comedy's middle. Studying the structures of sexual identity, she argues that the plurality of the middle extends beyond its duration to offer a "radical challenge to patriarchal values by disrupting sexual difference itself" ("Disrupting Sexual Difference," 180). Yet after offering a dazzling account of the unfixing of social and sexual norms in both society and literature, even Belsey must conclude with qualifications. She ends her essay by retaining a hope for change in conventions and their interpretation while acknowledging that even in Shakespearean comedy the happy ending is not necessarily "happy" for the women (190). I am less optimistic about even the unfixed middle of traditional comedy (though, like Belsey, I see Shakespearean comedy as potentially revolutionary). Ultimately, I find that as Shakespeare guides his female characters through the Scylla and Charybdis of revolution and reaction, he offers at best limited change. In other words, intense experience doesn't yield appreciable change either in character or in genre.

The middle of Shakespeare's play presents possibilities for female linguistic power and community; but as I have shown, these possibilities exist side by side with strategies for disrupting them. Ultimately, the disruption of power, community, and autonomy for women is completed by the ending, in which marriage dissolves the temporary triumph of possibility.

## The Return to Order

I argued in chapter 1 that the comic ending is the most significant cause of women's compromised presence in traditional comedy. For Shakespeare, as for other writers who have shaped the British comic tradition, marriage determines the overtones of that ending.

In Shakespearean criticism, as in general criticism of comedy, marriage has been portrayed as everything from a "beneficent arrangement through which mankind achieves a maximum of human joy" (Charlton, *Shakespearian Comedy,* 117) to an imposition on comic characters, both male and female. Several recent feminist investigations of Shakespeare's portrayals of marriage in the context of Renaissance attitudes to marriage have added social scrutiny to such literary study. After suggesting that both patriarchy and mutuality were possible models for Renaissance marriage, Marianne Novy finds that in Shakespeare's comedies "mutuality," or the sharing of responsibility, respect, and love, is the general guide for defining romantic relations between men and women (*Love's Argument,* 21–44). Carol Thomas Neely also details conflicting opinions on the role of women in Renaissance marriage. Yet she concludes that despite the new egalitarian ideal of the compassionate marriage that arrived with the Reformation, "the woman had unequal status at every point in the process of wooing and wedding" (*Broken Nuptials,* 11). She adds, however, that a "continuing dialectic" between Renaissance women's gains in power and status and the restrictions such gains called up make definitive conclusions about Renaissance women and marriage "difficult" (19).[7] Thus, in each Renaissance comedy the actions offer but a single portrait of the complex social terrain of marriage. The marriages at the end of *As You Like It* are both defiant of and acquiescent to contemporary practice. They are also firmly dependent on generic convention. And they offer a final example of the intractable limitations to women's power in Shakespearean comedy.

In *As You Like It,* marriage is more an assumption than a visible institution. Although marriage is the goal of at least nine characters in the play (the four couples, plus William), no character is known to be married, though Duke Senior and Duke Frederick can be assumed to have been. Marriage, thus, exists as an abstract idea with the potential of becoming an ideal. Although the play is overflowing with critical evaluations of life in the country, life at the court, the age itself, and even love, marriage is rarely spoken of. In 3.3, as Touchstone's love for Audrey is to be translated into marriage by Sir Oliver Mar-Text, the first image of marriage is one Touchstone embellishes with a cuckold's horns (3.3.42–55). A brief exchange between Touchstone and Jaques adds to this a picture of marriage as a contest of animal desires (3.3.68–71). Yet when Jaques refuses to let Touchstone's mockery of a wedding take place, the sanctity of the institution is preserved, curiously, by the biggest cynic in the play. Rosalind is the only other character to consider fully, before play's end, the transformation of love into marriage; and her view, like Touchstone's, is mockingly brutal. As she foretells her life as Orlando's wife in 4.1, her portrait of marriage promises little more than infidelity and animal passions. Orlando's firm response stands as proof against her charges, however, as do Rosalind's own pleas with Celia to "marry" her and Orlando. The play absorbs Rosalind's mockery as it absorbed Touchstone's cynicism. Marriage is rescued once by the realist Jaques and once by the idealist Orlando, and is, in both cases, preserved intact for the play's final scene where the would-be marriages of 3.3 and 4.1 are transformed into real marriages. Marriage remains an ideal unblemished by example.

The less obvious but more pervasive presence of marriage lies in the long-anticipated happy ending of the play. Familiarity with comic convention has led an audience to expect an ending in marriage, at least since Rosalind and Orlando fell in love in 1.2; and Shakespeare's only interference with such expectations comes in the teasing of his aborted marriages and in his omnipresent ironies. The drive toward marriage controls much action, as I have shown; friendship between women, for example, must finally take second place to the search for a mate and to the physical demands for regeneration. Comic endings in marriage are not simplistically happy—as even Shakespeare's array of comedies shows. And extensive criticism has confirmed that there can be no equation between marriage and a happy ending; yet the two remain, even if only ironically, attached and inseparable. The pressing question, however, is what marriage as the ending of comedy symbolizes for the women of *As You Like It*.

This brings me back to a consideration of convention and the power of an expected ending. Northrop Frye finds that the new society created in the marriages at the end of Shakespearean comedy is a changed one where a younger generation triumphs and gains the right to assert its fresh answers to life's dilemmas (*Natural Perspective*, 130). The joy of the comic ending is affixed to the promise of social renewal and regeneration. Both Rosalie Colie *(Resources of Kind)* and Heather Dubrow *(Genre)* extend the possibilities for some such sort of change, noting that because genres (such as comedy) create expectations, writers can use them to question those expectations and create a climate where actual change can occur. But the changes promoted by comedy are different for the women characters than they are for the men and for the society that these men control. The possibilities for change that do exist for women are severely reduced by an ending in marriage, in large part because comedy's reversals utilize a double standard, as I have previously argued. Thus, the application of what Rosalind learns about love and self in the middle of the play is limited by the fact that she cannot choose to avoid marriage. Her choice is binary: either she retains the illusory power and freedom of a Ganymede, or she gains the love and predictable comfort of a married Rosalind. The comic genre as Shakespeare adopted it— *Love's Labor's Lost* notwithstanding—does not allow for the possibility of combining Rosalind's linguistic power, her friendship with Celia, *and* her marriage to Orlando. The play ends, rather, with her silence, her apparent distance from Celia, and her marriage to Orlando. Like many other comedies, *As You Like It* investigates the effect of changing power structures, gender structures, and even generic structures. But for Rosalind, Celia, Audrey, and Phebe, any participation in change will be funneled through marriage.

### *As You Like It* on the Contemporary Stage

I conclude my study of Shakespeare's play and its women with an optimistic qualification. Although the women in *As You Like It* gain a circumscribed freedom, production of this and other Shakespearean comedies in recent years has offered enhanced possibilities for reducing the power of comedy's reversals and ending. The 1978 Ashland Festival Production of *The Taming of the Shrew* is a case in point. As Martha Andresen-Thom reports, the production placed great faith in the play's ability to counteract its own sexism. For instance, the action that preceded Kate's final treatise on marriage focused the audience on equality, not hierarchy:

> In tone and action she [Kate] conveys to us and to the incredulous audience on stage that her alliance is with Petruchio (Rich Hamilton) who attends to her, subdued and moved, until she starts to kneel so as to place her hand beneath his foot. He then goes to her and kneels too, catching her hand in his. Slowly they rise together, face to face, the bond between them enacted in this public ritual and soon to be consummated in the private domain of their bedchamber. ("Shrew-Taming," 123)

The 1983 Royal Shakespeare Company production of *Much Ado about Nothing* employed a similarly bold and unconventional ending to announce its refusal to accept wholeheartedly the final couplings that are part of the comic tradition. The expected male-female coupling of the festive ending was replaced with a series of circle dances where combinations of men, of women, and of men and women made male-female couples only a minor part of a spectrum. In this broadened range of relationships, the final focus on Beatrice and Benedick was placed in context, with the lovers' relationship retaining its romance not because of but in defiance of traditional assumptions.

The 1985–86 RSC production of *As You Like It* at the Barbican Theatre in London offers a translation of such feminist staging to *As You Like It* itself.[8] The production was an even more thorough attempt than those I have just mentioned to counteract the forces of traditional comedy. Most important, director Adrian Noble took great pains to imply not only that Duke Frederick's court never disappeared, but also that it was a *patriarchal* court from which the characters could not escape. Toward these ends, the roles of the two dukes were played by a single actor; he and his men simply covered the elegant tuxes of Duke Frederick's court with blankets to become Duke Senior and his banished men (the blankets later disappeared to reveal tattered tuxes). Visually, in other words, the audience was told that the court (and all it implies) is never really gone or forgotten. This compression of roles helped point to what one reviewer called the production's "consistently bleak view of the male competitive world" (Ratcliffe). Such a critique of the play's status quo world helped Noble and his actors strengthen the radical potential of the production's Arden. Orlando, for instance, was a very strong presence, stronger I would say, than his words. Not only was the actor physically muscular enough to make his wrestling victory in 1.2 more than convincing, but he also exuded during his discussions with Rosalind a strength of presence, an intelligence, that was a match for her powerful, controlling language. Orlando's strength challenged the simplistic sex-role reversals of the play. The treatment of the production's two main women—Rosalind and Celia—was, however, the most forceful attack on the traditional *As You Like It*.

Reviewer Irving Wardle connected the loss of a traditional pastoral world directly to the enlargement of Rosalind's presence—"Whatever pastoral elements this approach excludes, it is precisely in harmony with the heroine's line of development." I agree. As Rosalind exchanged her evening dress of act 1 for the white pants of Arden, actor Juliet Stevenson came into her own. It was immediately clear that the elaborate dress had physically inhibited her—she moved with energy and athleticism in Arden. As Stevenson puts it, "Literally and figuratively the disguise releases her [Rosalind]: you have to imagine her going into doublet and hose from Elizabethan petticoat and farthingale and a rib-cracking corset. . . . Rosalind can stretch her limbs, she can breathe properly, and so she's able to embark on increasingly long sweeps of thought and expression that take her ever deeper into new terrain" (Rutter, *Clamorous Voices*, 104). In addition to changing costumes, Stevenson completely discarded physical poses or mannerisms one might associate only with women. She seemed, indeed, a woman freed from confining gender roles. Yet despite the monumental efforts undertaken by Noble, Stevenson, and others to transcend traditional sexual roles and traditional genre expectations, this production too made its compromises.[9]

In the RSC program, for example, there appear four collections of quotations. One is entitled "In Search of Her Self." While this gesture toward the recuperation of a female subjectivity is laudable, the prose and poetry presented is all written by men and fails to approximate anything like a female point of view. A much more significant determinant of the production's compromises was the choice made about the play's ending. Surprisingly, the enlightened approach that characterized the early and middle portions of the production gave way to a very traditional happy ending. The physical onstage coupling, for example, was all heterosexual, with but a brief moment in which Rosalind and Celia confirmed the continuation of their bond. More surprisingly, Hymen took form as a disembodied, omnipresent voice; he commanded

(and exacted) a reverence for marriage. Stevenson defends this production choice in arguing that the "miraculous" appearance of the god Hymen suggests Rosalind's "direct access to the gods" and thus confirms
her power. Yet Stevenson also acknowledges that this celebration is a
difficult one for Rosalind to take part in (Rutter, *Clamorous Voices*, 118–
19). And indeed, the production's final gestures toward the preservation
of convention allowed the audience to forget the careful construction of
Rosalind's power. For example, reviewer John Barber admired Stevenson not for her challenge to but for her compliance with the traditional
portrayal of Rosalind. As he put it, Stevenson "combines a handsome
femininity with the leaping vitality of youth, but her 'sex and sexuality'
are never in doubt." Stevenson's own comments, finally, suggest the
perpetual tension involved in the project of bringing the women of
comedy to fulfillment:

> The *frustration* of the play-endings in the comedies is a continuous
> one—with Isabella in "Measure for Measure" . . . we could never
> arrive at a solution and I don't believe we have on "As You Like It"
> either. I find myself constantly (and isolatedly) arguing in rehearsal
> *against* the Happy Ever After choices, because inevitably the heroine
> is left in a deeply compromised position in order that the status quo
> should be restored. Such arguments, on occasion, relate not just to
> the ending but to the whole play, in fact . . . for 18 months I played
> a Rosalind that I never felt I'd been allowed to make truly my own.
> (Letter, 20 July 1986)

Other recent productions of *As You Like It* have also stood as efforts
to reclaim its strong women and disruptive potential. In the 1986 production at the Royal Exchange in Manchester, Janet McTeer apparently
managed to create a Rosalind who was able to retain the affections of
both Celia and Orlando (Coveney review). Yet even McTeer's Rosalind,
whom most reviewers found refreshing and independent, was found by
at least one reviewer to be nothing more than a predictable and risible
female type: "It was an angular, archly-humourous portrait of a woman
in love with her ability to manipulate men" (O'Neill). Taken together,
both of these productions of *As You Like It* suggest first that performance
offers a conduit for transcending the power of traditional comic structures and their effect on women, and second that even in contemporary

production, the traditions so central to the play make such transcendence a slippery and illusory business.

As You Like It invites producers and scholars to question their own definitions of comedy and to grapple with the incongruities of women's place in the comic world. In her strength, Rosalind promises possibilities that critics, directors, and actors are struggling to realize.

*Chapter 3*

# The Way of Millamant: The Endangered Female Self in the Comic Tradition

In dedicating the first edition of his comedy *The Double-Dealer* to Charles Montagu, William Congreve regrets that the women in his audience were reported to have taken offense at his portraits of women in the play. Defending his play against such gender-specific response, the playwright notes that "the Business of a Comick Poet" is "to paint the Vices and Follies of Humane kind" and that any work would be "imperfect" without a treatment of both sexes (*Letters and Documents* [1693], 168). In other words, comedy must take as its province the foibles of both men and women. In a letter to his friend John Dennis, Congreve later qualifies such an equal vision of women in comedy, suggesting that they, unlike men, evoke comedy only from their "affections," not from any "humours." He appends to this limited connection of women and comedy some backhanded praise of the sex: "We may call them the weaker Sex, but I think the true Reason is, because our [men's] Follies are Stronger, and our Faults are more prevailing" (*Letters and Documents* [10 July 1695], 183). As these two responses suggest, Congreve has an ambivalent attitude to women in comedy, seeing them as both like and different from the men in the genre. In his comedies, and most especially in his final comedy *The Way of the World,* Congreve does make central the "Vices and Follies" of women. But as centuries of criticism attest, he also manages to create at least one woman whose intellectual and moral allure clearly outweighs her follies and faults. Congreve follows Shakespeare in making a strong woman the center of his play. He also forecasts twentieth-century comedy in understanding the destructive pressure comic structures place on female community and self.

Congreve's *The Way of the World* is often considered the apotheosis
of Restoration comedy. In his dedication, also to Montagu, Congreve
himself removes this, his last play, from ordinary considerations of stage
success or generic conformity: "That it [the play] succeeded on the stage
was almost beyond my expectation; for but little of it was prepared for
that general taste which seems now to be predominant in the palates of
our audience" (*Way of the World*, 5). While Robert Hume has noted that
in its original production the play was a respectable success and not the
artistic failure critics seem to want it to be (*Development of English Drama*,
436), the tradition of the play's undervalued complexity continues un-
abated among students of Restoration drama. A 1987 study introduces
the play as the "summation of Restoration Comedy" (Burns, *Restoration
Comedy*, 205); and critics continue to conclude books on Restoration
drama with an appraisal of the play (Markley *[Two-Edged Weapons]*,
Powell *[Restoration Theatre Production]*, Holland *[The Ornament of Ac-
tion]*), implying its special status. Over and over, this critical privileging
centers on the play's women, and on its heroine Millamant in particular.

The tributes to her superiority form a lengthy tradition of their
own. Colley Cibber praised Anne Bracegirdle's original Millamant—"all
the faults, follies, and affectations of that agreeable tyrant were venially
melted down into so many charms and attractions of a conscious beauty"
(quoted in Lynch, introduction to *The Way of the World*, x). And direc-
tor/actor Nigel Playfair suggests the similar twentieth-century exaltation
of the character—"Here is a character rendered sublime by the poignancy
and the sincerity of its wit. And I repeat that there has never been on or
off the stage a woman so sublime in the same way as Millamant" (*Story
of the Lyric Theatre*, 230). Margaret McDonald adds the critic's seal of
approval in concluding that Millamant is "the apotheosis of the witty
independent woman in Restoration comedy" (*Independent Woman*, 154).
I too have found Millamant an attractive candidate for critical review;
but as a preface to my study of her character and the specifics of her
comic environment, I need to stress that the exalted position of *The Way
of the World* does not detach it (or its heroine) from its theatrical era or its
generic tradition.

Several recent studies have analyzed the connections between the
position of Restoration women and the portraits of women on the Restoration stage.[1] The ambiguous advances women enjoyed offstage were
matched onstage by four theatrical developments: the appearance of professional women actors, an increase in the number of women writing

plays (Weber estimates that 72 plays by fourteen women were performed between 1660 and 1720 [*Restoration Rake-Hero,* 15]), the supposed influence of women in the audience on play production, and the growing dominance women characters held in the plays proper. Yet each of these new theatrical opportunities for women is less promising than it initially appears. For the privilege of acting on stage, for example, women were expected to offer their bodies to influential male audience members. Women playwrights fared slightly better in establishing playwrighting as a female occupation, though I will suggest in chapter 6 how Aphra Behn's career was compromised by her sex. (Congreve himself, it should be noted, was supportive of several women playwrights, especially Mary Pix and Catherine Trotter (Morgan, *The Female Wits,* 24–27, 46). Similarly, the power of women in the audience was slighter than most critics have assumed. David Roberts's 1989 study of women in Restoration audiences *(The Ladies)* makes a convincing case against the long-standing assumption that women audience members forced major changes on the Restoration stage.[2] He suggests first that women exerted very little theatrical influence, even as patrons, throughout the Restoration, and second, that the changes slowly transforming the nature of Restoration comedy were not demanded by "moral" women but rather developed out of a broad range of social and political debates. According to Roberts, in other words, women's influence on the Restoration stage has been overrated. In the pages to follow I will suggest, finally, that the power accorded female characters in Restoration comedy is equally ephemeral. It is not surprising that out of a theatrical world divided on the value and position of its women should come a comedy full of powerful women in compromised positions.

Such theatrical circumstances caution against too simplistic a view of *The Way of the World's* powerful women. Similarly, this play's grounding in standard literary forms must qualify its reputedly remarkable nature. Its dating in 1700, the first year of the new century, has encouraged commentators to study it as the death knell of an era; it has become the Restoration comedy of manners enriched beyond its means to absorb nuance. As Scouten and Hume ("'Restoration Comedy,'") have demonstrated, however, 1700 does not mark the end of bawdy and the beginning of sentimental comedy; rather, the year stands as part of several decades during which the nature of English comedy gradually changed. *The Way of the World,* then, is not an anomaly but a work conditioned by its times and its form. And as Peter Holland *(Ornament of Action)* and other critics have amply demonstrated, the play is fully understood only with attention to the exigencies of production.

These notes on context should indicate that I join the rich tradition of those studying the play not by focusing on its uniqueness, but on its consonances with tradition. As with *As You Like It,* so with *The Way of the World* my consideration is broadly outlined by an analysis of the play's structural basis in inversion and its movement toward an ending in marriage. Again, I have highlighted such traditional structure in full cognizance of widespread critical opinion that this play proceeds on an original conception of plot.[3] I will study the persistence of the status quo in Congreve's world, the place of women in its inverted frolic, and the acquiescence of its ending. I will end my discussion with a consideration of *The Way of the World* on the twentieth-century stage. Notably, to move from the Renaissance to the Restoration is to enter a comic world that forecasts Shaw and Ayckbourn more than it echoes Shakespeare. Congreve's sensitive portraits of women suggest resignation to convention more than joy at its possibilities.

## Persistence of the Status Quo

The comic world of *The Way of the World* builds its rarefied interactions on a foundation of stereotypes and roles that reflect conventional definitions of men and women. In fact, the often-touted differences of the play depend on the presence of standard social protocol as regards sex roles. The most obvious and pervasive stereotyping attaches to women. It comes from both male and female characters and persists through all sections of the play, suggesting that the typing is not dependent on one sex or the result of one phase of the action. Its omnipresence also suggests its resilience, in spite of the transformations that come to the characters and the relationships in Congreve's play. But as my previous argument will have made clear, the typing is in no way unusual; it simply confirms the conventional gender assumptions operating in this comic world. In the course of the play, women as a group are found to be unforgiving (Fainall, 15) and frail (Mrs. Fainall, 43); they are identified as flirts (Witwoud, 23) and incessant gossips (Witwoud, 47); they are shown to be obsessively concerned with their looks and their age and in constant search of sexual gratification (these latter qualities most obviously appear in Lady Wishfort). The contribution of the play's women to this reductive thought clarifies how typical assumptions about gender influence the women's own behavior. Mrs. Marwood, Millamant, and Lady Wishfort, in fact, deliver the least flattering conclusions about women.

In act 3, for example, Mrs. Marwood reflects on the machinations of Foible and Mrs. Fainall (which she has just overheard) by concluding that the better part of the devil must be female: "Man should have his [the devil's] head and horns, and woman the rest of him. Poor simple fiend" (60). Shortly after this, Millamant likewise turns to vicious typing of women as an insult. As she and Mrs. Marwood trade some obvious and some less than obvious accusations, Millamant tells her rival, "I'll take my death, Marwood, you are more censorious than a decayed beauty, or a discarded toast" (63). While these two ladies of wit find it necessary to ridicule other women through debased typing, Lady Wishfort's commanding presence in the play insures that such typing can clearly be connected to life. As James Neufeld argues, Lady Wishfort stands as brazen evidence of Congreve's ability (despite his protestations to the contrary) to create a female character of "humours" ("Indigestion of Widdow-hood"). In fact, she is little else than a character whose actions depend on her stereotypical concerns about aging, her looks, and her chances for marriage. In their various ways, then, these three women reinforce the play's dependence on gender typing.

Mirabell's seeming abstention from such conventional thinking is of note. In the first three acts of the play, there is no evidence of his taking up the tendency of all those around him (both men and women) to generalize about women's behavior. His opening discussion of the play's women with Fainall is miraculously free of such thinking: he indeed treats women, even Lady Wishfort, as individuals. Yet in the "proviso scene" of act 4, when he is finally confronted with the reality of his tie to Millamant, even Mirabell turns to types. His provisos, in fact, provide a convenient recapitulation of the female behavior that has been demonized throughout the play. When he demands that Millamant drop subversion, masks, and makeup, that she abstain from drink and female cabals, he reveals his fears of woman as frail, unfaithful, and susceptible to overweening desires. Mirabell has no clear evidence that Millamant in particular is prone to any of these stereotypical failings—indeed, he has shown earlier that he knows otherwise—but his reliance on them for his provisos suggests the limitations that must attach to even the exceptional heroine of this play.

As I suggested earlier, critics have tended to reach nearly opposite

conclusions about the play's women. Mrs. Marwood is seen as an exceptionally evil version of the antagonistic witty woman. Mrs. Fainall is
"unconventional" according to Lynch (introduction to *The Way of the
World,* xiii). Holland singles out Millamant by noting that the original
casting of Congreve's play suggests he collapsed in her (for the first time)
two previously discrete female characters; in short, the playwright inno-
vatively connects virtue and true wit (*The Ornament of Action,* 234). The
women of *The Way of the World* may be distinguished from their dramatic precedents; they are not, however, free from conventional typing.
Such typing is the first way in which this play establishes the power of
standard social behavior.

The reverse side of this typing is the persistence of a powerful male
order in the play. And the prominence of male-directed actions and
concerns constitutes the second and perhaps the more commanding expression of the status quo throughout the drama. Three recent studies
have detailed the several dimensions of the male order and control in this
play, each concluding that the play's witty veneer grows out of patriarchal social and cultural constructs. Richard Braverman, who connects
his analysis to political and economic changes of the late Restoration,
asserts that the central struggle is the conflict between Mirabell and
Fainall. That struggle—and Mirabell's eventual victory—should be read,
he suggests, as emblematic of the changing locus of political power at
the turn of the eighteenth century. Fainall represents the "old" patriarchal order and Mirabell represents a new "way of the world" based on
trust: "Their [Fainall and Mirabell's] fates enact the eclipse of kingly
prerogative by the new sovereign relations of property, for Fainall, the
vestigial Restoration rake, is thwarted by the reformed rake Mirabell,
who has learned the new 'way of the world'" ("Capital Relations," 134).
Braverman goes on to show that this new order will accord to women
some additional power (148); but his main point is that the transfer in
orders reflects men's persistent power base. Harold Weber's study parallels Braverman's in reading Fainall and Mirabell as representatives of old
and new orders. Weber's critical context includes a focus on seventeenth-
century sexuality; and for him Fainall represents the destructiveness of
the "libertine rake" while Mirabell represents the more constructive,
more controlled sexuality of the "philosophical libertine." In this reading, as in Braverman's, Millamant's union with Mirabell is an important
certification of Mirabell's ascendancy. In addition, Weber finds that the
ending is controlled by Mirabell and best understood as his assertion of

power (*Restoration Rake-Hero,* 119–29). Robert Markley joins the two other men in acknowledging the historical (and theatrical) contexts of the play in his analysis of the role of male power in the drama. He sees the play as a battle between Fainall and Mirabell for control of Lady Wishfort's family, a family that presents itself as a vacuum since it has no men, and especially no man at its helm (*Two-Edg'd Weapons,* 237). A subtext of all three readings is that despite the seeming prominence of the play's women, all female actions and relations are subject to forces outside their control. In *As You Like It,* Rosalind determined action and presided over games of disguise and wit. In *The Way of the World,* Millamant exerts emotional power, but functions as an ornament in the unfolding of the male-determined plot and its reverberations.

In *As You Like It,* Shakespeare marked a clean division between the status quo world of the court and the inverted world of Arden, even though the norms of the status quo continued to determine the characters' choices in both worlds. I have just suggested that in *The Way of the World* too the norms and privileges of the status quo continue to operate throughout the action. Yet here the presence of inversion is more subtle. The characters of *The Way of the World* do not leave one world and travel to another. They do not, in fact, travel very far from the real life of their audience—the case has been made that there was little distinction between the onstage world and that of the Restoration audience. Despite such indistinct boundaries, however, the dimensions of this play's inverted world remain clear as regards its women. While the men's control ultimately prevails in the events at the Chocolate-house, at St. James's Park, and at Lady Wishfort's (the play's three settings), the women claim power at least temporarily: Lady Wishfort is ostensibly the power-broker who must be tricked; Mrs. Fainall and Mrs. Marwood both accept responsibility for the movement of the play; and Millamant feverishly defends the power of her youth and beauty through both her invitations to the chase and her deliberately flippant attitudes. In the inverted world of this comedy, then, women will exercise their power; but they will ultimately be overshadowed by factors they do not control.

## The Inverted World

As critics and reviewers have noted for nearly three hundred years, Millamant is the single most commanding presence in *The Way of the World.* In studying the middle world of this play, I too will focus on her celebrated navigation of the comic action. Yet the fate of women in Congreve's comic world extends beyond Millamant's brilliance. Thus, I preface my concentration on her with a consideration of the connections between and among the play's several women. Here, as in *As You Like It,* female community is but an illusion that reflects the influence of traditional comic structure and contributes to women's truncated power.

Besides Betty the waitress, women do not appear in the male enclave of the Chocolate-house in act 1. Yet from the beginning of Mirabell and Fainall's discussion there, the play's women are portrayed as a group whose cumulative presence is inherently intriguing. The women are first introduced not as individuals but as a group when the two men recount how the previous evening's social engagements were spoiled by the women's "cabal," an event from which the two men were excluded. Both men show disdain for the practice of such female socializing (the women do include innocuous men like Witwoud and Petulant in their gatherings), and they unknowingly offer the women power in their pressing curiosity to know about the conversations they have missed. Mirabell recounts his run-in with the group to Fainall:

> *Mirabell:* Seeing me, they all put on their grave faces, whispered one another; then complained aloud of the vapors, and after fell into a profound silence.
> *Fainall:* They had a mind to be rid of you.
> *Mirabell:* For which reason I resolved not to stir. At the last the good old lady broke through her painful taciturnity, with an invective against long visits. I would not have understood her, but Millamant joining in the argument, I rose and with a constrained smile told her, I thought nothing was so easy as to know when a visit began to be troublesome.
>
> (13)

Women, including Millamant, are thus introduced as granting first priority to their female friends. The men clearly do not like it. The second time the men in the Chocolate-house turn to the subject of women, those women again appear as a group. This time there are three gentlewomen who have driven up outside the Chocolate-house in search of Petulant (24). It is significant that in both cases of female grouping, the power that might be accorded such a multiple female presence is immediately discredited. As he chafes at his exclusion, Mirabell deflates the female cabal in guessing the vain Lady Wishfort to be its "foundress" (14). And

Petulant's gentlewomen are dismissed as a joke when Witwoud reports
how Petulant has hired the coach full of women to come in search of
him. The first act thus sets the tone for the play's continuing attentions
to women. It sets up female-to-female connections as a working option;
yet it simultaneously raises doubts—in this case, men's doubts—about
the value of such relationships. As the play progresses, the women will
come to share these doubts with the men.

As the first act registers the men's reservations about female community, the second records similar misgivings by women. In the first
physical appearance of women in the play, Mrs. Fainall and Mrs. Marwood directly discuss their particular friendship as well as the broader
issue of women's loyalty to one another. At first glance, it seems the
women concur that only women can make one another happy. Mrs.
Fainall begins the act asserting, "Aye, aye, dear Marwood, if we will be
happy, we must find the means in ourselves, and among ourselves. Men
are ever in extremes, either doting or averse" (32). Mrs. Marwood responds first with a denial, stressing a woman's need for male love, but,
when pressed by Mrs. Fainall, reverses her assertions to conclude of
men, "I have done hating 'em, and am now come to despise 'em; the
next thing I have to do, is eternally to forget 'em" (33). Mrs. Fainall then
crowns this agreement with a feminist reference to Amazons and Penthe-
silea (33). Yet the female friendship thus sealed is even more illusory
than the community the men have speculated about in act 1. For as soon
as a particular man—Mirabell—is mentioned, the camaraderie disinte-
grates. It is immediately clear that the two women both desire Mirabell
and that these desires have made their friendship a sham. Fainall (who
enters with Mirabell to interrupt the women's conference early in the
act) correctly assesses the situation to Mrs. Marwood: "Your mutual
jealousies of one another have made you clash till you have both struck
fire" (37). Ironically, Fainall's accusations bring Mrs. Marwood back to
her professed (and seemingly hypocritical) allegiance to women over
men; she concludes to Fainall that women's friendships are "more tender, more sincere, and more enduring, than all the vain and empty vows
of men" (38). This movement by the two women back and forth between attachments to women and a competing love for men is not as
confusing as it may sound in summary, however. That the protestations
of female allegiance are muddied by insincere thoughts (and are thus to
be discredited) is clear in the accompanying choreography of the scene.
In particular, as soon as Fainall and Mirabell enter the act, the women

separate to confer privately with the men, Mrs. Marwood with Fainall and Mrs. Fainall with Mirabell. As this separation and coupling predicts, the women are in fact enemies. These two women join the men of act 1, then, in considering female friendship only to discredit it.

When Millamant appears shortly after the tête-à-têtes of Mrs. Marwood and Fainall and Mrs. Fainall and Mirabell, the play's heroine thus enters an environment where a woman's friendship to other women has been presented as hypocritical at best. Appropriately, then, she enters with a male suitor in tow and a maid who (however loyal she will prove) never reaches the equal status of a friend (43). Upon her introduction, Millamant is safe from what have proved to be the vicious confusions of female companionship. Congreve will probe further her alliances with the play's women, but from her entry Millamant's focus is Mirabell, not other women.

The play's third and final setting at Lady Wishfort's provides moments, as act 2 does, of female-to-female encounters. These serve, however, only to prove the inability of women to be friends and to underline the women's overriding need for men. As Mirabell has asserted in act 1, Lady Wishfort is the purported center of the women's cabal. And yet the opening of act 3 reveals that any connections she seeks with women are only made in her ultimate effort to gain a man. A series of scenes between and among women shows, in fact, that Lady Wishfort's home is the primary battleground for female fighting, not female camaraderie. In the first of these scenes, Lady Wishfort's discussion with her maid Foible makes clear that the servant's loyalties are not to her mistress, but to Mirabell and Mrs. Fainall. Indeed, when Foible is forced into lying about her assignation with Mirabell in the park, she aligns herself with Mirabell by displaying great skill in inventing insults about her mistress, Lady Wishfort. After Lady Wishfort exits and Mrs. Fainall enters, Foible does show her loyalties to another woman, Mrs. Fainall. Although this allegiance is reasonably placed, Foible's clandestine scheming with Mrs. Fainall against Lady Wishfort and Mrs. Marwood connect the two women (Mrs. Fainall and Foible) in a less than flattering manner. Additionally, their exchange underlines the hostility that separates Mrs. Fainall and Mrs. Marwood. But the encounter between Mrs. Marwood and Millamant, which follows shortly after (62–65), best typifies the female infighting that characterizes the women's behavior at Lady Wishfort's home.

The bright banter that smoothes over most other rocky moments in the play barely maintains civility here. The two women are harsh and direct with one another. Mrs. Marwood, for example, tells Millamant to confess her love for Mirabell—"If you would but appear barefaced now, and own Mirabell, you might as easily put off Petulant and Witwoud as your hood and scarf" (63)—and later presses further for the confession of love:

> Mrs. Marwood:  You are nettled.
> Millamant:  You're mistaken. Ridiculous!
> Mrs. Marwood:  Indeed, my dear, you'll tear another fan, if you don't mitigate those violent airs.
>
> (64)

Millamant brings the confrontation to a close by requesting a song that—especially in its final verse—vindictively signals to Mrs. Marwood her (Millamant's) forthcoming victory as concerns Mirabell:

> Then I alone the conquest prize,
>   When I insult a rival's eyes;
> If there's delight in love, 'tis when I see
> That heart, which others bleed for, bleed for me
>
> (66)

The song also brings to an end the succession of all female encounters that has marked the first half of the third act. The overwhelming effect of these scenes is to portray women as their own worst enemies.

In the play's last two acts, final comments on women's friendships further suggest the women's inability to transcend either self-interest or interest in men during interactions with one another. The single most telling index of the play's portrait of women's relations is the moment during which Millamant and Mrs. Fainall appear alone together. Despite the fact that these two women have become allies in their battle to allow for Mirabell and Millamant's wedding, they have nothing to say to one another. They share a love for Mirabell and a reasonable attitude about it, yet they cannot convert the common emotion into camaraderie. In their brief encounter in act 4, Mrs. Fainall is next to silent, and Millamant is preoccupied with her verses and her need for privacy (80). If these two have nothing to share, then the other women can hardly have the foundation for true friendship. In addition, given the inability of Mrs. Fainall and Millamant to connect, it is no surprise that Millamant does not make the preservation of specifically female camaraderie a part of her proviso demands to Mirabell. Finally, after a play full of indications of women's isolation from each other, the play's closing reflections on female community can only be laughable. For example, during the final series of revelations and accusations, Lady Wishfort turns to Mrs. Marwood and idealizes female retreat from a world of such social treacheries—"Dear Marwood, let us leave the world, and retire by ourselves and be shepherdesses" (106). Neither of them, the audience knows, finds real comfort in such a vision, merely defeat. And shortly after, when Lady Wishfort reveals that her daughter, Mrs. Fainall, was raised apart from the presence of men, the idea of such isolation is decidedly comic (107).

The men in the play initiate the concept that female community is both threatening and silly. But more important, any power that might come to women via community is erased by the women's own aversion to one another. The drive toward marriage is not nearly as strong in this play as in *As You Like It;* nevertheless, female bonding is never offered as a viable alternative to heterosexual coupling. To turn to the play's heroine Millamant, then, is to turn to a woman who exists in a world where she is isolated from other women. Consequently, her trajectory through the world of comic inversion is distinguished by separation as well as by her more celebrated independence. Millamant's disengagement from other women is an index, in fact, of her strong desire for autonomy. Congreve's often praised portrait of her rests on his understanding of her need for self-expression.

Critically, Millamant has been accepted as a mystery that too few have wanted or needed to spoil with close scrutiny. As McDonald puts it, "the delicate fabric of her appeal seems to fray when subjected to analysis" (*Independent Woman,* 154). Thus she can be "one of the most blinding visions of character that have ever been dramatised" (Playfair, *Story of the Lyric Theatre,* 230) at the same time that the mere existence of her intelligence is an issue of debate. Yet Millamant can, of course, be analyzed. And what has been noted as her mysterious appeal can be clarified by a feminist scrutiny of her role as a comic heroine. Like Rosalind, Millamant is a bright, witty, and assured woman who has acquired the skills she needs both to defend her against and to enable her to reach the inevitable ending in marriage. Millamant, however, is also intensely aware of the pressure under which she must struggle to ensure self-definition in her predictable world.

Millamant's "difference" is the theme of her introduction in act 1. Although, as suggested above, she is initially referred to as a part of the women's cabal, she is presented as its most singular member. She is "mistress of herself" (13), a woman whose very faults command Mirabell's love (17–18). When she makes her entrance in act 2, however, her individuality is momentarily qualified by her affectations of frivolity. She fashions herself the lady of leisure; and in so strongly aligning herself with a conspicuous leisure, she devalues her worth in a conventional manner (see Roberts, *The Ladies,* 5–10). Millamant stands apart from other stylists of leisure, however; for at the same time she masks her power in such predictable ways, she makes countermoves to display it. Definitions of power and self, in fact, preoccupy her. For example, when Mirabell suggests that her vanity lies in the "power of pleasing," she retorts not only that her power more potently lies in cruelty but also that a woman would be crazy to part with such power. As the lovers' debate continues, Millamant extends her definition of a woman's power to note that she owes none of it to a lover: "One no more owes one's beauty to a lover than one's wit to an echo. They can but reflect what we look and say; vain empty things if we are silent or unseen, and want a being" (47). Yet Millamant's trace of doubt here, her mention of the woman who "wants a being," betrays her fear of losing both her power and her individuality. She asserts shortly after that, "I please myself" (48), as if to reconfirm her ability to define her self. When Millamant exits shortly after these exchanges, Mirabell describes her as a "whirlwind" (49). And that concept of her changeable self has been accepted as an accurate measure of her character in this act and later. Yet her variability can more profitably be seen as the result of the paradoxical roles she must accept as a woman in comedy and as a result of her battle against those roles. In the inverted world of courtship, Millamant acquires power over men, events, and words; but what makes her such a fascinating character is her recognition that such powers presume a weak, even erasable, self and a willingness eventually to sacrifice both power and self in marriage. She battles both assumptions. Her seemingly skittish behavior here, then, is an indication of her simultaneous accommodation to and repulsion from conventional female roles (see Markley, *Two-Edg'd Weapons,* 244). She establishes her fight to maintain a self of her own definition in this second act. Later, in her memorable appearance in the proviso scene of act 4, she displays her thoroughly prescient vision of her present and future status, self, and power.

The proviso scene in which Millamant and Mirabell explore the
possibilities for their married life has often been praised as an expression
of both wit and equality. Yet this scene is as much conditioned by
traditional contexts of gender and genre as are earlier ones. Thus, while
this is a scene of rarefied high comedy, it is not one of equality, nor does
it position Millamant to demand the power and the autonomy she seeks.

In keeping with her earlier demands for recognition, Millamant
initiates the interaction of this act 4 scene by demanding that retention
of her autonomy be the first condition of marriage. She expresses this
indirectly at first, in demanding maintenance of the power she has ac-
crued through the chase—"I'll be solicited to the very last, nay and
afterwards" (84). Her demand is more direct moments later: "I'll never
marry, unless I am first made sure of my will and pleasure" (84). As she
specifies the grounds on which she might hope to retain both will and
pleasure—both power and selfhood—her particular demands are all attempts to separate herself and her marriage from convention. Her first
fear is that her self, her "faithful solitude," and her "daring contempla-
tion" (85) might be lost; thus she demands the right to "lie abed in a
morning as long as I please" (85). Her demand that Mirabell address her
with no traditional terms of endearment also draws from her fear of
being co-opted by the institutionalized roles of marriage (85). As she
goes on to list further liberties she will demand—ranging from the freedom to write letters to the sanctity of her own room—her theme continues to be the preservation of a distinct life she might call her own. This
is not a scene about Millamant's freedom; rather, the subtle yet dominant
focus is on threats to that freedom. While Mirabell agrees to each demand she makes, his own demands make clear the power imbalance that
exists even at this point in the lovers' relationship. As both Weber *(Restoration Rake-Hero)* and Markley have shown, his demands underline the
control he maintains even here. And his control translates into a direct
threat to Millamant's cherished autonomy.

Markley points out, for example, that all of Millamant's demands
concern *her* domestic rights *(Two-Edg'd Weapons,* 245); Mirabell's demands *also* concern *her* domestic rights. Mirabell realizes, in other
words, that he has no need to demand the preservation of his own
liberties (marriage by definition ensures those), and thus he concentrates
on limiting Millamant's. Her responses to his demands are equally representative of the inequality of the proviso exchange. While Mirabell has
responded to Millamant's demands by generally acceding to them (he

has little to lose, even here), Millamant does not seem to possess an equivalent, beneficent power. She responds to his demands with a rhetoric she is not fully in control of, with exclamations and curses, the strongest of which implicitly registers her recognition of his power and her powerlessness: "Oh, horrid provisos! filthy strong waters! I toast fellows, odious men! I hate your odious provisos" (88). As Markley notes, she has no language of her own at this crucial moment, and that lack means she has no power to preserve the subjectivity she cherishes (243). The inequalities built into this exchange are finally indicated by the closure Mirabell brings to their bartering. Immediately after Millamant's final protest about his demands, Mirabell mocks her with "then we're agreed." In the next few lines, Millamant practices various responses, and her final acceptance—as full of aversion as joy—marks for a final time her ambivalent position: "Well, you ridiculous thing you, I'll have you—I won't be kissed, nor I won't be thanked—here, kiss my hand though.—So hold your tongue now, and don't say a word" (88). While she has just demanded conditions that might allow her to retain autonomy, Millamant's final vacillations mark her recognition that she is losing, not gaining power. She demands Mirabell's silence and gets it; but the victory is temporary. She will be the silent one as the play ends, and he will direct its final movements.

My study of the tenuous groupings of women in the play can add a final highlight to Millamant's compromised position in this central scene. Just before the proviso scene (when she is seeking solitude) and also during her listing of demands (when she demands future solitude), Millamant deliberately separates herself from others, especially other women. Consequently, the liberties she seeks concern only Millamant, as an exceptional woman. Her situation is similar to that of Rosalind in *As You Like It:* Millamant's distinctiveness means that her extraordinary achievements remain hers alone. Women in general are no threat to the conventional order in *The Way of the World.*

After the proviso scene, Millamant's role in the play changes substantially. Act 5 brings the labyrinthine strands of the plot back together, and Millamant is reduced to playing the part Mirabell instructs her in. For example, she pretends to offer her hand to Sir Wilfull at Mirabell's behest. And although she is present through the accusations and reversals that tie off the play's complicated involvements and schemes, she is silent, with but a short and characteristically ambivalent response to Lady Wishfort's giving her (Millamant) away to Mirabell: "Why does not the man take me? Would you have me give myself to you over again?" (122). Thus the inversions of this play have affected its perceptive heroine in a conventional way. In spite of Millamant's strong campaign for self-preservation, her power and individuality are in the end subsumed. Millamant's journey through the world of this play is not a mystery. Instead, the play tells the story of a woman's compromised response to social patterns that allow her temporary dominance as a prelude to more permanent subservience. Most important, Congreve has created in this character a woman who is conscious of but does not fully articulate the losses she will suffer in marriage. Rosalind seems relatively comfortable with the terms of existence marriage will offer her; on the contrary, Millamant is never comfortable with the possibility or the reality of marriage. She cannot fit the person she would like to be into a mold others have fashioned. This comic heroine is, thus, never at ease with the limited power comedy can allow her.[4]

## Marriage as Ending

Congreve's discouraging picture of female friendship and his portrait of Millamant's isolated struggle for independence both suggest his awareness of the limitations that attach to comic women's search for power and autonomy. His recognition of drawbacks also characterizes his portrait of comic marriage. Yet marriage remains both the goal of enlightened characters like Mirabell and Millamant and the end of the play itself. In addition, Burns notes that this is one of few Restoration comedies to connect marriage to the procreation of children *(Restoration Comedy,* 209). Congreve's combination of a cynical attitude to marriage with a dependence on it as a symbolic standard of future happiness results in a comic ending that highlights the paradoxes of the love relationships determined by comedy. Although the characters know it is difficult to make marriage the home of love, they can envision no alternative. To suggest how Congreve's ending reiterates a comic structure that confines women, I will first review the portrait of marriage that emerges from the play's five acts, and then consider the specific articulation marriage receives in the play's concluding moves.

From servant to master, from man to woman, marriage is characterized throughout the play as an institution that restricts freedoms, invites hypocrisy, and forces manipulation. Only rarely is it connected with happiness. The first marriage mentioned is that of the two servants

Waitwell and Foible, a union Mirabell has engineered to ensure the success of his scheme to wed Millamant. The newlyweds appear to be happily mated when they enter together in act 2 (50); yet Waitwell closes the act with his complaint that this arranged marriage has meant the end to his control of life—"I am married and can't be my own man again" (52). The first married couple to actually appear together are the Fainalls. Their greetings upon meeting at the park—"My dear!" and "My soul!" (35)—are rapidly shown to be evidence of the venom, not the love, they share. As such couples signal, marriage serves as a tool and is suffered as an impediment: this is especially evident in the tête-à-têtes that constitute the wandering action of act 2. And as the action of the play progresses, the cynical assumptions that the characters make about the institution only intensify. Both Mirabell's persistence in his campaign to gain Millamant and Lady Wishfort's overpowering desire for a marriage (to any one who fits her minimal standards) preserve the typical comic plot's drive toward marriage. But such progress stalls often in the play's later stages, when the recriminations against marriage multiply.

For example, Fainall and Mrs. Marwood close out the third act with some of the play's most ugly images of marriage. Fainall describes his own marriage as a mixture of pain and cruelty:

> Let me see. I am married already, so that's over. My wife has played the jade with me; well, that's over too. I never loved her, or if I had, why that would have been over too by this time. Jealous of her I cannot be, for I am certain; so there's an end of jealousy. Weary of her I am, and shall be. No, there's no end of that; no, no, that were too much to hope. Thus far concerning my repose; now for my reputation. As to my own, I married not for it; so that's out of the question. And as to my part in my wife's, why she had parted with hers before; so bringing none to me, she can take none from me. 'Tis against all rule of play that I should lose to one who has not wherewithal to stake. (76–77)

His summary leads him to conclude with a bitter renunciation of his role as husband:

> I am single, and will herd no more with 'em [husbands]. True, I wear the badge, but I'll disown the order. And since I take my leave

of 'em, I care not if I leave 'em a common motto to their common
crest:

> All husbands must or pain or shame endure;
> The wise too jealous are, fools too secure.

(78)

Fainall brings such private ruminations to public attention at the end of
the play when he drops his facade of caring for his wife and admits it is
her family's money he desires. His accusations against her are some of
the most vicious lines delivered in a generally brutal play: "You thing,
that was a wife, shall smart for this! I will not leave thee wherewithal to
hide thy shame; your body shall be as naked as your reputation" (118).
Such actions are, he has pointed out shortly before, "but the way of the
world" (117). It is suitable that Fainall's accomplice in his devious de-
signs, Mrs. Marwood, expresses a similar cynicism about marriage.
Early in the play she suggests that if she were to "do myself the violence
of undergoing the ceremony" of marriage again, she would at least make
her husband believe he were a cuckold ever "upon the rack of fear and
jealousy" (34). Yet Millamant's words and actions provide the best evidence that such sentiments, while extreme, are only exaggerations of the
general attitude to marriage expressed in the play. The song she requests
in act 3, for example, counsels that love must be tempered by ambition
and that success in love entails the wounding of others in one's own
social ascendance.[5] More forcefully in the proviso scene, Millamant re-
lays her conclusion that marriage is an institution she must take great
measures to protect herself against. Finally, Millamant too is ready to
make marriage a game, as she shows in agreeing (though only temporarily) to contract herself to Sir Wilfull.

Despite the bleak image of marriage in the play, *The Way of the
World* nonetheless concludes with marriage. For Mirabell and Millamant, marriage is meant to crown their sophisticated expressions of
attraction and repulsion. Even with its institutional baggage, marriage
is their vehicle to togetherness. While both parties know that the chances
for their long-term happiness are slim, they approach their union willingly. But Congreve does more than expose the bleak prospects of marriage. In this final return to the institution, he stresses that its connotations are different for men than for women. For Mirabell, as representative of the play's men, the play's several conclusive comments on

marriage articulate his control. Not only has he engineered his marriage to Millamant and proved to Lady Wishfort that she shouldn't marry unless under his guidance, but he also pretends to counsel the Fainalls back into some sort of truce by returning the deed of trust to them. He then concludes the play with four lines of warning about what may make marriage go wrong.

> From hence let those be warned, who mean to wed,
> Lest mutual falsehood stain the bridal bed;
> For each deceiver to his cost may find,
> That marriage frauds too oft are paid in kind.
>
> (123)

For most of the play's women, the final vision of marriage that Mirabell superintends means loss of status and control. Mrs. Fainall may retain her deed of trust, but will be subject to vicious recriminations from her husband in the future; Lady Wishfort is dazzled into compliance by Mirabell's complicated scheme and must acknowledge her foolishness; and Millamant is silenced, as I have already noted. In spite of Congreve's awareness that comic marriage is founded on hypocrisy and inequity, he can only express despair at (as opposed to rejection of) the gender hierarchies of comedy. Marriage is grossly defective and male-determined, but it serves a purpose. Even though this play ends with but a single new marriage, all of the play's characters are affected by the conventional definition of social relations that marriage represents.

## The Way of the World on the Twentieth-Century Stage

The play's production history offers a final vantage point from which to consider the way Congreve conjoins comedy and women. Holland (The Ornament of Action), Powell (Restoration Theatre Production), and others have demonstrated the critical profitability of understanding the Restoration staging of such a play as The Way of the World. Yet I propose to focus on more recent productions in which the portrayal of the play's women has been a major indication of the work's grounding in the limited elasticity of comic convention.

Kenneth Muir ('Congreve on the Modern Stage") has noted that audiences in this century have proven the most receptive of Congreve's drama; and in chronicling famous twentieth-century productions, he records how Millamant's portrayal has been the crux of critical appraisal. When the play has succeeded, it has most notably been because the actress playing Millamant has found a compelling way of presenting the character's complexity. The 1924 Nigel Playfair production in London, for instance, was carried by Edith Evans, who offered an attractive fusion of "power and beauty" (136, quoting Hubert Griffith from *The Observer*). Yet reviewer Griffith's elaboration on the portrayal hints that Evans succeeded only because her power was held in check, diffused: "She [Evans] kept Millamant an eighteenth-century flirt, and because she is of the line of great tragic actresses, transformed her also into a poem" (136). Griffith's relief at Millamant's flirtatious poetic nature suggests that Evans's Millamant remains a standard to the present day because the portrayal was a comfortably conventional mixture of strength and acquiescence. When the play has failed to live up to its reputation as the apotheosis of Restoration comedy, production problems have often also been traced to Millamant. In John Gielgud's 1953 production, for example, Pamela Brown's Millamant caused substantial disappointment, apparently because the actress claimed too much power. Brown was chided for being "an ice maiden" who overestimated Millamant's intelligence—"Miss Brown cannot bring herself to enter into the delicious make-believe of such an essentially empty mind, and this imperfectly concealed antipathy is ruinous to the comedy" (140, quoting from review in *The Tatler*). Such disparate responses to portrayals of Millamant suggest both her power and her powerlessness. In this century, a successful production of the play depends on an effective portrayal of Millamant; theatrically the character/actor holds great power. But less successful productions suggest that such power has its limits, for theatrical success seems also to be premised on the assumption that Millamant knows how to take her restricted place in the marriage that orders the play's end.

Productions of the play in the 1980s have consciously explored the issue of women and power that has been so central to the portrayal of Millamant. These productions map out—even more clearly than did the productions earlier in the century—the paradoxical nature of women that suffuses Congreve's comic environment.

In 1984, two major productions of the play outlined the contemporary possibilities for Millamant and her world. At the Greenwich Theatre, the social and monetary forces shaping love relationships were the focus. Lawyers and accountants continually swarmed in the "severe black and white" room of the set (see Wardle review) to serve as constant reminders that the banter and actions could not be separated from the characters' need to survive in a vicious, economically determined world. During the proviso scene, the lawyers even recorded the particulars on the pseudocontractual promises. This attention to the social and monetary contexts of the play allowed for a radically different Millamant, one who could openly suggest her predicament as a woman and clearly display her powers for dealing with it. On the whole, reviewers found this feminist Millamant refreshingly powerful. Robert Hewison, for instance, noted that the dominant Millamant of Paola Dionisotti filled the vacuum caused by the production's lack of love. Irving Wardle recognized further that Dionisotti changed the terms on which the character of Millamant (and the play) must be judged: "And Paola Dionisotti works a radical transformation of Millamant from the traditional hothouse creature to an arch-calculator forever dropping her pretense of feminine languor for brisk business-like statements of her sexual terms." Perhaps just as predictably, the reviewers also sensed that this powerful heroine displaced the more familiar contours of comic love relations. Michael Ratcliffe noted that Dionisotti's radical Millamant was powerful, but at the price of being unbelievable:

> Miss Dionisotti plays Millamant as a butch, firm chinned Victorian woman of the world . . . and when she collapses all of a feminine heap on the floor for love of her man, there is not a heart in the house, male or female, that will believe it.

This production, then, presented a heroine cognizant of both the limits and the possibilities of her control. Reviewers recognized the forceful presence of the women in the Greenwich production. And like their predecessors early in the century, they made this strong female contingent the basis for general, though not unqualified, praise.

The second 1984 production, opening at the Chichester Festival in the summer and later traveling to London's Haymarket Theatre, seemed also to probe beneath the play's traditional veneer, again primarily through a timely portrayal of Millamant. Reviewer Michael Coveney most unambiguously noted the feminist dimensions of this production: "Never before had I realized how much of the play is a discussion of liberty within marriage, women's liberty especially." More specifically,

Roger Warren remarked that in the proviso scene Mirabell and Millamant "are not quite so evenly matched as their symmetrically balanced
speeches in the proposal scene suggest." In his review he goes on to
report that the proviso scene is all *hers*. Coveney and Warren, along with
most other reviewers, located the center of the play's female strength
and liberty in Maggie Smith's triumphant Millamant. Yet just as the
Greenwich production called up recognition of the (not always welcomed) changes necessitated by a self-directed Millamant, so with this
production the great power Smith claimed remained open to ambiguous
interpretation. The implicit question, once again, was how much power
the heroine could be allowed to claim if she was to remain within comic
boundaries. Reviewers Jack Tinker and Kenneth Hurren, for example,
praised Smith's Millamant by defining her performance as brilliantly
capricious. Thus both placed this Millamant within the tradition of her
variability, though Hurren's comments are the more revealing. He
praised Smith as "the embodiment of all the whims and caprices of
woman at her most beguiling." The desire to keep Smith's Millamant
within recognizable female territory was most obvious in Francis King's
review, where King conjectured that Millamant's assertiveness may be
rooted in "some deep-seated sexual inhibition." Finally, those reviewers
with less conventional judgments about Millamant marked the limitations to Smith's Millamant. Irving Wardle, for example, noted Millamant's relinquishing of power when he recorded how she "bravely cuts
out all the satire when she comes down stage to bid farewell to her
liberty." Of Congreve's Millamant, director Gaskill remarks that it is
"as sophisticated a part as has ever been written" (quoted in Masters
review). Reviews of his production suggest that such sophistication allows for both a powerful Millamant and the simultaneous—and apparently still necessary—reduction of that power.

   For a final look at continuing attempts to translate the play's slippery approach to women, I turn to the 1989 production by the Cambridge Theatre Company at London's Young Vic. The set of reviews
that greeted this production may be most notable for the reviewers'
conscious efforts to respond to the women within a feminist frame of
reference. Several reviewers made an effort to highlight Congreve's
strong portrayals of women (Osborne, Darvell). And at least two went
further and attempted to study Millamant from a feminist perspective.
Martin Hoyle, for example, remarked on Millamant's "early-feminist
conditions." And as he detailed her struggle to be more than "chattel,"

he found "positively joyful" her "refusal to be kissed." He then concluded that the production projected more happiness than most, most
notably because of Millamant's feminist glimmerings. Along the same
lines, Nicholas de Jongh remarked on Congreve's "male-chauvinist
mind" and concluded: "In his empire of love, men are the rulers, women
the pining victims." Yet these responses do not give a complete view of
the play, the production, and the various possibilities for understanding
this play's women in 1989. For along with such feminist appraisal still
came traditional responses and expectations. Milton Shulman, for example, wished that Susan Brown, the actress playing Millamant, had displayed more "coquettish high spirits and submerged love." He wished,
in other words, for the stereotypical variability so long associated with
Millamant. Peter Kemp expressed similar regrets that Brown had not
transmitted "the seductive and unsettling flurry of flightiness she
should." But most tellingly, James Christopher's reference to Millamant
as "cock-teasing" reveals the vestiges of conventional gender expectations that continue to surround the play's women. Overall, reviews of
the production were mixed. Through these contradictory extracts, however, one can see that Congreve's play—even in this Young Vic production—still rests firmly in the comic tradition. Its conventionally based
blueprint for women remains one of its most enduring features.

Both the play text and its productions suggest that Congreve was
aware of the treacherous possibilities comedy presents its women. His
Millamant is certainly a sharp observer of the way her rarefied culture
makes different demands on men and women. And contemporary directors, actors, and reviewers have continued to explore the possibilities for
portraying the play's women to an audience conversant with the constraints of gender. For them all, the play remains a place where women
exist in a state of contradiction and ambivalence.

## Chapter 4

# Shaw's *The Philanderer:*
# The Reformer's Women
# and the Contradictions of
# Comic Freedom

Like his predecessors Shakespeare and Congreve, Bernard Shaw seems conscious of the compromised position of comedy's women. Yet Shaw's work is distinguished from that of the other two playwrights by his often-stated desire to transform women both in comedy and society. Reform was his mission in his comedy as in his life. Yet his crusading about women did not make Shaw's self-appointed task of remaking comedy substantially easier. And like the earlier writers, he leaves a comedy less radical than has often been assumed. In a few pages, I will turn to Shaw's early play *The Philanderer,* which provides evidence of his full engagement with the challenging and treacherous particulars of combining comedy and strong women. Given his ample extra-play pronouncements on the issue of women and comedy, however, I preface my specific textual study with a general consideration of the way Shaw envisioned the aesthetics and politics of women, comedy, and change.

## Shaw, Tradition, and Reform: The Contexts
## for His Comic Women

The several incarnations of his play *Pygmalion* suggest the tenaciousness of Shaw's belief about women's role in comedy. From the premier production of the play in 1914, Shaw found himself repeatedly censoring others' desires to make the comedy end with the romantic coupling of the two main characters, Henry Higgins and Eliza Doolittle. The impulse to rewrite his play persisted, in spite of Shaw's clear point that Eliza's love interest is the less central, less mature Freddy. In the 1914 production, Shaw denied permission to actor Herbert Beerbohm Tree (who played Henry Higgins under Shaw's direction) to perform an ending in which Henry blows kisses and throws flowers to Eliza. Yet after the opening, when Shaw journeyed to Yorkshire during the run, Beerbohm reinstated his romantic gestures against Shaw's wishes. In 1938 Shaw wrote the screenplay for a movie version of the play and found his wishes ignored in a similar manner, again during his absence. Instead of the ending Shaw wrote, which offered clear indications of the union of Eliza and Freddy, the producers pointed to a romantically framed reunion of Henry and Eliza. Shaw had not changed his mind about the comedy's ending even in 1948, when at ninety-two years of age he unequivocally responded to the Minneapolis Civic Theatre's request to modify the ending toward a coupling of Henry and Eliza: "I absolutely forbid . . . any suggestion that the middleaged bully and the girl of eighteen are lovers."[1]

On the one side stands Shaw, consistent in his belief that to romanticize the Higgins-Doolittle relationship is to negate the development of the play's more radical characters and ideas. On the other side stand generations of actors, directors, and producers, drawn not to Shaw's hard-edged message in the play, but to the possibilities of the conventional happy ending they seek—love, romance, the promise of marriage. This confrontation between reform and tradition is at issue in most of Shaw's work. And as he brings his full genius to bear on the theory as well as the practice of women in comedy, Shaw analyzes the conflict from all angles. Specifically, he is attuned to issues of women's rights, and he is heavily invested in effecting social change out of drama.

Shaw's attention to the women of comedy is a natural outgrowth of some of his most basic beliefs about human behavior and is connected to his lifelong campaigns for sexual equality and social change. Barbara Bellow Watson *(A Shavian Guide)* and Margot Peters *(Bernard Shaw)* have both offered book-length studies of Shaw's connections with and sensitivity to the women in his life. Both writers document that his relationships and friendships with women were always conditioned by his personal campaign for women's rights. In explaining the "secret" of his "extraordinary knowledge of women," Shaw himself calls attention to his simple assumption that men and women are the same—"I have always assumed that a woman is a person exactly like myself"

("Woman—Man in Petticoats," 174). However, some doubts have always been attached to his feminist zeal. Michael Holroyd, for example, reports that the various unorthodox ways in which Shaw supported the campaign for women's suffrage alternately endeared him to and alienated him from suffrage campaigners *(The Genius of Shaw)*. And as Watson reports, Shaw's unusual portraiture of women has raised alarms both from "ladies" and "sensualists" *(A Shavian Guide, 18)*. Even considering the objections that have been raised against Shaw's feminism (many of which a feminist can dismiss easily), the evidence points to his support of women. He saw the establishment of sexual equality as the only way to improve and ultimately to save the world.

In his plays, Shaw's efforts on behalf of women's rights are inextricable from his belief in the necessity of social change and in the power of drama to effect such change. Writing in *The Quintessence of Ibsenism,* Shaw argues that a step toward the new demands a demolition of the old:

> The point to seize is that social progress takes effect through the replacement of old institutions by new ones; and since every institution involves the recognition of the duty of conforming to it, progress must involve a repudiation of an established duty at every step. (28)

Although he goes on to admit that even his revolution can make but "crablike progress" (28), he has dedicated his playwrighting life to the forwarding of social progress. Shaw's belief that the drama was not merely a possible conduit for social reform but rather an essential one is set forth in his 1895 comments on the problem play. In his methodical way, Shaw first states that "every social question . . . affords material for drama." Second, he notes that many dramatists avoid social questions out of a "political ignorance" often shared with the audience. Third, he argues that the "hugeness and complexity of modern civilizations" have simultaneously pressed upon people more facts than they can process and burdened people with "the urgency of social reforms." Given this urgency, he concludes, writers must participate in the process of saving the world. He adds a fourth point as an optimistic coda, promising that this "tendency to drive social questions onto the stage, and into fiction and poetry" will lead, eventually, to the requisite improvement in social organization and to the solution of grave social problems ("The Problem Play," 65–66). For the majority of British playwrights who wrote problem plays at the turn of the century, the genre was not considered comic. Yet for Shaw, whose primary dramatic genre was comedy, this prescriptive study of problem drama applied especially to comedy. It is Shaw's combination of the urgency of problem drama with the pleasure of comedy that allows his portraits of comic women to stand alone.

Shaw's unequivocal pronouncements on women and on the drama's potential for change have made his work particularly important for feminists. He is enthusiastically welcomed into their ranks. Barbara Bellow Watson has been the most articulate in explaining the far-reaching possibilities that are allowed to Shaw's comic women, arguing that "Shaw changed radically the structure of comedy itself" ("The New Woman," 2). She parallels Shaw's belief in social evolution and his transformation of comedy:

> Shaw sees society, and even nature, as capable of genuine evolution, of an escape from recurrence, and his comedy reflects that view in its very structure. Both the nature of the conflict and the nature of its resolution differ in Shaw from the traditional comic pattern, even when the events of the plot seem most conventional. (4)

Looking to a host of Shaw's plays—*Pygmalion, Getting Married, Man and Superman, The Millionairess, Major Barbara, Candida, The Apple Cart,* and others—Watson details how women characters command Shaw's comedy in multiple ways. Her argument has been extended by Sally Peters Vogt ("Ann and Superman"), who concentrates on *Man and Superman* to demonstrate that the inversions of the play help produce its revolutionary message.

Shaw's combinations of feminist vision and a drama of change have their limitations, however. For even his comedy is not immune to the powerful forces of convention. The difficulty with Watson's argument, for example, is that she bases her assessment of Shaw's comedy on two main assumptions: (1) that traditional comedy, with its cyclic movement to a new, but not so new, order has allowed little room for women; and (2) that the inversions and subversions of Shavian comedy have little precedent. Both are erroneous. Not only has comedy long made a place for women, but that place has been dependent on both inversions and subversions. I am sympathetic with Watson's argument, for I share her belief that traditional comedy limits its women. Yet I find her claims for the "revolutionary and feminist structure" of Shavian comedy ("The

New Woman," 10) misguided since they fail to take into account the dependence of traditional comedy on both strong women and inversion. In studying *The Philanderer*, I will join Watson in advocating the novelty to be found in Shaw's comedy and comic women, but I will also argue that Shaw's comedy comes out of the British comic tradition and is—despite his efforts and his consciousness—restricted by the genre. Without doubt, Shaw supported women's equality and social reorganization; but in choosing comedy as his major vehicle for such social campaigns, he adds his own paradoxes to a paradoxical tradition.

As Watson's study makes clear, many of Shaw's plays offer evidence of his creative approach to joining women and comedy. *Man and Superman* is a logical candidate for the study of his comic invention, since in it he joins the theatrical instability of his Don Juan in Hell act to his three other highly conventional acts. Similarly, both *Major Barbara* and *Pygmalion* would allow for investigations of equally adventuresome combinations of women and comedy. Instead, however, I have chosen to study Shaw's comedy through the lens of his second play, *The Philanderer*. Like *Man and Superman, Major Barbara,* and *Pygmalion, The Philanderer* makes radical assumptions about the theatrical and social worlds it investigates. But to a degree unequalled in these other plays, *The Philanderer* is intensely self-conscious about how the elements of reversal and ending define women's portrayal in comedy. Shaw himself is prescient about further connections to be made between this comedy and life, suggesting that *The Philanderer* is "unpleasant" not only because it exposes the grotesque results of contemporary marriage laws, but also because it directs these "attacks" against the audience ("Preface Mainly about Myself," 33–34).

Several factors account for the play's relative obscurity in Shaw's canon. Although written in 1893, the play was not produced until 1907 and rarely thereafter. In an uncharacteristically short "Prefatory Note" written in 1930, Shaw himself admitted that the play was already "dated." As Alfred Turco, Jr., reports, many critics have joined Shaw in a quick dismissal of the play (*"The Philanderer,"* 47); it is rarely studied, even in extensive works on Shaw. In addition to those who have ignored the play as dated and insubstantial, others have limited it to autobiography. Margot Peters is among the biographical critics who have probed the play primarily as a comment on Shaw's relationships with Jenny Patterson and Florence Farr. As Peters reports, the philanderer Charteris is in part Shaw's self-portrait (*Bernard Shaw*, 115). In spite of all efforts to discard the play, however, it has not been forgotten. Four prominent productions since 1976 have attested to its durability. And Turco has claimed *The Philanderer* as one of Shaw's "best dozen-and-a-half plays" (*"The Philanderer,"* 61). I intend to show that *The Philanderer* is not so much a neglected masterpiece as an exposure of the compromised way comedy and women coexist, even for Shaw.

Set in the early 1890s, the play details several love affairs that have developed in a gathering place called the Ibsen Club. Act 1 introduces the two main characters, Leonard Charteris (the eponymous philanderer) and Julia Craven, struggling through the current dislocations of their love relationship. True to his reputation, Charteris has responded to Julia's possessiveness by pursuing a relationship with Grace Tranfield; and the play opens on Charteris and Grace's amorous embraces in her drawing room. Julia has responded to Charteris's philandering by tracking him to Grace's home. Most of the first act, then, records the collision of the three characters and the awkward situation that arises when they are interrupted by Joseph Cuthbertson (Grace's father) and Colonel Craven (Julia's father), both returning to the drawing room unaware of their children's goings-on.

Act 2, which takes place the next day in the library of the Ibsen Club, is the heart of the play.[2] In the shadow of Ibsen's bust, all of the characters from act 1 gather, joined by Sylvia—Julia's manly younger sister—and Dr. Paramore, the medical specialist who has made his reputation by diagnosing in Colonel Craven a rare and fatal liver condition. As Cuthbertson and Craven provide a chorus of the conventional, complaining about the silly, egalitarian liberties on which the Ibsen Club is based, the younger generation continues its dizzying scurry for companionship. Grace rejects Charteris, although she continues to be charmed by him; Julia continues her pursuit of Charteris, although he continues to discourage her; and Charteris talks of his love predicament to everyone, including Dr. Paramore, whom Charteris pushes into active pursuit of Julia.

Act 3 commences in Paramore's reception room where Julia and Paramore—alone together—become engaged to be married. The others arrive shortly after to judge the play's one pending marital union. Shaw's title points his audience toward what I consider a somewhat misleading concentration on Charteris's course through the three acts. In this brief synopsis as well as in the discussion to follow, I offer a broadened focus on the philanderer, the three women around him, and this play's concern about women in comedy. As in chapters 2 and 3, I will study the play in three segments. I will consider Shaw's "Old Order," his inventive reversals of that order, and his brutal ending. To conclude, I will consider both the play's theatrical self-consciousness and its recent production history as final comments on the play's women. Shaw does not remake comedy, but his intense scrutiny suggests how attuned he is to its contradictory impulses toward women.

## The Old Order

At the very end of the play, Charteris debates the existence of an "Old Order" with Cuthbertson and Craven. Cuthbertson expresses his relief that he is of the Old Order, only to be contradicted by young Charteris, who asserts that Cuthbertson is only "symbolic" of it: "Dont persuade yourself that you represent the Old Order. There never was any Old Order" (226). Although their debate fades before it is resolved, Shaw himself answers the question they raise about the existence of a status quo. Aware as any comic playwright of the pervasive and deadening nature of established order, Shaw still presents that order as the foundation of his play. For Shaw, the Old Order *does* exist, primarily in the persons of Cuthbertson and Craven.

Throughout the play, both Cuthbertson and Craven take it upon themselves to defend and preserve the traditional. They celebrate their reunion in act 1 by railing against the new social behavior the play is about. Craven recounts Cuthbertson's words from earlier in their evening: "You said the whole modern movement was abhorrent to you because your life had been passed in witnessing scenes of suffering nobly endured and sacrifice willingly rendered by womanly women and manly men" (159). Consistently they cling to stereotypical ideals of men, women, and family life: men deserve a smoking room to themselves; women need "strong, manly, deep throated, broad chested" men (169); and marriage must be a woman's major goal. They exercise the power that rests with such traditional opinion as frequently as they can, even in environments (such as the Ibsen Club) not receptive to their ideas. Craven, at the end of the play, speaks to his daughters "as your commanding officer" while Cuthbertson takes it upon himself to speak *for* his daughter Grace (224). Such comments and actions typical of the established order infect even those characters who have taken care to distance themselves from it. Charteris, for example, assumes that

women tell lies better than men (155). And even Sylvia partakes in such
conventional stereotyping, defiling the type of woman who will keep a
man dangling just to prevent "any other woman from getting him"
(182).

Shaw, of course, undercuts such beliefs and behavior at every turn.
Although both Cuthbertson and Craven champion the traditional marriage, neither *had* one: Cuthbertson and his wife eventually separated due
to irreconcilable families and life-styles; and Craven, at best, "got to be
very fond of" the woman he married for money (171). The men also
display personal knowledge of the philandering they seem to abhor.
Both fought over the same woman (eventually Cuthbertson's wife) in
their youth, and Craven has knowing advice for Charteris and his juggling of women: "It's well to be off with the Old Woman before youre
on with the New" (176). Shaw does not take the two men seriously.
But his comedy, in a formal way, does. The play is about changes in the
traditional system of sexual and marital relations. But those changes,
those reversals, are consistently judged against the system they replace,
the system that Cuthbertson and Craven stand behind.

**Reversals**

The reversals of comedy provide Shaw with an inviting locale for his
main concerns in *The Philanderer,* the testing of new orders, specifically
new sexual orders. And through a series of sex-role reversals, he con-
ducts his primary exploration of women and comedy.

The Ibsen Club is the heart of the play's reversals. Established as a
social and dining club for both sexes, it is an organization dedicated to
principles its members have extracted from Ibsen's work. Most central
is the club founders' interpretation of Ibsen's drama to mean that traditional stereotyping of men and women is debilitating. Thus the club
operates under one basic rule—that only unmanly men and unwomanly
women (i.e., those *un*stereotypical) can be admitted. Charteris details
the membership process: "Every candidate for membership must be
nominated by a man and a woman, who both guarantee that the candidate, if female, is not womanly, and if male, not manly" (159). The club,
then, in theory, establishes for its women exactly what comedy does:
an atmosphere where sex roles are reversed, where women can claim
power and status.

But instead of creating an androgynous utopia, those founding the

Ibsen Club have unintentionally distorted both male and female types. Because it is based on reversing a system rife with double standards, the club has not erased sexual differences but perverted them. Most significantly, the men and women have not undergone equal or even comparable changes. For the men, the reversals only *appear* to represent a loss of status. As is typical in comedy, the men in the play have apparently given up power to the women. As act 2 opens, Sylvia has both Paramore and Cuthbertson cowering before her charge that they have unwittingly dismissed her: "What I protest against is your assumption that my presence doesnt matter because I'm only a female member" (167). But only moments later Cuthbertson is unleashing his unrelenting disgust for Ibsen: "I sometimes feel that I should like to take the poker, and fetch it [Ibsen's bust] a wipe across the nose" (169). This disgust rather than an acceptance of women's power more accurately illustrates the role the men have carved for themselves in their relation to the "new" woman. All four of the play's men, in fact, have but tenuous connections to the club's ideals and reversals. As I have already noted, neither Cuthbertson nor Craven believes in the principles of the club (Cuthbertson has joined only to protect his daughter, and Craven is a visitor). Paramore neither dismisses nor embraces the principles of the club. And most notably, Charteris uses Ibsenism not to support women so much as to advance his philanderings with them. He even suggests that the club founders had as much in mind—a social environment where unruly women could be kept in line.

> You know what breaks up most clubs for men and women. Theres a quarrel—a scandal—cherchez la femme—always a woman at the bottom of it. Well, we knew this when we founded the club; but we noticed that the woman at the bottom of it was always a womanly woman. The unwomanly women who work for their living, and know how to take care of themselves, never give any trouble. So we simply said we wouldnt have any womanly women; and when one gets smuggled in she has to take care not to behave in a womanly way. (161)

Watson maintains that androgyny is a common feature of Shaw's ideal world (*A Shavian Guide,* 213; "The New Woman," 16). Through the men in *The Philanderer,* however, Shaw suggests how much self-interest stands in the way of any such equality. Shaw understands that in his

Ibsen Club, as in Shakespeare's Arden, androgyny benefits men more than it does women.

While their position is compromised by the limited change the men undergo, the women in the play do benefit from the reversals institutionalized by the Ibsen Club. They have freedoms here that they could not find elsewhere. The smoking room, for example, is "always full of women" (170). Women and men sit down for serious discussion (of nonromantic matters) several times in the play. And the behavior of Sylvia and Grace is unstereotypical. Sylvia has benefitted most, finding at the club acceptance of her brash ways and an allowance of her breeches. Grace too has learned to turn the reversals of the Ibsen Club to her advantage. Yet Julia, who is clearly not an unwomanly woman, is a problem both for the club and for Shaw's comedy. To examine further the contours of the sex-role reversals inspired by the club's idol Ibsen, I turn now to a detailed examination of play's two main characters, Charteris and Julia. In his preface to *Plays Unpleasant,* Shaw suggests that *The Philanderer* is about the perversions that result from outdated marriage laws; and he objects to the ways in which " 'advanced' individuals" evade marriage ("Preface Mainly about Myself," 33). Both Charteris and Julia are the objectionable results of a relational system Shaw finds is out of control.

Not only does Shaw's title point toward Charteris, but Charteris is also the main promoter and philosopher of Ibsen-inspired reversals. As such, he proves himself master of any rhetorical situation; and in turn, he is vitalized by his manipulation of this world of reversals. In act 1 as he describes the Ibsenist ideal to Julia, he cleverly makes *her* seem the philanderer:

> As a woman of advanced views, you were determined to be free. You regarded marriage as a degrading bargain, by which a woman sells herself to a man for the social status of a wife and the right to be supported and pensioned in old age out of his income. Thats the advanced view: our view. Besides, if you had married me, I might have turned out a drunkard, a criminal, an imbecile, a horror to you; and you couldnt have released yourself. Too big a risk, you see. Thats the rational view: our view. Accordingly, you reserved the right to leave me at any time if you found our companionship incompatible with—what was the expression you used?—with your full development as a human being. I think that was how you put

the Ibsenist view: our view. So I had to be content with a charming philander, which taught me a great deal, and brought me some hours of exquisite happiness. (147)

Like Horner in Wycherley's *The Country Wife,* he takes from the "philosophical" situation exactly what he needs to involve himself with as many women as possible. With Julia, Charteris is always willing to lie when necessary. But he is consistent in finding the wit to protect himself from others also. When Grace refuses to steal Charteris from Julia (as he proposes), he skillfully converts her feminist loyalty into an illogical response:

| | |
|---|---|
| *Charteris:* | I cannot deny it, my love. Yes: it is your mission to rescue me from Julia. |
| *Grace:* | *(rising)* Then, if you please, I decline to be made use of for any such purpose. I will not steal you from another woman. *(She walks up and down the room with ominous disquiet.)* |
| *Charteris:* | Steal me! *(He comes towards her.)* Grace: I have a question to put to you as an advanced woman. Mind! as an advanced woman. Does Julia belong to me? Am I her owner—her master? |
| *Grace:* | Certainly not. No woman is the property of a man. A woman belongs to herself and to nobody else. |
| *Charteris:* | Quite right. Ibsen for ever! Thats exactly my opinion. Now tell me, do I belong to Julia; or have I a right to belong to myself? |
| *Grace:* | *(puzzled)* Of course you have; but— |
| *Charteris:* | *(interrupting her triumphantly)* Then how can you steal me from Julia if I dont belong to her? . . . No, my dear: if Ibsen sauce is good for the goose, it's good for the gander as well. (142) |

Yet with Grace, who embraces the principle of the manly woman and the womanly man in earnest, he also frequently drops such masking rhetoric. When in act 2 Grace asks him, "Does your happiness really depend on me?" he answers openly:

| | |
|---|---|
| *Charteris:* | *(tenderly)* Absolutely. *(She beams with delight. A sudden revulsion comes to him at the sight: he recoils, dropping her hands and crying)* Ah no: why should I lie to you? *(He folds his arms and adds firmly)* My happiness depends on nobody but myself. I can do without you. (185) |

Throughout the play, Charteris combines the cant and candor he needs to control the actions of those around him. Most of the time the others object to his behavior. Both Craven and Cuthbertson are shocked by Charteris's caddish behavior toward their daughters (175). Paramore is similarly offended when Charteris broaches the delicate subject of Julia with him (195). Julia and Grace vary in their responses, their mixture of love and disdain dependent on their emotional involvement at the moment. But Sylvia's relationship with Charteris reveals the most about his place in this world of gender role reversals.

Thoroughly manly woman that she is, Sylvia has no personal interest in Charteris, nor he in her. That frees her to evaluate objectively his behavior with women. Charteris's play-opening discussion with Grace reveals that he is neither handsome nor well-dressed, neither romantically mysterious nor gallant (143). He is, as he wants to convince Grace, the opposite of the traditional romantic hero, and in that case not responsible for women's attachment to him. Yet in act 2, Sylvia gets Charteris to admit that it is his basic disregard for women that in fact draws them to him:

> *Charteris:*  Then you know that I never pay any special attention to any woman.
>  *Sylvia:*  *(thoughtfully)* Do you know, Leonard, I really believe you. I dont think you care a bit more for one woman than for another.
> *Charteris:*  You mean I dont care a bit less for one woman than another.
>  *Sylvia:*  That makes it worse. But what I mean is that you never bother about their being only women: you talk to them just as you do to me or any other fellow. Thats the secret of your success. You cant think how sick they get of being treated with the respect due to their sex. (180)

As Sylvia intuits, Charteris's behavior points to two conclusions about the play's reversals: (1) that they are easily manipulated for this man's benefit, and (2) that, as a consequence, they are less manipulable by women.

While central to the play's establishment and operation of sexual reversals, Charteris remains a static character little changed by the events he orchestrates. Julia, however, is the play's dynamic character. Ellen Terry identified Julia's strategic part as a tragic one—"Julia is a very tragedy."[3] Terry's is a response Shaw would seem to have encouraged, for he also marks Julia as tragic from his first description of her—"a beautiful, dark, tragic looking woman, in mantle and toque" (144)—to his last, in which he notes that the rest of the cast (minus Charteris) feel "the presence of a keen sorrow" while regarding Julia (227). I propose, however, that the darkness that attaches to Julia in this play is a result of comedy, not tragedy. Through Julia especially, Shaw notes that the reversals not only at the Ibsen Club but also at the heart of comedy fail to liberate women.

Julia's changes in the play are not the expected ones: she does not learn to be the unwomanly woman she sets out to be, the woman the play's reversals seem to favor. Instead, she comes to accept the womanly woman she is. In act 1, when Julia breaks in on Charteris and Grace, she is already realizing the limits of her involvememt in Charteris's Ibsenist views. As Charteris linguistically betters her with his clever arguments against their union ("Advanced people form charming friendships: conventional people marry" [150]), she stubbornly sticks to her demand for Charteris's exclusive attentions, for marriage. In this scene, Julia seems little more than the "jealous termagant" Charteris accuses her of being (150). Yet her unflattering confrontation with Charteris is also the beginning of her self-education. Charteris obviously has been attempting to indoctrinate her into the beliefs of the Ibsen Club to suit his purposes. Act 1 shows that she has failed as his student. As the play progresses, she moves—steadily—toward her own understanding of women's role in love relationships.

Yet Julia's changes are extremely slow throughout the second act, as she persists in her intense pursuit of Charteris. Her introduction in this act is as melodramatic as before—"her face clouding, and her breast heaving" (176–77)—and she spends her first minutes onstage chasing Charteris in and among the others present. Later in the act when she returns from lunch, she is momentarily distracted from her chase by the news that her father is not, after all, terminally ill, that he can expect to live a normal life. But she is not so distracted that she forgets to flirt with Paramore (194) or to express jealousy over him (200). At the end of the act, this series of events leads Grace to charge Julia with womanly behavior that is in clear violation of club rules. In the course of her ensuing debate with Grace over the issue, Julia pits her emotion against Grace's logic. Predictably, Julia fares quite poorly. Yet just before the two women are interrupted by Sylvia and others, Julia speaks the first words she has found to express the kind of woman she is: "Thank

Heaven, I have a heart: that is why you can hurt me as I cannot hurt you. And you are a coward. You are giving him [Charteris] up to me without a struggle" (203). The Julia of acts 1 and 2 is unsympathetic—jealous, childish, rude. In the terms provided by the Ibsen Club, she is a womanly woman to be scorned. Yet what Julia learns in the first two acts is that the club reversals and their implied judgments have made her miserable. In the third act she accepts her womanly self. Significantly, the key to understanding Julia's role in the comedy is to note that she makes her acknowledgment in pain, not triumph.

Julia defines her position as a womanly woman with growing clarity in act 3. In the opening tête-à-tête with Paramore, she identifies the general way men have demeaned her, treating her more as "a Persian cat" than a human being (211). Her comments are even more incisive later in the act when she is ready to stand up to Charteris. When he expresses his joy (and relief) over her engagement to Paramore, she is prodded into her most cogent responses of the play. Charteris still commands the lion's share of the dialogue, but for the first time Julia calls his bluff—"You fraud! You Humbug! You miserable little plaster saint!" (220). Later and more publicly, she is self-possessed enough to object to her continuing treatment as an object—"Must I stand to be bargained for by two men—passed from one to the other like a slave in the market, and not say a word in my own defence?" (222). Yet in spite of her advances, Julia is not triumphant at the end of the play. Having vented her anger, she collapses into tears and submission.

Charteris himself stands as evidence that the command of and benefit from the play's reversals lies with men. Julia's course through the play amplifies the operation of the same reversals as they affect women. Her initial distress is not traceable solely to principles of unmanly men and unwomanly women, yet undeniably the reversals offer her illusory power, not because she is a womanly woman but because she is a woman. Yet when Julia denounces Charteris and his cant, she fares little better. She engages herself to a man she does not love (to get even with the one she does) and is, at the end, both weepy and quiet. Julia rejects the reversed world of the Ibsen Club because it offers her false power. She accepts a "normal" role in a "normal" world, knowing that it cannot make her happy either. Through Julia, Shaw exposes not only the paradoxes but also the undesirable choices that comedy offers women.

The two other women in the play, Sylvia and Grace, fare quite differently in the tangle of reversals. Though static like Charteris, both in fact have profited from the world of unmanly men and unwomanly women. Sylvia is less a representative than a parody of the new woman: she prefers to be called by her surname, Craven; she lounges in her breeches; and she has discarded manners completely. Her demeanor puts her clearly outside the loop of sexual activity. While the others are fond of her, she is incidental to their goings-on. Grace is an infinitely more complex character and a more important indication of Shaw's attitude to reversal. She shares with Julia strong sexual desires just as she shares with Sylvia commitment to a world of unwomanly women. Like Charteris she can command rhetoric and reason: for example, she convincingly finds her way out of loving him, through words—"That is why I will never marry a man I love too much. It would give him a terrible advantage over me: I should be utterly in his power. Thats what the New Woman is like" (185). She stands up to Charteris, claims her independence, and is able to express concern for her rival Julia in the last moments of the play. If, in Julia, Shaw explores the limitations of reversals, in Grace he argues for a connection between reversal and women's empowerment. Much more than Julia, Grace is in the tradition of Rosalind and Millamant, making the most of her extraordinary world for herself and those around her.

In a small way, Shaw argues through Grace for the power of reversal in women's lives. In a much larger and more central way, he notes through Julia the difficulties of looking for change through reversals. In his preface to William Archer's *The Theatrical "World" of* 1894, written just shortly after he completed *The Philanderer,* Shaw identifies the oppositional forces set in motion by the theatrical study of women in the 1890s: "Now it is not possible to put the new woman seriously on the stage in her relation to modern society, without stirring up, both on the stage and in the auditorium, the struggle to keep her in her old place" (50). In *The Philanderer,* Shaw's awareness of such battles is expressed through his beleaguered women characters. As he ends his play, he offers a final comment—again centered on Julia—on the troubled confluence of women and comedy.

## Ending

The conclusion of Shaw's play has been forecast by his attention to two concerns present throughout the play: marriage and happy endings.

From the early moments of the play, when Charteris proposes marriage to Grace, matrimony exists as a relational option everyone but Sylvia strives for or has experienced. Cuthbertson and Craven, as I noted above, have been married; and despite their marital failures, they see marriage as a desirable option for the younger generation. Even after he has seen Charteris, Julia, and Paramore transform marriage into a method of retaliation, Cuthbertson can offer his "heartiest congratulations" to the newly engaged Julia and Paramore at the end of the play. Paramore is similarly enchanted by the idea of marriage to Julia and allows Charteris to direct his wooing. Charteris may never be serious about marriage, yet he has Grace believing he may be. And finally, both Julia and Grace—despite the Ibsenist reversals they flirt with—desire marriage. Grace (who is a widow) rejects Charteris before he can reject her, but maintains a loyalty to the institution, as noted above, by declaring that she would entertain the idea of marriage, just not marriage to a man she loves "too much." Even in the confines of Shaw's comedy, then, marriage persists. Shaw had anything but a simplistic or romantic notion of the institution. He makes clear innumerable times in his writing that he would just as soon have seen marriage abolished. Yet as Watson points out, Shaw the artist and Shaw the sociologist do not always draw the same conclusions about marriage (*A Shavian Guide,* 103). Shaw does not condone marriage in *The Philanderer;* rather, he reports its stubborn presence.

The pursuit of a happy ending is an equally persistent influence on events in *The Philanderer.* Not surprisingly, consideration of happy endings is inextricably tied to the play's portrait of marriage. Julia is the first to present marriage as a desirable standard of future happiness, referring to it twice in her first appearance. With Grace present, she reminds an alarmed Charteris that "it is not two days since you kissed me and told me that the future would be as happy as the past" (145). Julia does not make explicit reference to marriage here, but does soon after. After Grace has departed, Julia makes her request for marriage synonymous with a happy future. She tells Charteris, "One word from you will make us happy for ever" (151). In act 2, as he prods Paramore into a romantic pursuit of Julia, Charteris (ironically) makes the same equation of marriage and a life happy-ever-after. Referring to Paramore's theory "that it would be pleasant to be married to Julia" (197), Charteris concludes in his logical way, "at least youll admit that it's amiable and human to hope that your theory about Julia is right, because it amounts to hoping that she may live happily ever after" (198). But for all the idealistic and optimistic belief throughout the play that marriage and happiness are indivisible, the conclusion of the play suggests that the combination of marriage and endings is far from fortuitous, especially for women. Shaw's many references to marriage and to happy endings, in other words, are intentionally undercut by his actual ending—where marriage represents resigned resolution.

All the final actions in the play revolve around the engagement of Paramore and Julia. While Cuthbertson and Craven see themselves gaily in charge of a traditional ending in marriage, only the play's men seem to have profited from the institution. Paramore is proud of his new commitment to Julia. Charteris relishes his freedom from Julia's chase. But in traditional terms, Julia should have been the one to reach happiness. Grace knows better. She, in fact, forges a shaky alliance with Julia by succinctly voicing Julia's unhappiness—"They think this is a happy ending, Julia, these men: our lords and masters!" (225). The final moments of the play, which follow shortly after, reinforce Grace's reading of marriage not as the happy ending the play has falsely predicted but as defeat and despair. After Julia collapses into Grace's arms, wounded a final time by Charteris's impudence, Shaw ends his play with the following stage direction: "Charteris, amused and untouched, shakes his head laughingly. The rest look at Julia with concern, and even a little awe, feeling for the first time the presence of a keen sorrow" (227). Turco finds this ending ambiguous (*"The Philanderer,"* 57). However, it is only indeterminate if one is expecting the combination of marriage and happiness that several of the characters—in true comic form—have sought. I find the ending an exceedingly clear sign from Shaw that happy endings in marriage are as false in comedy as they are in life. Shaw's *The Philanderer* is such a vital addition to his canon because in it he shows, with so little ambiguity, the damage the comic ending can do. Ever aware of men's stranglehold on power, Shaw knows that the comic burden is almost always women's.

## *The Philanderer* as Theatrical Meta-Commentary

Shaw is clearly self-conscious about the operation of comedy in his play: he both depends on and perverts the expectations that traditional comedy calls up. But it is through a meta-commentary on theater that Shaw

most cleverly confirms his sensitivity to the vicissitudes of comedy as
they affect women.

Theatrical events and lives are a main context for the action of the
play. Ibsen, his drama, and his philosophy stand as the basis for relationships among all the characters. In act 2, Ibsen's bust—reverentially
placed—dominates the set. Charteris, as I noted above, gains his stature
as a promoter of Ibsenist ideals. Cuthbertson, too, is steeped in theater.
His drawing room, the scene of act 1, is defined by engravings, photographs, and statues of playwrights and actors, including Henry Arthur
Jones, Sir Arthur Pinero, Shakespeare, Sir Henry Irving, Ellen Terry,
Sarah Bernhardt, and Macready. The decorating obsession is explained
by Cuthbertson's profession: he is a dramatic critic. The first two acts,
then, present a world in which theater is the basis not only for decorating
but also for viable theories about the world. In spite of the fact that
Cuthbertson is the dramatic critic, however, it is Charteris who defines
the audience's perception of this theatrical motif.

Charteris's dependence on theater and on the theatrical is in fact
most understandable if he is seen as an image of Shaw the dramatist. As
I noted earlier, several commentators on *The Philanderer* have drawn
parallels between Shaw's personal relations with women and Charteris's
relations with Grace and Julia. Peters, for instance, notes that the first
act confrontation involving Charteris, Grace, and Julia paraphrases an
episode in Shaw's own life (*Bernard Shaw*, 115). I would suggest, more
generally, that Shaw offers a commentary—through Charteris—on the
impulses of a young dramatist. At the end of act 1, for example, Charteris obliges critic Cuthbertson's questions about the strange events that
have just transpired by transforming his [Charteris's] life into drama:

> I tell you, seriously, I'm the matter. Julia wants to marry me: I
> want to marry Grace. I came here tonight to sweetheart Grace.
> Enter Julia. Alarums and excursions. Exit Grace. Enter you and
> Craven. Subterfuges and excuses. Exeunt Craven and Julia. And
> here we are. Thats the whole story. Sleep over it. Goodnight. (165)

Charteris parodies dramatic plotting and jargon, but also finds them a
perfect vehicle for explaining his life. Much later in the play, he calls up
his playwright's awareness of multiple points of view in responding to
Julia's mocking self-deprecation:

| Julia: | According to you, then, I have no good in me. I am an utterly vile worthless woman. Is that it? |
| Charteris: | Yes, if you are to be judged as you judge others. From the conventional point of view, theres nothing to be said for you, |
| Julia: | nothing. Thats why I have to find some other point of view to save my self-respect when I remember how I have loved you. (218) |

Like a playwright, Charteris is ever aware of the different ways different characters choose to see the same events.

Such theatrical self-consciousness comes to bear on the issue of the play's women at two critical points. The first comes early. Near the end of act 1, as Charteris and Julia attempt to explain their curious presence in Cuthbertson's drawing room to both Cuthbertson and Craven, Charteris twice refers to Cuthbertson as a theater critic, the "leading representative of manly sentiment in London": "Nonsense! he's [Cuthbertson's] a dramatic critic. Didnt you hear me say he was the leading representative of manly sentiment in London?" (163). The comment is part of Shaw's complicated inversions in the play; but even so, it can be taken as a notation from Shaw that the theater is too predominantly a battleground for the manly. The second self-conscious comment on the gender play of this comedy is more resonant, since it ends the play. And this time Charteris is the object rather than the source of criticism. Earlier I quoted in full the play's final stage direction, in which Shaw separates Charteris from the others. He is laughing; they are not. I also noted that I find this moment an emphatic mark of Shaw's self-consciousness, a recognition that comedy provides a poor environment for women. But Charteris's laughter also represents a harsh indictment of the playwright as represented throughout the play by Charteris. Like a dramatist, he is the power who has engineered both the frolic of the play's inversion and the marriage at its ending. He, however, is the only one laughing at the close, the only one who finds such narrative pleasurable. Because his laughter contrasts with the concern of all the others, not his joy but their despair is privileged as the appropriate ending as far as women are concerned. Charteris is no Prospero, self-consciously reigning over a playwright's final theatrical efforts. He is a cad that Shaw created in order to magnify the gender disparities of comedy.

Until recently, *The Philanderer* has rarely been produced. Mander and Mitchenson report that after the Royal Court production in 1907 (the first professional production of the play), only four more followed between 1908 and 1951 *(Theatrical Companion to Shaw)*. Since the mid-1970s, however, the play has commanded surprising attention. It was performed at the Roundabout Theatre in New York in 1976, at the National Theatre in London in 1978, at Houston's Shaw Festival in 1982, and at the Yale Repertory Theatre in 1982 (Turco, *"The Philanderer,"* 47). As they coincide with increasing cultural awareness of women's roles, such revivals reinforce my argument that the play is pertinent to an understanding of women in comedy. The Yale Repertory production suggests how paradoxically and true the drama still plays as a statement on gender roles.

Both the actors and the director of the Yale Repertory production agreed that the play was *not,* as Shaw had conceded in 1930, dated. Christopher Walken, who played Charteris, noted the timeliness of the play for an American audience in the 1980s—"Even though this play is almost one hundred years old and is set in a foreign country, what happens in this play still goes on every day" (Zelenak, "Philandering with Shaw," 75). More to my purposes, the Yale Repertory actors reported that the most palpable responses to the play were generated by its gender roles. Walken noted that response to Charteris seemed to be determined by the mix of men and women in any one night's audience. Tandy Cronyn (the actor playing Grace) amplified this observation when she added, "Yes, the women thought you [Walken/Charteris] were a cad" (Zelenak, 75). Brooke Adams, the actor playing Julia, complained that for her character, 1980s assumptions about gender roles led to a negative response—"it hurts when they laugh at me, because this woman [Julia] is suffering so much" (Zelenak, 76). Both Director David Hammond and the actors concurred, based on such observations, that the production was effective because it exposed patriarchal assumptions that still influenced most of the audience. The play was not dated, in other words, since the patriarchal world on which its inversions are based still persists.

For a 1980s audience as for an 1890s one, the play thus depends on desires for both the predictability of convention and the allure of change. Shaw, who understood clearly the tradition of comedy, makes the two impulses inextricable. In *The Philanderer,* Shaw does not reform comedy for women, but he has written a play that openly confronts the limited options it offers them.

# Chapter 5

## Ayckbourn's *Woman in Mind:* Contemporary Despair and the Comic Woman

Shaw's theatrical crusade for women has not become the distinguishing component of twentieth-century British comedy. Far from following Shaw's lead and championing a gynocentric existence, twentieth-century comic authors have, instead, offered a predominantly male world darkened by institutionalized human cruelty and the destructive forces of technology. In the contemporary theater, Beckett, Pinter, and Orton are among the most recognized voices of a diminished comic world. As recognition of human cruelty has increased, gender relations and their procreative potential have accordingly been devalued in or dropped from much contemporary comedy. Yet attention to the connections between men and women has not disappeared from all comedy. If anything, both writers and their audiences are more painfully aware than ever of the need for and the difficulties of defining fulfilling social relations for men and women. However, the contemporary writers who continue to focus their comedy on social relations are producing plays characterized by a deepened awareness of women's compromised role in the genre. Both in general and on the specific topic of women, even this comedy is despairing.

Tom Stoppard is among those contemporary comic writers who have continued to deal with gender relations. Stoppard is also, for many critics, the unrivaled master of contemporary British comedy. His plays are intellectual, inventive, complex, and successful. His comic women, however, too rarely break from type. Even the more sympathetic women characters, such as Annie in *The Real Thing* (1982), bear substantial resemblance to the more traditional female types of *Dirty Linen*

(1976). Thus, to find a contemporary writer both concerned with gender relations and sympathetic to women's plight, I turn to Alan Ayckbourn.[1]

At the age of fifty, Ayckbourn has already written more than thirty-five plays, a prolific output that has been a signal for many critics to devalue his work. His early plays, widely acknowledged to be brilliant though lightweight farces, led critics like John Russell Taylor to dismiss Ayckbourn as a writer with no potential to become "an important dramatist" (162). Taylor was writing in the 1970s. In the late 1980s, however, Ayckbourn had become recognized as one of the British comic stage's most significant voices. Reviewers of his work have labeled him "our most ingenious stage craftsman" (Kemp, review of *A Small Family Business,* 1987), the "maestro of suburban adultery" (de Jongh, review of *Relatively Speaking,* 1986), Britain's "most popular playwright" (Billington, review of *Woman in Mind,* 1986), and—many times over—"our leading comic dramatist" (Nightingale, review of *Way Upstream,* 1982).

Two developments in Ayckbourn's now widely acclaimed work make it appropriate ground for a study of women in contemporary British comedy. First, Ayckbourn is moving (deliberately, he suggests) away from farce and toward a darker, more serious comedy. His model is the modal complexity and "tremendously human" comedy of Chekhov (interview with Robin Thornber, *Guardian,* 7 August 1971, 8; as quoted in Page, "The Serious Side of Alan Ayckbourn," 37). Second, tied to his more sophisticated comic vision is a more insistent sympathy for his women characters. Ayckbourn is frequently concerned with women's positions in life as well as in comedy; and he is recognized by one of the most prominent London critics as "our leading feminist dramatist" (Billington, review of *Woman in Mind*). As a function of both developments in his drama, Ayckbourn has joined the ranks of comic writers exploring both the potential and the problems of comic form. Richard Allen Cave finds such formal exploration an indication of Ayckbourn's liberation from comic form: "Ayckbourn's prolific output seems designed to question whether what till now were believed to be *necessary* limitations in these styles of comedy . . . are really necessary at all" (*New British Drama,* 65–66). I offer the possibility, on the more pessimistic side, that Ayckbourn's formal probing has deepened both his understanding and his acceptance of the limitations that attach to women in comedy.

*Woman in Mind,* the play I will study in this chapter, is both pre-

ceded and followed by other Ayckbourn plays that demonstrate his recognition of the peculiar status of comic women. In *Sisterly Feelings*
(1980), the toss of a coin at the end of act 1, scene 1, determines which
of two sisters leaves with their common extramarital love interest, Simon. Although the rest of any one night's production of the play is
contingent upon that toss for determining which of the play's scenes are
staged, Ayckbourn himself seems to be under no illusion that his women
have been offered "real" choices. Regardless of which version of the play
is staged, the drama ends with both women back in their marriages. As
a very traditional order is re-established, the effect is to show that the
choices the women make exist only for the duration of the play's middle.
Ayckbourn's limited world of choice in *Sisterly Feelings,* then, is not
unlike that in Shakespeare's Arden. In *Henceforward . . .* (1988), which
follows *Woman in Mind,* Ayckbourn leaves no doubt that his comic
vision rests on a realization of women's compromised role. The play
centers on Jerome, an unlikable, selfish, recluse composer. When Ayckbourn presents both of the women in Jerome's life—his estranged wife
Corinne and a hired companion Zoë—as (literally) robots, he leaves little
room in his play for hope, love, or real companionship between men and
women. The play's dark and lonely ending results largely from Jerome's
inability to see women as more than tools designed for men's conven-
ience.

The mixture of sympathy and despair that has distinguished Ayckbourn's comic portraits of women is most compellingly present in his
1986 *Woman in Mind.* Reviewers of the London production were consistently impressed with Susan, the central character. While male reviewers
of the play, notably Billington, proclaimed Ayckbourn a "leading feminist dramatist" (as I already noted), women reviewers were, if anything,
stronger in their applause for Ayckbourn's play. Victoria Radin, after
she admits her reservations about "the terrain of Alan Ayckbourn's
tight-arsed suburban archetypes," goes on to admire his "imaginative
sympathy" for Susan. She sums up: "He has created a greatly appealing
Everywoman, who shall haunt me for some time." Joan Smith includes
a lesson on R. D. Laing's theory of a family's mental health and then
concludes that the play offers an important example of the mental strain
that most often comes to women—"Ayckbourn's Susan speaks for all
the women who have been driven to the brink by the dreariness of their
lives. If you want something to make you think, see it." As these reviewers suggest, in Ayckbourn's play—as in those of Shakespeare, Congreve,

and Shaw—the woman at the center serves as an example of the qualified power that comes to comedy's women. A final review, this one of the production that brought *Woman in Mind* to New York City in 1988, serves as a reminder that Ayckbourn's Susan—however strong—survives in a theatrical environment still basically ambivalent to comedy's women. Sylviane Gold writes:

> Mr. Ayckbourn often has included women on the verge of breakdowns in his comedies—always good for a laugh, a hysterical woman. But here, in the person of Stockard Channing, a woman at her wit's end is a figure of compassion as well as humor.

I detect irony in Gold's summary; nevertheless, as she praises actor Channing, Gold reduces Susan by introducing her within the realm of dismissible comic women.

The contours of Ayckbourn's comic world in *Woman in Mind* and the play's main woman, Susan, are primarily determined by the two structural components I have noted in other landmark British comedies, reversals and ending. While Ayckbourn's sensitivity to women's qualified positions is most ingeniously present in the play's complicated inversions, his more radical permutations of the comic ending offer a still stronger critique of comic allocations of power.[2] With *Woman in Mind,* Ayckbourn maps the intersection of contemporary despair and comic women.

### Reversals

The play slides between two worlds, the first inhabited by Susan's real-life family, the second by her fantasy family. In the first, Susan is joined by her solemn, middle-aged vicar husband, Gerald; her estranged, grown son, Rick; her incompetent sister-in-law, Muriel; and her family practitioner, Bill Windsor, who inspires more laughs than confidence. Few identifiable events transpire in Susan's real life—for basically Susan is losing her grasp on sanity. As she does, the mundane goes on: Bill Windsor appears several times to treat her; Rick returns home after a long absence to announce his marriage and forthcoming departure for Thailand; and Muriel prepares a horrendous meal. The one climactic moment occurs offstage, late in the play, just before Susan loses control: she burns her husband's treasured manuscript on the parish history and mocks Muriel's belief in her dead husband's continuing "presence" by scribbling a crass message on the ceiling. In contrast to this disturbed first version of family life, Susan's second, fantastic familial world approximates her view of perfection. Andy, her devoted husband, Tony, her doting brother, and Lucy, her loving daughter, all offer Susan unqualified love in this place insulated from reality. This second Susan and her second family live on a spacious estate, complete with swimming pool and tennis courts—they sip champagne on a lark. With them, Susan is uncharacteristically relaxed and charming. She also believes she is happy.

Roughly speaking, this second world is a comic inversion of the first, for in it the heroine Susan blossoms—she finds her professional self as a historical novelist and finds loving acceptance for personal traits (clumsiness, for example) she is only berated for by her actual husband Gerald. More generally, Susan's fantasy world is recognizable for qualities standard in the more conventional inverted worlds of other comedies. As in *As You Like It* and *The Way of the World,* for example, Ayckbourn's other world—for all its differences—is not so much a reversal of norms as an idealization of them and of the status quo. In Susan's fantasy world, the men still determine consequences and marriage is enthroned. The difference in *Woman in Mind*'s structure of inversion is primarily marked by the back and forth movement between Susan's two worlds. The traditional single move into and out of an inverted world is replaced by an increasingly frantic oscillation between the reality of her life and the desperate hope of her dream world. Through these repeated journeys from one world to the other, Ayckbourn offers an inversion with limited possibilities for female control. Perhaps most tellingly, when the play terminates in Susan's fantasy world (and not in the status quo world), the despair that comes increasingly to be associated with her mental escapes predominates. As a result of such alterations in conventional comic plotting, the power and control that would ordinarily come to Susan during comic reversal are not embraced, but critiqued. Ayckbourn's sequencing of events suggests that the power Susan gains in her fantasy world is nothing more than fantasy; and such fantasy is obviously detrimental to her ability to function normally. In the end, her forays into fantasy prevent rather than enable her normal functions. In addition to denying the supposed liberation of comic inversion, Ayckbourn's zigzagging reversals—which seem to be beyond Susan's control—also suggest that Susan has no choice. Both at the very beginning and at the end of the play, while Susan is passing into or out of consciousness (and simultaneously into and out of her fantasy), her name is distorted into "choose'un." Far from celebrating her freedom, this melding of "Susan" and "choose" marks an ironic collision of self and choice.

While Ayckbourn eschews the conventional inversions of comedy, he does—through an alternate route—explore this collision of self and choice. Through a narrowing of his theatrical point of view, he studies the possibilities for his heroine's sense of identity, her ability to choose, and her claim to power. In the play's most telling "reversal"—his presentation of the action through Susan's viewpoint—Ayckbourn begins his play with this stage direction:

*Darkness.*

*We hear the sound of a woman moaning as she regains consciousness. As she opens her eyes, there is bright, afternoon garden sunlight. Throughout the play, we will hear what she hears; see what she sees. A subjective viewpoint therefore and one that may at times be somewhat less than accurate.*

*The woman is* Susan. *She is lying on the grass in the middle of her small, tidy, suburban garden.* (9)

This directive implies that the play's stage action throughout involves only those actions and characters Susan is immediately aware of. For example, when Susan is wrapped up with her fantasy family, the audience (like Susan) sees only their gaiety and well-heeled ease. There is even a moment when the strong presence of her fantasy family allows Susan to block out the entrance and exit of Muriel. The audience does not see Muriel either, and reconstructs her appearance only through a later comment from Bill (18). Similarly, when Susan must deal exclusively with her real world, the audience joins her in a recognition of its mundane qualities. Ayckbourn's description of the initial appearance of Gerald and Muriel reflects Susan's despairing view of her life:

*She* [Susan] *stares at the two who have just entered. First, the* Reverend Gerald Gannet, *a solemn man in his middle forties. With him his sister,* Muriel, *much as described by Bill earlier. She is a woman who has known her share of suffering and is anxious others should know about it too. Certainly, as seen through Susan's (and therefore to a large extent our own) eyes, the two present an unattractive picture, entirely lacking the lightness and ease of her earlier family.* (22)

Susan's two worlds also often appear simultaneously on stage. In the early moments of the play, Susan is in control of the double reality, aided by her second family, who, like Susan, is aware of both presences. Braced by the nonchalant courage of Lucy, Tony, and Andy, Susan is even moved during several of these "double" moments to fight back against the oppression of her real existence. Having been prompted by both Tony and Lucy (48), she tells a meddling Bill to "drop dead." Later, she again draws strength from Lucy and Tony to call Gerald a "smug," "self-satisfied," "conceited . . . bastard" (58). Yet, predictably, such confidence building has its limits. Only moments after she has found the courage to tell off Gerald, Susan's precarious double existence begins to disintegrate, as does her control. First she finds herself helplessly repeating everything Andy says (62–63). When she then tells him, "Please, go away," she and Andy seem to switch personalities—again against Susan's will (63–64).

In the paragraphs to follow, I will analyze more thoroughly the setbacks that continue to mark Susan's confused mental existence until the end of the play. My point here is that Ayckbourn's dependence on Susan's divided subjectivity, while it accords Susan the complete power of determining events, simultaneously—and ironically—records not her accrual of power, but her ultimate lack of it. While the creation of a fantasy world enables her to get through the trials of her ordinary life, it does not increase her capacity to function, but in fact blocks her from developing lasting strategies for real-life survival. In fact, when Ayckbourn describes Susan's subjectivity initially as "somewhat less than accurate" (9), he implies from the beginning that there is something *lacking* in Susan's view of the world. And finally, Ayckbourn's awarding of the play's subjectivity to Susan, while it allows an audience to sympathize with her, also comments on the comic world she is created in and confined to. First, the inversions that make Susan the center of the play mark (as usual in comedy) the normal point of view as both healthy and male. Second and more important, the subjectivity Susan gains from the play's structure isolates her; it does not liberate her. To see the play from Susan's point of view is to see failure, not choice or control. Thus, Susan is not a subject with either an understanding of self or an ability to understand others. Ironically, then, Ayckbourn's construction of the play around Susan's point of view highlights her lack of self, choice, and power, *not* her acquisition of these qualities. The destructive nature of Ayckbourn's comic reversal was clear in the New York production, as

Frank Rich's review attests. Throughout his review, Rich finds himself mildly disturbed. He does not make explicit connection between his disappointment and the play's altered comic structure. However, he does mark the limited nature of Susan's choice in the play:

> The play doesn't run very deep in its view of Susan's psychology or her alternatives for liberation. The complex issues of marriage and family are ignored or tightly circumscribed as Mr. Ayckbourn asks his protagonist to choose between good and bad husbands and children rather than to question her own enslavement to the roles of wife and mother.

Rich, like me, finds himself as aware of what is missing in the play as of what appears. Real choice, self, and power for Susan are not present.

Within his own variations on comedy's inverted world, Ayckbourn's attention to traditional comic concerns of both sex and marriage takes on a distinct hue. Susan's concerns about and implications in both matters suggest not only her difficult position in the play, but also Ayckbourn's awareness of this difficulty.

Early in the play, Susan confronts her husband Gerald with the complete lack of sex and physical contact in their present lives. Wanting him to understand the implications of such deprivation, she describes her own need for the intimacy of sex:

> What I'm saying is . . . All I'm saying is, that once that's gone—all *that*—it becomes important. Over-important, really. I mean before, when we—it was just something else we did together. Like gardening. Only now I have to do that on my own as well. It was something we shared. A couple of times a week. Or whatever—" (26)

Susan's later conversation with her son Rick suggests that she has always been forthcoming in her discussions of sex, frequently wanting, for example, to take Rick's girlfriends aside to offer advice on contraception and orgasm (55). Thus there is nothing new in the concern she voices to Gerald. Yet faced with the lack of physical connection in her real life, sexual intimacy becomes an essential part of the compensations in her fantasy world. When husband Andy first departs from Susan in that other world, she looks longingly after him, exhaling "a little strangled

moan of pleasure" (16). This clearly sexual bond between Susan and her
fantasy husband plays a key role in the play's dizzying climax. Just before
Susan, in her real life, sets fire to Gerald's manuscript, she and Andy
succumb to their sexual desire and abandon themselves to passionate
lovemaking on the lawn (76). Susan has some cognizance that she is
losing, not gaining, power through this sexual fantasy—she cries out,
"Oh, dear God! I'm making love with the Devil" (76)—but her desires
and needs prevail over her conscience.

As many theorists have noted, sex is a staple of comic plot and
action. This play is unusual neither in its privileging of sex nor in its
ironic use of it. Yet the consistent correlation between Susan's despair
and her fantasized sex life only adds to the sense of limitation that surrounds her presence in the comedy. Interestingly, other options for connecting sexual desire and action have been available to her in the course
of the play, but these she finds inadequate. For example, in her developing relationship with Bill there is the clear potential for a rather typical
comic love affair. Near the end of the play, in fact, Bill is about to kiss
her and to begin what seems to be a mutually inspired physical connection. But Susan's desire for the safe escape of sexual fantasy stops them.
Lucy interrupts their tête-à-tête just before the kiss (70–71). This intrusion of fantasy into Susan's only sexual outlet in her real world again
underscores her precarious position.

The play's portrait of marriage, like its portrait of sexuality, is in
tune with the restricted comic scope of this play. I have alluded already
to the deficiencies and unhappiness that mark Susan and Gerald's marriage. Susan notes that their marriage lacks love as well as sex (25). In
the frenzy of events late in the play, she actually musters up enough
courage to ask Gerald for a divorce (77). More significantly, the dynamics of the marriage are unambiguously to blame for Susan's failing grasp
on reality. In an early stage direction, Ayckbourn notes that Susan has
assumed for her own personality the common wifely role of "second
fiddle" (9). That role is not inevitably a problem, but the action of the
play suggests that this role accounts in large part for the crisis Susan
faces. Her very enthusiasm for her marital role has, in fact, brought her
into her mid-forties completely unequipped to understand the vacuum
of self she now faces. She tells Gerald:

I don't know what my role is these days. I don't any longer know
what I'm supposed to be doing. I used to be a wife. I used to be a

mother. And I loved it. People said, Oh, don't you long to get out
and do a proper job? And I'd say, No thanks, this is a proper job,
thank you. Mind your own business. But now it isn't any more.
The thrill has gone. (24)

Thus, for Susan, the promises of marriage have worn thin. And the
restricted role she has taken on has left her with a limited repertoire of
devices for coping with the world.

Yet despite her own difficulties with the institution, Susan continues
to idealize marriage; and she maintains an ambivalent relationship to it,
expressed through her responses to the marriages of her children, both
real (Rick) and imagined (Lucy). Of Rick's childhood, Susan bitterly
recalls his nightly prayers of "'Please God, don't make me have to get
married'" (32). Thus, in act 2, when Rick unceremoniously tells his
mother that he is newly married to a woman named Tess, she is alternately surprised and hurt. She responds first by assuming the worst of
the situation—Tess is pregnant or Rick has married as an act of revenge
against his mother. She will listen to Rick's explanation that he married
out of love only after exhausting these other cynical possibilities (53).
While Susan holds out little hope for Rick's marital happiness, however,
she simultaneously desires the impossible—a storybook wedding. She
backhandedly expresses this desire to Bill when she mendaciously
dresses up the tale of Rick's marriage to report to the doctor, "He's just
told us some wonderful news, actually. We were very thrilled . . . He's
getting married" (69). In her real life, then, Susan has found her hopes
and dreams for marriage thwarted by both husband and son. Her need
for the institution and the happiness she wants it to connote are fully
expressed, however, in her fantasy life.

Susan's own marriage to her fantastical husband Andy is, of course,
near to her view of perfection—the union is loving and sexual. It exists
in direct contrast to the failing union with Gerald. Daughter Lucy's plans
for marriage similarly give Susan a necessary counterweight to Rick's
plodding moves. Interestingly, Lucy brings Susan news of her engagement in act 1, before Susan even knows of Rick's attachment (36). And
from that point on, the more that the events of Susan's real life disturb
her, the more she depends on Lucy's impending marriage to promise a
resolution of love and contentment. In the disjunctions at the end of the
play especially, Susan clings to the idea of Lucy's wedding more stubbornly than to anything else. It is her only remaining lifeline, as even her

fantasy world crumbles around her. Andy knowingly remarks, "Susie's got this thing about a wedding. She wants a wedding, for some reason" (85). But even in her fantasy world, Susan's dream of perfection through marriage sours. Lucy's marriage nightmarishly transmogrifies into a horse race, and Lucy, the victor, appears not only in animal ears, but also sporting none other than Rick as her new spouse. Ironically, then, even in her fantasy, Susan eventually faces the sordid side of marriage. And when her dreams for marriage are destroyed even on the level of fantasy, Susan loses her tenuous grasp on sanity. She is annihilated by the connection that conventionally undergirds women's role in comedy—i.e., marriage does not redeem her but destroys her, both realistically and fantastically.

Susan is a character who has attempted to live her life based on a conventional view of sex, love, and marriage. Despite her own experience of failure, she believes in the ideal of marriage as an institution of companionship, passion, love, and happy endings. Ayckbourn's play is uniquely structured, in part, to suggest that Susan's beliefs are not only unrealistic, but also unhealthy, especially for a woman rendered so powerless by marriage. Comedy too rests on a belief in the positive power of coupling and compatibility, if not in love and passion. Thus, in finding fault with the world that molded Susan, Ayckbourn is also finding fault with a comedy that is based on the beliefs of such a world. The darkness that pervades the inversions of the play does not dissipate with the play's conclusion; in fact, the ending offers nothing but despair.

## Ending

*Woman in Mind* does not have a typical comic ending. In fact, the unusual reversals of the play begin to look ordinary next to the difference of its ending. Many reviewers of the initial London production were troubled by an ending whose apocalyptic qualities they could not frame in familiar terms. Billington is gentle with his suggestion that Ayckbourn "hasn't quite cracked the problem of the surreal climax," but Giles Gordon reads failure in the frantic accelerations of the end: "Here his frenetic lurch into Alice-in-Psychiatryland seems a cop out."

In my preceding comments I have offered a piecemeal vision of the play's final events. Yet I can indicate the scope and power of the unusual conclusion as they affect women only if I detail the length and variety of this ending. The movement toward the apocalyptic events of the

ending is gradual, which makes it difficult to precisely mark off the
ending from the action that precedes it. By one calculation, the changes
that lead to the ending begin when Susan finds herself, alarmingly, unable to separate her self from Andy's self (63). Yet since this moment is
followed by a long and intimate conversation between Bill and Susan—
one of the most normal and comfortable exchanges of the play—I feel
more assured in marking the dislocations of the ending after that talk.
From the moment Lucy interrupts the conversation and prevents Susan
and Bill's kiss (70), any conventional coherence in the play evaporates
for good: Bill is absorbed into Susan's fantasy world for the first time
(73); Susan's conversations with fantasy husband Andy turn into an
incomprehensible jumble of the real day's events (75); and Susan aban-
dons herself to surrealistic lovemaking with Andy (76). Susan's en-
trenchment in her other, fantasy world is interrupted long enough for
the audience to discover that she has taken her revenge on Gerald and
Muriel in real life (this is when she nearly burns the house in torching
Gerald's manuscript and when she decorates the ceiling with a message
to Muriel from her dead husband).

But the turmoil she brings to Gerald, Muriel, and Rick pales in
comparison to the disorder Susan confronts when she moves irrevocably
into her fantasy life (81). It is important to note that this is a disorder
over which she has no control. Ayckbourn's stage directions stress the
difference that attaches to the closing moments: *"Everything from here on
is in a slightly heightened colour and design, suggesting* Susan's *own extreme
mental state"* (82). The irrational events that follow—the wedding that
becomes a horse race and the appearance of Bill, Muriel, Gerald, and
Rick as a part of the fantasy world—conjoin with Susan's loss of command and volition. In part through her will and in part against it, Susan
has completely lost touch with her real world. Consequently, she has
also conceded control of her fantasy.

The disturbing events that constitute the end of the play unsettle all
that comes before. Without any sign of reassuring closure, for example,
the play's labyrinthine inversions seem even more to be signs of instability and failure. I am most concerned, of course, with the impact of these
final events on Susan herself. One way to read the cataclysmic events
(the wedding / horse race and the erasure of a boundary between real and
fantasy) is to suggest that Susan pays a huge price for her escapes into
fantasy. In other words, the penalty for claiming control and power is
the complete loss of control and power. Thus, as Susan's dreams turn

to nightmares, so evaporates any sense she may have of herself as a powerful presence. In fact, she is much weaker than she had been before the play opens. Yet the comic tradition provides ample evidence that such wholesale destruction is not necessary for the subjugation of women. The ordinary happy ending can bring women back into traditional roles with much less obvious disruption. The nightmarish quality of Ayckbourn's sprawling ending does, however, seem a necessary corollary of the treatment his comic woman has been accorded throughout the play. In particular, the conclusion stands as a final indication of the interconnection between Susan's weak comic existence and her tenuous sense of self.

Susan has the final speech in the play. It begins, ironically, as her toast to the marriage of her children, Lucy and Rick. Yet this attempt to call up the certainty of a traditional comic ending cannot be sustained. All too quickly, Susan sinks into the verbal incomprehensibility with which the play began. As she senses her oncoming loss of consciousness and control, she pleads with both families—real and fantasy—to stay with her. Her pleas then disintegrate into a last despairing hope for the retention of her self. As she calls out, "December bee? Choose'un. December choosey. December bee? December bee?" (92), she calls for her self—"Remember me? Susan. Remember Susie. Remember me? Remember me?" No one responds to her call. Instead, Ayckbourn's play seems to answer in silence that Susan's self has been lost. As this final moment makes most poignantly clear, she has not found happiness, strength, or self in the play. The ending emphatically seals her off from any hope of "fantastical" perfection or even from any glimmer of real-life compromise.

I don't believe that Ayckbourn has designed his play to stand as an indictment of women in comedy. Yet the conjunctions of this play's woman and its comic structure mark once more the great difficulty women characters have in the genre. In other words, it is no coincidence that the playwright's comic despair attaches to a central female character. As Ayckbourn struggles with the dark side of comic power and structure, he signals not only "impatience with easy laughter" (as one reviewer of *Woman in Mind*—Grant—suggests), but also an acknowledgment of the inadequacies of comedy, especially as a vehicle for critical social commentary. Cave concludes, very differently, that Ayckbourn at his best is "reinvigorating the forms of domestic comedy" (*New British Drama*, 70). I would argue that as he has investigated the role of women in comedy, Ayckbourn has counseled not hope but despair. Ironically, several of the techniques that distinguish this play have become common features of contemporary comedy by British women playwrights. Most prominently, the reliance on the extrareal connects Ayckbourn's play with the work of his female contemporaries. The play's extreme expression of despair, however, and not its technique, is what makes it representative of dominant trends in contemporary comedy. In a number of the reviews of Ayckbourn's most recent plays, reviewers have begun to describe him as a writer of contemporary morality plays. In its way, *Woman in Mind* comments on the patriarchal morality that continues to govern women's role in comedy.

Shakespeare, Congreve, Shaw, and Ayckbourn have been among the many writers of British comedy who have been fascinated by and drawn to the special relationship between women and comedy. In studying *As You Like It, The Way of the World, The Philanderer,* and *Woman in Mind* in the last four chapters, I have emphasized the understanding and sympathy that have molded the women as well as the power these women have known. Yet in each case this understanding, sympathy, and power have been compromised by comedy's generic constraints. In the final chapter of part 1 I will turn for the first time to a woman writing about women in comedy. In studying the comedy of Aphra Behn, I will argue that she fashions a departure from comic tradition that frees her women, in part, from the limitations of comedy. But even with Behn, the paradoxical role of women in comedy remains operative. As Ayckbourn makes clear some three hundred years later, there are few satisfactory ways to bring comedy and strong women together.

## Chapter 6

# Aphra Behn and the Possibilities for a Countertradition

Like most Restoration dramatists, Aphra Behn depends on her pro-logues, epilogues, and dedicatory epistles to register her consciousness of the dramatic forms she employs and the gender issues she explores. The volatile reception of her plays forced her to defend her abilities as a female playwright in the addenda that sometimes preceded and some-times followed the play text itself. And in the process of bracketing her work with gender-related commentary, she distinguishes hers as a dra-matic aesthetic with new possibilities. In the representative epilogue to *Sir Patient Fancy,* for example, she claims that this is "a Woman's Com-edy" that challenges the conventions of the theater:

> Your learned Cant of Action, Time and Place,
> Must all give way to the unlabour'd Farce.
> . . . . . . . . . . . . . . . . . . . . . . . . . . . . . . . .
> And if you're drawn to th' Life, pray tell me then,
> Why Women should not write as well as men.
>
> (4:116)

Such declarations, also found in *The Forc'd Marriage* and *The Lucky Chance* among others, have encouraged many to take special note of Behn's departures from convention. But when her work is studied in the context of comic tradition, her drama proves to be less rebellious than her claims suggest. For Behn's plays are both dependent on as well as disruptive of the genre. And it is this double nature of her ties to comedy that makes her drama a turning point in my study of women in British comedy.

Aphra Behn occupies a unique place in British comedy both because she is the first woman to make playwrighting her profession and because she intensifies the exploration of women in comedy in an age that invited such consideration from all its writers. Relying primarily on her late play *The Lucky Chance* (1686), I will argue in this chapter that Behn creates a comedy identifiably different from that of her comic colleagues. However, I will also assert that her work remains primarily in the tradition she so consciously rejects. In short, Behn has a complicated double connection to comedy. Yet despite the qualified nature of her comic rebellion, in her controversial women and their unorthodox behavior Behn still manages to sketch the outlines of what I would like to call a "countertradition" of comedy. In her shaping of women characters and especially in her frank portrayal of women's sexuality, she prefigures contemporary British comedy by women, a comedy that still more clearly asserts a tradition of its own.

## Aphra Behn and the Comic Tradition

In her biographical study of Behn, Vita Sackville-West concludes that Behn's drama was disappointingly conventional (*Aphra Behn*, 80–81). Recent criticism, however, has focused on the pioneering vision of Behn's work: her novel characterization of the female self, her feminist understanding of sexuality, her direct eroticism, her rethinking of comic plot, and her reconsideration of stage representations of men and women (see, for example, Burns *[Restoration Comedy]*, DeRitter ["Gypsy"], Diamond ["Brechtian Theory / Feminist Theory"], Langdell ["Aphra Behn and Sexual Politics"], Mendelson *[Mental World]*, Musser ["'Imposing Naught'"], and Zimbardo *[Mirror to Nature]*. Such studies indicate that Behn has been revived for the late twentieth century through a focus on her difference; and in particular, through attention to her sex, her sexual ideology, and her feminist politics.

I too turn to Behn because of the differences that distinguish her work. But because these differences are grafted onto the dramatic conventions she inherits, I have organized my study of her comedy around a consideration of the way her work intersects with the comic structures I have focused on in the preceding chapters of part 1. I will analyze the connections of Behn's *The Lucky Chance* to traditional comic structure in three parts. First I will detail her subversive but dependent relationship with the comic status quo. In her preface to the play, Behn finds herself divided between competing needs to identify with the status quo and to mount a challenge against it. Similarly in the play itself, she creates a world both bound to and suspicious of convention. Second, I will analyze the inverted middle of Behn's play and its trailblazing portraits of women. While Behn presents both conventional and nonconventional women, in her character Julia she tests unprecedented new possibilities for the comic heroine. And third, I will turn to Behn's conventionally based ending and the hesitation with which she approaches it. This three-part analysis of the play's accommodation of comic structures will prepare the way for the chapter's final segment, in which I assess the extent to which Behn establishes a countertradition for comedy. As I concentrate on revivals of Behn's plays in the 1980s, I can specify the legacy she leaves to the women playwrights who have followed her to comedy.

## The Lucky Chance and the Status Quo

As nearly every student of Behn has noticed, Behn herself represents a disruption of the dramatic status quo since she has little precedent as a woman playwright. In a time when the effects of revolution and social decadence were juxtaposed, a woman like Behn—who combined her belief in women's rights with a strong need to explore sexuality—could not only exist but flourish. Acutely aware of the unique position she occupied, Behn began her first play, *The Forc'd Marriage* (1670), with an announcement of her intent to be not just a dramatist, but a *woman* dramatist. The prologue begins with one actor (presumably male) warning that with this play women are about to make dramatic wit their own weapon. Significantly, this first actor is followed by a second, a woman, who triumphs in the now gender-coded situation by asserting that the new theatrical presence of women is in itself a victory:

> Can any see that glorious Sight and say *[Woman pointing to the Ladies.]*
> A Woman shall not Victor prove to day?
> Who is't that to their Beauty would submit,
> And yet refuse the Fetters of their Wit?
>
> (3:286)[1]

Behn's challenge to her audience is a coy, but nevertheless clear, request for recognition of her sex and its difference. Most of Behn's succeeding prologues and epilogues similarly point to the playwright's sex.[2] It is in the preface to *The Lucky Chance* that Behn most fully plays out her role as a sexual outsider in the theater; she is an outsider, however, intent on becoming a part of theatrical convention. For in the preface it is clear that Behn finds herself divided by her dramatic aspirations: her desire to be accepted as a writer is at cross-purposes with her allegiance to women.

Behn wrote the preface after the play's first production, and spends the lion's share of her time responding to the many complaints that had greeted the production. Most prominently, she argues that she should be given unqualified acceptance as a writer, that her work should be considered the equivalent of men's. Any "unprejudic'd Person" who reads her play and compares it to "others of this Age" would find in it, she contends, not "one Word that can offend the chastest Ear" (3:185). In other words, it is just like the work by her male dramatic peers. As she answers specific charges against the play's alleged sexual indecencies, she repeats her argument that her play is no different than the "Celebrated of your Plays" and concludes, as before, that she is censured solely because she is a woman—"such Masculine Strokes in me, must not be allow'd" (3:186). She ends her preface with an extension of the same argument, contending one final time that her skill as a writer equals men's although her graciousness may be greater:

> All I ask, is the Priviledge for my Masculine Part the Poet in me, (if any such you will allow me) to tread in those successful Paths my Predecessors have so long thriv'd in . . . If I must not, because of my Sex, have this Freedom, but that you will usurp all to your selves; I lay down my Quill, and you shall hear no more of me, no not so much as to make Comparisons, because I will be kinder to my Brothers of the Pen, than they have been to a defenceless Woman; for I am not content to write for a Third day only. I value Fame as much as if I had been born a *Hero;* and if you rob me of that, I can retire from the ungrateful World, and scorn its fickle Favours. (3:187)

In sum, Behn argues that in spite of her sex, her work is best understood in its connections with the status quo of her theatrical world. As these excerpts suggest, throughout her preface Behn defends her position as a writer whose sex should be irrelevant; however, when—at the same time—she also defends herself as a *woman* writer she argues against herself. She maintains, on the one hand, that her work is the same as men's—indeed, at the end of the preface she even speaks of "my Masculine Part the Poet"; on the other hand, she never relinquishes the difference that her sex represents. This second aspect of her defense, the moments when she marks herself as a woman, are nothing less than a subversion of the status quo.

Behn's subversive insistence on sexual difference manifests itself in two main ways in the preface: first, in her appeal to the women in her audience; and second, in her discussion of the play's portrayal of sex. In commenting on the women in her audience, Behn proposes a revision of standard Restoration assumptions about female audience members. She recognizes, to begin, that one charge against her—that she has offended the women in her audience—has little validity. She responds to the charge by noting the vindictiveness that accompanies it: "and when they [her detractors] can no other way prevail with the Town, they charge it [her play] with the old never failing Scandal—That 'tis not fit for the Ladys" (3:185). Later in the preface Behn elucidates her comment by proposing that women may just as naturally support her play as condemn it. Whereas her detractors assume that all women are automatically offended by such a sexually explicit play as *The Lucky Chance,* Behn assumes that women have a variety of responses to the play, as she knows from her own experience. For example, when she specifically addresses women for the first time late in the preface, she tells them that "several Ladys of very great Quality" responded favorably to reading the play and that several women who viewed it "more than once . . . found an Entertainment in it very far from scandalous" (3:187). In other words, she had ostensible support from women for her play. Her conclusions about the women in her audience are thus, first, that the women do not as a whole represent a moralistic, prudish element, and second (though this conclusion is implicit), that the play has a special appeal for women.

Behn's conclusions about her female viewers are supported by the most recent studies on the Restoration audience. David Roberts demonstrates that while women were invariably treated as a homogeneous group in Restoration prologues and epilogues, the women who actually attended plays were a broad and varied group. Those in attendance were women from nearly all classes who might have come alone or in groups, who might or might not be accompanied by men, and who might or might not appear masked (*The Ladies,* 28–31, 65–94). The most significant conclusion Roberts draws from these findings is the one that Behn also projects in her preface: one can't make the female theatrical audience monolithic just as one cannot assume its aesthetic was prudish (*The Ladies,* 140). Thus it is also possible to conclude, as Behn does, that women support her play. It is significant, however, that in claiming women's support, Behn removes herself from the critical mainstream whose approbation she so desires.

Behn also subverts her claim to the theatrical status quo in her defense of the play's portrayal of sex. In her preface, Behn reports that when she asked her detractors to identify specific objectionable moments in the play, they pointed either to the moment when "Mr. Leigh [the actor playing Sir Feeble Fainwou'd] opens his Night Gown" or to the scene "when the Man [presumably Gayman] takes a Woman [presumably Julia] off the Stage, and another [man] is thereby cuckolded" (3:186). Behn offers defenses of both scenes. Of the first, she responds that Mr. Leigh, she hopes, has his "cloaths on underneath" his robe (in other words, she suggests that although the *character* presumably exposes his genitals, clever staging would prevent the *actor* from having to). To legitimize the second scene, she replies with a list of celebrated male-authored Restoration plays that include similar scenes, noting their supposed appropriateness: "yet they so naturally fall into the places they are designed for, and so are proper for the Business, that there is not the least Fault to be found with them" (3:186). Neither the charges nor the defenses are, on the face of it, directly connected with Behn's sex. Yet as she goes on to note, such issues are raised solely because she is a woman who is held to different sexual standards than a man. In effect, by holding firmly to her right to be a woman writer who takes a close look at sexuality, Behn is directly challenging the sexual double standard that applies to the theater as to life. Catherine Gallagher, in her essay on *The Lucky Chance,* comes to a similar conclusion by noting that because of the sexually explicit writing she does, Behn is in fact asking for an equation of female playwright with whore ("Masked Woman," 26). My conclusion, like Gallagher's, is that Behn, by so flamboyantly pointing not just to her sex but also to the sexuality of her characters, does more to highlight her differences from than her continuities with the male comic tradition she ostensibly seeks to enter.

In her discussion of Behn's focus on sexuality ("Aphra Behn: Sexuality and Self-Respect"), Judith Kegan Gardiner finds that Behn was perpetually divided between her identifications with a male dramatic aesthetic and a female sexuality. Behn's need to move between these two poles of gender identification is clear; and indeed, the divided sensibility on display in her preface is evidence of this bifurcated allegiance. The effect of this division goes far beyond the preface, however. For throughout her plays, Aphra Behn's singular presence as a woman playwright means that her attempts to align herself with comic tradition are always accompanied by the disruption she represents as a woman and which she magnifies in her highly sexualized action. Thus, as I turn now to *The Lucky Chance* itself and its portrait of the status quo, I want to stress that its gestures to the status quo are always complicated by the gender-specific shadow the playwright herself casts.

In *The Lucky Chance,* as in *As You Like It, The Way of the World,* and *The Philanderer,* the inversions of comedy are dependent on the presence of the standard order. In Behn's version of the conventional, men remain predictably in power. Yet Behn stresses the way generational differences fracture the seemingly monolithic nature of the male-determined status quo. The shift in power from the older generation to the younger is standard comic fare. Behn's rendition of the shift, however, is distinguished by her attention to the impact of such generational complications on women. Thus Behn's portrait of the status quo in *The Lucky Chance*—like her assumptions about playwrighting in her preface—both is and is not convention-bound.

As in Shaw's *The Philanderer,* members of the older generation in *The Lucky Chance* serve as representatives of the traditional social and moral order. Sir Feeble Fainwou'd and Sir Cautious Fulbank have money and status, enough that they serve as city aldermen and carry sway through their money. They also serve as repositories of conventional stereotyping of women. When they first appear in act 1, scene 3, they introduce the subject of Sir Feeble's new marriage to the much younger Leticia by finding women both "discreet" and sexually insatiable (3:203). When the two converse later about women's faithlessness, they add to such conventional assumptions their fears of being cuckolded (3:219–20). But Behn strategically places her strongest image of the older men's traditional beliefs and fears about women in the middle of the play. In act 3, scene 5, Sir Feeble shows up at Sir Cautious's house in the middle of the night, under the mistaken notion that the city is threatened by siege and in need of its elders' counsel. The mismatched conversation that ensues shows the men to be foolish in matters of both state and heart, and particularly worried about the possibility of being cuckolded.

The old men are recognizable comic figures, both in their stereotyping of women and their unself-conscious nonchalance about their power and position. As in most comic worlds, there is a price to be paid for such egocentrism.

In addition to portraying the two as foolish old men undeserving of their power, Behn removes them from power by the end of the play, first by demoting money (their main source of power) as a factor in human relations and second by the much more radical move of having both give up their wives. Having failed to consummate his marriage, Sir Feeble agrees to hand his bride Leticia over to the man she loves, Bellmour; and only a bit less dramatically, Sir Cautious agrees that Julia, his wife of some months, "belongs" to her loved one, Gayman. I will discuss the details of these relational transactions later. My present point is that Behn invests her two male members of the older generation with conventional power and ideas, but allows little status of any kind to attach to them. In consequence, issues of gender and power shift to the male representatives of the younger generation; but with these young men, Behn's attitude to the status quo lacks definition. Behn is experimenting with nonconventional portraits of male behavior, and in so doing she creates a volatile situation.

In her portraits of Sir Feeble and Sir Cautious, Behn presents and then rejects conventional attitudes toward women. Yet the two men are such foolish characters that the criticism of their attitudes is diluted. In Gayman and Bellmour, however, Behn directly confronts the complicated realities of gender politics and the status quo. In these two young men, in other words, she more realistically studies the male attitudes to convention that undergird the changing relationships in the play. From the opening scene, which consists almost solely of Gayman and Bellmour's talk, it is clear that the world of this woman's play remains dominated by men. Behn seems to parody male bravado when she has the two friends—unaware as yet of each other's identity—draw swords against one another (3:192). But after Gayman and Bellmour recognize one another, they resume their close connection, their confidences, and their trust—and all three qualities are presented positively. As the action of the play unfolds from this point, the two go to some admirable lengths in looking out for one another. Gayman, for example, will later on pretend to be the ghost of Bellmour to frighten Bellmour's rival Sir Feeble. Many other moments in the play follow suit, establishing the men's friendship—as well as their concerns and desires—as prominent. As several reviewers of the 1984 Royal Court revival of *The Lucky Chance* noted, even under the feminist guidance the production received, the play seemed to be dominated by male connections and concerns.

The young men's struggle between the conventional and the unconventional in their thinking about women is still more important to my argument than their dominance in the action. Gayman's situation is particularly instructive. In his initial encounter with Bellmour, for example, Gayman flatly refuses to accept traditional thinking about women's sexual proclivities—"No, no, Pox on't, all Women are not Jilts. Some are honest, and will give as well as take" (3:195). Yet such thinking, which appears to stem directly from his love for the unconventional Julia, is compromised by his concomitant tendency to rely on traditional stereotyping. For example, when he reflects on women who are neither young nor handsome (i.e., other women besides Julia), he is dependent on conventional thinking. Trying to guess the identity of the woman wooing him in secret (it *does* happen to be Julia!), he makes the wrong conclusions because his operative assumptions about women are based on traditional stereotypes: "No—'tis a Woman—I am positive. Not young nor handsom, for then Vanity had made her glory to have been seen. No—since 'tis resolved, a Woman—she must be old and ugly, and will not balk my Fancy with her sight" (3:233–34). As such variable behavior might predict, the relationship between Gayman and Julia is resolved at the play's end through a combination of traditional and nontraditional thinking. What the narrative dominance of the young men and the vacillation in their thinking about women primarily suggest, however, is that Behn's world is based, though not totally dependent, on standard gender-based distinctions. She presents characters who look beyond their own world but never leave it.

Behn's relationship to the status quo is slippery. While she herself personifies disruption, both her preface and her play alternately depend on and challenge the conventional. As I will detail in the next section, even in the freewheeling upheaval of comic reversal Behn mixes portraits of standard behavior with pioneering efforts to thwart convention. But in her midplay rebellion as in her presentation of the status quo, her dedication to women leads her to experiment with changes in structure and character that exceed those I detailed in chapters 2 through 5.

## Women in the Upheaval of Behn's World

Like Shakespeare and Congreve, Aphra Behn fuses her study of social
and personal change with her portraits of exceptional women. Like
many accomplished comic writers, she promotes her heroines' enhanced
vision in a comic world they control even while she recognizes their
handicapped social and generic status. The women Behn creates, however, are measurably (though not exceptionally) different. I will trace
this difference by analyzing first Behn's unmistakable condemnation of
the social disadvantages her women face and second her examination,
through her character Julia, of nontraditional behaviors for women. The
conventional disruptions of comic inversion allow Behn to build on her
unusual status as a female Restoration playwright. The result, in *The
Lucky Chance,* is a comedy that extends the radical possibilities comedy
offers its women.

There are three principal women in Behn's play. Julia is married to
Sir Cautious Fulbank, a man much her senior. She is in love, however,
with Gayman. Yet since Gayman is penniless, she has had to consent to
an arranged marriage with Sir Cautious for the sake of survival. Leticia
is in a similar position. She goes through a wedding ceremony with Sir
Feeble Fainwou'd early in the play, another arranged marriage, which,
in this case, the bride consents to not only because she has no wealth but
also because she believes her beloved, Bellmour, is dead. The first scene
establishes, however, that Bellmour is alive. The third woman, Diana,
is less prominent than the other two and faces the exigencies of her
pending arranged marriage with less assertiveness than they. Diana's
father, Sir Feeble, is in the process of arranging her marriage to Bearjest
while Diana is in love with Bredwel, Leticia's brother. Behn obviously
intends to emphasize the similarities of these three love triangles, but
also distinguishes the plots and their implications through the particular
embellishments she adds to each. The entanglements of Diana, Bredwel,
and Bearjest, for example, provide the lightest comedy and involve both
the eloping of Diana and Bredwel and the tricking of Bearjest back into
a marriage he had previously deserted. With Leticia, Bellmour, and Sir
Feeble, the focus is on Bellmour's farcical attempts to prevent the consummation of Leticia and Sir Feeble's marriage; his schemes include an
assumed identity, false messages, and ghosts. The most complicated and
most thought-provoking events in the play surround the third group of
characters: Julia, Gayman, and Sir Cautious. As both Julia and Gayman

plot to connect themselves to one another in spite of the imposing barrier that Julia and Sir Cautious's marriage represents, they rely on a variety of intricate disguises and schemes. I will examine in detail the events through which Julia and Gayman advance their cause, for the most radical possibilities of Behn's comedy lie here. I preface that study, however, with a brief look at the presences of Leticia and Diana in the play, for through these two women Behn notes the power of tradition even in her inverted world.

Both Leticia and Diana find themselves at the mercy of conditions that make it hard for the women to control their own relationships. Through both women, Behn condemns those conditions and studies one way to reject them. Leticia initially faces her union with Sir Feeble hopelessly and with loathing, remarking of him on her first exit, "Heavens, what a nauseous thing is an old Man turn'd Lover!" (3:205). When she discovers Bellmour is alive, however, her revived belief in their love gives her the strength to protest more vigorously against her marriage, despite her financial plight. Speaking to Bellmour, she rejects the marriage to Sir Feeble as, in fact, invalid and even unlawful:

'Tis not a Marriage, since my Bellmour lives;
The Consummation were Adultery.
I was the Wife before, wo't thou deny me?

(3:217)

As she is about to abandon Sir Feeble later, she declares even more boldly that his claims to her do not count; her true love with Bellmour justifies her rejection of her previous social and legal vows to Sir Feeble. Speaking of Sir Feeble to the audience, she declares,

Old Man forgive me—thou the Agressor art,
Who rudely forc'd the Hand without the Heart.
She cannot from the Paths of Honour rove,
Whose Guide's Religion, and whose End is Love.

(3:230)

Thus Leticia rejects marital unions based on money and demands recognition of her match with Bellmour, a match based on what she considers the overriding principle of love. Arranged marriage must make way for marriage by consent.

Diana is less vocal than Leticia in her protests against arranged

marriage; but since Behn actually shows the transactions involved in Sir
Feeble's attempts to marry Diana to Bearjest, the degradations she suffers are more clearly indicated. After a discussion with Sir Cautious, Sir
Feeble proudly announces the sale of his daughter to Bearjest: "Mr Bearjest, your Uncle here and I have struck the Bargain, the Wench is yours
with three thousand Pound present, and something more after Death,
which your Uncle likes well" (3:207). Diana is not present at this moment, but Bearjest later translates to her the crude message of her trans-
actional value. When she asks how he would use her as a wife he responds, "Very scurvily, that is to say, be always fashionably drunk,
despise the Tyranny of your Bed, and reign absolutely—keep a Seraglio
of Women, and let my Bastard Issue inherit" (3:220–21). Such beliefs
drive even Diana, an inexpressive young woman, to declare her independence from the traditional arranged marriage—"Sure nothing is so
bold as Maids in Love!" (3:265)—and to join Leticia in laying responsibility for her rebellion on an inhuman system. Again, not to her father, but
"of" him she declares: "Father, farewell—if you dislike my course, /
Blame the old rigid Customs of your Force" (3:260).

In the case of both women, arranged marriages are rejected on the
grounds that love must command a higher social status than money or
tyrannical fathers. Yet this love is expressed within substitute marriages
in which the women are willing to accept traditional wifely roles. In
other words, Leticia's and Diana's rebellions are fierce but limited, as is
clearest when their transformations are compared with that of Julia.
Gallagher probes the differences between Julia and the two other women
by suggesting that the true crisis in the play is not that involving monetary transactions (i.e., the arranged marriages of the Leticia and Diana
plots) but that involving the female self (the issue in the Julia plot). She
finds that Leticia and Diana represent unitary selves that were regularly
negotiated in the seventeenth century. However, she asserts that Julia
(like Behn) assumes a fractured self, an assumption that puts a wholly
new and threatening valuation on issues the other characters have taken
for granted (28–34). Behn offers in Julia, says Gallagher, "a different
idea of identity" ("Masked Woman," 28). As I discuss Julia in the following paragraphs, I join Gallagher in arguing that Julia is the key to this
play because of her attitude toward self as well as toward sexuality. As
in *As You Like It* and *The Way of the World,* there is one extraordinary
woman in this play. In a play dominated by the plots, acts, and concerns
of men, this one heroine manages to raise fundamental questions about

women's roles. Through Julia, Behn offers possibilities for comedy that strain the genre and that, in doing so, leave a rich legacy for women writing comedy in the twentieth century.

From the first, Julia is characterized as a woman who fits no known mold even in this rebellious play. While the act 1, scene 1 reunion of Gayman and Bellmour is primarily taken up with Bellmour's quest for Leticia, Gayman's first reference to Julia introduces her as sexually faithful to her husband in a climate where little value is placed on such loyalty. Gayman complains to Bellmour: "I am for the faithless [faithless to Gayman, that is] Julia still, the old Alderman's Wife.—'Twas high time the City should lose their Charter, when their Wives turn honest" (3:193). All of Gayman's appeals to Julia—his swearing, weeping, vowing, writing, praying, raving, and lavishness—have brought him debt, not love from the steadfast Alderman's wife (3:194–95). When Julia herself appears in the second scene, she fulfills expectations of her different presence, but not exactly as Gayman has indicated. For she reveals herself to be not the cold and virtuous paragon Gayman's comments may call up, but a thoughtful, giving woman who has fashioned her own principles and responses for dealing with her difficult personal situation. After reading a letter from Gayman in which he pleads that he is waiting for the financial means to woo her once more, Julia tells her maid Pert unequivocally that it is Gayman, not his money, she cherishes—"Charles [Gayman] . . . you are as welcome to me now, Now when I doubt thy Fortune is declining, / As if the Universe were thine" (3:200). She continues insistently when Pert doubts her, "I prize my Honour more than Life, / Yet I had rather have given him all he wish'd of me, / Than be guilty of his Undoing" (3:200). The picture of Julia's carefully considered and individual response to her situation intensifies in the rest of this scene. Like Leticia and Diana she bemoans "forc'd Marriages" (3:200), yet she takes the initiative in the battle against her marriage by setting up a scheme both to replenish Gayman's diminished funds and to test his loyalty (she cannot avoid an arranged marriage like the other two; for she is already in one). She steals from her husband, Sir Cautious, and sends Bredwel to offer the money "from an unknown hand" to Gayman (3:202). With this gift, significantly, she begins laying the groundwork for what turns out to be a probing of Gayman's sexual faithfulness. It is important to note that Julia finds herself in a superior position during these undercover actions early in the play: while she has compromised her sexual loyalty to Gayman by marrying and sleeping with her husband, she expects Gayman to remain sexually loyal to her. In other words, she has instituted a reversed sexual double standard. When this first appearance of Julia ends, the audience has thus been introduced to a woman who writes her own behavioral rules and remains true to them. She will, if she can, maintain her honor in marriage to Sir Cautious, express her love to Gayman, and—above all—remain in control.

Confirmation of Julia's differences continues throughout the next several scenes. Her husband, Sir Cautious, for example, compares his marriage to Julia with Sir Feeble's impending union to Leticia by contrasting Julia's lack of orthodoxy to Leticia's more standard behavior. Where Leticia is modest in her drink, Julia, says her husband, "would prodigally have took it off all" (3:204). Where Leticia appears obedient and judicious, Julia, bemoans Sir Cautious, is "a wit" (3:204). When Julia joins the scene later, she toasts the union of Sir Feeble and Leticia with responses formally courteous but simultaneously critical of Sir Feeble's bullying of Leticia into marriage. Similarly throughout the second act, Julia continues to uphold her own opinions, in opposition to the conventional responses of others. She asserts herself by betting with Sir Feeble over bowls. And when the issue of arranged marriage is raised once more, she publicly chides her husband for his behavior on their wedding night. She then instructs both Sir Feeble and Sir Cautious: "Wise Men . . . should not expose their Infirmities, by marrying us young Wenches; who, without Instruction, find how we are impos'd upon" (3:220). Her first meeting with Gayman closes out the second act and offers a display of her survival strategies as they condition her most important relationship, that with Gayman.

By this point in the action, Julia holds the advantage over Gayman, having sent him a large sum of money anonymously; and she toys with him on the basis of this discrepancy in their knowledge of each other's actions. Much more important in the development of this relationship, however, are her attempts at the end of act 2 to replicate for Gayman conditions in which he, like Julia, will have to face the hard choice between money and love. For in sending him the money, she has led him to believe that some woman (as the audience knows, Gayman presumes it is an older woman) asks his kind embraces in exchange for the money. Since Julia knows his assignation with this "unknown" woman is to follow shortly, she pleads with Gayman to stay instead with her, accusing him—as he no doubt accused her in the past—of being unfaithful in his hurry to be off to another. Julia is not much on stage in the first two acts; but she is—through her ingenuity and assertiveness—established as the locus for this play's challenge to order.

During acts 3 and 4, Julia not only proceeds to test Gayman's faith and principles, but also continues to display her control. At the same time, Behn continues to delineate her strongest character in some notably unconventional ways.[3] For example in act 3, scene 4, as Gayman is ushered into his clandestine meeting with his unknown beneficiary (Julia, as the audience knows), Behn discards the realism of previous scenes to surround him with a pageant of music, dance, ritual, and song. With Gayman as their captive audience, Pert (Julia's maid) and a "Shepherd" direct the feast of music and song during which they give Gayman first gold and then a ring. This ring, they chant to him, is a symbol of his vow to the unknown lover. They exit with their host of dancers, verbally alluring Gayman to the assignation to come: "The joy of love without the pain, / The joy of love without the pain (3:233)." In such action, Julia's apartment, where the mystical wooing of Gayman transpires, becomes a place that allows for departures from realism and plot-driven narrative as well as from standard vows. The distortion of reality unhinges the play's events from their basically conventional narrative development. It also allows Julia to frame the issue of faithfulness in her own way. Later Julia will confront Gayman with her charge of his faithlessness. In this scene, however, she encourages him to approach the issue in an environment where standard protocol does not seem to apply. While she makes her move primarily to force him into a recognition of her unorthodox worth, she also opens up possibilities for displacing other conventional responses. In act 4, scene 1, when Julia finds herself alone with Gayman the next day, she capitalizes on the situation she has arranged the night before: she puts him through the agony of having to separate pursuit of money from pursuit of love. Again he is being urged to respond unconventionally. Yet the control Julia has worked so creatively to gain—both in her fantastic pageant and in other, less exotic, actions—is not absolute.

In act 5, Julia will most thoroughly establish and define her self. This definition, however, is preceded by two incidents that cause her to lose ground in her power play with Gayman. First, she finds him describing the beneficent woman he has embraced as a worse bedfellow than "a Canvas Bag of wooden Ladles" (3:246). The unexpected degradation sends her reeling. Second, this blow to her self-esteem is followed by another she will not be cognizant of until well into act 5: her husband and Gayman have engaged in a gambling bet and the stakes are a night in bed with her. While Julia knows only of the first incident, both modify her ascendancy in her love struggle with Gayman; and yet they also serve to intensify her final battles, in act 5, to control and define her life.

In the preceding analysis of Julia's presence in the first four acts, I have suggested that she disregards convention to define a social role that protects her self but that also allows her to critique practices she abhors. She is a pragmatist who fashions her own way through honesty, fantasy, bluntness, and coyness. She goes beyond most comic heroines in her boldness and independence, though she is vulnerable, like them, to the desire for happiness and love. It is act 5, however, that sets Behn's play and her Julia apart. The events of this final act confirm that Julia's power draws directly from the bedroom and is predicated on her understanding of her sexual difference. The events at the end of act 4 make Julia vulnerable for the first time in the play. The events of act 5 serve as a counterweight; they reveal the strength in her unusual expressions of sexuality.

Critics have long recognized the sexual component in this play as well as in Behn's entire canon. She has been both praised and condemned for work termed everything from bawdy to erotic, from pornographic to sensitive, from intimate to immoral. But even in the Restoration, when bawdy scenes and characters were prevalent, *The Lucky Chance* drew special attention from the beginning. As I have suggested, in her preface to the play Behn offers a modest reading of its sexual explicitness in response to a hostile reception. Yet this play and others have continued to necessitate special explanation to bolster her self-defense. For nearly two hundred years Behn was summarily dismissed as an immoral writer. Morgan offers a representative example of the dismissal, in noting that in 1832 John Genest described *The Lucky Chance* as "too indecent to be ever represented again" (*The Female Wits,* 19). In this century students of the Restoration have repeatedly searched for ways to redeem her, though with limited success. Some have suggested that Behn was moral rather than immoral (see Sackville-West, *Aphra Behn,* 48; Woodcock, *Incomparable Aphra,* 148; and Link, *Aphra Behn,* 156), but such attempts to save her by aligning her with conventional morality are artificial and hollow. Behn, even for all her own protests, was not "moral" in the traditional sense. I want to follow a different line of reasoning to argue that her explicit sexuality may be most efficiently understood through a recognition of her departure from conventional morality and conventional comic portraiture. The difference in Behn's attention to the sexual dimension of her characters' lives may, in fact, be the most novel and powerful quality of her comedy.

Others have preceded me in noting such differences. Zimbardo, for example, has argued that Behn's plays are so disturbing because she is among the first of her contemporaries to portray characters who are psychologically full; as a result, her eroticism takes on additional dimension (*Mirror to Nature*, 157–63). Similarly, Burns has noted that Behn led the way in refining a theatrical language of sexual difference through her attention to props and women-directed plots (*Restoration Comedy*, 123–41). But Holland introduces the differences I wish to explore when he notes that Behn far exceeds other Restoration dramatists in the number of discovery scenes she uses, most of them (eighteen of thirty-one) "scenes of undressing, dressing or bedrooms" (*The Ornament of Action*, 41). Three such bedroom discoveries, he notes (41 n. 63), occur in *The Lucky Chance*. It is Julia's performance in the bedroom scenes in act 5 that I wish to focus on here; for in them Julia claims her true power, a power rooted in her sexual desires. The self that she has asserted so insistently in the first four acts is shown, in an emphatic ending, to be founded on the acknowledgment and understanding of her sexuality. Since John Harrington Smith's seminal 1948 study ("Shadwell, the Ladies, and the Change in Comedy"), students of Restoration drama have assumed that women represent the "moral" force in Restoration theater (and by "moral" he means chaste). My point is that through Julia, Behn claims just the opposite, a disruptive role for the woman of Restoration comedy. For Julia is a female who is inherently concerned with her own sexuality and who will define chastity and morality on her own, very physical terms.

A sizable portion of the action that precedes act 5 foretells its reliance on the sexual to resolve plot and character complications. Most obviously, the Leticia–Bellmour–Sir Feeble plot revolves around one man's plans to get Leticia to bed and another's counterplans to foil such action. At one point during the men's tug-of-war, Sir Feeble shamelessly throws open his dressing gown to scare off the women surrounding Leticia (act 3, scene 2); his disrobing makes explicit Behn's attention to the physical (even genital) details of lovemaking. Soon after this, at the end of act 3, scene 5, both Julia and her maid Pert enter in states of undress; and since the audience knows Julia is coming directly from the encounter she has arranged with Gayman, the women's appearance can be construed as a sign of the physical intimacy with which Julia has just entertained Gayman. And finally, as I detailed earlier, Julia's various complaints about her marriage to Sir Cautious have, as often as not, made direct reference to their sexual relationship. Thus it is no novelty when in the final act Behn puts such emphasis on her heroine's sexuality.

Julia's most crucial expressions of her sexual self come in two main parts: the first in act 5, scene 4, as she and Sir Cautious discuss their marriage; the second in act 5, scene 7, as she and Gayman disagree about the sexual encounter they have just had. Both take place in the "antechamber" to her bedroom. The location is of crucial importance because this is one of the only places in the play that a woman could call hers. Except for act 3, scene 4 (the scene during which Julia stages her fantasy of song and dance for Gayman in her apartment), the action has all transpired within the spaces that Sir Cautious, Sir Feeble, and Gayman control—namely, the men's homes and living quarters. In such male-dominated locales, the women are visitors and comport themselves accordingly. The privacy of her own sleeping quarters allows Julia wider privileges, however. And significantly, she asserts privileges that only the intimacy of the bedroom can make possible.[4] In the first of the two bedroom scenes, the location carries further connotations: when Julia talks with Sir Cautious, the location of her bedroom acts as a reminder of her physical duties as a married woman. What are to Julia unwanted, even distasteful duties seem to have prompted her to understand her needs and desires so well. In both scenes in her own space, the first with Sir Cautious and the second with Gayman, Julia claims a power beyond that she has displayed heretofore. In short, she is free to explain to the two men in her life the principles by which she will live her private life.

Julia's discussion with Sir Cautious in scene 4 is occasioned by his request that she make love to him that night. Not knowing what the audience *does* know at this point—that Sir Cautious is only trying to procure his wife to pay off his bet with Gayman—Julia deals with her husband's request by initiating a serious discussion about the couple's sexual relationship. Julia's frank comment that Sir Cautious is not much agreeable to her bed leads to a discussion of her faithfulness. Here the pragmatic approach that has characterized Julia's earlier responses to her husband and others comes into play. While Julia has in fact been physically faithful to her husband, she declares that she reserves her right to act otherwise. To her, honesty and loyalty have less priority than freedom—"But I'll not change my Freedom and my Humour, / To purchase the dull Fame of being honest" (3:267). She even claims a right, in this marriage, to acknowledge that her desires do not attach to her husband. Speaking of Gayman, she says, "We cannot help our Inclinations, Sir, /No more than Time, or Light from coming on—/ But I can keep my Virtue, Sir, intire" (3:267). In response to her comment, Sir Cautious wants to explore the possibility of "allowing" her some discreet loving outside of their marriage, but Julia will not negotiate with him. She has separated her legal loyalties to one man from her sexual desires for another and ends their discussion retaining her integrity. The way she has negotiated with the world has its discomforts; yet her unorthodox morality and chastity still mark a revolutionary presence in the comic world.

In act 5, scene 5, the brief scene that follows this one, the action moves from the ante-chamber to Julia's actual bedroom. Here she is in bed; and Gayman, at Sir Cautious's direction, joins her there. The scene lasts only as long as it takes for Sir Cautious to usher Gayman into the room, but it points unmistakably to a sexual encounter about to occur. Both the brief scene and what it points to are significant. Julia does not control this moment as she does the more verbal encounters that precede and follow it; in fact, here she is tricked into bed by both husband and lover, a trick that she only discovers offstage. But in spite of Julia's relative disadvantage, Behn's decision to include this scene underlines the forceful presence of sex and desire in the play. As I discussed earlier, in her preface Behn somewhat sheepishly scrambles to defend this scene which signals that her two main characters are about to consummate their love. But when it is connected to Julia's campaign to define her own existence, the scene can be highlighted more appropriately as a reminder that this woman has gained control of her life only by understanding her desires in the real give-and-take of the bedroom. As a reference to actual lovemaking, this scene stands concretely, then, at the core of Behn's investigations of her heroine's sexuality. Specifically, when Julia and Gayman emerge from her bedroom in scene 7, Julia makes unmistakable her agenda for connecting the exigencies of such sexual encounters to the abstraction of love.

For the audience, the most perplexing issue in this scene (act 5, scene 7) is the degree of intimacy Julia and Gayman have experienced in the bedroom. Have they or have they not consummated their love? On the one hand, Gayman's use of the conditional and his references to imagination suggest that the act of love was approached but aborted. On the other hand (and more often), both characters seem to be responding to a completed though truncated sexual encounter. Julia bewails the loss of her honor and sees herself as an "adult'ress." And Gayman talks of his "Excess of Love" (his erect penis, according to Gallagher, "Masked Woman," 40), and his discovery of "new Worlds of Charms" (3:272). As Julia has intimated in her earlier talk with Sir Cautious, however, such details are not the issue. The true issue is the motives and desires out of which the characters have acted; the true issue is the honesty and integrity that should accompany such encounters. The issue of principles is raised by Julia when she discovers that her husband and Gayman have acted together in setting up the bedroom rendezvous. After she determines that her husband is in fact the more to blame for his part in the bet—he acted out of avarice whereas Gayman acted out of love—she shifts her loyalties decisively from Sir Cautious and her marriage vows to Gayman and love. She declares, "And here I vow—by all things just and sacred, / To separate for ever from his [Sir Cautious's] Bed" (3:273). Just as earlier she has told Sir Cautious she would remain loyal to him because it served her honor best, here she tells him (Sir Cautious has joined Julia and Gayman in the later portions of the scene) that she will remain his wife only in name because he has not respected that honor. Simultaneously, she tells Gayman that in spite of his indiscretions, he is best suited to be a partner in her sense of honor. Of course, she also desires Gayman sexually; and in deciding on Gayman here, she is deciding that to follow her desire is now both honest and honorable. The issue throughout this series of three scenes in Julia's bedroom and its antechamber has been her sexuality. As she regains control in this, the play's final scene, she is reasserting her claim that her honor and her faithfulness will continue to be judged by her alone. It is now established that Julia defines her self, her independence, and her honor through her understanding and exercising of her sexual desires.[5]

In Julia's bedroom behavior, Behn highlights her disruption of established codes in *The Lucky Chance*. The enduring potential of such upheaval was suggested in the 1984 Women's Playhouse Trust production of the play. In a stylized production that made the play accessible through broad strokes, the play's bedroom scenes were stressed visually through an overstated staging device by which a large bed was lowered on stage from above. In a slight revision of Behn's text, the bed was present not only for the short scene in which Julia and Gayman actually join one another in bed but also for the two scenes in her ante-chamber.

In effect, the bed became Julia's pulpit, a place in which she was free to voice her self with authority. Thus, in this production, Julia's proclamations about her honesty, freedom, and faithfulness were visually rooted in the free exercise of her sexuality. For any production, Behn has molded in Julia a woman who is fierce about her independence and unashamed to demonstrate the way desire has shaped her actions. Behn has also provided a model of the heroine that significantly swerves from the comic tradition, a model that sets an important precedent for the women writing for the contemporary British stage.

I have separated my discussion of the play's three main women to show Behn's gestures to and departures from comic convention. However, I would like to conclude this analysis of women in Behn's inverted world with a consideration of the connections among the play's women. In analyzing the four plays in chapters 2 through 5, I noted that the isolation of women has traditionally been a limiting factor for the comic heroine. To some degree, Behn's three main women are also isolated in their battles to secure happiness; yet a network of women exists, a network the playwright depends on at crucial points in the play. Behn intimates that there may be power in such woman-to-woman connections, but she rarely utilizes it. In early sections of the play, for instance, she repeatedly stops short of bringing her women together. When Julia and Leticia first appear together, Julia offers Leticia a formal greeting—"Give you Joy, my dear Leticia!" (3:208),—but the two women do *not* converse further. A similar distance is marked when Leticia's maid Phillis seeks out her melancholy mistress in Sir Feeble's garden and Leticia responds by asking only to be left alone (3:216). And even when Leticia pretends to faint later on in this scene, the women who gather to aid her do not talk with her (3:218). Such teasing references to the women's connections are more distinct later. Julia enters act 4, scene 1, asking to meet with Leticia, but the scene immediately turns into her confrontation with Gayman, and she later finds Leticia's company only offstage. In this latter scene especially, it is almost as if Behn wants to demonstrate the difficulties of her women ever finding time alone together.

Such missed opportunities for the women to be together sharply contrast with two occasions on which the connections of the women *do* provide a forum for consideration of their situations. On the first of these occasions, the women of Sir Feeble's household, including his daughter Diana, surround the new bride Leticia, preparing her for her wedding night. The other women are not vocal, but Leticia has obviously collected them around her as protection from the sexual advances of her new husband, Sir Feeble. When he enters, complaining of the "prating Women" (3:227), Leticia attempts to use the community of women she has gathered about her as a shield: "you wou'd not have me go to Bed before all this Company" (3:228). This group of women quickly disperses when Sir Feeble scares them off with his opened gown, but the gathering has suggested the possibilities for power (in this case a power to be used against men) that lie with the collected women. Behn makes the feminist potential of this power clear in the second major occasion on which the play's women conjoin. Buried in the middle of act 5, scene 1, is the one and only moment in the play when the three main women are alone together on stage. Left to themselves, they immediately turn to an issue of basic importance to them all—their entanglements in forced marriages. Julia and Diana both sympathize with Leticia's precarious situation, Julia by offering condolences—"I was sick to know with what Christian Patience you bore the Martyrdom of this Night" (3:251). And in an even stronger show of support, both Julia and Leticia counsel Diana to risk anything to avoid the marriage her father wants to arrange for her. Julia's words once more best express the urgency of their advice: "Let our two [Julia's and Leticia's] Fates warn your approaching one: / I love young Bredwel and must plead for him" (3:251). The women do not have long together, yet during their brief encounter they affirm that they share central concerns.

For most of the play, the women are dealing with joys and setbacks singly or in the company of men. Only occasionally does Behn depend on the power women can gain through their connections to one another. In other words, her portrayal of a community of women is, finally, limited. As with her portrait of Julia, with her collective treatments of women Behn recognizes women's unusual situation; but with her groupings of women, she does not choose to magnify that concern. Her comedy enlarges the power of women in comedy—particularly through her attention to one woman's sexuality—but the play remains much more in the comic tradition than out of it. Behn's instructive relation to the comic tradition can be traced, finally, in her wrestling with comic closure.

Marriage and Ending

In this play, as in several of her others, Behn emphasizes the disasters that invariably follow from arranged marriages. According to Maureen

Duffy, Behn registered the play under the title *The Disappointed Marriage or the Generous Mistress* (*The Passionate Shepherdess,* 247), a title that seems to point first to Leticia's close call with an arranged marriage and second to Julia's attempts to make her own arranged marriage palatable. With her final title, *The Lucky Chance,* however, Behn expands the marital dimensions of the play, indicating (perhaps in ironic reference to Gayman and Sir Cautious's bet) that luck and happiness have a place in this world. And corresponding to the upbeat title is a second view of marriage, one in which the institution is offered as the traditional capstone to romance. In this play, as in Shakespeare's and Congreve's, marriage marks happiness as the play ends. But Behn's portrait of marriage is complex, with the institution simultaneously romanticized and vilified; once more this places her both within and without the comic tradition.

It is at the end of the play that Behn's various responses to marriage are most clearly set forth, but the kind of plot that leads up to the ending has a direct bearing on the way Behn's marriages are interpreted. Her plot in *The Lucky Chance* has often been looked on as peculiar or lacking; like Congreve, Behn has often been accused of offering *no* plot. Even reviewers of the 1984 London production complained of a plotting deficit. Sheridan Morley charged, "The problem is that from the opening exposition *The Lucky Chance* has nowhere to go but around in ever decreasing circles; once we have been told at the very out set what everyone is up to, and whose bed they wish to get themselves into, all that's left is for us to watch that happen which it does, often very slowly indeed." Michael Billington linked what he also saw as deficiencies in the plot directly to Behn's competency as a comic writer when he noted, "What she doesn't have is real comic rigour and the ability to push situations to their logical conclusion." I would like to suggest, to the contrary, that Behn's plot is not evidence of her lack of skill, but rather a demonstration of her unconventional comic strategy.

Edward Burns argues that what may appear random plotting to some is one of Behn's trailblazing ways of disrupting generic (in this case comic) convention: "In all Behn's plays the characters are joined in a complicated and unschematic mesh of relationship, to be knitted even more closely by the ever evolving, even random interplay of which the plot consists. Her systematic disarrangement of a received dramatic language dislodges plot nodes and conventions only to find a new validity in them" (*Restoration Comedy*, 134). As Burns's final words concede, Behn does not range too far from Restoration plotting convention, but her departures can be directly connected to her reshaping of comedy and of its women. For example, the scene in which Julia treats a somewhat confused Gayman to an exotic diet of song, dance, and riddles (act 3, scene 4) does not advance the plot in a conventional way. But like the several other scenes that sport the appearances of ghosts and devils, it counters the play's realism with a fantastic element. This mode change clearly opens up options for the play's women by suggesting that their actions may liberate them from the depressing realities of the marriage market. Such loosening of the standard plot is often connected to the women's efforts to determine their own lives. Julia especially disrupts Gayman's drive toward their union by repeatedly placing reality-distorting obstacles in the way of that union. She does not necessarily have a goal in mind (i.e., her goal cannot be marriage), except perhaps the testing of Gayman's love. And thus the times she spends toying with Gayman do not point forward, but turn in on themselves self-consciously, to point generally to the terms on which men and women in love can hope to meet. *The Lucky Chance* is still recognizable as Restoration comedy with its parallel plots and its series of sexually motivated encounters, but Behn's resistance to certain dimensions of standard plotting create a context in which marriage and its meaning for women may be viewed from more than one point of view.

When her characters do arrive at the end of the play's action. Behn rewards four of her young lovers—Leticia and Bellmour, Diana and Bredwel—with the institutionalized union they have sought—marriage.[6] The two marriages, in fact, easily resolve most of the relational complications that have concerned the four characters. In simple though ironic terms, this culmination means that the way for these characters to beat arranged marriage is through marriage. But significantly, the marriage that triumphs in the end is based on mutual love and desire. That difference is crucial. For when love and desire can be combined within the institution, women in Behn's world find their greatest chance for both fulfillment *and* protection (see Langdell, "Aphra Behn and Sexual Politics," 119; Root, "Aphra Behn, Arranged Marriage, and Restoration Comedy," 4–5). Very little irony attaches to the sentimental unions Leticia and Bellmour, Diana and Bredwel obtain. Marriage is unambiguously their happy ending. With Julia, Gayman, and Sir Cautious, however, marriage cannot be the final answer, for Julia and Sir Cautious are married while it is Julia and Gayman who share love and desire. Thus it is once more in the complications of the Julia plot that Behn qualifies what is, even to her, a too-rosy view of the benefits of marriage.

One way to interpret Julia's actions throughout the play is to suggest that all along she has been crafting intimate relationships (with Gayman primarily, but also of necessity with Sir Cautious) that can function outside of conventional marriage. Yet despite her hard work and her proselytizing of both of the men with whom she is connected, her happiness in the play's last moments remains qualified. For all her creativity, she is not completely successful in reformulating her world. She has declared her allegiance to Gayman for both love and desire early in the final scene when she denounces Sir Cautious's bed. Yet she remains married to Sir Cautious, whatever that now means. And although he "bequeaths" Julia (along with the bulk of his estate) to Gayman upon his death, the old man remains alive. A solution to the tricky situation the three face has been proposed, but it lies in the future, not the present. It is possible that Julia could decide to carry on a sexual relationship with Gayman prior to Sir Cautious's death; indeed, she has left such a possibility open in her act 5, scene 4, discussion with her husband. To outline such possibilities is only to speculate, however. I can sum up the final situation for this threesome by suggesting that Julia still remains legally married to Sir Cautious while she has declared a "spiritual" marriage to Gayman. But it is not clear how she will express that most important side of herself, her sexuality. If I seem particularly tentative in outlining Julia's situation here, it is because at this crucial moment she is silent on these matters. She does banter with Gayman in some of the play's final lines, but nowhere does she directly address her marital/relational situation. Like Rosalind and Millamant, she relinquishes her voice. Yet unlike them, she does not do so while accepting a traditional marriage. Julia's presence at the end of the play thus qualifies the rejoicing in marriage that the other couples indulge in. She stands as evidence that marriage is *not* automatically the road to happiness and that women can fashion other, however ambiguous, "endings" for themselves. Through her focus on Julia, Behn challenges the traditional comic ending. Yet at best she raises questions about what else may be possible; she cannot define a new course of action.

## Aphra Behn, Women's Comedy, and Contemporary Women Playwrights

In analyzing Behn's relationship to the tradition of comedy, I have argued that while she operates largely within and from the conventions she inherits, she has still been able to explore approaches that set her work apart from the tradition, especially as it portrays women. In studying *The Lucky Chance* as I have studied other plays in the comic tradition, I have noted Behn's approach to the constraints imposed and the liberties allowed by typical comic structures. But as I have recorded the differences that attach to her work, I have found many of the same qualities that (as I will argue in chapters 7 through 12) are defining a new comic tradition in the contemporary theater. Those aspects of Behn's play that forecast the nature of contemporary women's comedy include the following: her loose conception of plot, a plot that in favoring lateral movement and fantastic elements is more adaptable to women's concerns; her less-than-resolved ending; her direct and substantive treatment of women's sexuality as it is tied to women's sense of self; and her recognition of the power women may gain from one another. Yet Behn has certainly not solved the problems that comedy traditionally presents for women; her example shows, in fact, how difficult it is to leave the comic tradition behind.

Contemporary reception of Behn's work offers a final angle for gauging the subtle difference in Behn's comic world. It also clarifies her connection to comedies now being written by women.

Both *The Lucky Chance* and *The Rover* (Behn's most well-known play) were revived in London in the 1980s; responses to both were mixed. While some reviewers saw the plays as scions of the old order and others cited them as precursors of the new, Behn's comedies proved (even on the contemporary stage) to be repositories of convention as well as radicalism. The Women's Playhouse Trust revived *The Lucky Chance* as its inaugural production in 1984. I found the production to be inspired—a stylized, upbeat, light affair that managed to make the play accessible at the same time it underscored Julia's modern, feminist appraisal of her compromised situation. Dale Spender, in her book *Mothers of the Novel*, was also enthusiastic about the production, finding in it a unique theatrical voice she attributed directly to Behn's sex:

There was a significant difference, because the women were not presented as fools—and the men were not flattered. . . . it was the men who were being measured by women's standards, and this provides a welcome and refreshing change. When women are the reference point, men do not have it all their own way. (53)

Yet such positive response to the play and its production was rare, partially because—as both Sue Parrish and Maureen Duffy have pointed out—even on the Royal Court stage, with support from the Women's Playhouse Trust, the director Jules Wright had little methodology for making theatrically concrete the differences Behn's play depends on. Parrish, who was associated with the production as associate director of the Women's Playhouse Trust, noted in an interview that the actors—both men and women—had a difficult time discarding the sexist codes that have become standard for staging such sexually oriented plays. Thus the play's differences in its portrait of women were often contradicted by the familiarity (and conventionality) of the acting and presentation. Duffy's perception of this production as a diluted success was similar. She noted that the men took on an inordinate dominance in production because a theater language that could signal more sexual equality was not accessible to the actors: "The hero, Gayman . . . is allowed to be too dominant and upsets the play's balance. The problem isn't in the writing but in finding a theatrical idiom which allows hero and heroine to stand up to each other as vocal equals" (review). Even for feminists in 1984, then, *The Lucky Chance* remained a comedy full of contradictory possibilities for women.

Most reviewers of the production, while not so consciously concerned with the play's relation to a male theatrical tradition, implicitly made the play's conformity to tradition a standard for judging it. This happened most obviously as several reviewers combined their review of the Women's Playhouse Trust *The Lucky Chance* with their review of Behn's *The Rover,* as revived at the Upstream Theatre, also in July of 1984. Almost every time the two productions were brought together critically, the Upstream production and *The Rover* were rated superior, in large part because *The Rover* was recognizable as a much more conventional comedy. Michael Coveney summed up the difference by noting that "none of the writing [in *The Lucky Chance*] is as impressive as in the best scenes of *The Rover*. . . . there is a vivacity here quite lacking in *The Lucky Chance*." Michael Ratcliffe was more adamant in suggesting the inherent inferiority of *The Lucky Chance:*

> That it [the Women's Playhouse Trust] has chosen to do so [to inaugurate its life] with a far from convincing production of the wrong play by Aphra Behn . . . will come to be regarded in time as no more than a temporary setback, willfully self-induced. That Mrs. Behn's equally rare masterpiece, *The Rover* . . . is also to be seen in London . . . merely exposes the perversity of the WPT in staking their first throw on *The Lucky Chance* (1686).

As such critics detailed their guarded responses to *The Lucky Chance*, they continually pointed to Behn's failure to measure up to their conventional expectations of a comedy.

Those who reviewed the two Behn plays together could temper their critique of *The Lucky Chance* by praising *The Rover*. But even those reviewing just *The Lucky Chance* were basically making the same judgment—*The Lucky Chance* perverts comic convention and suffers from what was perceived as sloppy, eccentric playwrighting. For example, I suggested above that several reviewers objected to the unfamiliar contours of the plot in *The Lucky Chance*. Reviewers also complained of a lack of character development (Giles Gordon), a lack of the wit Behn's contemporaries Congreve, Dryden, and Wycherley are known for (King), and a lack of linguistic sophistication. Milton Shulman's comments display the harsh tone common in such reviews: "Unfortunately, the prose sounds as if it had been knitted with words being clicked out primarily to get to the end of the story without displaying much feeling for real wit or true style."

Not all reviews of the production were negative. But interestingly, most of the positive reviews (such as Spender's [*Mothers of the Novel*] and mine) grew from appreciation for, not dismay at, the departures from convention. Both Behn's prescient feminism and the structural changes were cited as pluses in such responses. Naseem Khan, for example, found "an independence of spirit that is fitting to present times," and Ned Chaillet summed up the sexual politics as "very modern." In short, positive and negative reviews stemmed from opposite applications of the same assumption about the play's conformance to convention. When the play was praised, it was for being out of the mold; when criticized, it was for its failures to present standard dramatic fare.

Such divided criticism reaffirms my assertions about the play's difference by highlighting the contemporary dimensions of that difference. As the 1984 production demonstrates, Behn's play remains controversial because of its departures from comic and theatrical tradition. The 1986–87 Royal Shakespeare Company (RSC) production of *The Rover* adds a significant footnote to consideration of *The Lucky Chance,* the comic tradition, and contemporary theater. As with the 1984 productions of *The Lucky Chance* and *The Rover,* reviewers found themselves on unfamiliar territory with this later *Rover.* In fact, not one of the more than thirty reviews collected in the *London Theatre Record* analyses of the production mentioned the two 1984 productions, and many proceeded under the assumption that this was the first Behn play aired in Stratford and London for some time. It is not surprising, then, that reviews of the original Stratford production echoed the 1984 reviews by combining a recognition of Behn's distinguishable female voice with a disappointment in her playwrighting skills.

Yet it is in critical response to the London transfer, late in 1987, that the fragility of Behn's comic rebellion can be most clearly measured. During the transfer from Stratford's intimate Swan Theatre to London's more expansive Mermaid Theatre, some changes in casting were made, one in particular with an eye to the production's commercial viability. While Jeremy Irons and most of the rest of the RSC Stratford cast remained with the transfer production, TV soap opera star Stephanie Beacham was added in the central role of Angellica. As a result, the worst fears of Parrish and Duffy seem to have been realized; the transfer production welcomed a vamping and a flaunting of bodies that reviewers showed to be sexist. For instance, reviewer John Merriott described the production's focus on conventional sexual typing in his summary of the new star's role: "Meanwhile Stephanie Beacham transplants her full lips and even fuller bosom from the Colbys, hoisting her skirts all the way." The power of this play's two central women was clearly undercut by such staging. Even more telling, however, were those reviews that focused on the inadequacies of England's first major female dramatist.

Influenced by the commercialism of the transfer production, women reviewers especially came away from this *Rover* displeased at what a woman writer had added to the dramatic repertoire and confounded by the evasiveness of the play's feminism. Carole Woddis, for example, suggested that a sugar-coated production had made the potentially radical message on sexual politics palatable even to Yuppies. Victoria Radin questioned the extent of the difference Behn's sex brings to her writing: "Benn [sic] is now labelled a 'feminist,' by which is meant that she sometimes, but not always, used her own eyes to describe the world about her. . . . But Benn's failure to develop her observations and Barton's [the director's] determination to romp where a bit of rumping might have done better conspired to lose my interest well before its natural end." Claire Armistead's point is more specific, but she joins Woddis and Radin in questioning the reclamation of the play as women's territory: "It is problematic because, despite attempts to claim the play as proto-feminist, the two women [Angellica and Hellena] are inevitably the losers." In noting the thinness of the play's attention to women, all three women identify the precarious nature of the changes Behn has brought to comic drama. This London production seems to have reduced the scope of the play's positive orientation to women through its reliance on the traditional sex appeal of its new star. Yet I would suggest that this dilution of the play's feminism only clarifies the double nature of Behn's ties to comedy; i.e., Behn brings a new perspective and new techniques to her comedy, yet while they foretell of new uses of comedy, they remain a part of her dependence on comic tradition.

In the 1984 production of *The Lucky Chance,* clear efforts were made to magnify the way Behn's female voice parallels the contemporary call for women's equality. The mixed reception of the production marks the way traditional assumptions and expectations can mask or demote this play's radical moves. Similarly with the 1986–87 production of *The Rover,* Behn's support of women is easily cancelled out by hyperconventional casting. As I will argue in the next six chapters, a comedy in which women can claim their selves, their independence, their love, and their power—a comedy that runs counter to tradition—can and does exist. Aphra Behn offers an example of early adventures in such comedy and stands—despite the limited nature of her theatrical and generic rebellion—as the earliest example of a British comic playwright who attends to women in an attempt to make a comedy for women.

*Part 2*

# Women *Writing* Comedy

## Chapter 7

# Charting New Comic Traditions: The Need for a Diversified Critical Approach

In the six chapters of part 1, I have argued that British comedy must be approached as a genre created in and conditioned by a patriarchal society. Focusing on the female characters in comedy, I have shown how their comic power and glory are circumscribed by the comic structures that culture-bound expectations have generated. The strong woman in comedy, for example, proves a phantom who can disappear, voiceless, in the final moments of comic community. The autonomous female encouraged by the unorthodoxy of comic reversal fades before the reality of marriage. The gender reforms promised by the relational experimentation of comedy prove unnecessary in a return to the status quo. In other words, comedy's women are more punished by its reactionary aspects than rewarded through its revolution. Even from my analysis of the enlightenment brought to comedy through twentieth-century production, I have concluded that comedy restricts the power of its women. And yet, despite the persistence of comic structures and their containment of women, possibilities for a countertradition of comedy do exist.

Aphra Behn, for example, has realized a comedy that magnifies her women's power. While she is ultimately thwarted in her attempts to sustain a comedy fully receptive to women's sexuality and agency, she establishes a vision of comedy that offers women more than marriage and truncated power. Her work is prototypical of drama that runs counter to comedy's gender biases both because she calls for changes in the treatment of women and because she has confidence in the possibility of changing comic conventions. Predictably, the countercomedy that Behn produced has infrequently been resuscitated. While Behn's work has contributed an alternative to the received vision of women in comedy, it has exerted little pressure on the male-determined architecture of the genre. Behn remains on the margins of comic tradition. She is, however, no longer alone. My analysis of Behn in the context of the male tradition of British comedy points to two hypotheses about women and comedy, both of which I will test here in part 2: (1) that comedy can—under certain conditions—do more than negate women's power, and (2) that women playwrights have been the most attuned to the chances for combining comedy with female power and autonomy. These hypotheses point to a very different kind of comedy. When women and comedy come comfortably together, for instance, both comic structure and characterization necessarily change. And basic conceptions of what comedy can be must broaden with the recognition of women playwrights and their comedy.

Throughout part 2, I will be outlining the contemporary manifestations of the comic countertradition Behn initiates, a tradition built on an enduring power for women. The radically different nature of this tradition mandates a critical approach of its own, though one that must be reconciled with my approach in part 1. I have argued in part 1 that for all its alluring promises to women, comedy has an inherently sexist basis. I will be arguing in part 2 that contemporary British women playwrights are finding ways to author a woman-centered and woman-supportive comedy. I see the two arguments as complementary, not contradictory. I can best explain my methodological separation of comedy's sexism (part 1) from comedy's potential for women (part 2) by drawing from Catherine Belsey's thoughts on Shakespearean comedy. Belsey sketches a connection between the loosening definitions of family in the Renaissance and the ascendancy of a comedy reflecting multiple options for social relationships. As a consequence, she finds, in the transformative middle of Shakespearean comedy, that traditional definitions of the sexes are disrupted and other, radical options for connection explored. She acknowledges, as I have shown in chapter 2, that the ending of a play such as *As You Like It* closes off a "glimpsed transgression" and reinstates a "clearly defined sexual difference" ("Disrupting Sexual Difference," 188); but nevertheless, she insists on the power of comedy to propose new definitions of social and sexual relations. It is the possibility of such new definitions as they occur in the realm of contemporary British comedy that I will be exploring in part 2. In the first half of this book, I have asserted that both comedy's reversals and its ending qualify the apparent freedom and power comic heroines traditionally experience. Both structures keep comic women from establishing a changed world or retaining unorthodox roles. I am not retracting that argument here. However, I intend to argue in the chapters to come that the unfixing of conventional gender definitions that Belsey locates in Renaissance comedy's inverted middle stands much more powerfully at the center of contemporary drama by women. Because of the still-evolving approaches to structure and character that these contemporary writers employ, the women in this contemporary comedy are not irrevocably compromised by comic inversion *or* conclusion. These writers have, on occasion, made traditional comic structures work for women; but more often, they have proposed new configurations of comic organization and character to support vigorous, revolutionary women. I am arguing, in short, that comedy can be an instigator of social change as well as a blueprint for plurality, and that the contemporary theater has been most receptive to such radical possibilities for comedy and its women.

The portrait of the comic genre that emerges from my study of contemporary female playwrights is one of comedy as the location for multiple definitions of female self, sexuality, and relationship. Women playwrights are finding themselves progressively more skillful in using comedy's complicated, transformative middle to redefine its ending and to produce a theater promising openness and options. With its unstable, unpredictable, and ever-changing coalitions of writer, actors, and viewers, the theater has always held great potential to threaten the status quo. With increasing confidence, women now writing comedy are finding that this revolutionary potential can provide a way around the traditional limitations of the genre. At the same time, the women are preserving the celebration only comedy can promise. Susanne Langer defines comedy as an energetic, vital celebration of life that promotes happiness. Writing in 1953 ("Comic Rhythm"), she is necessarily working from and in the male tradition of comedy, but her focus on a sanguine worldview that transcends conventions of narration and character does presage the joy, power, and life of woman-authored comedy.

To study this demonstrably different comedy in the chapters to come, I have adopted a critical methodology more diversified than that in part 1. In the first six chapters, I offered a structural analysis of individual plays, an analysis complemented by consideration of production. A predominantly structural analysis is my concern in chapters 8 and 9, where I analyze the varied organizational qualities of the comedies now being written by women. My goal is to present the traditional comic inversion and ending as but part of a range of organizational principles now being tested in women's comedy. In the two subsequent chapters I will examine qualities in addition to structure that contribute to the novel architecture of these plays. Specifically, I will turn to portraits of sexuality and self (chapter 10) and attentiveness to communities (chapter 11). Both sex and community are long-standing attributes of comedy; and in part 1, I have considered both as a part of my analysis of individual plays, noting that sex was an activity to which women had only limited access and that community was a concept designed to discourage female friendship. But by focusing on these subjects anew in chapters 10 and 11, I will be demonstrating how the changing balance of power in contemporary comic plays by women depends on a theatrical recasting of women's sexuality and of their options for community. Besides these additions to my earlier focus on structure, I have increased my reliance—throughout part 2—on productions of plays and the critical reception of such productions. In fact, attention to the context of production is so central to my analysis of contemporary drama that I turn to an analysis of this context as a primary component of chapter 12. In that last chapter, I study the theatrical and critical environment in which contemporary plays come to the public, and I speculate about how the nature of production continues to influence and compromise the reception of women's comic drama. I end the final chapter with speculation about the future of women's comedy in the British theater. And I will return there to the notion of paradox with which I began chapter 1: for just as I can detail the maturing vision now to be found in women-authored comedy, I can accompany it with a chorus of voices lamenting the declining state of the contemporary theater. The methodological and organizational differences in part 2 are mandated by an exciting and volatile theater; such differences are also conjoined to two related changes in my play-by-play discussion.

First and most notably, the second half of the book is not organized around single authors or extended discussion of single plays. In considering the tradition of British comedy in part 1, it was easy to turn to the influential works of comedy's most renowned practitioners. There were models for writers to follow and for critics to evaluate. In contrast, contemporary comedy by women puts the idea of tradition itself in question. Not only is it difficult to identify which writers will be the most influential or enduring, but it is also antithetical to the enterprise of women's drama to consider any writers canonical. Indeed, the assumptions guiding the maturing women's theater still insist on the exploration of new methods, not the adoption of prescriptive models. Second and more important, I do not focus on the heroine of comedy in this analysis of contemporary comedy. As in part 1, female characters are still my main concern. For example, I do continue the investigation of the comic woman's self, especially the self so at issue in the Restoration drama of Congreve and Behn; chapter 10 is devoted to analysis of the complicated ways in which the self of contemporary comedy is a reflection of female sexuality. Yet this further investigation of women characters and their subjectivity can only take place within broader considerations of the comedy women are writing—considerations of everything from women's cabaret to theater reviewers' gender. Essentially, the women in comedy are being transformed from objects to subjects in the plays now being written by women, and the transformation has meant an alteration not only of the women characters but also of play construction (comedy's inversions and ending), of relationships among characters, and of the relationship between those on the stage and those off. This methodological shift is meant not only to highlight current constructions of female subjectivity but also to make those constructions the primary vehicle for considering the three kinds of change that infuse contemporary comedies by women. Most central to my study is a change in the genre. As Belsey points out in her study of female subjectivity, to enfranchise the female subject is to change nearly everything about the text ("Constructing the Subject," 50). Through their new breed of comic women, women playwrights are writing some very unorthodox comedies that suggest a radical rethinking of what comedy may be. This conventional change—which essentially defines women's comedy and is at the heart of my argument—is tied to two other kinds of change pervasive in women's comedy: changes for the characters and changes recommended for the society the plays scrutinize. In general, these plays chart the growing agency of their female characters and offer a broad endorsement of social change. Part 2 of *Women and Comedy* is notably different from part 1 because the comedies women are now writing are different enough to demand a new critical approach.

The plays and theater I will discuss in chapters 8 through 12 will often not seem comic. Some of the changes in structure, characterization, and presentation are so radical that the qualities of the comic tradition so identifiable in part 1 will disappear. The magnitude of the alterations suggests once more the deep-seated nature of the limitations to traditional comedy and explains in addition the skepticism with which many of the recent plays have been met. To root out all comedy's misogynist nature is to root out a good deal of what critics have assumed comedy is.

Before I turn to specific plays by contemporary British women and to the countertradition of comedy they extend, I need to introduce three related contexts for my part 2 study: (1) the history of women in the contemporary British fringe theater, (2) contemporary stage portraits of comedians and what these suggest about the parameters of studying women in contemporary comedy, and (3) feminist critical attention to women and comedy, specifically to women playwrights and comedy. My goal in this chapter, as throughout part 2, is to indicate both how many ways contemporary writers are finding to reclaim comedy's joy for women and how the lion's share of such reclaiming has been done *by* women.

## The Politics of Women in Contemporary British Theater

In the history of British theater, women writers have never been common. There was a significant showing of female authorship initiated by Aphra Behn in the late seventeenth and early eighteenth centuries; and as Michelene Wandor points out, some four hundred women wrote plays from 1900 to 1920 (introduction to *Plays by Women,* 1:7). Yet such eras have been rare. While women writers have never yet claimed their fair share of the theater, they have undeniably become a notable, perhaps permanent, presence in the last twenty years. Their presence remains problematic, however. Of the 327 playwrights listed in 1980 in the British Alternative Theatre Directory, 38 were women; 103 of the 547 listed in 1983 were women. Wandor believes that the increase of women playwrights from 12 to 19 percent of the total indicates a blossoming in women's writing for the theater; and yet the numbers are deceptive on two counts. First, the directory is self-selected, so anyone wishing to consider herself or himself a playwright can be included. Second, the percentage of plays published and/or produced by women is significantly lower than the number of women playwrights would suggest. Indeed, Wandor estimates that fewer than ten percent of plays by women currently get published (*Carry On,* 124). The Conference of Women Theatre Directors and Administrators has produced similar numbers from its survey study, showing that in the year September 1982 to September 1983, only 11 percent of plays produced in alternative, community, fringe, repertory, and national theaters were by women (and a large share of the 11 percent consisted of plays by Agatha Christie) (*The Status of Women in the British Theatre*, 6). Caroline Gardiner's 1987 study reinforces such figures; she finds that in the late 1980s, only 11 percent of performed works were original works by women playwrights (Remnant, introduction to *Plays by Women*, 7:7). In subsequent pages, I will suggest some reasons for the ambiguous increase in the number of current women playwrights. But more to the point, I will detail the particular theatrical and political atmosphere that has conditioned women's multiplying connections to current stage comedy.

The increase in the number of women writing for the theater since 1970 is one result of the feminist movement. But it was the concomitant birth of British alternative theater in 1968 that created a place for the politically aware theater of both women and men. Catherine Itzin *(Stages in the Revolution)*, John Bull *(New British Political Drama)*, Steve Gooch *(All Together Now)*, Andrew Davies *(Other Theatres)*, and John Elsom *(Post-War British Theatre)* have meticulously documented how the political ferment of the 1960s called for a new theater where small-scale, socially aware productions could result from new theater talent, new theater strategies, and bold political agendas. But as Wandor *(Carry On)* and Helene Keyssar *(Feminist Theatre)* have indicated, this alternative theater was at first not especially attentive to women or their special concerns. While almost all of the new theater groups were progressive and/or socialist in their outlook and most made attempts to be egalitarian in their policies and operations, women were consistently cast as supporters and rarely given control. Carole Hayman remembers that in the early days of Joint Stock, one of the most important and enduring fringe collectives, her suggestions that the group produce women writers were discarded with objections like, "Women haven't got anything to write about . . . because they haven't done anything in the world" (interview).

Though women were included in almost all of the early, influential alternative theater groups (e.g., 7:84, Red Ladder, and Hull Truck), it was not until women began to organize their own productions and companies that they could begin to define the terms of their own theater and could identify the need for women writers. The early phases of women's theater, from 1969 to 1973, are chronicled by Wandor in *Carry On*,

*Understudies.* Wandor traces the movement from agitprop to the formation of the Women's Theatre Group and Monstrous Regiment (still the
two most visible women's groups) in the mid-1970s. It is important to
note, however, that even at the first "Women's Theatre Festival" of 1973
(which spawned the Women's Theatre Group, Monstrous Regiment,
and other collectives), women had to learn how to barter for the artistic
control they had never had. Ed Berman, artistic director of the theater
hosting the festival, "insisted on having a final say on selection" of plays
(*Carry On,* 47); and his tight control created hostility among the women
who were, paradoxically, grateful for being offered a chance. Pam Gems
notes that Berman "asked me for two nice sexy pieces and I was fed up
with that request so I wrote two very black pieces, one about a girl who
killed her baby. . . . And I really dared him to put them on" (interview).
The reawakening of a woman's theater in the 1970s, then, had a double
legacy: it enhanced attention to politics and it demanded recognition of
theater's patriarchy.

     The politics that characterized the new women's theater groups was
in turn conditioned by the socialist-feminist debate that helped shape
British feminism in the 1960s and 1970s. Wandor surveys the diversity
of this political background by outlining three broad categories of femi-
nist/theater politics: radical feminism, bourgeois feminism, and socialist
feminism (*Carry On,* 130–39). What Wandor chooses not to survey in
any detail, however, is the sometimes messy intersection of socialism
and feminism that conditions each of her three categories and that has
influenced the political perspectives of most playwrights now writing.
Although I risk simplifying a bit, I would like to augment Wandor's
analysis by suggesting that the general tension between socialism and
feminism outlined by Sheila Rowbotham, Lynne Segal, and Hilary
Wainwright in their 1979 *Beyond the Fragments* remains at the base of
theater women's political awareness. The three authors argue that the
creativity for changing forms and organization that energized the
women's movement of the late 1960s and early 1970s presented a model
for the reorganization of the socialist left, whose radical agenda women
found too impersonal and "underdeveloped" in its analysis of relations
between the sexes (52). In American feminist terms, their message was
that the personal is political and that the personal, specifically gender
politics, had not been factored into socialist policy.

     In recent years, theoreticians have expanded the terms of this de-
bate. Angela Weir and Elizabeth Wilson ("The British Women's Move-

ment"), Michele Barratt ("Rethinking Women's Oppression" and *Women's Oppression Today*), Johanna Brenner and Maria Ramas ("Rethinking Women's Oppression"), Jane Lewis ("Debate on Sex and Class"), and Sheila Rowbotham *(Women's Consciousness, Man's World)* have brought the issues to a more sophisticated level by focusing, on the one hand, on new Marxist attention to ideology (the influence of Althusser) and to the possibilities for a pluralist approach to society's structures. On the other hand, these writers have investigated charges that feminists now are both too essentialist (i.e., they rely too heavily on biologically determined sex differences) and not material enough (i.e., they overlook economic and class considerations). Janelle Reinelt has examined the collisions of feminists and socialists in the special context of women's theater and suggests how women writers have employed Brechtian techniques to bring this debate to the stage (see "Beyond Brecht").

Yet most women playwrights—although their work and attitudes are conditioned by the debate—do not engage themselves in the debate directly. Fewer now than in 1970 find it necessary to announce themselves as socialists. But both the prominence of socialism on the British political scene and its centrality in alternative theater ensure that the women writing must be aware of those places where advocacy for women and advocacy for society's underprivileged intersect. In fact, the issues being debated by theoreticians affect even the work of those women claiming to be neither socialist nor feminist. The writers themselves, however, often use caution in talking about any political goals connected with their work. Timberlake Wertenbaker, for example, notes that theater "has a very, very slow influence," and Louise Page has learned that her political statements can be translated to her audiences only through emotions. And yet Pam Gems's belief that "words change everything" marks the avowed political activism of many theater women. Sandy Bailey (Monstrous Regiment), Jane Boston (Siren Theatre Company), and Julia Pascal (Pascal Theatre Company) all join playwright Jude Alderson in the effort to raise "people's consciousness" through the theater (interviews). The growing number of women writing for the British stage is part of a theater movement whose existence is a direct result of political commitment. This does not mean that all women writing comedy intend their work as political engagement. But it does mean that they write and produce their work in an environment of political awareness and leftist advocacy.

### Comedians on Stage: Male and Female

While the current political scene has special resonance for women, there
is no clear line that separates the work of contemporary women writers
from that of their male counterparts. In fact, the most recent literary
criticism conditioned by the socialist-feminist debate argues against the
pitfalls of such essentialist thinking. Judith Newton and Deborah Rosenfelt specifically caution against the philosophical division of a tragic male
essentialism from a comedic female essentialism (*Feminist Criticism*, xvii;
see also Moi, *Sexual/Textual Politics*). Reinelt and others have carried
such warnings about essentialist thinking into the specific context of
contemporary theater (see "Feminist Theory"). However, women's
comic writing can be profitably studied apart from that of men.[1] While
several male playwrights are currently producing plays with the qualities
that more generally distinguish women's work, the generic modifications transforming comedy are most clearly associated with women. Let
me suggest, by analyzing three recent stage portraits of the comedian—
two by men and one by a woman—why it makes sense to study women
in contemporary comedy by studying plays by women.

Trevor Griffiths's *Comedians* (1975) is the most well-known of these
three. Griffiths presents a penetrating portrait of contemporary comedy
and its politics in this play by yoking together eight would-be male
comedians—six students and two professionals. Through the eight,
Griffiths comments on the ramifications of three different attitudes to
comedy. First there is Bert Challenor's professional, entertainment-
world definition of comedy as an escape, a social safety valve. His comedy is clearly reactionary. Second, teacher Eddie Waters offers comedy
to his students as a vehicle for social awareness and change. His comedy
is a safe revolution that proves too good to be true. Third, student
Gethin Price threatens Challenor, Waters, and the audience with a comedy of violence, confrontation, despair, and abuse—comedy with an
uncontrollable revolutionary potential. Griffiths's own sympathies lie
largely with Price, and his play endorses the necessity of Price's hate and
violence (Carlson, "Comic Collisions"). As Griffiths himself notes in
discussing the historical context of his play, in the late 1960s and early
1970s the contemporary comedian was "about to become something
quite different . . . . they brought a heightened cynicism and a heightened
bitterness into the common colloquy" ("Transforming the Husk," 44).
As his play traces the devolution of the comic genre to a form that has

lost its joy and innocence, Griffiths joins other writers, like Peter Barnes and Harold Pinter, for whom the issues of comedy are not its revolutionary or reactionary potentials, but its inability to reflect anything other than the world's angst and despair. But in both Griffiths's premises and conclusions, women play a minimal, almost invisible role. There are jokes based on stereotypes of women, but no women characters and little consideration of the gender issues so central to the long tradition of theatrical comedy.

Both Terry Johnson in *Unsuitable for Adults* (1984) and Catherine Hayes in *Not Waving* (1982) focus their analysis of comedy on a female comedian; and with this switch in gender, the two writers make clear the one-dimensionality of Griffiths's play as it concerns gender. While the conclusions to be drawn about women's relation to comedy are ambiguous at best in these two female-centered plays, the presence of women in each broadens the range of issues comedy is attached to.

In Johnson's play, the comedian Kate delivers sex-oriented monologues that are a direct reflection of a life in sexual turmoil. In life, her relationship with Nick is threatened by the abortion she has just had (and that he would like to forget) and by the philandering that Nick insists that he can't help. Additionally, the bitterness of her feminist politics has been recently sharpened by a brutal rape in the neighborhood where she works. Onstage, she seems to be doing little more than translating into comedy the anger her social status as a woman has engendered. For example, in the rehearsal of her act before her friends, she succinctly sums up her position: "The problem for women in general, and female comedians in particular . . . is they can't piss in public and maintain their dignity at the same time" (29). Kate's later performance in front of an audience, in act 2, is equally confrontational, and its anger is like that of Price in Griffiths's play. The difference is that in her anger, Kate accuses the audience not of disregard, but sexism: "You're bored because I'm a woman, you can't see my tits, and nobody's about to dismember me. I only talk about it, right?" (56). For Kate as for Price, comedy is a weapon for attack, not a vehicle for joy. But while Johnson's play, like Griffiths's, treats comedy as a vehicle for portraying a society whose decadence threatens its integrity, the central presence of two women in *Unsuitable for Adults* completely changes the way an audience may respond to the comedy and its anger.

The most interesting and most important relationship in the play is that between Kate and Tish, a young stripper working in the same pub.

In spite of the sexual rivalry both Nick and Keith force upon the women, Kate and Tish engage in a series of conversations driven by their sincere attempts to understand and support one another. And significantly, the play's epilogue allows the warmth of this relationship to replace the accusations of Kate's comedy act. The two women end up together in a Dartmoor cottage where Kate's desire to "cuddle up" to Tish (63) leads to the hug that concludes the play. The simple joy of this ending, found nowhere in the play's earlier scenes, points to a bond between women as a way around the collapse of comedy, as a way to revive its hope. Johnson does not connect his play's joy directly to comedy, but he does connect it to women.

Hayes, in *Not Waving,* develops a similar contrast between a comedy of despair and a comedy with intimations of the hope and community that women may spawn. Hayes rejects the idea that the sex of her comedian makes a difference ("Up to Now," 79); nevertheless, as in *Unsuitable,* differences that are directly traceable to comedian Jill's gender give her comic pessimism a distinctive hue. For Jill as for Kate, comedy is not an abstraction, but a by-product of emotional and sexual entanglements with family and friends. And in this play, as in Johnson's, the female comedian's obsession with her body establishes the basis for her comedy. Jill, even more than Kate, focuses on women's sexuality by drawing from a self-deprecatory impulse. Whether she jokes about her corpulence, her aging, her birth experience, or her fear of VD, she accepts stereotypes of women's physicality and sexuality that both belittle and anger her. Yet even through the ambivalence of her comic, Hayes can transmit a discomfort with traditional comedy and its treatment of women. This play lacks the joyous release that comes with the hard-won epilogue of *Unsuitable,* but it does press for a similar conclusion about comedy: Comedy's traditional release is deceptive because it depends on an acceptance of stereotypes restrictive to women.

The distinctions to be made among these three plays by Griffiths, Johnson, and Hayes are of degree more than of kind. All three authors seem to accept as a given the prevailing attitude to comedy in the contemporary theater: i.e., they display comedy no longer as a conduit for happiness but, at best, as a format for exposing a fraying social fabric. In all three plays, comedy is an escape from what is pressing. Yet there is a crucial difference in the two that concern themselves with women. In Johnson's and Hayes's plays, the prevailing view of comedy is modified. In both, the authors demonstrate that to couple comedy with women as protagonists is to change both the questions contemporary comedy pursues and the answers it tests. My examples suggest that such a change of vision is not restricted to women playwrights; in fact, Johnson finds more of a difference in his female comic and her world than does Hayes. But a necessary ingredient for the difference in both plays is the presence of women as subjects, not just as subject matter. Because women are makers of comedy in both *Unsuitable* and *Not Waving*, comedy's staples of relationship, sexuality, and community are viewed from a fresh perspective. Even Peter Barnes's attempts in the more recent *Red Noses* (1985) to integrate women into his investigation of comedy and change seem meager because his women are more objects than subjects. And by and large, the examples of Griffiths and Barnes are representative of what still transpires in contemporary comedy by men. It is mostly the women making comedy who have been able to open up new vistas on comedy for today's stage. Contemporary women playwrights, like comedians Kate and Jill, focus on women to give comedy not just new notions of relationship, community, and self, but also to explore new and believable options for comic joy. What Hélène Cixous concludes about women's writing in general also applies to these women writing comedy: "A feminine text cannot not be more than subversive" (from Gilbert's introduction in Cixous and Clément, *Newly Born Woman*, xviii).

While Jill and Kate do not gravitate with premeditation toward issues of relationship, community, and sexuality, women now active in theater writing and directing generally desire to claim such issues in their concentration on comedy. There remain some playwrights—Louise Page, Timberlake Wertenbaker, and Bryony Lavery, for example—who are wary of aligning their work with comedy; not surprisingly, they want to distance themselves from a genre that is easily dismissed for being lightweight or frivolous. But many others are unabashedly enthusiastic. Playwright Nell Dunn declaims comedy as "such a wonderful thing"; actor Katina Noble of Spare Tyre preaches that comedy is "the best way to go about" putting women's concerns on stage; and playwright Sue Townsend is proud that "I can only write comedy, in fact" (interviews). While writers and actors find themselves energized by comedy's potential, women directors have been the most articulate in analyzing the powerful bond between contemporary women and comedy. Sue Parrish, who finds herself attracted to directing plays with a high comic content, finds laughter "the most liberating thing in the

theater" (interview). And director Carole Hayman has established herself as a spokeswoman for the necessary connection of women and comedy. In Hayman's experience, "the women who are emerging as theatre
writers . . . are almost all comedians." Finding comedy "common to all
the women writers" she has worked with, she is bold about asserting
that comedy is particularly female: "Comedy is women's business. I *love*
comedy. I *resent* being told that women can't do it. It's a whole area of
their lives that's been blotted out. *That's* my major reason for directing"
*(City Limits)*. It is a long way from Johnson's and Hayes's brief visions
of a female comedy to Hayman's equation of women with comedy, but
constant is the connection between women's subjectivity and a changing
concept of comedy.

## Comic Women Playwrights and Criticism

While signals of the importance of comedy to women (and women to
comedy) have become increasingly apparent to all kinds of theater practitioners (especially women), critical appraisals have been sparse. As I
noted in chapter 1, comic theorists have done little to account for the
special presence of women in traditional comedy. Feminist criticism has,
however, allowed students of comedy to frame new questions about
women's role in the genre. My analysis in part 1 owes much to the
specialized awareness of genre and context that feminist criticism has
encouraged. As I have noted, in part 2 I will be extending such analysis
with additional attention to the political, generic, communal, and psychological contexts in which contemporary women's theater occurs. As
my final introduction to my own analysis in the next five chapters of
part 2, I would like to outline briefly the way other feminist critics have
begun to attend to women and comedy. A growing number of writers
are noting the unusual options comedy offers women.

The essays Regina Barreca has recently collected in *Last Laughs:
Perspectives on Women and Comedy* map out the presence of comedy in the
work of many women writers. Barreca herself offers an important overview of the affinity of women for comedy, collecting and analyzing
prescriptive conclusions about women and comedy that define the limited thinking of several disciplines. She does not restrict her analysis to
theatrical comedy, as I have done, but she comes to many of the same
conclusions I do.[2] Barreca's introduction and the collection she has compiled are important contributors to the little-explored field of women

and comedy. Yet her collection deals primarily with the nontheatrical, and thus the work extends the study of comedy in the theater mostly through analogy. (Aphra Behn, Delariver Manley, and Wendy Wasserstein are the only women playwrights whose work is explored, and in much of this analysis the connections to comedy are oblique.) The generally nontheatrical predilections of this volume are, in fact, forecast by the nature of the feminist work on women and comedy that predates it. Judith Wilt ("Laughter of Maidens") and Judy Little *(Comedy and the Woman Writer),* for example, have studied fictive comedy and women, and Nancy Walker ("Do Feminists Ever Laugh?"), Naomi Weisstein ("Why We Aren't Laughing"), and Emily Toth ("Female Wits") have explored women's humor; but stage comedy has still rarely been explored. Feminists have begun connecting women and comedy, but with incidental attention to theater.

Among feminist theater critics, comedy has gained increasing attention. Three representative appraisals of women and comedy suggest the range of treatments women-authored comedy has received; they also suggest the hesitancy with which women's comic efforts in the theater are still treated. Helene Keyssar, in her book *Feminist Theatre,* groups together several British and American writers with comic tendencies under the chapter title "Success and Its Limits." She considers writers whose comedies have succeeded on Broadway and in the West End and is rightly alarmed by the reactionary power of the humor that is standard in such locales (158). In other words, she finds herself disappointed by the possibilities of women's comedy as they have been played out on many stages (see 150). When Michelene Wandor, the most important contemporary chronicler of women's theater in Britain, analyzes comedy, she turns not to comic plays or playwrights, but to the comic performer—that figure re-created by Johnson and Hayes. And while Wandor finds the female comic a quickly developing source of power and subjectivity for women (*Carry On,* 108), she considers these performers only briefly. Whether intentionally or not, both Keyssar and Wandor, like many of the women playwrights themselves, underplay the connection of women to stage comedy. Morwenna Banks and Amanda Swift have been the first to contribute a book-length study *(The Joke's on Us)* on the connections between women and the performance of comedy. While they argue for an affinity between women and comedy, their book is an incomplete analysis of the connections of women and comedy since its attention is scattered from stage to cabaret, from

TV to film.[3] Comedy has rarely been first on the agenda of feminist theater critics. But as writers such as Keyssar and Wandor have begun to assert, comedy can only benefit women when its potential for revolution and change is conveyed in receptive conditions.

While critics such as Keyssar, Wandor, Banks, and Swift have realized the promising connections between women and theatrical comedy, most feminist critics, like most comic theorists, have sidestepped the issues one must confront to fully understand women's connections with stage comedy. Study of women and comedy is still rare, I suspect, because women's appearances in and uses of comedy remain paradoxical. I approached such paradoxes from one point of view in part 1, detailing the dangers women have faced in the conventional comic world. There are dangers to female self, female community, and female power. Such dangers are inherent in traditional comic structure and are all too easily still translated in production. The hesitation with which critics continue to approach women's attachment to comedy may be an unstated recognition of the burden women in comedy have carried.

Here in part 2, I will approach the paradoxes of women and comedy from a second point of view, one that appreciates the diversity and plurality contemporary women playwrights are establishing in their comedy. Thus, in chapters 8 and 9, I will approach comic structure by showing how the power of conventional comic inversion and ending is being fractured by the women's concept of comedy as a texture that replaces linear plotting with juxtapositional, episodic, and metaphoric movements in narrative; that substitutes multiple heroines for an isolated one; that enlarges the extrarealistic possibilities always latent in comedy; that invites unconventional casting against gender and number; that relies on music to interrupt comfortable audience responses; and that draws from women's cabaret its disruptive privileging of a vocal, female self. The structure of contemporary women's comedies is as dynamic as the transformation it both displays and encourages. In chapter 10 I will return to the issue of women's identity in comedy. Relying on recent feminist investigations of the complex interrelationship of female self and sexuality, I will catalogue ways in which women playwrights are breaking the patterns of traditional comedy to empower selves. These selves are often multiple and rooted in a mutable sexuality; they are literary constructs that reflect the unsteady real-world intersection of language, gender, and society. With chapter 11, I move on to community, another basic ingredient of comedy, and argue that women playwrights have altered the comic equation in a radical way by writing *in*, offering plays *about*, and producing plays *for* women's communities. Women's theater groups both on the fringe and in the most established venues have experimented, with varying degrees of success, with models for institutionalizing collaboration among theater women. The mixed results of such collective work as well as the blemishes and danger that are apparent in the plays' onstage communities document the complicated nature of community as it is conveyed in women's comedy. Finally, in chapter 12, I close with a range of extratextual investigations. My attention to Doug Lucie's play *Progress* allows me to begin the chapter by recapitulating, a final time, my argument that women's comedies remain different from men's in their strategies, characters, and concerns. Yet my main goal is to speculate about the future of women's comedy by detailing the audiences women playwrights have both imagined and found and by analyzing the still unpredictable realm of reviewing (where gender plays a major role). Women's comedy is a genre built on and committed to change. But the extent of that change remains an issue. For me, Timberlake Wertenbaker's *Our Country's Good* stands as the culmination of the comic theater that women have built in the last twenty years, although the play's positive look forward is not the only current view of the future.

Pam Gems, Wandor, and Wertenbaker all agree that there is now some pressure on women playwrights to turn to comedy. All three share an apprehension about this coercion, feeling that a reification of connections between women and comedy would mean that women's work will never be taken seriously (Betsko and Koenig, *Interviews*, 209, 410; Wertenbaker interview). Thus, it is against critical advice, against the odds of attracting the attention of the theater establishment, that women playwrights pursue comedy and its illusory power. Yet ever more firmly, women are establishing a comic realm that is all their own. In the chapters that follow, I want to outline how the contemporary female creator of drama is transforming the comic tradition by claiming what Catherine Clément describes as a laughter that "breaks up, breaks out, splashes over" (Cixous and Clément, *Newly Born Woman*, 33).

## Chapter 8

# A Textured Comic Drama:
# Transformations in Structure,
# Character, and Mode

I spent one whole scene admiring Miss Pogson's legs. I mention this
only to suggest what a very tricky arena the theatre is for the discussion of sexism. One of the occupational hazards of my job is falling
in love four times a week.
—Robert Cushman reviewing Sarah Daniels's *Masterpieces* in 1983

When a journalist like Robert Cushman reviews such an intensely feminist play as Sarah Daniels's *Masterpieces* with such unabashed sexism,
there can remain no doubt that the relationship between women playwrights and the predominantly male community of reviewers is troubled. Unfortunately, that does not mean Cushman and his generally
more tolerant brethren can be dismissed, for their work registers the
sanctioned response of the theater community to women's theater work.
Thus, in spite of the idiosyncratic nature of reviewing, I begin my study
of the structures of women's comedies with the critical response to those
structures. Such critical response highlights both the radical
modifications women are bringing to their drama and the threat such
changes pose.

   While the polemic feminism and leftist politics of many women's
plays can irritate audiences, reviewers generally will not attack a play
on the basis of its politics alone. Instead, the most common criticisms
of contemporary women's comic plays are based on structure and form.
The following seven excerpts are representative of the failure reviewers
commonly attach to the structure of recent comedies by women:

John Barber on Sue Townsend's *Are You Sitting Comfortably?:* "The play offers no story but only incidents."

Kenneth Hurren on Caryl Churchill's *Cloud Nine:* "The play, if I may use the term of a work that is almost totally innocent of any formal structure, may be about nothing at all."

Jack Tinker on *Cloud Nine:* "Sloppy construction."

John Barber on Sarah Daniels's *Masterpieces:* "[Sarah Daniels] has trouble organizing her anger into a play."

Charles Spencer on Pam Gems's *Aunt Mary:* "Vestigial plot."

Ned Chaillet on Gems's *Up in Sweden:* "[Pam Gems] is not a play-wright but rather a composer of dramatic scenes."

Eric Shorter on Louise Page's *Salonika:* "[Enid's seduction of Peter is] just another rather incredible consequence of this author's idea of plotting."


Colin Chambers, from his perspective as the Royal Shakespeare Company's (RSC's) literary manager, concurs that "what many women are going to write doesn't actually fit what . . . many people think of as good theatre" (interview). Summing up the worst case, playwrights Michelene Wandor and Pam Gems both conclude that the reviewers who have complained of the lack of basic structure see women's drama as "nonplays" (Betsko and Koenig, *Interviews,* 409, 203). Occasionally the connection between a reviewer's criticism of structure and a playwright's feminist agenda is made directly. As Mark Lawson reviews Sarah Daniels's *Byrthrite,* he makes explicit the basic terms of the female playwright–male reviewer conflict over structure: "Ms. Daniels has a gift for provocative invective but she is a poor storyteller: perhaps linear narrative is too phallic."

The cross-purposes of reviewers and playwrights extend even into less condemnatory responses to the organization of women's plays. In fact, any play that wanders at all beyond the standard parameters of comic plot seems to confuse even the best of reviewers. Reviewer Irving Wardle, who found Gems's *Dusa, Fish Stas, and Vi* "the best written and most penetrating new feminist piece that has come my way," finds himself in a linguistic morass when actually attempting to describe the play's construction: "They have individual plot lines (Dusa's abducted children, Fish's unfaithful man) interwoven in a pattern of mutual dependence, with strong and weak continually changing sides instead of hardening into a fixed pecking order." Others have avoided Wardle's tangle of words by comparing women's comic play structures to models from radio, film, and TV; but the comparisons are tentative, as if the reviewers were apprehensive, not fond, of the admixture of forms. Comic plot and structure are, as I have myself assumed in earlier chapters, the basis for audience expectations in comedy. And ever since Aristotle's abbreviated discussions of comedy emphasized plot, it has been common to evaluate comic plays first on the basis of their plots. Yet in evaluating women's drama against traditional standards of plot, reviewers and the established theater community they represent dismissively conclude that women's plays lack structural integrity.

I have begun with reaction to women's dramatic structure only in part because professional audience response begins and stalls there. Analysis of plot is the keystone of my study in part 2 also because the construction of these contemporary plays—unrecognizable, surprising, alarming, and enjoyable all at once—is the foundation of the transformative enterprise women playwrights have undertaken in their comedies. These plays do not lack structure, as the reviewers charge.[1] They depend on unfamiliar structures. When the structure is unsuccessful, as still often happens, the play's other qualities and innovations are of academic and critical but not theatrical interest; the play fails. But when the structure succeeds in convincing an audience to accept its new formats, it also argues convincingly for new attitudes to the world and its women. To begin this study of the contemporary theater with formal considerations is also, then, to privilege the politics of women's theater. For there is no way to separate a study of form from the ideological implications of that form. Rachel Blau Du Plessis has argued that form is equal to ideology *(Writing beyond the Ending)*. In the specific case of dramatic comedy this translates into an awareness—keen for some writers and unconscious for others—that the way a play is put together is as important a statement as any polemical speech in it. Deborah Levy, a playwright intensely aware of the implications of her form, notes the crucial importance of devising new forms:

> The structure, the foundations, on which our world and society are built, is a bad one and we can't stop it. What we say is important and how we say it, in terms of the theatre anyway, is equally important. And I don't think enough women have taken it on. (interview)

Women's plays are—even more than Levy is willing to credit—filled with formal reconsiderations that in themselves convey political statements. And while all women playwrights are not leftist in their politics, it is more common than not for their comic reconstructions to facilitate commentary on sexism, racism, and classism.

Before I examine the plays themselves, however, I want to delineate the assumptions about comic form operative in the reviewers' difficulties with these plays, for these assumptions have a bearing on the altered dramatic formats women are trying out. In part 1, my analysis of comic plays was based on my assumption that inversion and a happy ending are the companion driving forces of comic structure, especially as it concerns women characters. The assumptions reviewers are making about women playwrights' comic structure are related to though not identical with mine. The assumption underlying most reviewers' complaints about structure is that plots should have a clear progression. While the adjective *linear* is often attached to the idea of progression, this idea seems to be, basically, another way of looking for an identifiable journey to the happy ending. I would suggest, in other words, that when reviewers complain about plot, they are complaining about a play in which a standard inversion is not maintained and/or a recognizable ending is not forecast. A few examples should suffice. Barber, in charging that Townsend's play "offers no story but only incidents," values a strong story line over an episodic construction. Similarly, Michael Billington's dismissal of Townsend's "cut-and-come-again technique" in *The Great Celestial Cow* and Martin Hoyle's charge that "the thread of the plot is thin" in Louise Page's *Golden Girls* also begin from the critical standard that a good comic plot is identifiably linear. Clearly, these indicted plays have none of what Colin Chambers described in an interview as the "vigorous narrative" that the theater establishment prefers.

Feminist critics have recently concluded that such standards of narrative, based almost exclusively on the study of literature written by men, are themselves male (de Lauretis, *Alice Doesn't;* Du Plessis, *Writing beyond the Ending*). And those studying drama in particular have similarly linked the demand for linearity to male perspectives. Susan E. Bassnett-McGuire finds theater itself "male" and explains that women do not construct their lives linearly because their lives are not linear ("Theory of Women's Theatre," 462–64). Josette Féral concurs that the lack of a linear plot marks most women's drama ("Writing and Displacement"). Speaking from practice and not theory, playwright Page joins Bassnett-McGuire and Féral in making this gender-based distinction. Since women "are expected to split up their time," she says, women play-wrights' fractured "time structures" predictably reflect their life patterns (Betsko and Koenig, *Interviews,* 359). This argument that traditional dramatic structures are male runs through most studies of women's dramatic form. For example, in studying plays by Churchill, Benmussa, and Duras, Elin Diamond argues that a feminist plot must interrupt standard, linear male plots that collude in "female subjugation" ("Refusing the Romanticism," 276). In studying lesbian theater, Harriett Ellenberger finds that lesbian writers are often in search of radically different forms to house radically different characters ("The Dream Is the Bridge"). In studying American and British women's drama, Helene Keyssar concludes that women's plays refuse to move toward the recognition scene that has been the expected climax of Western drama for two thousand years (*Feminist Theatre,* xiii). And Sharon Willis, in contending that Hélène Cixous's *Portrait de Dora* forces its audience to be conscious of the ideology of any narrative form, identifies a consciousness about form present in much women's drama ("Hélène Cixous's *Portrait of Dora* "). The standard assumption that acceptable plays must take on a certain form and the feminist countercontentions that such assumptions (and the forms they privilege) are sexist define the parameters of the critical debate on women's dramatic forms.

In chapter 1, I turned to the work of Bakhtin, Davis, and Turner to argue that comic inversion, while potentially liberating for women characters, has almost always offered only limited freedom. To begin pursuing the specific question of the difference that attaches to structure in women-authored comedies, I would like to extend that chapter 1 consideration briefly by turning to the work of Judy Little. In studying comedy in women's fiction, Little draws on Turner's notion of the liminal to argue that the rebellious middle of comedy, in fact, cancels out an apparently conventional ending. At the end of her book, she makes her case for a "feminist comedy" by suggesting that a strong "inversion" can replace a conventional status quo ending by substituting a "lack of closure," a "lack of resolution" (*Comedy and the Woman Writer*, 187). As valuable as Little's explorations of women and comedy are, however, I find a direct transfer of her conclusions to women's drama and its structure problematic. In short, redefining dramatic comedy for women will be more radical than retheorizing inversion. On two counts, Little's optimism about the possibilities of inversion must be qualified.

First, Little, like Turner, expresses her own reservations about the staying power of the inverted world. Turner very clearly cautions his readers about locating social change in the liminal. Liminal moments, he writes, "invert but do not subvert the *status quo,* the structural form, of society: reversal underlines to the members of a community that chaos is the alternative to cosmos, so they'd better stick to cosmos, i.e., the traditional order to culture" (*From Ritual*, 41). Little's apprehension is less clear-cut, yet early in her study she too acknowledges that inversion may *not* be enough to effect a changed order (*Comedy*, 14). Like Turner, Little recognizes that new forms necessarily have a relationship to those forms that precede them; thus, even though she concentrates on making the best possible case for finding comic inversions progressive, she too has registered her doubts about such findings. Second, since Little concentrates her study on inversion, she does not and cannot, in the end, escape it. As E. Ann Kaplan insists, critical dependence on inversion is, in effect, self-defeating, for inversion, by definition, depends on the status quo and is a poor basis from which to seek change *(Woman and Film)*. While inversion will continue to be an important consideration in my investigations in this chapter, I want to show that it is but one structural possibility for comedy, one approach to change. I follow Turner and Little in searching for a drama that effects change, but I do so by looking at features other than inversion that can make up comedy's construction and by focusing on a substitute for plot that I will call "texture." Pursuing this notion of texture allows me to provide a basis for explaining the continuing rift between women playwrights and the critical community they must work in.

"Anarchy," says writer/director Lou Wakefield, "is at the core of most women's writing." Director Carole Hayman adds that what women are now writing is "quite anarchic . . . quite subversive"[2] (Wakefield and Hayman interviews). I will pursue this notion of anarchy as I begin to suggest how a study of comic structure and social change can extend beyond a grounding in reversal and conventional endings and move toward texture. I will do this mainly through the examination of specific plays that follows in this chapter and the next. As a final prelude to that investigation I would like to offer the example of Greek Old Comedy as a precedent for a comedy that is both anarchic and textured.

Recent feminist attention to Greek Old Comedy is well represented by Froma Zeitlin's essay "Travesties of Gender and Genre in Aristophanes' *Thesmophoriasouzae*." While she details the ramifications of comic inversion in her study of the women in the play, Zeitlin's central deliberations on the play's powerful women focus on mimesis and transvestism. She concludes that Aristophanes' play forecasts the feminization of Greek aesthetics soon to be valorized in Euripides' plays (327). She acknowledges the power accorded the women of Aristophanes' Old Comedy, but she studies these women primarily as predecessors of the more influential women in New Comedy, romance, and pastoral. Zeitlin concludes that Euripides' women-centered, swiftly plotted, melodramatic plays—and not Aristophanes' dramas—hold the special significance for women in future generations.[3] I would like to suggest, instead, that the elusive, anarchic formlessness of Old Comedy that she is ready to dismiss holds the more special significance for women in comedy. Indeed, the qualities of Old Comedy's unusual composition are strikingly similar to what are emerging as the common qualities of contemporary women's comedy.

In terms of plot or structure, Aristophanes' Old Comedy defies conventional categorization. Through the years his plays have been described as everything from chaotic to condensed. There is a reversal in Old Comedy in that any recognizable order to motivation and events disappears. But the resultant chaos is much less controlled than in later comedy (most of which we owe to the heavily plotted New Comedy), both because of a reliance on the supernatural and because individual scenes are connected in a focus on a particular idea or character and not in a drive toward the ending. Such unfamiliar plotting marks Myrrhine's teasing of her husband Cinesias in *Lysistrata*. This interaction, which stands as the primary example of the difficulties created by the women's sex strike, is there not so much to develop the characters or to clarify the development of the strike as to concentrate audience attention on how the strike feels to the people it affects. Just as the construction of the play does not privilege plot or character in a familiar way, the ending of Old

Comedy is dissonant to the modern audience because it refuses to return
to order. In *Clouds,* instead of the reconciliation an audience might expect between the father and son—Strepsiades and Pheidippides—the play
ends with Strepsiades setting fire to the Sophists' school and driving
away its teacher and students. In addition to its loose narrative and
unpredictable endings, Old Comedy's openness about bodies and their
functions, its self-consciousness (especially its choral interruptions), and
its "discontinuity of character" (Dover, *Aristophanic Comedy,* 72) all also
parallel similar qualities in contemporary women's comedy.

But while the most notable structural elements of comedy by contemporary British women are also apparent in Old Comedy, the parallel
between the two theaters is less than exact. To begin with, since Aristophanes was eminently conservative by most accounts, his comic structure was most probably not designed to challenge the status quo. Satire
of the standard order certainly was within his purview, however. Second, I have found no evidence that women writers are consciously in
debt to Old Comedy. Thus, Old Comedy is not so much a model to
contemporary playwrights as my reminder to reviewers and critics that
dramatic comedy began with a very loose structure. Most important,
Old Comedy provides a precedent that suggests how the construction
of women's plays—though not recognizably based on inversion or predictable endings—may indeed have structural integrity. Old Comedy
shows that a textured play can be significant and lasting.

Old Comedy long ago made stageworthy an anarchic combination
of voices; contemporary women playwrights are now producing a similar combination of effects in their drama. Old Comedy thus provides,
for my study of structure, a model of organization at odds with traditional notions of comic plot. I will expand on this model by focusing
my study in this chapter and the next on the structural notion of texture.
*Texture* carries with it connotations of a composite, a weaving together
of many discrete items that results in a unified dramatic effect. It describes the effort in women's comedies to blend together seemingly
disparate effects, including those (such as episodic plots, fantasy, direct
expressions of sexuality, and self-consciousness) that characterized Old
Comedy. It refers not to a single form or formula in the comic plays
women are now writing, but to a mood and a feeling that repeats itself
in a variety of forms. Echoes of traditional inversion remain but do not
dominate. Endings, often happy ones, persist. And strong comic heroines appear in many of the plays I will discuss. Yet these plays by women

are more recognizable by their new visions of comic structure than by their reconstitution of standard forms. Women playwrights do not want a complete escape from the standard inversion and happy ending of comedy; they do want a comic environment in which any reversals and all happiness come on their terms.

Before I turn to the plays and their formal innovations, a final comment about the place of models is in order. Most British women writing drama today are wary of any models or patterns and unsure of influences. In the interviews I conducted with writers, Caryl Churchill was the only contemporary women writer to be cited more than once as a model. And while a wide range of other influential writers was mentioned (Mary Daly, Bertolt Brecht, Angela Carter, Anne Sexton, and Cora Kaplan), most writers were uneasy about identifying influences. Jane Boston of Siren Theatre found, on being asked who had influenced her, that no "female playwrights immediately come to mind." And Sue Townsend was adamant about the vacuum she writes in: "I haven't got any models, no. I am not influenced by anybody." In addition, writers are hesitant to class their work by genre. In fact, as I noted in chapter 7, thinking in terms of "comedy" at all was troublesome to most. What follows, then, is my attempt to make connections among writers and between writers and formats when the writers themselves are reluctant to do so.[4]

A lack of understanding—centered on play structure—surrounds the current work of British women dramatists. Reviewers' response is only the most visible indication of the gulf between practice and critique. But as I have pointed out in this critical overview, at issue here is not a simple war between the sexes. At issue are the power of forms, the relationship between form and ideology, and the relationship between theater and social change. There are dangers in attempting to list the qualities that characterize such a dynamic and political arena as contemporary women's theater. But it is important to begin describing the texture of women's comedy so that its significance can be assessed.

## A Textured Comic Drama

Before she settled into her feminist voice, playwright Bryony Lavery created comic women who existed in what she refers to as the "Yesbut Park": "My women characters were brave, intelligent, funny, loving, real . . . *yes but* at the end of every play they ended up as the losers. I

wanted them out of that park" ("But Will Men Like It?" 29). When she
realized that she and her characters were victims of comedy's traditional
reversals and endings, Lavery began experimenting with a comedy
closer to cabaret, pantomime, and musical than to Shakespeare, Shaw,
or Maugham. Her move is emblematic of a general shift in women's
comic writing. Yet there is no tidy label for the formats in which Lavery
and other women create comic drama, having left the Yesbut Park. The
writers' descriptions of their formal efforts, in fact, feature the tentative.
Catherine Hayes, for example, describes the plot of *Skirmishes* (1981) as
"a conversation that goes around" and notes of *Not Waving* (1982) that
the structure reflects the inside, not the outside, of her characters' lives
(interview). Timberlake Wertenbaker is as cautious of formulas as is
Hayes; but she is more willing to acknowledge that her sex has dictated
her departures from conventional form: "I suppose I am conscious of
wanting to do something different. If somebody won't write the play
for you, you have to write it yourself. So it is not that I have decided to
be different, but I am quite conscious of that need from my point of
view" (interview).

Those monitoring the women's formal experimentation join the
writers in searching for ways to describe the difference in their play
structure. Philip Palmer, literary manager at the Royal Court in 1986,
generalizes about a special, gentle mood he attaches to many women's
plays he has seen or read: "[They have] almost a lyrical quality. . . . There
is a tranquility at the heart of them, enchanting" (interview). From her
position as director, Carole Hayman has identified the difference as boldness: "Women writing theatre . . . are eroding all the time the frontiers
of what you can get away with. They are crossing taboo lines all the
time in both content and structure" (interview). And Lou Wakefield
stands by her concept of anarchy in judging the difference in women's
work: "Women are much more content to see confusion, or worse, the
chaos. . . . Our bodily cycle . . . we know that things change and that
there is no threat in change" (interview). Such provisional descriptions
suggest that there exist too few plays from which to delineate something
called a female aesthetic of comic form. But it is exactly women's new
arrival on the scene, says playwright Louise Page, that nourishes the
difference women have to offer:

> I think you have to be very big and very bold on the stage now, and
> women are taking those risks. They are not tied down to conven-

tion, and in a sense, can get away with something that isn't naturalistic, because there is that slightly quirky thing of people saying
"well, you are a woman." It's an area in which we women are freer
for not having role models. (Betsko and Koenig, *Interviews,* 360)

When referring to the "textural" strategies of contemporary
women's drama, those writing on theater have offered many terms in
an attempt to capture the variety of form that exists. These terms include
such adjectives as "episodic," "circular," "diffuse," "multi-directional,"
"juxtapositional," "naive," "impressionistic," "metaphoric," "wandering," "TV-inspired," "fluid," "sectional"; and such nouns as "collage,"
"cabaret," and "cavalcade." None of this terminology is new in discussion of drama. But this current search for appropriate descriptions, while
it does not always suggest confidence in the women's work, identifies
the variety of directions the plays themselves are taking. Barreca, in
summarizing the directions taken in women's comedy, notes that "mul-
tiplicity" and "process" are common (introduction to *Last Laughs,* 17).
In this chapter and the next, I have divided my consideration of the
variety and flux in women's comic structures into two segments. First,
in the rest of this chapter, I will consider the more dominant aspects of
women's formal approach to comedy: their organizational strategies,
their grouping of characters, and their departures from realism. Second,
in chapter 9 I will consider other strategies by which to measure the
advance of women writers beyond traditional comic structures. I will
analyze cross-gender and multiple-role casting, the use of music, and the
incorporation of cabaret. Also in chapter 9, I will conclude my look at
structure with a return to the stubborn ending of comedy, arguing that
the radical changes in organization, character, and mode, as well as the
novel uses made of casting, music, and cabaret, have opened up the
possibilities for a comic ending that does not encumber women.

## Beyond Inversions: Organizing Women's Comedy

Pam Gems's *Loving Women* and Caryl Churchill's *Cloud Nine* offer two
complementary models of the organizations now prevalent in women's
comedy. Both authors are conscious of generic structures, and in consequence both measure out, even evaluate, strategies women have recently
used in approaching the treacherous structures of comedy.

Gems bases her play *Loving Women* (1984) on conventional comic formulas. And like most writers relying on comic tradition, she walks a fine line between using and being used by comic convention. Most of the play depicts the relational changes in a familiar love triangle in which two women—Crystal and Susannah—battle over Frank, the one man. The women are even typed so that Gems can heighten their stereotypical competitiveness: Susannah is a plain, nervous, heady social campaigner and Crystal is an accepting, beautiful, working-class hairdresser. But as the play advances predictably through its ten years, it gradually becomes clear that while the women alternate at "having" Frank, the central relationship is that between Susannah and Crystal. At the end of the play, Gems relies on this novel emphasis not only to alter the comic formula but also to prompt the two women to decide that they can live together. Frank's presence or absence has become irrelevant. To make her point that it is the unconventional connection between the two women that constitutes a happy ending, Gems relies on her audience's experience with the comic tradition: i.e., viewers expect one of the women to get Frank and one to lose him. There is dissonance in the pattern of expectations when this does not happen; and in catching her viewers off-guard, Gems can more convincingly discredit conventional relationships. Gems is keenly aware of the ideological power of comic structure and has noted that "comedy is the most potent weapon." About *Loving Women* in particular she asserts that her structural twist is a clear statement about relationship: "But the main thing . . . in the end, that interested me, was new ways of living. New ways, because we haven't found any way you see, dismissed marriage. . . . It wasn't the fashion. But nothing better has replaced it, in fact, it's much worse" (interview). In choosing to tell her story of Susannah, Crystal, and Frank in such a recognizable comic form, she calls for a conventional response before she demands a critical self-consciousness of the familiar responses and their attendant values.

Judging by reviews of the play, Gems generally succeeded in directing a clear understanding of her characters and their choices and in gaining an audience receptive to her feminist message. There were those reviewers, among them Sheridan Morley, who were offended by the play's feminism ("If you're going to end up a Greenpeace wimp, Miss Gems seems to be telling us, you'd probably be better off gay in the first place"). But most professional viewers made sense of that feminism by pinning it on a recognizable structure: they wrote of "farce," "comedy,"

and "triangular comedy," all standard comic patterns. Ironically, however, these receptive responses reflect not the feminist power of Gems's
work so much as the dilution of that power in a conventional format.
In other words, reviewers' praise for the comfort of recognizable forms
effectively cancelled out the threat of Gems's radical conclusion. Comedy and a feminist agenda are *not* incompatible, as I will argue for the
whole of part 2. Yet what Gems's play shows is the burden of bringing
the two workably together, even for someone fully aware both of comedy's patriarchal dangers and of its feminist potential. A critique of form
and convention, in other words, can be overpowered by the vestigial
presence of convention, especially for those—like the reviewers I've just
remarked on—searching for the familiar, the conventional. Reviewer
Ros Asquith, in aligning the play with the West End, suggests, in fact,
how easily co-opted the play's revolution could be: "[It is a] sex-farce
for aging hippies. Well, maybe this is the West End of the future." Of
Siren Theatre Company's similar attempt (in *Pulp* [1986]) to use conventional generic structures, Jane Boston remarks that "it is a fine and risky
line" between altering a form and being consumed by it (interview). In
*Loving Women,* Gems demonstrates how women can take conventional
comedy and deftly use it to reinforce an idea. But Gems's ability to speak
to issues of social change is muted by her choice to retain a clearly
recognizable comedy.

Caryl Churchill is more deliberate and systematic about her relationship to comic form. In fact, in *Cloud Nine* (1979) she works from a
hostility to comic form and its ideology that Gems, with her accommodations, avoids. *Cloud Nine,* one of the most widely known comedies
by a contemporary British woman, makes traditional comedy one of its
primary concerns (and targets) through the sharp contrast between
Churchill's two acts. Act 1 is a farcical portrait of a Victorian family
upholding the empire in nineteenth-century Africa. By her exaggerations in song, her stereotyping, and her innovative casting (double roles
and cross-casting of gender and race), Churchill displays how the social
and sexual conventions these people live by in 1880 confine and distort
their lives. The best example of the crippling effect of convention is the
characterization of Betty, wife of Clive, the family patriarch and resident
British officer. Since she is played by a male actor, Betty's presence
immediately raises radical questions. And through Betty's self-deprecatory description of her role as wife at the play's opening, Churchill
highlights the precarious nature of Betty's self:

I live for Clive. The whole aim of my life
Is to be what he looks for in a wife.
I am a man's creation as you see,
And what men want is what I want to be. (4)

Her confused sense of identity is more concretely expressed later in the act when she agonizes over her adulterous love for family friend Harry.

The connection between such distortions of character and Churchill's critique of comedy is clarified in act 2, set up in extreme contrast to act 1. Act 2 is set in 1980 where act 1 was in 1880. Act 2 is reflective and ruminative where act 1 was frantic. Act 2 is loosely organized as a series of episodic encounters among sexually confused characters, where act 1 was tightly, linearly pointed toward a conventional heterosexual climax. Churchill makes use of these changes to underline her central notion that sexual identities have been severely damaged by conventional assumptions about sexuality and that by recognizing the restrictive nature of these assumptions, characters can begin to repair the damage. Betty is again exemplary; in this second act she realizes that her marriage is confining and that her sexuality has gone unexpressed. The most touching speech in the play is her long, heartfelt confession about masturbation.

The formal shifts that personally liberate Betty and the other characters also carry a parallel message about the play's comedy. First, in act 1, Churchill invites criticism not only of repressive Victorian morality, but also of the farcical formula it so neatly fits into. Then, in act 2, she proves that a comic concentration on sex, joy, and laughter can and should be packaged, instead, in a nonlinear narrative. Churchill's radical restructuring goes far beyond Gems's comic revisions. And because she creates an unfamiliar dramatic world, Churchill, unlike Gems, received widely varying reviews. Many critics liked the play's farcical opening, were baffled by its second act transition, and were hostile to the difference of act 2. Peter McGarry complained that "an air of indecisiveness pervades the latter stages," and Peter Jenkins joined him in marking a falling off: "Its most constant danger is degeneration into a mere sequence of acting exercises, or cabaret turns, loosely plotted together." As the discomfort surfacing in these reviews suggests, Churchill's play declares war on the structures of conventional comedy. It asks an audience to recognize both the inadequacy of old formulas and the liberating, still untested, and potentially disruptive possibilities of new ones.

*Loving Women* and *Cloud Nine,* then, represent the two main strategies women are using in their structural appropriations of comedy.
Gems attempts to use traditional form unconventionally so as to alter its
meaning, and Churchill does her best to destroy the form and locate its
joy elsewhere. The two approaches to the politics of form provide useful
markers for thinking about other comic plays. A second play by Gems,
Michelene Wandor's *Aid Thy Neighbor,* and Andrea Dunbar's *Shirley*
provide variations on *Loving Women*'s more temperate subversions of
comic tradition.

In *Aunt Mary* (1982), Gems is more destructive of the comic format
she employs than she was in *Loving Women. Aunt Mary*'s story of two
transvestites (one gay, one bisexual) moves through a traditional comic
series of witty exchanges and sexual intrigue to the untraditional three-
way marriage of the two transvestites—Mary and Cyst—and their
woman friend Muriel.[5] The early portions of the play are familiar and
unfamiliar at once: an audience is encouraged to accept the unusual sexual orientations of the characters because of the characters' familiar engagement in relational intrigue. But Gems's version of a wedding, which
comes near the end of the play, is offered not as the parody one might
expect, but as an indictment. While her onstage wedding offers a brides-
maid, the wedding march, traditional vows, and flowers, marriage is
presented as a nonreligious, nonheterosexual institution. Thus, instead
of confirming the status quo, this wedding sets a seal of approval on
actions and characters society has often sought to exclude. With this
shattering of the comic conclusion, Gems moves closer to Churchill's
formal razing. This play, more than *Loving Women,* shows how those
women who make use of standard comic patterns can still find revolutionary potential there.

Michelene Wandor's *Aid Thy Neighbor* (1978) relies, similarly, on
an altered but familiar comic development as she tells the roughly parallel stories of two couples considering whether or not to have children.
Like Gems, Wandor bends the narrative formula by plugging new variables into a familiar equation. Wandor offers two couples, one
heterosexual, one lesbian. When the play ends with only the lesbian
couple, not the heterosexual one, opting for children, Wandor denies the
traditional, happy-ending promise of children as the future product of a
grounding in the status quo. *Aid Thy Neighbor* is an exception for Wandor in that it is, as she notes, the "one play in which I did self consciously
write a comedy, in a particular comic tradition" (interview). While her

other plays range far from traditional formats, *Aid Thy Neighbor* is a reminder that even the most ideologically aware writers can be lured by a more traditional comic construction.

I do not find, among women writing comedy, that there is any identifiable general move either toward or away from such comedies as Gems's and Wandor's. Yet because all of the examples I have given are from an older generation of women playwrights, I would like to offer one final example from a younger writer, Andrea Dunbar, who is in her twenties. In *Shirley* (1986), Dunbar demonstrates the continuing attraction of the more traditional comic format for women playwrights. She also offers a final example of the women playwrights' need to alter that format. Dunbar's story is of Shirley, a teenage girl who comes to an awareness of her self through her relationships with boys and with her mother. There are familiar comic scenes in bed and in bars; but the ending, which has Shirley and her mother together, each having dropped the man in her life, is another modification of the conventional comic trajectory toward happiness. Gems, Wandor, and Dunbar all adopt some form of comic inversion and its subversion; and all hope to mitigate against the conventional eucatastrophe through their often radically different endings. But in all of these plays, the chances for viewers to interpret them as conventional are high. *Loving Women* is again exemplary; reviewers responded favorably because they recognized the play, not necessarily because they supported its altered relational schemes or ground-breaking ending.[6]

Those plays that, like *Cloud Nine,* develop new structural frameworks for comedy are not necessarily better or more important than the parodic, more tradition-dependent plays of Gems, Wandor, Dunbar, and others. But it has been the structurally more adventuresome plays that go the furthest in transforming the comic world. The trade-off, of course, is that those writers taking on the greater formal risk are also more likely to fail. I presented *Cloud Nine* as exemplary of women's comedies that seem to be battling against convention, not only because it is a good play, but also because it was Churchill who wrote it. For Churchill, besides being the most well-known of current women playwrights, is also the most brilliant experimenter in form.[7] Churchill herself asserts that she does not set out to create comedy: "I don't think I set out to be funny. Things that end up being serious or being funny I usually set about in exactly the same way. And it isn't clear which it's going to be until I'm quite far on into the material" (Truss, "Fair Cop,"

9). And with the exception of *Cloud Nine* and *Serious Money* (1987), her plays have not been wholly comic. But with her scrambling of conventional narrative in *Top Girls* (1982)—a play in large part comic—Churchill offers another instructive transformation of comedy to stand beside *Cloud Nine*.

Like *Cloud Nine, Top Girls* has two radically different sections. In the long opening scene, businesswoman Marlene throws a celebratory dinner party for her friends, who are, somewhat inexplicably, great women from the past: Pope Joan, Dull Gret, Isabella Bird, Lady Nijo, and Patient Griselda. In the four following scenes of a very different mood, Marlene deals with her professional and familial responsibilities. The opening scene, with its joyful gathering, its camaraderie, and its anarchic disregard for chronology, is clearly a comic feminist banquet. But unlike the comedy of Gems's play, and unlike even the comedy of *Cloud Nine*'s first act, it is a comedy unconfined by conventional structures. Several of the women are often talking at once, the talk moves from one story to the next depending on who can command attention, and the scene is there only for the moment: it has no past or future. The scene cannot even act as part of a comic inversion, for there is no "normal" to precede it, it has no ending, and—most important—it plays no directly observable role in the narrative about Marlene that follows. The feminist banquet stands apart, protected from the emotional turmoil Marlene faces in the latter stages of the play. This formal juxtaposition of such different moods, one so comic, one so serious, creates an obstruction for those wishing to understand the play in a conventional way. Reviews of the initial London production were lukewarm (it was not until after the play traveled to New York to become a hit that it was well received in London). And even Mary Remnant, who read the script of *Top Girls* for Methuen before the play was staged and who is quite sympathetic to women's drama (she has edited Methuen's fifth, sixth, and seventh volumes of *Plays by Women*), was initially "quite puzzled" by the play's connections (interview). The significance of this play's daring combination of effects is its demonstration that a time of comic joy and power—the first scene—can exist on stage without being subverted or discounted. While Churchill prevents such discounting by structurally isolating her banquet, she does use the comic mood of her first scene to introduce ideas about women and social change that persist beyond scene 1. The play, she contends, moves from the feminism so obvious in scene 1 to the socialism at issue in the debate between Marlene and her sister in the final scene (Betsko and Koenig, *Interviews,* 82). In each of her other major plays—*Objections to Sex and Violence, Light Shining in Buckinghamshire, Vinegar Tom, Traps, Fen,* and *Soft Cops*—Churchill also explores unconventional organizations. None of the plays on this list is comic, but to consider the more comic *Cloud Nine, Top Girls,* and *Serious Money* alongside *Fen, Light Shining,* and the rest is to see that this one woman's creation of new territory for comedy will not isolate comedy, but will attach it to other theatrical possibilities for investigating social and generic change.

While Churchill is the most widely known and respected British woman playwright, Sue Townsend may be the most successful comic writer. Significantly, Townsend takes pride in declaring herself a comic writer, a declaration most women are wary of. Yet Townsend's work, besides being wonderfully witty, is also formally aware; and her *The Great Celestial Cow* (1984) is another important example of the radical departure in form that Churchill has patterned out. In following the life of Sita and her family as they move from India to Leicester, Townsend adopts a plural structure. The model of social progress Sita's husband Raj has planned for the family (including arranged marriages, economic prosperity, and class mobility) is interrupted by an array of scenes not attached to this traditional plan. These scenes—which not surprisingly register the women's protest to Raj's plan—include music, dance, and nonrealistic staging (talking cows, rituals, monologues). The movement of the play, then, is far from straightforward or linear. The organization of scenes is essentially a dialectical contest between the traditional and the nontraditional. For example, a scene in which Raj attempts to arrange a marriage for daughter Bibi is followed by a monologue in which Bibi delivers a condemnation of the world that has driven her not to marriage but to sexual promiscuity.

Such intrusions on the traditional inversions of comic structure are most important for the changes they allow Townsend to bring to her conclusion. In claiming comedy as her métier, Townsend is unashamed to admit that the joy of comedy's happy ending is important to her (interview). So on the accumulated feminism of her intrusive scenes she ends her play on a "happy" *and* feminist note. For the marriage ending that would have pleased Raj, Townsend substitutes a surrealistic revision of scene 1. In the revised scene, children are raised in an atmosphere of equality and in a community of women. In finding this scene "an escapist, idyllic depiction of life back in the village, where conflicts are resolved and harmony reigns," reviewer Joseph Farrell offers one example of the many tradition-bound readings this scene provoked. My point, however, is not that the scene operates to suggest fantasy as the only location for these women's hopes, but that the novel arrangement of the play's middle sections points to the actual possibility that change could come to these women's lives. By ending with what is clearly a revision of her opening scene, Townsend invites comparison between one world women do not control (the opening scene) and a world they do (the closing scene). The result of such a comparison—following on the play's disjointed comic trajectory—is that the final joy and harmony seem not the result of an escapist dream but the attainable result of women in control of their imaginative lives.

Between the parameters represented by Gems and Churchill, women's comic plays follow an array of organizational patterns. In almost all of them, however, writers work from a shared desire to test the possibilities for connecting the various scenes and pieces of their plays. At the heart of the dramatic "texture" of these plays is the practice of connecting the pieces of a play with goals other than the teleological direction of the action. In other words, the parts of the whole do not exist primarily to serve in the goal of moving toward the ending. In the paragraphs to follow, I want to suggest the broad range of ways in which women are making the "process" of their plays the main determinant of action.

Many of the plays may be best described as dramatic concatenations of very short scenes. In *Rose's Story* (1984), Grace Dayley logs the struggle of a pregnant black teenager to keep her baby. There are seven scenes in this brief play, each of which is either one short episode or a string of short episodes. The abbreviated run of many of the scenes urges a response more symbolic than realistic. When, in act 1, scene 3, for example, Rose must confront the sanctimonious pity of the women in her mother's prayer group, the audience may register the conflict of belief systems without being burdened with complex character development. The focus remains solely on Rose and her development. While few plays rely wholly on short scenes, brief scenes very frequently punctuate narrative development by offering an interlude that retards forward movement. These condensed scenes often include other effects—fantasy, music, direct address—as I will elaborate in this chapter and the next.

The obvious complaint to be made about such brief treatment of material either throughout a play or in a single scene is that it is shallow.

Critic Lyn Gardner and director Sue Parrish are among those who have been troubled by the way TV may have encouraged such effects in the work of young writers like Dayley (interviews). But while familiarity with the structures of TV narratives may have blinded some new writers to the different requirements of and possibilities for the stage (many of the younger writers admit to having watched much more TV than theater), the relationship between TV and women's drama is more complex. TV is not necessarily the villain or the victor. Many of the current women playwrights who have in the past and will in the future write for TV (including Page, Wertenbaker, Lavery, Wakefield, and Alderson) are likely to bring a knowledge of that medium to bear on the theater. But the chances are good that this cross-media work will open up rather than close off the range of theater practice. For example, short scenes such as those in Dayley's play are often less an indication of lack of development than they are of different kinds of development. Since so many of these plays, as Keyssar *(Feminist Theatre)* points out, are no longer premised on confrontation and climax, brief encounters can serve more purposes than they might have in traditional narrative drama. TV undoubtedly has contributed to the abbreviated duration of scenes, but so too have the pattern of women's lives (women are directed in several ways at once, says Page [interview]), the influence of cabaret, and a general theater trend toward the shorter play and scene. Foreshortened scenes have also characterized plays by men. I offer the phenomenon here as but one feature of a changing theater landscape cultivated by women.

In some plays the length of the scene is not so noticeably different as is its placement. Again, I have found no terms that suitably describe the characteristics of such placement, though in the preceding paragraphs I have relied on descriptors such as episodic and juxtapositional. It is clear, however, that the placement of scenes often stems from an emphasis on principles other than linear plot development. Structures that are best described as juxtapositional frequently occur in plays with more than one group of characters. In Daniels's *The Devil's Gateway* (1983), for example, the story of Betty's feminist consciousness-raising intersects with the story of Fiona and Linda's lesbian relationship. There are connections between the two plot lines, since Fiona comes as a social worker to visit Betty and since Linda is the daughter of Betty's friend Enid. But the characters' developments do not bring them together in a dialogue or action. Although thematic commonalities exist, especially a concern for global peace, the stories basically exist side by side. The last presentation of Linda and Fiona, in the penultimate scene, shows them escaping a police constable after they have defaced a Soho sex shop. The last view of Betty shows her setting out, with friend, daughter, and mother, for the women's peace camp. Such parallel but integrated stories exist also in Daniels's plays *Ripen Our Darkness* and *Masterpieces.*

Juxtaposition in Jude Alderson's *Rachel and the Roarettes* (1985) and *The Virgins' Revenge* (1985) involves the splicing of time, not characters. In *Rachel,* Alderson doubles her feminist effect by telling the same story of a woman refusing marriage in both contemporary and eighteenth-century settings. The stories are not quite parallel (events in one time frame are sometimes the opposite in the other), but as Alderson slices one story into the other she makes it impossible, eventually, to separate the two. In *The Virgins' Revenge,* it is again a juxtaposition of different times, not different characters, that dominates the play's movement. Philomela and Psyche appear in each scene, but the scenes themselves jump from 2004 A.D. to Victorian London to ancient Greece to the present. The result is a comical study of women's sexual enslavement that insists on making comparisons between licensed prostitution in 2004, Victorian pandering, and contemporary political sex scandals.

Parallel plots and multiple time frames have long been part of dramatic construction; but if the reception of their plays is indicative, women writing today are using these techniques differently. Hayman's term "lateral" usefully describes this difference (interview); each discrete scene in these women's plays may not move the play forward in a conventional way but will, instead, explore a moment, create a mood, speculate on a topic. In short, the principle of organization is more often synchronic than diachronic. This refusal of a single line of development moving "ahead" has resulted in as many organizations as plays. To conclude this overview of the restructuring of comedy in women's plays, I will turn to three more plays that indicate the liberal interpretation women have brought to the basic construction of their plays.

*Time Pieces* (1982), authored by the members of the Women's Theatre Group and compiled by Lou Wakefield, is based on the framework of a family photo album. As an aunt and niece thumb through their family album, they allow for the presentation of the tales of several generations. The separateness of the scenes is reinforced by a range of presentation that includes realistic staging, monologue, musical interludes, and even group chanting. At the same time, connections are made through the frame and by the aunt and niece's analysis. This patchwork structure is particularly common in work composed by groups. And while *Time Pieces* is also representative of the oversimplification in many similarly structured plays, it offers a common pattern of organization.

The refusal of a single focus has also appeared in a more stylized form, of which Michelene Wandor is the most practiced. Her *To Die among Friends* (1973) moves in and out of comic moments, but still provides for comedy an important model of a more radical experiment in form. In the five sections of the play, Wandor presents five different situations and character groups that all bear some relationship to the idea of growth. The characters are rarely named (most are designated only by letters), and are offered as experimenters, not experts, in understanding the changing social fabric they act out. In these structural variations, Wandor disallows conventional expectations for both form and content.

Finally, I turn to Daniels, to her *Masterpieces* (1983), for a play that combines many of the intraplay connections I have considered above. The play has a central character, Rowena, who must come to terms with the role of pornography in her life. But Daniels does everything she can to prevent the reading/viewing of the play as a traditional narrative about Rowena. Time is jumbled, for example, as Rowena's trial for murder in scene 2 precedes the murder itself in scene 14. More noticeably, the unsettling concatenation that occurs in the first scenes continues through the entire drama: The play opens with one male actor doing three consecutive monologues of three different characters, moves to a restaurant setting for the discussion of pornography, offers a woman's monologue on her feminism, comes to Rowena's trial for murder, and then transfers to a school classroom. Once more, the reviewers suggest how difficult such formal connections have been to process. Michael Billington settled on the relatively neutral phrase "a zig-zag course" to describe the organization of *Masterpieces;* Nicholas de Jongh made sense of the order only by suggesting it was less than theater—"the play's form is sometimes untheatrical, perhaps written with radio in mind rather than the stage"; and even Wandor felt jostled by the combination of effects: "Although there appears to be a causal narrative, there is little to fulfill the naturalistic plot expectations set up by the domestic scenes." The plays of Daniels, Wandor, Wakefield, and others, which depart in large and small ways from the diachronic, do not fall neatly into identifiable forms. Many of the women are not even conscious of writing in new ways. And clearly, audiences are still struggling to make sense of it all. But

women playwrights continue to battle against traditional comic structures in as many ways as they can devise.

## From Heroine to Heroines:
## Female Comic Characters

I have avoided considerations of character so far because I think it is
essential to understand that structural changes are the foundation on
which women's comedy is asserting its independence. The accompanying changes in characterization can be considered only in this perspective. As Alice Rayner also notes, plot is the essence of comedy, and
changes in plot automatically condition changes in character (*Comic Persuasion,* 155). Recognition of the dependence of character on plot is
essential, for in a very basic way the women in these comedies are not
all that different: they remain the power at the center of the action. The
power is appropriated very differently, however, since the path these
women take through their comic world is not so strictly bound by the
male tradition. As I turn my attention to character now, I will look first
at new visions of the comic heroine and then at replacements for her.

There remain comedies written by women in which the heroine
cleverly outwits the men to win her man and her happiness. Fay Weldon's comedies, for example, focus on women who dedicate themselves
to relationships with men and achieve their goals through familiar subversive means (*I Love My Love* [1984] is a good example). In most
woman-authored comedies with one or two women at their core, however, the women characters pursue different kinds of happiness, and in
modified ways. First, for most of the women characters, happiness has
become the attainment of self-understanding, specifically an understanding of what it means to be a woman. And second, the central women
approach this understanding largely in the company of other women.

*Trafford Tanzi* (1978), with its cartoonlike clarity, stands as a prototype of the usually feminist journey to self-knowledge now at the center
of many female-authored comedies. Author Claire Luckham charts
Tanzi's movement from female babyhood to traditional marriage to
Tanzi's rebellion against the patriarchal system that has determined her
life choices. This is not a unique story, of course. What makes Luckham's version of the story unusual is her use of an exaggerated wrestling
motif to tell the story of Tanzi. The entire play takes place in a boxing

ring; the play is divided into "rounds" that end with a bell; the characters actually, physically, wrestle out the issues in each scene; and the audience members participate directly by booing, hissing, or cheering as they feel appropriate. In its final version, the play ends with Tanzi beating her husband Dean Rebell in the ring and translating that victory into their home—their bargain has been that if he loses he must become a house-husband. Luckham describes the action of the play as being about a woman who is "knocked back by conventional ideas of what a woman should be" and who learns "to take responsibility for herself" (17). This straightforward tale of feminist awakening does not venture far from familiar comic action, but Luckham does provide a heroine whose growth brings her not back to where she started, but forward into a whole new kind of relationship. Nor does Tanzi win her victories by subversion, but rather by direct confrontation.

Sharman Macdonald's *When I Was a Girl, I Used to Scream and Shout . . . (1984)* has enjoyed, like *Tanzi,* a West End success (*Tanzi* ran at the Mermaid in 1982–83; *When I Was a Girl* ran at the Whitehall Theatre in 1987). But Macdonald departs still further than Luckham from a traditional treatment of the comic heroine. Fiona and her mother Morag both sort out their lives with men in the course of the play, but they do so largely removed from men. Fiona's boyfriend Ewan, who is the only male in a cast of four, makes but a few brief appearances. The more deliberate focus of this play's feminist awakening is three women's relationships to one another. As Fiona, Morag, and Fiona's friend Vari sort out the events of twenty years, they set in order their relationships to husbands and boyfriends, but focus their greatest energy on re-inter-preting the alignments of their own troubled relationships. The togeth-erness and happiness that mark the end of this play stem from Fiona and Morag's hard-won confessions and final reconnection. The events of Fiona's life are the matter over which the three women laugh and puzzle; but to understand it all, Fiona must understand the life choices of her mother and her friend also. "I knew I had a choice," Morag tells Fiona in the end (62). Morag's statement reverberates in the lives of all three women, who know, by the end of the play, that they do control their lives through the choices they make. Happiness here is located in the women's newfound comfort in themselves and their friendships.

Handling events by direct confrontation, not subversion, is repeated in two recent plays by young black writers. As these plays sort out events of the present, not the past, they show how the exercise of choice

by women now often replaces subversion as the primary mode of operation. Both also repeat the focus on the heroine's growing autonomy.
While Jacqueline Rudet's *Money to Live* (1984) ends ominously, most of
young Charlene's education about life on her own is buoyed by the
laughter she shares with others. As Charlene explains to her mother her
decision to become a stripper, she displays her discovery of choice: "I'm
part of a generation of smartly-dressed, empty-headed girls who believe
that applying make-up is a form of art. . . . Out on these streets around
me I see girls pushing prams. For some of them, the birth of that child
was the death of them . . . people don't get married and stay together
anymore" (169). This moment is typical of the play's dedication to a
feminist consciousness and its characters' exercise of choice. Charlene,
in fact, refuses traditional parameters of the comic ending—marriage and
children. Grace Dayley's *Rose's Story* is an interesting companion piece
to Rudet's play, for Rose—who also finds her "self" through the play's
events—decides that, unlike Charlene's, her life will be triumphantly
domestic. A pregnant, unwed teenager, Rose comes of age by battling
for her baby against parents, social workers, and friends—"I've realized
that I will have to become somebody in my own right" (72). Both
Rudet's and Dayley's plays also show how these changes in the heroines'
role necessarily come hand in hand with structural alterations. Instead
of *Tanzi*'s tidy inversion of marital power, these two plays end without
major events to make an "ending." There is, instead, a sense of contentment that comes with a realization of the control a woman can exercise
when faced with the challenges life poses.

As these examples verify, the comic play of female awakening has
usually been politically aware. As a final example of a one-heroine play,
Timberlake Wertenbaker's *The Grace of Mary Traverse* (1985) shows how
direct the connection can be between the feminist self-consciousness of
these plays and a broader political agenda. In *Mary Traverse*, Wertenbaker takes the Faustian journey and converts it from an isolating, individual nightmare into a string of bizarre episodes that the main character,
Mary, shares with her maid Sophie and her Mephistophelian guide,
Mrs. Temptwell. Mary's journey toward feminist consciousness leads
her to realize, like Tanzi, Fiona, Charlene, and Rose, the confinement
of traditional female roles; and like the other women, Mary sets out to
acquire the happiness that she deserves and that she will define in her
own way. This play travels far from the comic as Mary confronts such
disturbing events as rape, riot, and gambling, but the play ends in a

garden with Mary relaxing with her father and her friend/maid Sophie and testing a tentative but comic acceptance of the world: "I'm certain that when we understand it all, it'll be simpler, not more confusing. One day we'll know how to love this world" (71).

Connected to Mary's comic, feminist transition are some far-reaching politics. Most obviously, Mary enlists herself in grand, revolutionary plans for changing the political order, including participation in bloody street riots against the established government. For Mary, there is an important connection between finding new options for women and changing the world. And for author Wertenbaker also, comedy is an important part of her political agenda: "*The Grace of Mary Traverse* is the most comic of the lot [Wertenbaker's plays] in that it also ends happily. . . . I would say I use a lot of comic things in my plays but they are not ultimately comedies because their purpose is probably different from a comedy. Their purpose isn't to be ultimately soothing or reassuring" (interview). Like so many others, Wertenbaker shies away from the label of comedy. But her often comic plays keep forging the connection between political awareness and female change. All comic plays by women do not approach Wertenbaker's conflation of feminist consciousness and political activism, but women creating comic heroines have made the feminist assertion of self the predominant action in their plays.[8]

In each of these plays centered on a single character there is also a strong contingent of other women who usually support the heroine through her changes or change with her. (There are exceptions, of course. Mrs. Temptwell, for example, never accepts Mary Traverse's visions about a reconstituted world.) Just as important, in many plays this group of women actually takes the place of a single heroine. Groups and communities have always been features of comedies, but traditionally there is a center or a hierarchy to the group while the group itself is in the background. In many women's plays, however, the group is in the foreground. Women playwrights' experimentation with foregrounding groups is currently both widespread and uneven. But the multiple female heroine is evolving as one of the most distinctive features of these plays and one of the strongest expressions of an active feminism. As Du Plessis notes, the use of a collective protagonist "may imply that problems or issues that we see as individually based are in fact social in cause and in cure" (*Writing beyond the Ending*, 179).

While she presents groups in most of her plays—*Womberang, The Great Celestial Cow,* and *Are You Sitting Comfortably?*—Sue Townsend makes it look deceptively easy to balance such multiple character por-traits in *Bazaar and Rummage* (1982). Here she presents the disastrous but endearing histories not only of three agoraphobiacs, but also of the two amateur social workers aiding them. Instead of a narrative that follows an arc in the life of one character, Townsend provides two acts in which a series of relationships are interwoven so that the events that mark progress or setback in one life affect the lives of others. Townsend identifies dealing with change on a group basis as her special skill, but only as she notes the problems with such construction: "In fact, it is very difficult to do because you have to keep them [the characters] moving, and saying, and interacting constantly" (interview). Nell Dunn was also conscious of the difficulties in creating a group protagonist in *Steaming* (1981). Inspired by her own warm and friendly experiences in London's Turkish baths, she was determined to offer six characters who could share the feminist growth of this play: "I wanted to show . . . the true companionship of women and the pleasure they could have in each other." But like Townsend, Dunn reported the strain of her attempts to realize all possible relationships among six people. Ironically, she found Jane, the feminist, the hardest to integrate (interview).

Although the group protagonist has presented a structural hurdle for playwrights, it is the core of a great percentage of the comic plays by women, largely because of the multiplied options for female growth such plays offer. Several successful plays, such as Gems's *Dusa, Fish, Stas and Vi* (1976) and Page's *Golden Girls* (1984) have brought the model of the multiple heroine before large audiences beyond the fringe. The fringe theater too has been full of group-centered plays, including Jackie Kay's *Chiaroscuro* (1986), Debbie Horsfield's *Red Devils* (1983), Lou Wakefield's *Time Pieces,* the Women's Theatre Group and Paulette Ran-dall's *Fixed Deal* (1986), Michelene Wandor and Gay Sweatshop's *Care and Control* (1977), Jane Thornton's *Amid the Standing Corn* (1985), and Charlotte Keatley's *My Mother Said I Never Should* (1987). I will suggest in chapter 11 that this structural preference is related to the writers' preoccupation with communities of women and redefinitions of the fam-ily. Here I would like to turn to *Golden Girls* to analyze fully the struc-tural pressures created in such popular plays.

Because it is about competition, Page's play stands as a paradigmatic account of the tensions that arise when a tradition of end-determined drama meets the collective female protagonist. As five young women train to place themselves in the four positions of Britain's Olympic four-hundred-meter relay team, Page relies on very little of the traditional comic plot. Romantic relationships, though present, are of marginal interest. Relationships among the women and with their training staff take precedence as there are at least five central characters. While the play has a clear climactic moment in the race at the Olympics, much of the play's action counsels the audience not to put too much value on its outcome. Instead, the scenes that lead up to the race reflect the shared focus by allowing for the monitoring of several characters and many relationships at once. Act 2, scene 2, is the best example of the several collective scenes that allow for a reconstitution of the ending. As the five women athletes try to relax on a hotel terrace in Athens the night before their Olympic run, Page has them and the members of their support staff wander on and off the stage, alerting viewers to the women's varying states of mind. The scene snakes from (1) Janet and Muriel (two of the runners) to (2) Janet and Muriel chatting with trainer Vivien and sponsor Hilary to (3) Hilary and Muriel to (4) Hilary, Muriel, and Dorcas (a third runner) to (5) Mike (Dorcas's boyfriend) and Dorcas to (6) Dorcas, Mike, and Janet (a fourth runner, who is romantically involved with Mike) to (7) the three in the love triangle joined by Sue (the fifth runner) and Noel (her father) to (8) Dorcas, Sue, and Janet to (9) Sue, Dorcas, and Tom (the coach)—and so on for several more intrascene variations. Page cannot always successfully manage this flow of characters and concerns, and this scene may be among those that prompted her to divulge that she does not consider this a very good play (interview). But the scene is illustrative of the texture of so many of these comic plays: the play's fabric is woven, slowly, from many strands of character and concern, none of which, alone, tells the story.

In such plays as *Bazaar and Rummage* and *Steaming,* such shared concern and action is largely unambiguous; the women need to work together to achieve their goals. But Page sets before her audience the necessary question of just how far such togetherness can go by having her five athletes compete against one another for the four spaces on the track team. They cannot all run together. Competition exacts a large toll—Dorcas has taken drugs to make the team and is responsible for disqualifying the whole team after they have, in fact, won the Olympic gold. But the failure Dorcas represents is outweighed by the way the women learn to work together—even though they all cannot run to-gether—and the way they remain together—all five of them—despite their setback. The tension and misunderstanding that does remain between characters parallels the formal tension that results, in a play like this, from the fusion of end-oriented drama and the diffuse focus of a group protagonist. In fact, many of the negative reviews I have cited earlier in this chapter are complaints about the diffuse structure a collective protagonist necessitates. While some of these complaints are clearly justified, my point here is not the success writers can have (and have had) with a collective protagonist, but the difficulties that still arise from a disjunction between audience expectation and authorial practice.

## Confirming a Difference: The Extrareal

The novel configurations of structure and character that distinguish contemporary women's comedy are not uniform, are still widely unrecognized, and consequently still constitute the basis for the suspicion and rejection that greet women's drama. Contributing to this gap between conception and reception is a third quality common in women's comedy—the use of nonrealistic staging. Disregard for stage realism, like revision of structure and character, is another indication of the combative nature of women's comic plays.

There is broad critical agreement that plays by contemporary women frequently depart from realistic staging. Of the many plays she covers in her book *Feminist Theatre,* Keyssar concludes that few "do not diverge significantly from conventional realism" (xii). And whether explicitly or implicitly, most other chroniclers of contemporary women's drama join her in finding women's theater non- or antirealistic (Diamond ["Refusing the Romanticism"], Willis ["Hélène Cixous's *Portrait de Dora"*], Curb ["Re/cognition"]). Reviewers, too, rely on terms like "surreal," "fantastic," and "antinaturalistic" to recreate the mood of what they've seen. Recent feminist investigations into the nature of theatrical realism suggest, however, that a slightly more complicated situation exists. Basically, critics are now suggesting that neither realism nor its alternatives can be pigeonholed as dramatic modes definitively pro- or antiwoman. For example, despite strong connections between realism and the maintenance of the status quo, women playwrights have often turned to realistic staging. The recent resurgence in women's theater began in a realistic mode, as Reinelt points out, with women eager to use the stage as a direct reflection of their newly transformed lives ("Feminist Theory," 48). And even within the present spectrum of presentational alternatives, realism continues to offer possibilities for

women. Forte suggests, for example, how plays by women can "mas-
querade" as realism, both allowing for familiar responses and at the
same time eliciting more radical re-interpretation ("Realism, Narrative,
and the Feminist Playwright"). Along similar lines, Diamond argues
that realism and mimesis can be "retheorized" as a site for feminist
intervention ("Mimesis, Mimicry, and the 'True-Real'"). Yet the complicated retheorizing that Forte and Diamond, among others, have undertaken testifies as much to the dangers realism still poses for women
as to the strategies it offers for redefining women's theater. Thus, while
it may be employed as a tool for the creation of a woman-supportive
drama, realism continues, in many contexts, to reinforce the dominant
ideology.

As its beginnings in Greek Old Comedy suggest, comedy has always had a skewed relationship to realism. Comedy's formal structures—reified in English-language drama as inversion and ending—have
provided it with a cushion from the messiness of life. Yet even in the
generally stylized milieu of comedy, realism's conflation of stage and
world have contributed to the limitations imposed on women and comedy. For it is precisely the parallel between stage and audience that makes
the strong women of comedy potentially so threatening. Thus, in spite
of the possibilities that a redefined stage realism may offer women, it is
through use of the extrareal that contemporary women playwrights have
sounded some of the most resonant notes in their own orchestration of
comedy. Echoing those critics and reviewers who have remarked on the
departures from realism in contemporary women's drama, the playwrights themselves highlight their excursions outside of "realism."
Some writers stress commonsense reasons for their reliance on the extrareal. Page notes that women's lives, simply by not conforming to the
recognizable pattern set by men, are "surreal"; and Wandor and Wertenbaker both credit their preference for the nonrealistic to its linguistic
potential (interviews). Many writers, however, have more rebellious
motives for adopting the extrarealistic. Writer Deborah Levy and the
women in the Women's Theatre Group, Monstrous Regiment, and Scarlet Harlets are among those who have found the naturalistic theater "a
series of codes that mean nothing" (Long and Neave interview). These
theater practitioners also see realistic staging techniques as largely responsible for women's traditional and confining stage domesticity. At
the extreme, Bryony Lavery contends not only that life refuses to con-

form to the naturalistic, but that for a feminist sensibility, "creating naturalism" is anathema (interview).

The message from critics, reviewers, writers, and others concerned about women and stage realism is twofold: first, that the continuing predominance of realism is a significant aspect of the theater establishment that has, more often than not, limited women's theater participation; and second, that women's theater, in response, veers far from the real. Not surprisingly, this movement away from standard forms of presentation may further jeopardize women's chances of production. Colin Chambers notes that both the RSC and the Royal Court have produced plays (by men and by women) with extrareal qualities (interview). Yet in general, women who continue to write nonrealistic plays continue to face a potentially hostile reception.

Many of the most successful recent plays by women are memorable for their extrarealistic invention. Among those dramas in which the nonrealistic has played a significant part in defining new constructions and nontraditional characterizations are Churchill's *Vinegar Tom, Top Girls, Cloud Nine,* and *Serious Money;* Louise Page's *Salonika, Golden Girls,* and *Beauty and the Beast;* Sue Townsend's *The Great Celestial Cow;* Deborah Levy's *Pax* and *Naked Cake;* Sarah Daniels's *Masterpieces, Ripen Our Darkness,* and *Byrthrite;* Maro Green and Caroline Griffin's *More;* Michelene Wandor's *Whores D'oeuvres* and *To Die among Friends;* Tasha Fairbanks's *Pulp;* the Women's Theatre Group and Paulette Randall's *Fixed Deal;* Jude Alderson's *The Virgins' Revenge, Madonna in Slag City,* and *Rachel and the Roarettes;* Charlotte Keatley's *My Mother Said I Never Should;* Anne Caulfield's *The Ungrateful Dead;* and Rona Munro's *Piper's Cave.* The nonreal is manifest in a distinct way for each play; the following description of its presence in five of these plays is an attempt to indicate a range of approaches, not a single model. And while these departures from realism bring the plays near the anarchic mood of Aristophanes' Old Comedy, such alterations also take the writers, at times, far from drama recognizable as comedy. In *Pax* (1985) and *Naked Cake* (1986), for example, Levy ventures so far from expected illusion that a generic norm is difficult to identify. In many of the plays now being written, however, the surreal, the fantastic, or the destruction of the realistic are parts of a fluid comic texture.

Sue Townsend describes the mood of her early plays as "heightened naturalism" (interview). But inspired by Churchill's nonrealistic juxtapositions in *Top Girls,* she approached her later, least naturalistic play, *The Great Celestial Cow,* assured that she could create anything she wanted. From the beginning, she knew that this portrait of women emigrating from India to England would cohere around "the cow theme," which she describes as the attachment of the Indian women to the animals they were forced to leave behind in India. But she did not foresee that her liberation from "heightened naturalism" would lead to such a "fantastic," concrete expression of that theme (interview). In the first scene in India, Sita talks to, photographs, and shows her love for the onstage cow she is being forced to abandon. But once Sita is in Leicester, Townsend indicates the increased value of the animal connection ("the cow theme") by offering, first, talking cows (act 2, scene 11) and then a cattle auction during which the women become cows who physically threaten the male auctioneers (act 2, scene 12). In addition to blurring the boundaries between humans and animals, Townsend also transcends the real with ritual: act 1 ends with Navrati music and a shrined goddess who comes to life to join the dancing women.

The power of these surreal effects can be measured through their transformation of the more realistic scenes. For in a context where animals talk and goddesses step to life, the arranged marriage of act 2, scene 4, and the patriarchal psychiatry of act 2, scene 1, seem both artificial and ludicrous. Most important, the transformative power of Townsend's departure from realism makes feasible her final scene, in which, as I noted earlier in this chapter, patriarchy is replaced by feminist-inspired equality. Recounting the original staging of the last scene, Lou Wakefield (who acted in the scene) noted that with carefully chosen music and peculiar lighting, director Carole Hayman wanted to convince the audience that fantasy was actuality (Wakefield interview). Townsend herself, in speaking of the play's magic, stresses how the breaking down of the realistic boundaries of character and narrative encourages a rethinking of one's perception of the world: "It has a magic. It had a real magic that I don't think I have seen before" (interview).

Sarah Daniels, in *Ripen Our Darkness* (1981), uses a well-placed nonrealistic scene to transform the reality of an entire play. After twelve fairly realistic scenes, the main character, Mary, commits suicide and arrives, in scene 13, in a heaven with a female deity. Director Carole Hayman describes the fantastic-comic mood of this scene in the premiere production: "The whole thing was a dance drama. These women danced around and they did silly things, and it was very funny. But it was a totally surreal moment in what was generally a naturalistic play" (interview). While Daniels had called for "a potentially quite difficult and possibly quite embarrassing scene" (Hayman interview), its successful original production proved that the risk could pay off. Audiences, although surprised by the sudden change, were responsive to the scene's feminist politics. By surprising viewers with a female, feminist heaven, Daniels insisted that they follow Mary in using this place as a touchstone to register how patriarchal the rest of the play has been.

Both Townsend's and Daniels's plays provide evidence that women's use of the nonreal often reinforces the call for a changing order. In these two plays the surreal is limited, although its influence on the play is pervasive. In Rona Munro's *Piper's Cave* and Louise Page's *Salonika* and *Beauty and the Beast,* almost all of each play's action is beyond the real.

Rona Munro's *Piper's Cave* (1985) is more lyric than comic; yet in its absorption with variations on mood, tone, and realities, it suggests how meditative the disruptions of the nonrealistic can be. Set outdoors, near a seashore cave in northwest Scotland, the play tracks an unusual relationship between Jo, a woman who finds herself in need of shelter from the weather, and Alisdair, a man who has exiled himself to a lonely life in this isolated cave. Munro opens up the possibilities of relationship far beyond those of a realistic encounter between Jo and Alisdair with the frequent appearance of a third figure, the spectral Helen. Helen is sometimes Jo's friend, sometimes her conscience, sometimes her dream; she makes tangible Alisdair's relation to the land; and to playwright Munro, she is, as somewhat cryptically described in the cast list, "the place, the landscape" (110). As the relationship between Jo and Alisdair develops through its bizarre twists and turns, Helen wanders in and out, sometimes appearing to one or the other of the characters, sometimes to the audience, and always detached from the action. Although both Jo and Alisdair talk to Helen, her reality is not the same as theirs. And crucially, this play's attention to issues of men, women, and violence is complicated by the enigma of Helen: Is she living? Dead? A ghost? A vision? The place? Munro offers no simple answer to such questions, but seems to expect her viewers, like Jo and Alisdair, to accommodate Helen's surreal presence. In fact, this accommodation seems to be Munro's primary goal: for to accept Helen is to accept the reality of a realm of experience beyond the everyday, the explainable. Munro urges her audience to consider violence as an occurrence that has dimensions beyond the physical and the tangible: She shows how such a nonnatural-istic presence demands new ways of thinking.

Louise Page's use of the surreal in her plays has set a standard for fluidity and gracefulness among current women writers. Page herself sees the extrareal as a useful tool, "a way of seizing the audience and saying this is here and this exists" (interview). And after the success of *Salonika* (1982), reviewers jumped to classify her as a surrealist with a clever insistence on the nonreal. Page is rightly bothered at being so pigeonholed (interview), but nevertheless, *Salonika* has become a model for successful experimentation in modes of presentation.

In *Salonika,* Page tells the story of eighty-four-year-old Charlotte, her lover, Leonard, and her daughter, Enid, on holiday to Salonika, where Charlotte's husband and Enid's father, Ben, died in World War I. Page unsettles her audience first with the all-too-real appearance of Peter, the naked beach bum (who will be dead by the play's end). But her masterstroke for redirecting audience expectations is the use of long-dead Ben. Ben "sits up out of the sand" (8) in the first scene as naturally as Peter has before him. And as wife, daughter, and others confer easily with him throughout the rest of the play, their exchanges with him open up their lives in deep yet believable ways. From his beyond-the-grave perspective, Ben pressures not only his wife and daughter, but also Peter and Leonard (Enid's new companion) to make precious use of love, sex, and life. The comic presence in this play grows not from belly laughs and farce, then, but from the focus on relationships and happiness and from the commitment—strongest in Ben—to community. The result of the play's fusion of the surreal with the real is a different feeling—almost palpable—that reviewers have labeled "dreamy," "fluid," "mystical," "ruminative and rambling," and "hypnotic." Excerpts from two re-views, which praise the play's transformations of construction, charac-ter, and mode, corroborate my conclusion that this play succeeds be-cause of its combination, its texture, of extrareal modes:

Rosalind Carne: "Louise Page makes an excellent job of weaving past and present into a fine mesh of feeling and memory."

Susie McKenzie: "The play has a dreamlike quality: the characters, their conversation and their actions move from mundane to mysti-cal and from sharply realistic to uncannily unreal, with equal ease and confidence."

Page's *Beauty and the Beast* (1985) had qualified success onstage, but in its adventurous failure it poses important questions about how far the modal changes in contemporary women's drama may go. In Page's interpretation of Mme. de Villeneuve's 1740 tale, fantasy is the basis onto which traditionally realistic moments are grafted. Talking animals and flying fairies come along with dancing monkeys and a whole new transitional reality called "middle air." Page stops short of acknowledging that a goal in the play was to revise one of the most basic literary blueprints, the fairy tale; but she does admit that she set out to offer "a different way of looking at it [the fairy tale] (interview)." To reviewer Valerie Grove, Page explained her interest as a curiosity about "what happened before 'once upon a time' and 'happily ever after.'" What she creates, in place of the kind of plot children are familiar with, is a surreal texture: As reviewer Tom Sutcliffe notes, "Page traces and embroiders the narrative threads." The play is not comic; in fact, at least four reviewers went out of their way to mourn its repression of humor. Nevertheless, the play's bold movement beyond dramatic conventions of construction, character, and mode suggests that comic experimentations in form have a long way to go before they are played out.

Not all women's plays with comic possibilities showcase a complete agenda for formal change. Some playwrights conceive of narrative in a new, nonlinear way, some follow the growth of an emerging feminist character, some offer a cluster of protagonists, and some experiment with departures from stage realism. Some do it all. But almost without exception, women choosing to write comedy are finding that such effects are basic to the plays they want to write. These plays cohere around an integrated collection of effects, not around bold lines of action or familiar characters. The end product is a texture audiences and reviewers are slowly coming to recognize. And with that recognition will come an acknowledgment of the many levels on which such plays encourage change.

*Chapter 9*

# Beyond Subversion: Further Restructurings of Comedy

Contemporary women playwrights have based their comedy on reformulated structures, characters, and presentational modes. The reformulations, sometimes tentative and sometimes bold, have combined both to challenge and to frustrate audiences and reviewers. Yet the women playwrights' most shocking interventions in comedy have involved less basic aspects of traditional comic structure. I have combined in this chapter a look at three such provocative interventions—the reliance on cross-gender and multiple-role casting, the incorporation of music, and the grafting of cabaret performance onto comic staging. These particular revisions—along with the major changes I outlined in chapter 8—work together in the women's experimentations toward a new comic texture. And finally, the various manifestations of such changes have allowed for the most crucial revision in women-authored comedy—the reformation of the comic conclusion. I end this chapter with a consideration of these endings; as I do so, I hope to suggest one final time the durability, vision, and radical politics that infuse the comic structures women are now producing.

## Casting against Gender and Number

When a playwright chooses to cast actors against gender, race, type, or number, the rearrangement is often the most notable aspect of the play. The scrambling of actors and characters has had two major manifestations in women's comedy. First and most disruptive has been cross-gender casting. Second, more common and more the child of necessity, has been the awarding of two or more roles to a single actor.[1]

Like many of the features that cumulatively distinguish women's comedy, casting against gender has a long theater tradition that again looks back to Aristophanes' Old Comedy. While women were barred from the legitimate Western stage until the Renaissance (and until the Restoration in England), their absence was a favorite subject. In Aristophanes' *Lysistrata* and *Thesmophoriasouzae,* for example, the casting of men in the many women's parts created much of the humor; it was incongruous and funny to see women (the characters) with abnormal power and men (the actors playing women) in the unusual position of powerlessness. Shakespeare takes graceful advantage of similar transpositions, making androgyny his subject in such plays as *As You Like It* and *Twelfth Night.* Even today, the tradition of all-male theater and its use of male actors for female characters is far from dead. Only in 1959 did the Cambridge University Footlights Club permanently "pass up the easy guffaws available in all public demonstrations of transvestism" (Cooke review) to allow women to play women's parts. And in gay theater, the traditions of drag and camp continue to flourish. At the end of her review of cross-gender casting in the Western theater, Wandor offers two observations about the history of cross-gender casting. She finds first that "cross-dressing, or transvestite theatre" blossoms when conventional attitudes to sexuality and women are challenged. This suggestion that the conjunction of cross-dressing and a culturewide questioning of gender roles is common provides useful background for an understanding of contemporary women's theater. Wandor's second conclusion, that cross-dressing can be either reactionary or revolutionary, is more important. According to Wandor, it must be the particular way women use cross-dressing that allows them to convert its power to promote social change (*Carry On,* 20–32).

Women are clearly conscious of the revolutionary potential in cross-gender casting, and they heighten that potential in their frequent reversal of traditional cross-gender casting; i.e., in women's plays, women play men more often than men play women. These radical substitutions force questions about the nature of sexuality and help highlight the arbitrariness of sex roles. When cross-gender casting amounts to little more than impersonation of the opposite sex, as is often the case in Aristophanes, it creates comedy out of dissonance. It is basically reactionary. However, when the sex substitution is part of an exploration of sex roles—as in Shakespeare, for example, when the same figure is a male playing a female and a female playing a male—the basis of gender itself is called into question. Two events in English stage history mark how threatening to the status quo has been the apprehension associated with ambiguous sex-swapping. A third example argues that when women play men, there is especial danger to the established order.

In 1662, when Charles II granted the only two royal patents for theater performance to Thomas Killigrew and William Davenant, he specified that only men could play men, and women women. The restriction, which had not before been necessary (since women were prohibited from the stage), was at least partly in response to the shock and confusion surrounding the sexuality of Edward Kynaston, an actor who in the 1650s performed women's roles and in so doing attracted amorous attention from women. Two hundred years later, when Gilbert and Sullivan formed their partnership in 1875, they agreed, "on artistic principles," that no man should play a woman's part and no woman a man's (Stedman, "From Dame to Woman," 20 and notes), to keep their work free of troubling sexual overtones. Significant in both cases is the attempt to retain traditional gender roles; both imply that it is as dangerous for women to play men as for men to play women. More to the point of my argument, Gilbert and Sullivan's contemporary Vesta Tilley suggests how dangerous women playing men could be. While Tilley was a male impersonator who clearly attempted to claim male territory, she was not motivated by feminist vision. In fact, she sought to erase her transgression of type by fiercely parading her femininity offstage. In spite of her innocent intentions, however, her appearance as a man unsettled major segments of Victorian society. Although her biographer Sara Maitland claims, from the example of Tilley, that "while there is a potential sexual radicalism in women assuming male dress, it has not worked to the actual advancement of women" (*Vesta Tilley,* 102), I will show that the reversals on which Tilley built her art—women playing men—have registered an unmistakable feminist protest in the contemporary theater.

Women writers' use of the potentially explosive technique of cross-gender casting has its contemporary roots in the artistic and political decisions of several fringe theater groups. While Joint Stock Theatre Group has done many more plays by men than by women, since its first play the group has purposefully cast women as men. Joint Stock administrator Jane Dawson explains that the practice probably began "as a limited necessity" since large cast lists had to be multiply cast to save money, but this multiple-role casting quickly became a policy decision.

By *Cloud Nine* (1979), the cross-casting included men playing women, women playing men, and whites playing blacks. Dawson comments, "The idea is that everyone can play everyone. . . . Men can play women, women can play men. The obvious example is *Cloud Nine,* of course: adults can play children, whites can play blacks. Lately we have also got blacks playing whites. We are taking it to its logical conclusions" (interview). In several of Joint Stock's women-authored plays—*Light Shining in Buckinghamshire, Cloud Nine, Fen, The Great Celestial Cow, Amid the Standing Corn*—the collapsing of gender has been significant (see Ritchie, *Joint Stock Book*). And in Churchill's collaboration with David Lan and Joint Stock, *A Mouthful of Birds* (1986), transformations of several kinds often become attempts to erase gender distinctions.

The connection between such innovative casting and a feminist aesthetic has been clearest in specifically feminist theater groups. Often these groups consist solely of women, so the decision for women to play men is unavoidable, although some groups rely on plays with only women characters. The work of a long-standing, successful group like Spare Tyre demonstrates how cross-gender casting has become part of the feminist politics in an all-woman group. In Spare Tyre's first show, men appeared only as disembodied voices on the telephone. In their second show, the women used token costumes—"a bowler hat, a little tie"—to suggest men (Noble interview). Later, in *Just Desserts,* group member Clair Chapman portrayed men naturalistically. And in the 1986 *You've Gotta Be Kidding,* men were represented by oversized puppets. In each case, the women's appropriation of men offered a slightly different critique of patriarchal society; for example, men could be represented by puppets in *Kidding* because from a feminist point of view men often act like "dummies." Other all-woman groups, such as the Women's Theatre Group, Siren Theatre, Scarlet Harlets, and Sadista Sisters, have also used women to represent men on stage. The technique has not been uniformly accepted, however. Wertenbaker reports, for example, that some members of the Women's Theatre Group were reluctant to take on the male roles her *New Anatomies* (1981) required (interview). Similarly, Monstrous Regiment has at times been wary of sex substitution. Since men were originally part of the collective, only in the last few years has the issue presented itself. In *Shakespeare's Sister* (by Théâtre de l'Aquarium) (1982), with men still in the group, the men played two older women who represented the "old order"; the play's comment on power was reinforced by the sex-role change. But lately the group has stuck to all-women plays, and administrator Sandy Bailey speculates that the group would only consider gender reversals now for a comedy in which the reversal "was part of it" (interview).

Yet in most cases, women's appropriation of male parts has allowed women's companies to accelerate their feminist explorations, especially explorations of sexuality. In Siren Theatre's *From the Divide,* for example, the character Harry, played by Tasha Fairbanks, was experiencing a "masculine crisis"—"the man hating the woman inside of him"—an experience the audience could visualize because of Fairbanks's sex (Boston interview). Lesbian theater groups such as Hard Corps have thoroughly integrated women playing men's parts, so that a show like Jill Fleming's *Rug of Identity* (1986) depends for its humor as well as its message on the device. Such shows promote the questioning of traditional assumptions about sex and sexuality throughout their action. Jude Alderson, who as a founding member of Sadista Sisters is among the most practiced scramblers of stage gender, theorizes that women's playing of men's parts is something of an aesthetic necessity as well as a feminist protest against traditional conceptions of gender. In analyzing her own succession of careers, Alderson has noted that because of her circus experience in the androgynous roles of trapeze artist and clown, upon her transfer to the theater she found conventional women's theater roles "patterned and wooden." Thus, in the theater she initially found it easier to play men than women "because people accept that you [if you are a man] are going to be funny" (interview). Alderson's reservations about women's limited comic presence on stage still have some basis, of course. But the sex changes that she herself found essential have continued to transform the texture of comic drama.

While many of the scripts that feature cross-gender casting have not been published (including many I have just referred to), three that are accessible in print—Churchill's *Cloud Nine,* Townsend's *The Great Celestial Cow,* and Wertenbaker's *New Anatomies*—demonstrate how such cross-casting has underscored women writers' broad concern with sex roles. As I suggested in chapter 8, in *Cloud Nine,* the playing of females by males and males by females in the first act clarifies Churchill's condemnation of traditional sex roles and her recognition of the perversity and unhappiness such roles lead to. In Townsend's *The Great Celestial Cow* (1984), the assignment of women to play men, like the alterations in the play's reality, alerts the audience to the possibilities for transcending old stereotypes of male and female. Reviewers' responses to

Townsend's play, however, signal the threat that many still find connected with such basic dramatic transformations. Milton Shulman completely missed the point of Townsend's altered sex roles, contending that the actors had taken on roles for which they were "embarrassingly not suited." And Francis King found the role changes trivial: "It was a whimsical idea to have Indians playing cockneys, the old the young, men women, and women men. But the effect is too much that of a Christmas charade."

Although it is less comic in its effect than Churchill's or Townsend's plays, Wertenbaker's *New Anatomies* (1981) may provide the clearest picture of the threat (and power) these gender-role switches hold. A play centrally about the possibilities in altering given sex roles, *New Anatomies* tells the Victorian story of Isabelle and Antoine. While as children the brother and sister share an indulgence in games that deny and transcend gender, as adults the two follow opposite courses. Antoine rejects his "feminine" nature, joins the foreign legion, marries, and has children, while Isabelle embraces her "masculine" tendencies to pursue adventure. In four scenes specifically about crossing the gender line, Isabelle continues her childhood experimentations, searching for ways to realize her dream of a genderless existence. First, in act 1, scene 4, Isabelle dresses her sister-in-law Jenny as a man and sets off a series of character cross-dressings that climax with Antoine's unanswerable question, "Is this male or female?" (314). In act 1, scene 6, Isabelle tests the viability of cross-dressing by passing for a man in the Algerian desert community. In the stunning act 2, scene 1, Wertenbaker collects, in a Parisian salon, five extraordinary women, four dressed as men, to provide commentary on such gender-swapping. In the course of repartee, the women declare their need to express masculine as well as feminine selves. Writer Severine informs the others that "lots of women have gone on stage dressed as men" (322), a fact that Verda Miles, the male impersonator corroborates—"It is . . . much more interesting, much more challenging to play men" (325). Writer Lydia brings cross-dressing to the literary realm, confessing that "in order to write seriously I must dress as a man. . . . when I dress as a man, I simply begin to think, I get ideas" (325). But Isabelle takes the salon-inspired claiming of male dress and roles to its furthest extent, declaring, "I'm not a woman. I'm Si Mahmoud" (327). Finally, in act 2, scene 2, when Isabelle is on the brink of joining the Qadria brotherhood in a zouaian desert monastery, she comes closest to her dreams of genderless existence. She is told of the brotherhood that it has "no dogma. We believe only in the equality of all men and gentleness of heart" (329) (the use of the word *men* here does signal some complications Isabelle chooses to ignore).

Wertenbaker reinforces this playlong gender-role discussion with her casting directions. The play, written for the Women's Theatre Group, was designed "for a cast of five women and a musician" (298). Four of the actors, Wertenbaker explains, play a parallel trio of roles; each plays a Western woman, an Arab man, and a Western man. The fifth, playing Isabelle, takes on a character who spends much of the play passing for a man. Clearly then, the play rivets audience attention to issues of gender roles through its cross-casting as well as its content. Much of the play is not comic. And the disintegration and death of Isabelle are especially distressing since it is Isabelle's failure to transcend gender-typing that crushes her. But the salon scene, with its rich canvas of gender reversal, connects this gender-laden play to comic casting reversals, as Wertenbaker clearly sees: "There is only one scene that is really funny . . . and that is the salon scene where, again, the audience sort of suddenly knew where it was and laughed. And there is a lot of mockery in it" (interview). *New Anatomies* demonstrates how the power of casting against traditional gender expectations has become a central tool in women's remapping of comedy. As is the case in this play, such casting often echoes characters' concerns about sex roles. In general, most plays that include cross-gender casting follow *New Anatomies* in testing new possibilities for the comic grammar of sex.

In each of these three plays, as in many more, cross-gender casting has come together with multiple-role casting, the placing of one actor in more than one role. For Wertenbaker, the multiple-role casting of four characters allowed her to scramble cultural as well as sexual types. Townsend made her original cast of eight—seven Indians and one white—play forty-one roles, again to bring her audience to consciousness of the role-playing that sexual and racial stereotypes necessitate. Churchill's multiple roles are yet more studied. In both *Cloud Nine* and *Top Girls* (1982), her doubling of roles reverberates with extra meaning for particular characters. Churchill does not prescribe a particular double-casting of roles. But when in the original production of *Top Girls,* for example, the same actor played Dull Gret and Angie, Dull Gret's reduced consciousness cast its shadow on Angie's "slowness." In her preface to *Cloud Nine,* Churchill notes how character doublings enable particular meanings:

> Different doublings throw up different resonances. I have a weak-
> ness for Clive-Cathy. Betty-Edward, Edward-Betty, throws an in-
> teresting emphasis on that relationship, while Betty-Gerry gives
> Betty her chance to be dangerous. In the second version the same
> couples reappear: Clive and Betty become Edward and Gerry, Ed-
> ward and Harry become Victoria and Martin. And so on—there is
> no right way, just various interesting possibilities. (viii)

Most prominently, such casting calls attention to the artificial nature of
roles and types; these authors' preoccupation with sexual and racial roles
is particularly well served. More fundamentally, however, multiple-role
casting raises radical questions about characterization and self.

As realistic expectations and illusions about characters are prohibited in multiple-role castings, there arises a Brechtian consciousness of
the theater process itself and a transfer of emphasis from emotional
engagement with characters to broader intellectual considerations. In
*Cloud Nine,* for example, the traditional, realistic response to Betty is
broken in several ways, but largely because the actor who plays Betty
in act 1 will be playing Gerry or Edward in act 2. Viewers are made
conscious of the social pressures that have molded the characters' roles,
both in 1880 and 1980. But the more important impact of multiple-role
casting on women's drama is the foregrounding of self, not character.
For the visible fragmenting of the actor's self acts as one of several strong
commentaries on women and identity. In three of the plays I have discussed in the preceding paragraphs, there is one central character concen-
trating on her self-definition—Marlene in *Top Girls,* Isabelle in *New
Anatomies,* and Sita in *The Great Celestial Cow.* Around the three, in
each case, collects a small number of actors whose several roles force an
awareness of the way women are often fragmented. Sita, at one point
in the second half of Townsend's play, sits alone with a mirror, literally
looking for herself: "Sita, where are you? I don't know where you are.
Come back to me. You've been away so long I'm afraid that I won't
know you when you come back" (22). Because the characters in search
of an integrated self, like Sita, are surrounded by actors whose roles are
multiple, the difficulties of wholeness are underscored. The emblematic
quality the multiply cast actors bring to their several parts enables the
audience to respond to Sita's torment with intellect instead of emotion.

The theater has always been ready to make use of multiple-role
casting as circumstances have warranted. Productions of Shakespeare,

which demand such huge casts, for example, are not economically feasible if actors cannot double up on parts. And on London's fringe, where money is always tight, multiple casting is frequently the child of necessity. On the one hand, Catherine Hayes reports that the commissions authors receive often stipulate no more than four or six characters (interview). On the other hand, those who venture into writing for large casts either weaken their chances of production or depend on multiply cast actors. For instance, with her epic *Madonna in Slag City* (1986), Jude Alderson could produce her Oval House show only by both cutting costs (there was a good deal of volunteer time and support) and doubling roles. While multiple-role casting, then, can be a matter of necessity as much as choice, women authors can utilize such assignments to highlight issues of role-playing, types, and self while they may also save resources.[2]

## Music as Intrusive Interlude

The frequent use of music and song in women's comedies, like the use of cross-gender and multiple-role casting, increases the distance between these plays and realistic theater. Keyssar *(Feminist Theatre)* and Reinelt ("Beyond Brecht"), studying specific plays by Churchill, Gems, Luckham, Megan Terry, and others, identify women's reliance on song as a Brechtian inheritance. Reinelt, for example, cites *Vinegar Tom* as one of the clearest expressions of Brechtian distancing through song ("Beyond Brecht"). Following such female stage predecessors as Joan Littlewood, today's women writers have made song integral to their interpolations of reality. A sampling of plays in which song provides a major subversion of realism includes *New Anatomies, Time Pieces, Pulp, My Mother Says I Never Should, Strike While the Iron Is Hot, Trafford Tanzi, Cloud Nine, Madonna in Slag City, Serious Money,* and *Byrthrite.*

As in the case of cross-gender and multiple-role casting, the group, or group-inspired, composition of so many influential women's plays has contributed to the strong musical element. For many of the women's theater groups formed in the 1970s and 1980s, music was understood to be a basic instrument for generating effective politics. The Women's Theatre Group, for example, made a "music director" one of its original permanent positions in the collective. In Monstrous Regiment, too, music was an essential tool from the beginning. Sandy Bailey explains that the group perceived of music as a way "of talking very directly to people's emotions," a bypassing of regular thought processes and prejudices. She contends that even in a generally serious play such as *Vinegar Tom,* the songs were offered in a comic tone that made the political message accessible (interview). For several other groups—including Spare Tyre, Scarlet Harlets, Parker and Klein, Sadista Sisters, and Siren Theatre— music has been not incidental but basic to performance. Siren's Jane Boston finds the group's roots in punk music as significant as its roots in theater (interview); Sadista Sisters evolved from experimentations in club rock and roll; and Spare Tyre has recorded and marketed its original music. In most cases the music becomes a way to ask the audience to pause over what it has just seen or is about to see. The Brechtian directness of such song is explained simply by Katina Noble of Spare Tyre:

> Sometimes it is so hard to say in a scene what you can say so easily in a song. It is either too weighty, too wordy, too complicated, too squirmy, too naturalistic. And yet you can suddenly sing it in a song and it is economy, you can say it in many less words, but you couldn't translate it into a little naturalistic scene without it being quite untheatrical. (Interview)

For those committed to a "theater by group," then, song acts as another way of interrupting the connections dictated by realism.

Because the use of song is not unique to women's work and because it is a fairly straightforward technique, I'll offer just two examples of the effect. In the Women's Theatre Group's early play *My Mother Says I Never Should* (1975), a character called Singer (played by several different cast members) appears periodically to fortify the play's fairly didactic message that teens should educate themselves about sex and birth control. The opening song directs attention to the coming critique of traditional sex education:

> My Mother says I never should
> Play with the boys down in the wood
> If I did, she would say, you'll
> Get yourself in the family way.
> Was she right?
> Was my Mamma right?
> Pity for me if she was right. (119)

Similarly, the final song leaves no doubts about the thinking a teen should adopt:

> We've been talking to you about choices
> 'Cause some day we think you'll find:
> If you don't control your body
> Somebody gonna screw your mind. (141)

The simple directness of its music is a crucial component in this play's campaign for social change.

A more recent and more well-known play, Caryl Churchill's *Serious Money* (1987), turns to song on a much more sophisticated level. In a play built on rhythm, sound, and pacing, Churchill turns to song to cap the furious action of both acts. The satire that fuels the entire play is bitterly clear in the songs. Churchill did not write the words to "Futures Song," with which act 1 concludes, but in any one of its verses, her damning portrait of life in London's futures trading markets is distilled:

> So L.I.F.F.E. is the life for me and I'll burn out when I'm dead
> And this fair exchange is like a rifle range what's the price of flying lead?
> When you soil your jeans on soya beans shove some cocoa up your head
> You can never hide if your spread's too wide, you'll just fuck yourself instead.
>
> (62)

What makes Churchill's climax in song so frightening is the way she uses the communal nature of music to envelop audience, actors, and characters in an uncomfortable aesthetic alliance at the act's end. Her indictment is broadcast and shared.

Group work has spawned so much of the music in women's plays because the music, while it does break stage illusion in a Brechtian fashion, compensates for that fissure by encouraging other connections. The direct address to the audience joins actors with audience, and the songs themselves enhance the sense of community on stage when—as is often the case—several characters sing together. The connection may also be ironic or uncomfortable, as in *Serious Money,* but in general, music encourages connections that are often dramatically unconventional.

## Women's Cabaret and Women's Comedy

Both altered casting and music are easily identifiable as intrusions into
the continuity of theatrical production. Neither is unique to women's
comedy, but both have become common components in women playwrights' strategies for creating comic plays. Both techniques allow for
some specificity in the social message these plays often carry. A third
significant quality of these plays' interventions against theatrical convention, although less easily labeled or categorized, is equally significant.
This third factor in women's protestive staging of their comedies is the
incorporation of women's cabaret, specifically its foregrounding of
women's selves and women's laughter. The move toward cabaret is
connected closely to the self-consciousness with which many playwrights present laughter within their plays.

Wandor pinpoints the crux in understanding the interplay between
cabaret and theatrical comedy when she writes of the late 1970s cabaret
work of Monstrous Regiment, Clapperclaw, Cunning Stunts, Hormone
Imbalance, Beryl and the Perils, and Sadista Sisters that the "semi-anar-
chic shows" of these groups "opened avenues for a freer female comedy"
(*Carry On,* 82). In her historical overview, however, Wandor does not
have time to sort out the overlapping spheres of cabaret and theater. Or
perhaps she realizes how difficult that kind of distinction is becoming at
a time when women's cabaret is growing rapidly and when the women
performing it are also performing theater (Gardner and Noble interviews). I do not pretend that I can disentangle cabaret from theater, for
the two do overlap. But it is helpful to determine ways in which each
draws from the other and how, as Wandor notes, cabaret has offered a
model to guide women playwrights to a freer comedy.

Karen Parker and Debby Klein, who as Parker and Klein have performed both cabaret and theater, isolate three basic differences between
the two (interview). Most obviously, the presentation differs. In cabaret,
performers must be prepared to deal with microphones, inattentive audiences, and (usually alcoholic) drinking. And while a show can be scripted
in part, the performers must ad-lib blocking and much of the dialogue.
As Parker and Klein put it, in cabaret you cannot rely on the decorum
the theater's "fourth wall" commands, and you must relate directly to
the audience. They stress, however, that the two more radical changes
in cabaret involve the two central components I stressed in chapter 8—
character and narrative construction. The cabaret actor is not, as in the

theater, playing a character different from herself. Nor is she exactly herself, but a stylized version of herself, what Lavery calls a "persona" (interview). Jeanie Forte, in her investigation of American women's performance art, reinforces the point, contending that the directly communicating female subject of such performance constitutes a radical ontological move ("Women's Performance Art: Feminism and Postmodernism," 221). And while a show based on the provocative reality of a persona may be integrated around a theme or idea, the connections between jokes, skits, and songs rarely recall traditional comic construction. Debbie Klein describes cabaret composition metaphorically, emphasizing the exigencies of production, not the command of narrative logic: "Everything does link, but in a theatrical way rather than a narrative way" (interview). Cabaret is clearly a performance of the moment, as theater, with its script, is not. Yet the fuzziness of a distinction between cabaret and theater is indicated both by the difficulty practitioners have in describing any difference (Klein says, "You realize that what ever you are doing in theatre is not quite the same" [interview]) and by the striking parallel between cabaret and qualities of women's comedies, parallels that include diffuse narratives and characters alert to the problems and possibilities for female self.

The shared aesthetic space of cabaret and comic theater also includes parallel, though not identical, reliance on the bonding power of laughter. In chapter 7 I noted that the presence of a female comedian in contemporary plays brings with it an altered milieu. Similarly, in cabaret, the conflation of the comic agent and woman is unsettling. The cabaret performers themselves are conscious of their need for an altered realm in which to produce laughter. Although Morwenna Banks and Amanda Swift *(The Joke's on Us)* have just recently recovered a whole twentieth-century tradition of British female comics, those women approaching cabaret in the 1970s found it necessary to re-invent the woman comic. Lavery explains that she found herself compensating for the novelty of the woman as comic: "You have to write slightly differently for women because you have to introduce the fact that they are going to be funny. Whereas with men, it is sort of assumed. . . . Women comics have a sort of invisible barrier to break down" (interview). Sandy Bailey corroborates Lavery's contention, reporting similarly that when Monstrous Regiment put together the group's first cabaret show, *Floorshow,* in 1977, they had actively to disabuse the audience of its assumptions that the stand-up comic was, by definition, male (interview). This need to reconstruct the female comic points to a paradox in the relationship between the cabaret comic and the comic heroine. Although in dramatic comedy women can be accorded all the power they want (because the comic inversion ensures a limit to that power), they are a greater threat in cabaret, where there is not the comfort of a comic reversal. That paradox may partly explain the small number of female comics and the cultural lack of memory about them. Since cabaret is "so up front and so punchy," as Spare Tyre's Katina Noble puts it (interview), a woman performing cabaret has an enlarged potential for challenging the order of things. This disproportionate power is what both the women in cabaret and the women playwrights whose plays are informed by cabaret are after.[3] The laughter that results from cabaret performance offers women enhanced power.

I turn now to two scripts that clarify the ways in which women's comedy and women's cabaret intersect. Monstrous Regiment's *Floorshow* (written by Caryl Churchill, Bryony Lavery, Michelene Wandor, and David Bradford) and *Time Gentlemen Please* (written by Bryony Lavery) demonstrate the ways in which the direct relationships of cabaret have contributed to the changing face of women's comedy. As it tests the border between cabaret and theater, *Floorshow* (1977) uses the explosive power of women's cabaret to make dangerous comedy.[4] This show plays an important part in the history of women's theater, as Bailey remembers: "We were about the first women's group that did a stand-up comic on that very male notion of a stand-up comic abusing his audience." She also recalls how the novelty understandably exhilarated the actors—"Each night was different and you had to be on your toes" (interview). While one of the show's four writers, Michelene Wandor, recalls nothing new in the show "in terms of comedic processes" (interview; in *Carry On*, 71, she does acknowledge the play's importance in advancing stage representations of sexuality), another writer, Bryony Lavery, remembers, like Bailey, that the show sparked excitement because of its novel explorations (interview).

More cabaret than theater, the show is an amalgam of sketches, skits, and song, all on the theme of women and work. In cabaret fashion, the actors use their own names for the "personas" through whom the various pieces are drawn together. The show begins with the bold assumption that women can be themselves and still create humor. The feminist dimension of this direct comedy is clear from the opening, a parody of Genesis, which ends on a recognition of women's work: "And on the seventh day, called Monday, God rested; after she had done the washing up, cleaned the house, done the ironing and bathed the dog." In an early monologue self-consciously about the show, this comic attack on the status quo is again evident: "In other words it's an ordinary everyday story of exploitation and misery, sexual prejudice and wage slavery told with a smile and a song." While this monologue is as direct as *Floorshow* ventures to be about its comedy and laughter, in the follow-up Monstrous Regiment cabaret, *Time Gentlemen Please* (1978), the conscious revision of comic and cabaret tradition is unmistakably highlighted in Clive's opening monologue:

> Everybody assumes that a cabaret should make you laugh, and by extension, a cabaret should include stand-up comedians and by tradition these stand-up comics have been men. They've always told jokes. . . . But there's no reason why we should do the same as everyone else. If you look at the jokes that are told by stand-up comedians, they are very often about sex, but they very seldom extend our knowledge of sex by the very nature of their format, delivery, subject matter and so forth.

But while the authors of both shows do, from time to time, flash an acknowledgment that an implicit subject is women and humor, it is the laughter generated by direct attack that is the heart of what is new about these shows and their women. The opening lines from *Floorshow*'s sketch on a whore are a graphic illustration of how hard-hitting the writers were:

> Okay, what do you want to know . . . I'm a whore—I earn £60 a night—tax free. If I can I work with Arabs—because you can get a hundred from them . . . but they're much more choosy . . . you have to go to to be looked over and if they don't like you they won't have you. I'd say I was in the middle to upper bracket in whoring . . . that's just below the House of Lords and people like that . . . which is good because we get mainly middle class men . . . and they treat you very well . . . because they treat their wives well, whereas working class men beat up their wives so they don't see why they shouldn't beat up their whores.

Such speeches are dangerous because so little separates the social critique from the audience. The significance of these two Monstrous Regiment shows and of similar cabaret-theater work by Spare Tyre, Parker and Klein, Scarlet Harlets, and others is that they put women in the realm of comedy unimpeded by conventional comic structures. A reversal in a vocal, strong woman's fortunes is not mandated, a situation emphasized by the actors' regular retention of their offstage names. And a comedy about women can freely focus on self-recognition, not self-deprecation. Cabaret shows such as *Floorshow* and *Time Gentlemen Please* stand as examples of the uncompromised, healthy laughter women can make by themselves.

Women's cabaret, with its direct expressions of the female self and its unpredictable structure, offers practitioners of more fully scripted theater a model for radical combinations of laughter and protest. In works that clearly remain plays, such rebellion is most evident in the way the plays present onstage laughter. Although self-consciousness about comedy is as old as the genre, women writers are revising specific conceptions about laughing women. Laughter itself is a principal part of women playwrights' ongoing meta-commentary about the comic genre they so often choose.

The traditional stereotype of the laughing woman calls to mind a person whose laughter eases pain. In writing of American women's experimental theater, Clare Coss, Roberta Sklar, and Sondra Segal have located such humor used "to ameliorate the pain of seeing the experience of women in the patriarchy" ("Notes on the Women's Experimental Theater," 239). Naomi Weisstein similarly concludes that when women make jokes, humor "is a weapon or a technique of survival used by the oppressed. It is the powerless fighting back" ("Why We Aren't Laughing," 88). Hayes's Jill, in *Not Waving* (1982), personifies the self-deprecating humorist. "You've got to laugh," she charges her audience during her routine (44), but her own laughter is little more than a sign of desperation. Her comic act has become a last-ditch effort to survive—"I put everything into this. If it's not in my act, then I haven't got it. I don't know it. It doesn't exist" (24). Jill represents a type and an attitude to laughter, however, that women comic writers are seeking to modify. Against a backdrop of women's cabaret, women writers are not only displaying new ways for women to make jokes but also charting the new reactions, the new laughter generated by a comic machinery women control.

Frequently in women-authored plays, a focus on sexist jokes has been used to critique traditional attitudes to women and laughter. In *Strike While the Iron Is Hot* (1974), one scene in which men tell sexist jokes (45) is clearly meant to underline the men's inability to sympathize with their female co-workers. In much greater detail in *Masterpieces* (1982), Sarah Daniels uses the telling of sexist jokes in the opening scene to prepare for a whole play about the undoing of the assumptions that give rise to such jokes. As Ron, Clive, and Trevor toss off jokes degrading to women, their onstage audience (three men and three women are in the scene) and the play's are confronted with material clearly meant to offend:

> Ron: Oh that's it, hang on. Two nuns walking through a forest, right? When a man jumps out on them and rapes them, one of them reckons, "How are we going to explain to the Mother Superior that we've been raped twice?" The other one says, "But, Sister, we've only been raped once." "I know," says the first, "but aren't we going back the same way?"
>
> *The men laugh, Trevor not as heartily as the other two. Rowena rather hesitantly joins in. Yvonne doesn't even smile, while Jennifer laughs uproariously and rather disconcertingly so.*
>
> Clive: The only one I know is about the nun who was raped but she didn't mind because he was a saint. "How do you know?" asked the other nuns. "Because he had Saint Michael on his underpants."
>
> *Same response only they don't find it as funny except Jennifer who laughs even louder.*
>
> Trevor: That's as old as the hills.
> Ron: What was the other one?
> Trevor: I don't know.
> Ron: Yes you do, I heard you tell it to Frank.
> Trevor: Oh *(He is rather abashed.)* "Help, I've been raped by an idiot." "How do you know?" "Because I had to tell him what to do."
>
> *There is the same pattern of response. Jennifer laughs raucously. Yvonne remains silent but extremely uncomfortable, wishing she could just walk out.*
>
> Ron: What's your idea of an ideal date? She screws until four o'clock in the morning, then turns into a pizza.
>
> *Response is as for the first joke.* (6)

But when Jennifer forces her way into the telling, the situation changes. Although no feminist, she claims power for women through

her joke and Daniels announces her intentions to split her play along
gender lines:

     *Jennifer:*    There was this vicar who was asked to give a talk about sex
                  to the fifth year of a school in his parish. However, when he
                  came to writing the appointment in his desk diary he didn't
                  want to write sex as his wife might find it.
       *Ron:*    *(trying to be funny)* Find what?
     *Jennifer:*    *(grimaces)* His diary. So he wrote Talk, at such and such a
                  school, on sailing. The time came to give the talk and it was
                  received very well. A couple of weeks later his wife met the
                  headmistress in Sainsbury's and the headmistress said, "Your
                  husband gave a wonderful talk to our fifth year," and the wife
                  replied, "I don't know how, he's only done it twice. The first
                  time he was sick and the second time his hat came off."

                  *Although the men laugh they feel less inclined to do so.* Yvonne
                  *smiles.*

     *Rowena:*    Mother, trust you.
     *Jennifer:*    Just wanted to prove I could hold my own.
       *Clive:*    *(flatly)* Very adequately too, darling. (7)

In the rest of the play, Daniels details the violence sexist jokes do to
women, and in the process she indicts conventional connections between
laughter and women. Most writers are not making their comments on
laughter as explicitly as Daniels does, but implicitly they are joining her
in showing that a reconstituted women's laughter may be something
used for, not against, women.

In the many comic plays focused on groups, laughter has become a
way for the characters to cement friendships and encourage social and
psychological breakthroughs. In act 1 of Townsend's *Bazaar and Rummage* (1982), the agoraphobiacs step delicately and politely around each
other's problems. The laughter comes from the audience laughing at,
not with, the characters. But when the women are dealing with difficult
conflicts onstage in act 2, their self-generated laughter comes to express
their growth and awareness. They laugh at Margaret's joke (21), giggle
at Katrina's unintended joke (22), and even laugh at themselves after an
open door simultaneously stirs in all of them a fear of the outside world
(28). Townsend finds laughter an outlet women have mastered because
"they have had far fewer outlets [than men] to enable them to come to
terms with what has happened" (interview). Laughter is even more than

an outlet in the play; as it occurs onstage, it is a sign of personal health and psychological progress.

Laughter plays a similar role in *Steaming* (1981). In this first act too, laughter is rare among the women, who are just becoming acquainted. Dawn's hauntingly misplaced giggles are a poor substitute. But in the second act, jollity and laughter see the women through their exhilarating campaign to save the baths, and even through their defeat; both the onstage feast of scene 3 and the final scene of bath frolicking are decorated with loving laughter. Dunn reports that while she did not intentionally set out to write comedy, "comedy came out of the situation" of a group of women sharing a goal (interview). As most comic plays with group protagonists offer their own variations on this pattern, it becomes obvious that women's comedy provides laughter not only for the audience, but also for the characters. And laughter, for the characters, has become an acknowledged mark of togetherness, of control.

Even in plays less group-determined, the conscious reliance on laughter remains for the characters—especially the women—a standard signal of triumph. In Daniels's *The Devil's Gateway* (1983), for instance, when Enid and Betty unknowingly become high on marijuana, they first affirm their friendship through giggles and only then find courage to make their life-changing decisions. In Thornton's *Amid the Standing Corn* (1985), one of the women campaigning for the miners realizes early on, "It's a laugh that's the main thing, and I like a laugh, it's good for you" (14). The rest of the play bears her out as periodic laughter allows both relief and psychological rebuilding. Even in Rudet's *Money to Live*, which ends with the report of a near rape and in which laughter is at moments little more than a survival tactic, laughter is specifically cited by the characters, at least three times, to register their sense of security.

In plays less clearly comic, even those that include death, laughter remains a signal of individual triumph and female-to-female connections. Pam Gems's *Dusa, Fish, Stas, and Vi* (1976) offers four women whose difficulties keep them from many happy moments. But even in this play, a party scene celebrating Fish's birthday and various other personal victories for the other women is full of laughter and a general recognition that each of the women is strengthened by their shared laughter. The joy is compromised by Fish's subsequent suicide, but nevertheless the group scene does mark the characters' generally healthy development. Marcella Evaristi's *Commedia* (1982) is similarly a non-comic play in which laughter retains its healing power for women. At

the end of the play, its three principal love relationships are suspended—
due to death in one case, desertion in a second, and affectionate incompatibility in a third. But as the play's title predicts, attached to the play's
stagnant relational outcome is a feeling, centered in Elena the mother,
that an ability to laugh is the key to resiliency.

Let me turn, finally, to two plays that suggest the far-reaching
quality of the laughter women are now writing into their plays. Timberlake Wertenbaker's *Our Country's Good* (1988) is not a play primarily
about women. As Wertenbaker tells the story of a colony of convicts
establishing itself in Australia in 1789, she focuses on three groups: both
female and male convicts as well as the all-male administrators supervis-
ing the two more unruly groups. As the convicts, under the guidance
of Lieutenant Ralph Clark, put together a production of George Farquhar's comedy *The Recruiting Officer,* laughter becomes a sign of power
for both men and women. As in other plays by women, the power
remains with groups, but here it is with groups of outsiders from both
sexes. Laughter, for example, is the convicts' response to hangings (18);
it is the social cement with which characters Mary Brenham and John
Wisehammer revel in the delight of words (33); and comedy is the genre
chosen by the convicts as they fantasize about their future theater company. As I will detail in chapter 12, comedy is at issue in many ways in
Wertenbaker's play; here I stress that the play may indicate how
women's reliance on the laughter of comedy may increasingly come to
transcend gender distinctions. Women playwrights may give men as
well as women a new way to laugh. In Deborah Levy's *Pax* (1985), it is
not gender distinctions so much as generic distinctions that laughter
seems to erase. Levy's play is beyond conventional categories of genre,
but in its defiance of convention it perhaps best demonstrates how basic
laughter is to all women's theatrical enterprise. As she describes one of
the archetypal characters, The Keeper, and the response this figure generated in the play's initial production, Levy offers a prototype of the
woman writer's comic woman: a woman who has moved from merely
surviving—like Hayes's Jill—to achieving an enviable, contented, and
understanding response to the world:

> I don't know whether humour is the right word, but she [The
> Keeper] had a particular way of coping. She was a survivor. So she
> has been through Hiroshima; she has been through Auschwitz; she
> has been through the Spanish Civil War. And I suppose the word I

would use to describe it is wit, is witty. And a lot of the male members of the audience who came up to speak with me said they thought The Keeper was like a man. So I said why? Oh, she is witty. And it seems that you can be funny as a woman and you can be comical and you can be all sorts of things, but wit, that word, is something that is a male prerogative. . . . she dipped in and out of the subjective and the objective, but she could wrap up pieces of history in four or five sentences and make people laugh at the most tragic things. (Interview)

Laughter has become, in plays by women, much more than a by-product of comedy. It has become an expression of power and a vocalization of community. The laughter generated by female comics and used by female playwrights shows the empowerment to be gained through female subjectivity. And central to the theatrical turf that comedy and cabaret share is a protest against standard distinctions of genre and gender.

## Endings in Women's Comedy: Marriage and Other Possibilities for Joy

Ann Jellicoe's successful comedy The Knack (1961) climaxes with a bizarre, perhaps sexual, encounter between the play's only woman, Nancy, and one or more of its three men. As Nancy persists in labeling whatever happened "rape," the men make the idea of rape the subject of their relentless linguistic playfulness. Tolen's conclusion that Nancy's charge is fantasy—"She has fabricated a fantasy that we have raped her. First because she wants us to take notice of her and second because she really would like to be raped" (84)—while it is what would now be called a male fantasy of rape, represents one important segment of that humor. Ultimately, whether or not a rape takes place is beside the point. For however real or unreal that rape is, Jellicoe makes it the focus of laughter at the play's end and uses that laughter as a conduit to her happy ending—the coupling of Nancy and Colin. In its offbeat way, Jellicoe's conclusion represents the traditional comic ending pushed to its extreme. Comedy dictates that man and woman must come together at all costs, even if the price is rape. Jellicoe herself now acknowledges that her drive toward comic coupling seems disturbed by Nancy's construction of events as rape; she notes, "I don't think I'd write that scene like that now. . . . it was something you certainly could joke about [then]" (interview). But my point about the play is that Nancy's female perspective and her persistent charges and complaints about rape are discounted with her final romantic connection to Colin. When she aligns herself, in her characteristically nonverbal way, with Colin, she negates the protest that her outsider status has accorded her all along. This woman does not give up a voice of wit and wisdom, as Shakespeare's Rosalind did; but in her silent way, she sacrifices the power she has had for the duration of the play. And thus, Jellicoe's play stands as an alarming example of the regularity with which comic writers—even women—can bring their plays to conclusion by suppressing, often violently, their women. I argued in part 1 that such comic endings curtail the short-lived power that comedy seems to grant women. I return to a consideration of the comic ending here because if women playwrights are to make comedy a hospitable environment for women, they must find strategies for deflating the great power of comic endings.

The drive toward an ending is inescapable in drama; as Eric Bentley summarizes, "it is, in fact, hard to put an ending on a play that does not have some . . . conclusiveness" (*Thinking about the Playwright*, 175). For women writing comedy (as *The Knack* shows), such conclusiveness is an especial danger, because in comedy that conclusiveness has most often been symbolized by marriage. As she writes about women fiction writers, Du Plessis finds that because most traditional narratives have a "telos in marriage," women writers have had to invent new fictive strategies to supersede and "write beyond" the ending (*Writing beyond the Ending*, 2). De Lauretis specifies further that such writing beyond the ending is the direct result of a new subjectivity—women's—in literature *(Alice Doesn't)*. In chapter 10 I will detail the changing dimensions of the female subject in women-authored drama, but here I turn more specifically to a consideration of women playwrights' structural strategies for writing beyond the ending of traditional theatrical comedy.

At least one critic, Josette Féral, has ventured that there is no ending to women's drama ("Writing and Displacement"). Although for very different reasons, and out of criticism, not praise, some of the reviewers with whose work I began chapter 8 would agree that these plays lack a satisfactory, recognizable conclusion. But as Bentley notes *(Thinking about the Playwright)*, whatever it is called, however it is interpreted, something must come last in a play. In her optimism over the power of a woman-directed comedy, Barreca has argued that women's comedy avoids traditional happy endings and produces politically and socially disruptive plays that offer little joy (introduction to *Last Laughs,* 8). While I agree with her that women writers have sought new ways to harness comedy's potential for disruption, I have found that much joy still accompanies the comic attack. None of the British women's contemporary plays I am considering are identifiably comic in conventional ways. Yet most of them spring from hope and offer inspiration and encouragement to those who want to envision a changed social order. These plays may not have a recognizable sense of closure, but they do end; and more often than not, the ending is upbeat.

I have grouped women's various strategies for transforming comedy's ending into three rough and overlapping categories, ranging from the embellishment of marriage at one end of the spectrum to the highlighting of various groups and communities to the valorizing of transformation at the other end. How these plays end is crucial. While the other transformations of structure I have studied defuse the powerful expectations of ending that guide action and response in traditional comedy, expectations of joy and final happiness remain and must be confronted by both playwright and audience.

## Retaining Marriage

Surprisingly, in the new comedy being written by women, marriage remains a primary option, a common starting point for the pursuit of happiness. In the first and most familiar strategy for reformulating comic happiness, writers retain an institution recognizable as marriage, but embellish it with uncommon connections.

When *Trafford Tanzi* (1978) played in London, playwright Luckham reversed the traditional marriage ending by converting a male-dominated marriage into a female-dominated one. When Dean Rebell loses his wrestling match with wife Tanzi, he must accept as a symbol of his defeat the role of house-husband. With this reversal of the traditional comic ending, Luckham parodies the limiting nature of women's normal place at comedy's conclusion. Yet such an unadorned reversal, can, as I have argued above, more easily be read as a reinforcement of tradition than as a refusal of it. In fact, participants in the original production of the play as *Tuebrook Tanzi* at the Liverpool Everyman (1978) felt it necessary to resist more vigorously a traditional comic ending. Director Lou Wakefield reports that the Liverpool cast deliberately chose not simply to reverse the comic ending, but to challenge it by having Tuebrook and Dean promise to live as equals (interview). Michelene Wandor, in *Aurora Leigh* (1979), adopts this more radical revision of marriage, choosing to pass up the possibility of female domination. She reports that she "could not see how it could be credible if male domination was simply replaced with female domination" (author's endnote to *Aurora Leigh,* 134). Thus Wandor alters the original ending of Elizabeth Barrett Browning's poem by saving Romney from his retributive blinding, so that she can make the final marriage of Aurora and Romney more clearly an egalitarian togetherness. Wandor further distances traditional concepts of marriage by having Aurora and Romney seal their togetherness in offering to share their home with Marian, Romney's old lover, and her young son. It is important that the inclusion of Marian and her son in the configuration of the communal ending comes just after Marian's complete rejection of marriage only a few lines earlier. In opting for a life devoted primarily to her child, Marian thus adds to the ending an apprehension, even a warning, about marriage. But Wandor makes clear in Aurora's epilogue to the audience that even this play's encumbered marriage is meant to be compared to the more traditional happy endings of comedy:

> The Greeks said grandly in their tragic phrase:
> "Let no-one be called happy till their death,"
> To which I add: "Let no-one till their death
> Be called unhappy." (133)

Wandor and the cast of *Tuebrook Tanzi,* like many of their contemporaries, want to retain the joy of comedy's ending and have attempted, through creative portraits of marriage, to avoid the compromise of the traditional ending. Almost without fail, when marriage is at issue in their plays, contemporary women writers display a self-consciousness about it. Yet more writers than not move beyond the acceptance of marriage to a more radical critique or replacement of it.

From Marriage to Groups and Communities

To distinguish this first rewriting of the comic ending in marriage from the second, which also draws on marriage, I turn to the dramatic conno-

tations of marriage. Conventionally, marriage has carried with it connotations of heterosexuality and the nuclear family (or, if not the postindus-
trial idea of the nuclear family, at least the notion of marriage as the
signal of the future generation of children). Yet many writers are now
showing that those associations can be separated from what are marriage's comic denotations of happiness, sharing, union, and community,
and can even be replaced by possibilities for homosexuality, transvestism, and other unconventional forms of togetherness. Thus in women
writers' second approach to the happy ending, while marriage may be
vestigially present, it is a radically changed institution and often but a
component of broader connections among people. The couple, although
still a significant component of the ending, is less important than a group
or community.[5] Women's relationships with men remain in the ending
of many of the plays I would place in this category, but the joy and good
feelings are anchored in untraditional combinations of adults and children and in constellations of relatives and friends that posit new meanings for the word *family*.

As I noted in chapter 8, Pam Gems's *Loving Women* and *Aunt Mary*
have particularly sensitive, revisionist endings. In both of Gems's plays,
the portrait of a new kind of happiness depends on an adjustment in the
drive toward marriage—specifically the replacement of a heterosexual
couple with a nonheterosexual connection. Certainly a critique of marriage is implied in such substitution; but Caryl Churchill, in *Cloud Nine,*
presents the premier example of an ending that combines a critique of
traditional happiness with an exploration of new configurations of togetherness. After a first act in which she brutalizes the Victorian family
and a second in which she deliberates over substitute familial models,
Churchill concludes the play by sketching the lines of one new family.
At the core is a trio of two lesbians and one gay man who share a bed;
and drawing from their connection are other household members—the
two children of the two women and (possibly) the mother of one of the
women. The ending of *Cloud Nine* is important not just because of
Churchill's ingenuity in bringing such a heterogeneous collection
together, but also because Churchill is honest about the viability of her
reconstructed family. The happiness of her characters remains more
hopeful than assured in their uncharted territory; and Churchill indicates
the fragility of their nontraditional life-styles through both the tenta-
tiveness of their actions throughout act 2 and the reappearance of act 1's

Victorian types at the end of act 2. The ghostlike visitations by
Clive, Betty, Maud, Ellen, Harry, and Edward are reminders of how
persistent and tangible are the traditional models of sexual and cultural
behavior.

   Churchill's comments on the various productions of the ending of
her play underscore further both the difficulty of and the urgency for
moving beyond the conventional expectations called up by comedy.
When the play transferred from London to New York and was produced
by Tommy Tune, the order of events in the closing scenes was changed.
Instead of ending with Betty's dinner invitations to Gerry, the play
concluded with Betty's emotional, confessional monologue on masturbation, followed by a song. While Churchill acknowledged the extra
theatrical energy generated by Tune's reorganization, she was troubled
by the shift from group to individual at the New York conclusion: "I
didn't really like it as much because it threw so much emphasis onto
Betty as an individual, while the other way seemed to be more about the
development of a group of people" (Betsko and Koenig, *Interviews*, 83).
By softening Churchill's broad-based cultural critique with such individual focus, Tune effectively de-emphasized the new and unusual connections Churchill's play is about. While the change did not negate Churchill's transformed comic conclusion, the ease with which the play could
be coaxed back toward a more comfortable, recognizable conclusion
demonstrates the power of the traditional comic ending, even in a play
as radically structured as this.

   While such plays as Louise Page's *Salonika* (1982) also translate
male-female couplings into other acceptable connections that breed happiness, plays that conclude with groups of women usually drop both
men and marriage from their definitions of happiness. Not surprisingly,
those plays with group protagonists provide the clearest examples of
drama in which the final joy grows out of nonfamilial and often nonheterosexual groups. *Amid the Standing Corn* (1985) is bracketed by
scenes that display the camaraderie of a group of women brought together through the political pressure of a miners' strike. May, Dot,
Maureen, and Lynn begin the play assembled at a 1984 protest march
on Buckingham Palace. But only after a narrative backtracking to the
events that have led to that march does the audience see—in the final
scenes—that the women's cohesion is the result of a hard-fought battle
against traditional gender prohibitions. May ends the play by promising
that the new communal connections the women have worked for will

carry great social weight: "The thing is, men and women and families are together now, and the government has got a bloody fight on its hands, we are united and we shall not be defeated, not now, not ever again" (106). A connection between solidly bonded groups and a power to effect change marks the group endings of several other plays in which men are still more marginal, both for the women and for any happiness the plays celebrate.

High spirits, cavorting in baths, and joy in friendship provide the ending to Nell Dunn's *Steaming* as the play's six women celebrate their power. While the women have just lost their battle with the council to save the baths, they find victory in the self-growth they have helped one another find. As they plunge, one by one, into the pool, each claims an identity for too long forfeited in her acquiescence to the expected roles of a woman. The power this group generates is more personal than social; but the group-oriented conclusion clearly signals the establishment of a base for potential political change. In Louise Page's *Golden Girls,* public defeat (here of a staggering nature) is less central than the private recognitions that have grown out of group interactions. Page, like Dunn, ends her play with the group of young women convened on stage, assessing their losses and gains. Although their group potential has been realized only in part, their individual growth remains intact. In *Steaming* and in *Golden Girls,* as in *Cloud Nine,* the final focus on groups does not stand as an unambiguous sign of joy, nor is it meant to. Yet it remains important that in many women's comedies happiness is located not so often in marriage as in realigned relations with men, new familial groupings, and such all-female gatherings.

The tension between individual and social change that Churchill takes note of in commenting on the two productions of *Cloud Nine* suggests, finally, how the groups of women so prominent in the conclusions of women-authored comedies are pushing against the established boundaries of the comic genre. Women playwrights are not the first to rely on communal presentations of happiness. Groups and communities have always been an essential element of comedy; they have been most notably present in comic conclusions. Groups of women—especially women without men—have, however, been rare at the end of comedy. Thus, while individual change is the ostensible focus of groups like Dunn's and Page's, the presence of a group usually disallowed by the genre holds the potential for social change that Churchill focuses on. The group conclusion favored by many women playwrights may easily include individual change, but it also threatens broad generic and social change.

## Transformations through Birth and the Extrareal

The third revision of comic endings, while it may include the marriage or the groupings of the first two types, will in addition focus on the transformation all of these endings highlight. This type of ending most clearly recalls the open-endedness of Old Comedy. And as the resistance to closure in Aristophanes' plays has disturbed many readers through the centuries, so too have these radically revised contemporary endings jolted their audiences.

While the more dramatic of these transformative endings depart almost completely from the confines of the conventional comic close, I turn first to the somewhat conventional but insistently subversive focus on birth that marks the conclusion of many women's comedies. While birth (or the more general expectation of new life) has been associated with comedy throughout its existence, women writers are now reclaiming birth, converting it from a final certification of the status quo to an explosive promise of the new. Ann Jellicoe's *The Sport of My Mad Mother* (1958) stands as something of a precedent for more recent women's plays dealing with the transformations of birth. In the unfamiliar syncopations of this play, the power the mysterious Greta holds over the other characters is largely attributable to her unexplained pregnancy. The play reaches its menacing conclusion with Greta giving birth in an atmosphere of fecundity and forced joy:

> *Greta:*  Birth! Birth! That's the thing! Oh, I shall have hundreds of children, millions of hundreds and hundreds of millions.
> *Fah:*  And shall we be happy, very, very happy? (168)

As both Greta's and Fah's responses suggest, this event, more strange than happy, propels the action beyond any comfort and conclusiveness at the play's end. Anticipated, in-the-future birth is containable, shared by men and women, and easily co-opted by the patriarchy. This is the birth that comedy traditionally alludes to. Actually birth, as Jellicoe shows, is messy, wild, and all female; it does not sit easily with a patriarchal agenda. Birth represents woman's power to control and transform the world, and in such plays as Jellicoe's it is no longer a sign of woman's acquiescence to male domination.

Like Jellicoe, Grace Dayley also uses the threat of birth to help her break through what she sees as the barrier of a play's end. In *Rose's Story*, Rose is still only pregnant and has not given birth by the play's conclusion, but her delivery threatens to be messy and disruptive because she is a teenager, black, and poor. When Rose turns to the audience with her final line, "And this is where the story *really* begins," she is refusing not only the boundaries of a traditional comic drama, but also the conventional, safe, reaffirmative conscription of birth. Dayley wants to convert birth from being a symbol of a woman settling into her role to an indication of new possibilities. The success both Jellicoe and Dayley have had in translating birth for women's comedy is not unalloyed, however. For both of them, as for any woman hoping to make comedy her métier, pregnancy and birth remain problematic. Traditionally, both processes—so inherently female—have come to be equated with the comic conclusion; and what might yet prove to be the most potent symbol of woman's power has been structurally absorbed, made a part of women's partnership in marriage. There is always the danger that such familiar social and generic connotations will outweigh the more radical connotations women are now bringing to their portraits of pregnancy and birth. Nevertheless, women are turning more and more often to this subject matter that allows them to disrupt generic and social convention. Sarah Daniels's *Byrthrite* suggests how powerful such disruptions can be.

In her 1986 play, Daniels challenges established comic attitudes about birth by proposing new woman-directed attitudes. And in appropriating birth and pregnancy as forces for women's good, Daniels rewrites birth not just in her ending, but throughout the play. Instead of ending with a birth, this play opens on one. As a group of women celebrate the arrival of their friend Ann's daughter, they sing of birth as a woman's right/rite:

Unto you a child is born
Unto you a daughter given
From this time forth go and to all women tell;
That the daughter's inheritance shall pass
Through you all, to be kept forever
Women's rite, women's right for choice in birth. (1)

As Dayley's Rose says, "This is where the story *really* begins"—in the joy and power of the women's community. Contrary to what is expected in comedy, this opening birth turns out to be the only physical birth in the play. But in its repositioned slot at the opening of the play, it invites other births just as important for the play's women, the births of independent selves. By the end of the play, the creativity and rite of birth have become principal metaphors for women's productivity. Rose (who gives birth to plays and not babies) asks at the end, "How many times are we to buy back our birthright?" (43). Although the answer is still "many," the women have acquired the power and control both to ask and to answer the question. They have done so through the transformations birth teaches them to control.

Though powerful, the transformation implied in and acted out through the birth motif marks the end of a small percentage of women's dramas. The most recurrent of the third type of ending, which focuses on change and transformation, is an ending characterized by a shift in stage representations of reality. In chapter 8, I discussed the regularity with which women writing comedy are molding plays of multiple realities. In two of the plays I examined in detail there, *The Great Celestial Cow* and *Ripen Our Darkness,* the extrareal is concentrated at the end of the play where it has the extra effect of moving the play beyond the traditional boundaries of the ending as well as beyond the expected correlations of literature and world. I also discussed how plays like *Cloud Nine* and *Salonika* make use of the "transformation" imbedded in a non-realistic presentation to alter plot trajectory and the expectations it arouses. There is no need to repeat that discussion here. But for a concluding example of the command women are taking over both the dramatic terrain of birth and the comic possibilities for transformation at a play's end, I turn to Michelene Wandor's *Wanted* (1988). Throughout its action, but especially at the end, it combines the extrareal with a focus on birth.

*Wanted* brings together the fate of three characters as it makes the transformations of both pregnancy and birth its main subject. There is Sarah, based on the biblical Sarah, a woman not-so-biblically endowed with a fertile Jewish sense of humor. There is Angel, a character of indeterminate sex who acts as liaison between God and Sarah: the Angel greets Sarah with news of her pregnancy at the beginning of the play and then tries to get her to agree to give birth. And finally there is "Someone," the soul to be born out of Sarah's body. Wandor has not marked her play with scenes and provides no stage directions, and thus *Wanted* eschews conventional comic narrative from the opening. But she does separate sections of her dialogue, first with nursery rhymes and children's songs and later with what—this only slowly becomes clear—are the thoughts of the unborn Someone. After a series of exchanges between Sarah and the Angel and between the Angel and the soul, the play ends with the birth of the soul, marked by the first conversation between Sarah and Someone. Their simple exchange carries the weight of a climax, since the two about to become mother and child have not previously spoken:

> *Sarah:*   Alright. I'll do it. I'll give it a whirl. What the hell. I said I'll—here. Where are you?
> Here I am
> *Sarah:*   Well, well, well. Just look at that. A little miracle. (72)

Yet the birth does not function to bring the play and its characters back into recognizable patterns or orders. For Wandor's whole play has been an attempt to suggest new meanings that may attach to pregnancy and birth. Sarah, for example, refuses to give up her identity, after 89 years, to the conventional selflessness of motherhood. As the Angel argues *for* her acceptance of pregnancy, Sarah counters with statements like "I've lived quite happily for eighty-nine years without any babies" (13). Sarah also considers the pros and cons of hiring a surrogate mother. The soul, too, speaks against the romanticism of birth and spends the play somewhat allusively arguing against life and babyhood. Through such multifaceted revisioning of what birth may mean, the play points toward two levels of transformation.

First of all, birth and pregnancy are transformed. They are brought beyond their traditional comic meanings as precursors of stability and heterosexual contentment. They become female conditions and events that the play's characters can express ambivalence about: pregnancy is enriching and fertile, burdensome and demanding; birth is both magical and painful. Second, the ending of the play is transformed. While there is a birth, the intense focus of the preceding dialogue on what that birth might signify precludes the birth from signaling the inception of a traditional order. The ending has an unusual openness: old types have been debunked, but what might replace them is sketchy at best. Most significant of all, this transformed ending powerfully suggests that transformation is central to women's lives. Far from being essentialist in its implications, the play points to aspects of life particularly female to study both the power and the restrictions they entail.

   Wandor's play suggests the extent to which transformation can be both subject and goal in women's comedy. By so intensely exploring the options for birth and comic ending, Wandor has set an example other writers will follow in various fashions. My prediction is that both the extrareal and the attention to women's life-giving potential will characterize much more women-authored comedy. There are likely to be more plays that end like Wandor's, with more explosion that containment. In part 1, I argued that traditional comic endings have placed the heaviest burden on comic women. While that burden remains a factor in the plays women are now writing, women's reorganization of comic structure has allowed them to test endings of their own definition. Reformulated plots and heroines, new combinations of presentational styles, novel casting, and the incorporation of music and cabaret have all enabled women playwrights to create these new endings. And Wandor's play demonstrates how women are beginning to prescribe new doses of both joy and revolt for the comic conclusion.

## Chapter 10

# Taking Back the Body:
# Self and Sexuality

When Siren Theatre Company was planning its 1986 "lesbian thriller" *Pulp* (written by Tasha Fairbanks), company members were deliberately moving beyond a familiar feminist critique of male sexual desire and its objectification of women to a less conventional analysis of the constitution of female desire: "This play is about placing our desire as women in the context of the culture we are a part of" (Boston interview). Central to the group's presentation was Jane Boston's appearance as "the film star" in high heels and a tight, suggestive dress. The company played a dangerous and not always successful game, as Boston admits, by combining a critique of traditional forms of desirability with an attempt to reclaim them for women. Similarly, in *Time Gentlemen Please* (1978), Monstrous Regiment's cabaret/theater show on women's sexuality, the women were "outrageously over-dressed" in long, low-cut, sequined gowns in counterpoint to their feminist jokes on sex (Bailey interview). As theater that troubled its audience by sending what seemed to be deliberately contradictory messages, both plays highlighted the complex issue of women's sexuality in the contemporary British theater. Timberlake Wertenbaker, who acknowledges the strong erotic component in her own plays, characterizes the ambiguity that writers now routinely encounter in bringing any sexually conscious woman to the stage:

> Desire is a move towards something. And possibly I have resisted the idea that women don't desire, you know are the objects of desire, but are not active in that sense. . . . I can't really put it more clearly than that. The eroticism for me is not just women's sexuality. It is a broader notion . . . it is the desire . . . [to] find what makes us continue. (Interview)

The issue of sexuality is further complicated by the fact that Siren Theatre, Monstrous Regiment, Wertenbaker, and other women involved in contemporary drama usually combine their attention to the body with an exploration of female subjectivity. In play after play, a character's affirmation of her personal or political self grows out of a rediscovery or confirmation of her sexual nature. This simple equation of self and sexuality, however, does not erase the difficult conjunctions I just noted. In fact, I will argue that to accept this conflation of selfhood and sexuality is to distort both the plays and the world they represent. For a close look at the plays themselves suggests that the connections of selves and sexualities are complicated by the presence of multiple selves and mutable sexualities. In the last two chapters, I have outlined how women playwrights are redefining the composition of comic narrative. In this chapter, I will study the dynamics of subjectivity in the women characters peopling this changing comic realm. To facilitate this study of the complexities that attach to the plays' women, bodies, and selves, I would like to outline the psychological context in which both female selves and sexualities are established.

In feminist developments of Lacanian psychoanalysis, both the early development of identity and the concomitant developmental force of language determine the parameters for understanding selves and sexualities. In her outline of Lacanian psychology, Jacqueline Rose stresses that sexuality and subjectivity come into being simultaneously and that an individual's control and understanding of both are subverted, from the beginning, by the unconscious (Rose, 27–30). Luce Irigaray adds that a female's problematic position is exacerbated by a male-determined system that further compromises the development of a female subjectivity: "The feminine occurs only within models and laws devised by male subjects" ("Cose Fan Tutti," 86).[1] The role of language is also crucial in the formation of such delimited selves; for Rose "the subject is constituted through language" (*Feminine Sexuality,* 31), or as Julian Henriques and colleagues put it, "entry into language inaugurates the production of subjectivity" (*Changing the Subject,* 215). In other words, Lacanian psychoanalysis begins by accepting the impossibility of an integrated self *and* by accepting the forceful role language plays in identity formation.

Important for feminists, this explanation of linguistically conditioned plural selves points to the possibility for a change in the self, women's self in particular. Henriques et al. point to the centrality of language and symbolic representation as the basis for transforming the understanding and representation of women's lives (*Changing the Subject,* 216–17). Catherine Belsey, who also focuses on the linguistically constructed nature of the Lacanian subject, adds that the positing of a linguistic *process* for identity formation encourages belief in change: "In the fact that the subject is a *process* lies the possibility of transformation" ("Constructing the Subject," 50). Many other researchers, including Jeffrey Weeks *(Sexuality),* Wendy Hollway ("Gender Difference"), and Carol Vance and Ann Snitow ("Toward a Conversation"), have made parallel cases that if historical, social, and cultural forces (in addition to linguistic ones) have helped to "construct" self and sexuality, then both are open to "investigation and judgment—and change" (Weeks, *Sexuality,* 208). Weeks in particular suggests that by adding social and cultural influences to the picture of the psychological construction of the self, researchers can focus on the controllable (and changeable) social constructions instead of on the problematic nature of the formation of the self:

> Firstly, psychoanalysis has established the problematic nature of identity. This was clearly there in Freud; the message had a curious trajectory through the work of other writers; it has been reaffirmed in the recent celebration of the flux of sexuality by feminist writings and by Deleuze and Guattari in their different ways. Whatever the vagaries of their thought, ranging from the pessimism of Freud to the anarcho-amoralism of recent writers, here is a gain which theorists of sexuality must increasingly take into account. Secondly, the debate around psychoanalysis has also demonstrated the potency of social norms and institutional formations. The possibility exists within the discourse of accepting them (as Freud did to some extent) or rejecting them (as many sexual radicals have sought to do). What cannot be done is to ignore them. (*Sexuality,* 180–81)

In privileging the possibilities for change, such arguments have made the study of linguistic and cultural constructs a primary site for feminists tracing women's literary efforts to reclaim their bodies and their selves. Kaja Silverman, for example, in *The Acoustic Mirror,* argues that the body always bears the stamp of its enculturation and that, therefore, feminist efforts to rewrite that body must begin with an understanding of discourse (146). Like Silverman, a key contributor to the feminist analysis of sexuality, Teresa de Lauretis similarly urges her

readers to broaden their analysis of sexuality. She notes that while the
search for a female self in a patriarchal society is continually compromised by the negative position that women have been expected to fill
(*Technologies,* 19), the necessary way to understand, even counteract,
that negativity is to recognize woman as a construct of a gender-sex
system. A woman-defined sexuality and subjectivity may be possible,
she suggests, only when women understand the forces of theory and
discourse in their lives. Finally, the feminist reclamation of female selfhood and sexuality, which both Silverman and de Lauretis analyze in the
specific context of film, will entail not just a simple reversal of the
practices that have shaped a sexist world, but the imagining of different
terms.[2]

De Lauretis, Silverman, Belsey, Weeks, and others do not consider
the specific applications of their ideas for women's work in the theater,
yet their assumptions have guided other writers, like myself, who seek
to explore the theatrical territory in which self and sexuality come together. The work of Hélène Cixous and Josette Féral has unambiguously
suggested the enhanced opportunity theater offers for such investigation.
Writing on women in theater in her essay "Aller à la mer," Cixous
writes: "It is high time that women gave back to the theatre its fortunate
position, its raison d'être and what makes it different—the fact that there
it is possible to get across the living, breathing, speaking body. . . . The
scene takes place where a woman's life takes place, where her life story
is decided: inside her body, beginning with her blood" (547). The body
is, for Cixous, the promising reason to think of women in connection
with theater. The further correlations that Josette Féral urges suggest
that for both women the conjunction of women and bodies in the theater
offers a unique opportunity for women to claim a self-generated sexuality: "Speak the body, express its sexuality, fill the void of NOTHING: 'They
invented all of their sexuality while ours was silent. If we invent ours,
theirs will have to be completely rethought. And this body of woman is
perpetually told and retold in women's plays'" ("Writing and Displacement," 552).[3]

In translating such concerns to the realm of English-language theater, American feminist theater critics have expanded the study of theater
as an effective location for generating an analysis of the complex conjunctions of self and sexuality. Sue-Ellen Case and Jeanie K. Forte have
stated the most optimistic case, arguing that "women in the subject
position" in theater offer the possibility of a whole new discourse, one

that would include the option of homosexuality ("From Formalism to Feminism," 64–65). Jill Dolan joins Case and Forte in believing that woman is the most promising site for the transmission, through theater, of radical ontological changes. Yet she adds a caution about the efficacy of relying on actual bodies for such transformations. In her study of performance art she finds, in fact, that the use of nudity may be counterproductive for such an agenda. Working from the Lacanian notion that both desire and sexuality are cultural constructs, she argues that the formation of alternate constructs are more a matter of language and perception than of flesh ("Dynamics of Desire").

More recently, Jeanie Forte, Elin Diamond, and Janelle Reinelt have contributed to the growing body of critical literature on the theatrical conjunction of self and sexuality in women's theater. Forte, for example, challenges Dolan's argument in calling for a reconsideration of the phenomenal presence of bodies; she suggests they needn't be discounted in Lacanian thinking ("Women's Performance Art: Construction of the Social Subject"). Diamond takes Churchill's *Fen* and *A Mouthful of Birds* as two plays in which the female body is a site for the revision of social and political repressions ("[In]visible Bodies"). And Reinelt argues that the third "reconstructive phase of feminist theatre"—the theater at the cutting edge of the late 1980s—gives its "concentrated attention to the subject" ("Feminist Theory," 52, 50). The various arguments do not harmonize. But for all those currently engaged in the theatrical study of female agency, the self and sexuality are considered in tandem. As such criticism attests, the theater's combination of the physical and the literary make it a fertile location for explorations of the female self. As the only literary form with options beyond language, theater provides an arena not simply for examining the complex psychological formation of identity, but also for returning to women the "potency of social norms and institutional formations" (Weeks, *Sexuality,* 180). As a challenge to other theorists of the theater, among them Herbert Blau *(Take up the Bodies),* who are cautioning that the self may no longer exist in the theater, these feminist critics have found that the theater constitutes one of women's best chances for self-definition.

This contemporary reconsideration of self and sexuality provides an important new perspective on comedy's very old focus on the physical and the sexual. The sophistication of this critical apparatus offers a needed background for charting and understanding the new expressions women authors are giving to comic drama's physicality. In part 1, I suggested that traditional British comedy builds from an objectification of women and depends for its effect on its women's destiny in marriage and procreation. But while current women playwrights are still attracted by comedy's promise of togetherness and procreation, they are creating characters who realize a much fuller and more troublesome range of bodily possibilities.[4]

For the men whose visions have guided the development of contemporary British drama—I think of the strong influences of Harold Pinter, Edward Bond, and most recently Howard Barker—a mixture of sexuality and violence has been the dominant expression of the physical. This mode of expression shapes the female as well as the male characters. The rape that informs Barker's work, for example, is considered disgusting but necessary. Although the more clearly comic work by Tom Stoppard, Doug Lucie, Anthony Minghella, and others masks the brutality of its objectification, it generally maintains the equation of a woman's self with her position as a sexual object. Jonathan Gems's play *Susan's Breasts* (1985) is not particularly retrograde in its treatment of women; yet when the play opened, its title was taken as a call for polarized responses to women's sexuality. On the one hand, feminists faulted the objectification and bodily dissection indicated in Gems's title. On the other hand, male reviewers proved the cultural validity of such objections by reading the play's title as a sanctioning of sexual objectification. Francis King punned, "The only boobs in evidence here are in dramatic technique"; and Kenneth Hurren joined him, quipping, "Actress Susan's breasts are so little in evidence as to be almost concave." As Lou Wakefield sums up, a gap remains between the perceptions of men and of women writing in theater. Of the men she notes, "The men who think they are feminists think they have to find a happy end for our bodies. Because for them we are trapped in our bodies" (interview). Of the women, I will suggest in the pages to come that they are finding new routes to subjectivity and that those routes incorporate bodies in a range of ways, almost all of which move women beyond the standard view of them as troubled objects.

## Celebrating the Body in Collective and Cabaret

In the work of several theater collectives, drawing attention to the physiucal presence and powers of women's bodies is a basic goal. Both the Scarlet Harlets and Spare Tyre are representative as they deal in a straightforward, sometimes naive way with connections of self and sexuality.

The hallmark of the Scarlet Harlets' work is their reliance on the body as an apparatus equipped with infinite capabilities. Their shows—usually an integrated series of skits—have been built around skills like dancing, tumbling, juggling, balancing, and tightrope walking. In the accompanying dialogue, the women's selfhood is clearly related to both the physical and the sexual, although the body is not paraded as a sexual site. Company member Sue Long, in talking of the 1986 show *Toe on the Line,* insisted not only on connecting the physical and the self, but also on shedding the distancing of naturalism, which splits actor and character. "You start from you," she notes, to emphasize that the bold statements on stage have an enhanced truth because the subject is unmediated (Long and Neave interview). Additionally, in Scarlet Harlet shows, the connection urged between the self and the physical is political. One number from early in *Toe on the Line* has two actors sharing a single tightrope as they recall the history of their lesbian love affair. The audience, on the one hand, admires the women's physical skill, balance, and trust; and on the other it will realize that the image of two lesbians teetering on a thin rope is an appropriate "living" metaphor for a sexuality unsanctioned by much of society. This conflation of social comment and physical representation also distinguishes a skit late in the show in which the three company members balance on one another to make beautifully shaped figures. Accompanying the balancing is the show's most overt political dialogue, condemning Margaret Thatcher and her Britain. Sue Long reads the combination of physical cooperation and an agenda for social change as saying, "Look, we all have got these ideas about how we want the world to change, but we can't do it on our own" (Long and Neave interview). This troupe, then, accepts an equation of a woman's self with her sexuality and asserts that the body can offer women whatever kind of power they want.

For the women who make up Spare Tyre, the focus is less on physical agility and more on the psychological effects of women's relationships to their bodies. As with the Scarlet Harlets, the comedy of Spare Tyre is uplifting, but its message is more complex. Although most of Spare Tyre's shows have been explorations of women's problematic relation to food (members were inspired by Susie Orbach's *Fat Is a Feminist Issue*), company members have made women and appetite fertile territory for their goal of helping women find selves. It is not the specific content of the shows, however, as much as the process of out-reach in which lies Spare Tyre's significant contribution to contemporary theatrical attitudes about the female body.

Collective member Katina Noble explains that the company has focused on eating disorders because through them women all too frequently try to cope with problems of self-image:

> We are all striving for that perfect body, and we never quite make it. I think it is so universal in Western women's lives, and it is also so bound up with an enormous lack of self-confidence, self-hatred. . . . In a way, if you start to do other things in your life to feel more confident . . . you will feel less self-hatred. You will not turn it in on your body. (Noble interview)

Not only do the shows directly address women's everyday problems of self-definition and food with songs like "Everytime My Mother Rings, I Want a Mars Bar," "Inside Every Fat Person," and "Putting It off til I'm Thinner," but the company has also helped establish a network of self-help groups for women with eating disorders. The actors append consciousness-raising audience discussion to the end of many performances. And compatible with this closeness to audience is the group's penchant for comedy. The ties so clearly established, in performance, between personal identity and comic response have, in fact, gained considerable praise for the work of Spare Tyre. Of *You've Gotta Be Kidding* (1985), a review in the *Portsmouth News* reported: "Every woman in the audience must have recognized some of the thoughts and feelings expressed here, and I defy even the most diehard anti-feminist to sit through the cabaret without enjoying it." The assumption that selves can be transformed by the increased understanding of social and cultural pressures on women's bodies is naive, as I have noted. Theoretically speaking, the change that Spare Tyre has brought to its loyal and enthusiastic audience is at best simplistically misleading; yet Spare Tyre's operations and beliefs predominate among theater practitioners. Noble, representing many, claims to have witnessed direct connections between self-understanding and a renewed attention to the "questioning of traditional structures and role models."

What the work of the Scarlet Harlets and Spare Tyre shows is how women's theater has responded to women's negative self-image. Both groups have demonstrated a success in improving the images of actual women in their audiences with their focus on the abilities of and the cultural distortions to women's bodies. Another collectively produced work, Bryony Lavery's *Time Gentlemen Please* (1978), written for Monstrous Regiment, also begins with women's negative self-image. Yet in this piece, the self-conscious atmosphere of comic cabaret allows for a further consideration of issues only touched on in the celebratory work of the Scarlet Harlets and Spare Tyre.

As Lavery describes it, *Time Gentlemen Please* evolved from what was, in 1978, "the enormously dangerous choice of doing a show about sex" (interview). From the distance of more than a decade, it is easy to note that the investigations of sexuality here are predictable. At the time, however, the entire operation was analyzed quite differently. For example, as I mentioned in my remarks on the play at the beginning of the chapter, costuming was provocative—the men were outfitted in dark, discreet suits, while the women were "exposed" in "exotic variations on the black and silver trappings of slinky cabaret costume" (Wandor, *Carry On,* 71). The show's exposure of traditional expectations in heterosexual sex was similarly controversial. The song "Time Gentlemen Please," addressed to men, criticizes male attitudes to sex as too urgent, quick, and harsh:

> Why all the hurry? Lay back for a little while
> Take all the time you need, do it with perfect style
> Why all the worry? Oh, why spoil a fine affair?
> Take all the time you need, I'll still be there.
>
>> Time Gentlemen Please
>> Taking time's not a disease
>> Taking time's aiming to please
>> Time Gentlemen, freeze.

The dialogue "Last Night" contrasts this male behavior with the show's more favored female response. In this segment of the show, one of the actors teases the audience with her detailed account of "weeks of patient work" with a seemingly shy man that lead her not to the "tender, friendly sex" she had longed for, but to a forty-five-minute gymnastic encounter that leaves her achy, bruised, and bored—and leaves him murmuring "terrific." The gap between male and female behaviors outlined in these two segments is representative of other material in the show. Yet as the show toured, this relatively tame feminist critique drew criti-

cism and misunderstanding along with support. Such direct talk about
sex from a woman's point of view was unsettling.

The combination of female subjectivity and sexuality was, in fact,
nothing short of explosive. First of all, as Sandy Bailey of Monstrous
Regiment reports (interview), in many of the places the show toured—
working-class men's clubs, trade-union halls, communist party conferences—the women's suggestive costumes were not read as parody.
Audience members took the exposed, accented flesh as they were accustomed to, as a sign of women's sexual objectification. This regressive
response was accompanied, secondly, by protest from progressive
women's groups and lesbian groups who objected to the show's almost
exclusive focus on heterosexuality. Lavery acknowledges the limited
sexual scope of the show, but notes that in this cabaret the sexuality
presented grew directly from the heterosexual experience of the six actors—"We were doing the show on our own experience of sex" (interview). Such a defense did nothing, however, to stop the protests against
the show, protests that climaxed in Leeds when feminist and gay pro-
testors succeeded in stopping one performance. Other objections to the
show were raised when detractors noted that the sexual discussion and
self-exploration were based exclusively on middle-class experience. Director Susan Todd answered this second charge by arguing that with
their grounding in a particular sexuality and a particular class, the performers were, in fact, claiming a sexuality for all women:

> The women performers deconstruct their traditional mode of stage
> presence and abandon coyness, terror and self-doubt for a direct
> expression of sexuality. . . . That particular transformation was
> fought for very hard and it represents a victory for each woman
> over self-denigration. (*Morning Star,* 28 November 1978; Wandor,
> *Carry On,* 72)

Both Lavery and Todd assume in their defenses that there is a direct
connection between the emerging sexuality of individual actors/charac-
ters and a stronger self. Objections were raised on the same assumption
that a change in self is to be equated with a change in sexuality. I will
conclude my study of *Time Gentlemen Please* by suggesting, however,
that the show encourages a more complex attitude to sexuality than
either its defenders or its detractors recognized during the heat of argument.

Michelene Wandor focuses on what she sees as the limitations of the show for effecting any lasting social change. She worries that most audiences read the play's message as, at best, a call for female sexual dominance to replace male sexual dominance. The audience would thus carry away nothing more than the very old image of woman as castrator (*Carry On*, 73). Unforgivable to Wandor is "the failure of the material to provide content strong enough to rupture the form" (*Carry On*, 72). Not having seen the production myself, I have difficulty in settling on a final judgment about the subversive possibilities of this comedy. Yet the text does provide openings that a performance or an audience could read as signs of a less traditional and more mutable sexuality.

In her opening monologue, for example, character/actor Mary introduces "identity" as a problematic concept. In particular, she expresses her fears of exposing her sexual nature to her mother: "I would hate my mother to see this cabaret. . . . if there's just one person like my mother in the audience tonight, I'm scared." The sexuality that will, throughout the show, serve as the basis for self-abnegation as well as for self-affirmation thus begins as a relative construct dependent on a tie as volatile as a mother-daughter relationship. This awareness of the constructed nature of sexuality extends to language in at least two numbers from the show. Mary, again, begins one such analysis by asking, "When you were a kid, did you have a special word for 'shit?'" Moving from the bodily to the explicitly sexual, she notes that the words for sexual pleasure, "orgasm" for example, aren't women's. After warning that "we shouldn't be afraid of using our own words for these things," she proposes her substitutions: "gloop" for vagina, "Wah hey" for orgasm. She concludes that the present vocabulary of sex fortifies a divisive (what is now called essentialist) male and female world. Implied in her analysis (comic here as elsewhere in the show) are some basics of feminist linguistic analysis, most importantly her assumption that language is patriarchal to such a degree that women can't know themselves through it. The show's male corollary to this female linguistic meditation is a brief exchange between two of the show's men, Keith and Clive; their "dialogue" on romantic and/or sexual involvement is nothing more than a pastiche of lines from pop songs. Once more the message is that sexual responses are conventionalized and coded almost beyond control, usually beyond consciousness.

Finally, author Lavery demonstrates a desire to move beyond conventional sex and beyond simplistic equations of self and sexuality, first in the song "I Went to a Marvelous Orgy," in which multiple sexual partners are celebrated. Such exploration is present, second, in a monologue full of admissions about sexual confusion. I won't overstate the case: none of the examples I have brought together in these last two paragraphs makes a clear-cut case for the privileging of complicated constructions of self and sexuality in this piece. Yet *Time Gentlemen Please* suggests that in women's comic cabaret, notions of women's subjectivity and their bodies can be complex. The portraits of women's selves and their sexualities are still more diffuse in fully scripted plays. What remains consistent in cabaret and scripted theater alike, however, is the excitement of comedy; through the recognition of self in the body, women increase their self-confidence, find love, and begin to change the world.

### The Body and the Self in Theatrical Transition

Almost any one of the plays considered in part 2 of this book could exemplify how women's bodies serve as the primary site of self-doubt, self-study, self-improvement, and self-love in plays by women. Many of them, including Michelene Wandor's *Wanted* (1988), Jude Alderson's *Madonna in Slag City* (1986), Timberlake Wertenbaker's *The Grace of Mary Traverse* (1985), and Grace Dayley's *Rose's Story* (1984) turn to pregnancy—as have countless plays by men—to study self and sexuality as the key to the human species. Page's *Golden Girls* (1984) studies the difficulties of transforming young women's bodies into fine-tuned machines primed for athletic competition. Gems's *Dusa, Fish, Stas, and Vi* (1976) makes heterosexual desires a counterpoint to the search for identity. But I will turn first to Sue Townsend's *Womberang*, Nell Dunn's *Steaming*, and Jacqueline Rudet's *Basin* as representations of the most significant attitudes toward the connections of self and sexuality as they are conveyed in recent comic work. I will then conclude with a look at the more exploratory and hence more problematic approach to the self in Alderson's *The Virgins' Revenge*, Wertenbaker's *New Anatomies*, and Sarah Daniels's *Byrthrite*.

Sue Townsend's first play, *Womberang* (1979), is pleasantly predictable. A group of people, mostly women, gathered in the waiting room of a gynecological clinic come to some startling self-realizations in a body-rich atmosphere. The central character, Rita, transformed into a feminist "activist" by her experiences with divorce, breakdown, and therapy, leads the other women in recognizing their bodies as their own. She motivates Mrs. Connelly to give up her corset and then dance, nearly nude, on waiting-room benches. She helps Audrey and James to consummate their marriage, for the first time, in the waiting-room changing cubicles. And she declares pregnant Lynda the joyous provider of "the next generation" (96). A good deal of talk about female medical conditions—menopause, dropped wombs, and fertility—accompanies the actual display of bodies (most notable in Mrs. Connelly). And a celebratory feeling grows from the play's multiple transformations, a feeling enhanced by gin and a rebellion against hospital administrators. This play's newly recovered selves appear too quickly to be taken as naturalistic portraits of self-affirmation, but the magic of comedy makes the changes effective in a different way. Theater reviewer Ned Chaillet reported that "the laughter seems motivation enough." As he notes, Townsend's idea seems to be that the recovery of self through body can be best offered as a real possibility for the audience through a shared laughter. Outside of intimations that Rita, like Mrs. Connelly, may be dying, the play is unclouded by shadows, including the recognition that recovering the self is not usually so easy.

While it too involves the discovery of bodies and self in a group environment, Nell Dunn's *Steaming* (1981) allows for a deeper probing of the possible pathways to self-discovery. As I mentioned in chapter 8, *Steaming* presents the relationships of six women who form alliances during their visits to a London Turkish bath. The atmosphere is charged with attention to sexuality both in the talk—which ranges from Josie's energetic fantasies to discussion of marital and extramarital sex—and in the display of bodies. Four of the six characters appear completely nude at some point, and the women invite attention to this bodily ambience through mirrors, hugs, massages, and kisses.[5] Without question, Dunn depends on this intensified physicality to depict a group of women rediscovering selves. Her epigraph privileges a bold subjectivity—"a warrior / Takes responsibility for his acts" (Carlos Castaneda). And character Nancy's move to personal understanding is exemplary. From hatred for her mirror-image—"God, is that face really mine?" (38)—she comes to a self-affirming thirst for "sexual desire and sexual experience, that melting"(70). As Dunn succinctly puts it, Nancy "had to accept herself physically in order to grow up." Dunn adds, speaking of all the women characters' progress to subjectivity: "I certainly think there is some idea of revealing themselves, of emotional honesty that went with physical nakedness. I wanted that lovely feeling, here I am" (interview).

Yet Dunn's correlation between self-discovery and bodily acceptance is far from direct, especially as this play is translated into a theater space. Dunn calls a "dig at men" her decision to keep the one male character, Bill, behind a glass door (interview). This restriction announces to the audience that men, not women, must accept shadow selves in this world. However, in the space thus declared fertile for female subjectivity, the multidimensional presence of bodies becomes a slippery rock on which to build selves. As Dolan suggests in her analysis of American theater, real bodies may not be the most effective material with which to study real bodies ("Dynamics of Desire"). In fact, successful production of *Steaming* depends crucially on the audience's acclimatizing itself to the fleshy environment by accepting its uninhibited stage action as wholesome, *not* titillating. Dunn herself underlines this point by having at least two of her body-shy characters—Dawn and Nancy— learn to undress unself-consciously in the course of the play.

As Dunn admits, however, production of the play has not always invited or allowed this vital transition. She found the original transfer of the play from East London's Theatre Royal to the West End Comedy Theatre reprehensible, as the production increasingly played to an audience's amusement with the women's bodies. In my own experience of watching the play at the Comedy Theatre, I noted a titillated hush in the audience, which was rivetted on Josie, the first to undress onstage. Dunn found herself unable to watch the transfer production (the Broadway playbill takes things a step further by making light of an audience populated by "lonely gentlemen with raincoats on their laps" [Morley, "*Steaming*," 36]). The problems created by the display of bodies were also exacerbated in the transfer production by the very traditional matching of body type to character type. The two most traditionally good-looking bodies belonged to the actors playing the more "successful" middle-class women, Nancy and Jane; working-class, man-pleaser Josie was fleshy; and Vi was as corpulent as she was pushy. Two later productions have suggested the continuing nature of the problems the play invites with its physical focus. In the Isle of Man, Henry Callow, the bailiff, prohibited the play's performance in 1986.[6] Dunn herself recalls how another theater company felt compelled to call for a matinee in which the audience was nude; in response, the town council banned the performance (interview). This play will always force its audience to connect self-growth to the acceptance of a character's body. But the seriousness with which its message is taken will be variable. Instead of clarifying the feminist link between subjectivity and sexuality, *Steaming* and its production history problematizes that link.[7] As the play demonstrates, the possibility of sexual objectification is an ever-real danger for women in the theater.

Finally, I would like to consider how the play's comedy adds to the ambiguity of its message. While the play is undeniably comic, the sexuality tied to that comedy is at once corrosive *and* stabilizing. In Dawn, the comic butt of the play, Dunn shows how, as she puts it, "sex is a black comedy, sometimes, after all" (Morley, *"Steaming,"* 36). Early on, Dawn's simple nature draws fond, condescending responses, from characters and audience, to her appearance in a plastic raincoat. Yet in the second act, her new attention to her body (and her "self") adds both recognition and menace to the laughter. In the first scene of this second act she sheds her comical plastic coat and paints her nipples red, to the other women's applause (53). In the next scene she moves beyond laughter, this time touching her breasts as she proclaims, "They say my body's beautiful" (60). Dawn's sexual repression is arguably the saddest in the play, since her adolescent attraction to men is connected with rape and perhaps abuse. In part because of this past, her recovery of a self full of desires is troubling and tentative. In this play, sexuality is not a panacea for individual progress toward self-definition. It remains, however, a site for comic sharing and community.

*Steaming* connects emergence of the self to a warm, though sometimes darkened, welcoming of bodies and sexuality. Yet its nudity and its comedy, two qualities that might be expected to ease the personal transformations, do just as much to introduce complications. The group context in this play and in *Womberang* also qualifies the deliberations over self present in these and many other contemporary plays. By placing all individual growth so firmly within a group framework, Dunn and Townsend offer something of an analogy on the subject and its multiple nature. These two plays are representative in that the selves they nurture do not mature individually but as components of group interactions. Just as psychoanalytic critics are now counseling for an understanding of the "self" as a plurality of attitudes and not as a unity, these playwrights are making self-affirmation a necessarily shared and multidirectional process.

Jacqueline Rudet's *Basin* (1985), like Townsend's and Dunn's plays, is aware of its feminist portraiture of self-growth and is, like the earlier plays, eased by its comedy and its community of women. But while Townsend and Dunn focus on the connections of self and sexuality in a white, heterosexual world, Rudet examines the emergence of a self conditioned by black culture and lesbianism.

Here again the lives of the play's three women, Mona, Susan, and Michele, are heavily conditioned by societal responses to and expectations about bodies and sex. Mona, Susan, and Michele chat early in the play about their often tempestuous and not quite satisfying relationships to men. Desire is unmistakably central in the women's lives. But a focus on the heterosexual sex the women have known begins to dissolve, first when Susan concludes a long speech with a hint of other possible sexualities: "What I'm struggling to say is that I think I'm growing tired of that lovable, household pet known as the boyfriend" (120). The transfer to a woman-oriented sexuality is considered metaphorically when Susan later talks of basins. Jamaican mothers give their young (four-year-old) daughters a basin in which to wash their "koolalook" before bed each night, training them in feminine hygiene as a preparation for marriage (129). Thus the basin represents women's enslavement to men's sexual desires. Yet the basin concurrently represents female tradition and community, and it is on this second connotation of the word that the play makes its major turn. As Susan and Mona give up their heterosexual lives to become lovers, they reclaim the basin for themselves. They also reclaim a Jamaican term, *Zammies,* which means close—intimate and perhaps sexual—friends; it is what these two women become.

Rudet, like Townsend and Dunn, uses this sexually charged world as a foundation for considering the female self. But unlike the others, Rudet draws a clear line between the selves that function in the heterosexual and in the lesbian worlds. On the one hand, the female self as defined in relations with men is considered weak and self-abused. Here Michele provides the primary evidence. Mona says of Michele first, "Like I said, you rely too much on men. You've never been alone for two minutes. You don't even know who you are and what you're capable of" (117). Shortly after, Susan adds, "You seem to upset me whenever I see you. You keep saying, 'Things will get better' but it's not 'things' that need to get better. It's you!" (119). And by the end of the play, Michele can only manage a feeble self-defense. She says to Mona, "I still love and respect you and Susan, but you mustn't condemn me for loving Michael. Sometimes people find themselves unable to resist things that are bad for them" (138). Mona, Susan, and Michelle have all been shortchanged in self-development while living their lives for men. Susan explains the confusing developmental situation of all three women, noting that the formation of the female self in a Caribbean culture prepares women for men, but also, inadvertently, aligns them with women:

> Do you know what really hurts? The fact that I wasn't given a choice how I should experience my first fuck. Caribbean girls don't have the chance to enjoy childhood, we're catapulted into woman-hood from an early age!
>
> How can I help but feel a special warmth towards other black women. You see, not only do I love you but I know how it is to be how you are. (124–25)

Thus, on the other hand, only the female self that is formed together with other women allows women understanding, freedom, and choice. It is this second female, often lesbian, self that the play celebrates. Finding the self and its sexuality crippled at best in the heterosexual sphere, *Basin* urges consideration of an all-female alternative. Rudet's portrayal of the interrelationship of self and sexuality is representative of many onstage efforts to establish women's subjectivity through separatist politics.

Rudet's radical politics are also in evidence in the second trio of plays I turn to now. Each of these plays goes beyond those of Townsend, Dunn, and Rudet to consider fully the institutional, social, and cultural forces that destabilize women's control over the development of self and sexuality. In *The Virgins' Revenge, New Anatomies,* and *Byrthrite,* Alderson, Wertenbaker, and Daniels acknowledge these complex forces and develop some provoking theatrical strategies for dealing with them. Concomitantly, they create a theater less stable, more angry, and more realistically forward-looking.

Jude Alderson's *The Virgins' Revenge* (1985) offers an even more direct assault on traditional concepts of female sexuality than is found in *Time Gentlemen Please* or *Basin;* it does so by shifting the grounds of investigation to examine how women's self and sexuality have become commodities.

The play is a collection of four scenes that move from 2004 A.D. to Victorian London to mythical Greece to the present. In each scene the two main characters, Philomela and Psyche, cope with events conditioned by some sort of sexual prostitution. In the first scene, both work in the "Sexual Services" division of a twenty-first-century department store, Selfridge's. The governmentally sanctioned sale of sex is effectively dissolving, for these women, the empowering connection of self and sexuality. As a consequence, Psyche's energies are expended in remembering a distant prehistoric time when women controlled both their selves and their sex: "When we worked in those temples we had so much power. We were chosen women. Goddesses" (8). She also remembers the loss of such female priority: "But they harnessed my power and built things that bent nature. And they built things that bent people's minds. And they started with language" (10). This contrast between what women have had and could have, on the one hand, and what they *do* have, on the other, is the major dialectic on which the play operates.

The contrast between the possible and the actual splits the women linguistically, temporally, and physically. Nonetheless, Philomela and Psyche perform a strangely harmonized duet. In the final scene, set in the present, Phil recalls other strong women and embroiders "an exquisite picture of matrilineal paradise" (43) that ends with this promise: "Mother your virgin is singing for revenge" (47). Psyche supports Phil's visionary journey with a contrasting, down-to-earth, feminist revision of history. Although this counterpointed dialogue introduces the triumphant ending in which the women bake their centuries-long pimp/lover Terry in a pie, their victory is compromised by the play's opening scene, which initiates action by signaling that even 2004 A.D. has not seen the end to the institutionalizing of women's bodies. The play's movement back and forth between women's subjection to male notions of desire and women's subject status in defining their own sexuality offers a more complicated model of female sexuality than evident in many other plays.

To enhance this counterpoint, Alderson depends on the dislocations of the many formal devices I catalogued in chapters 8 and 9: time is not chronological, the narrative moves laterally as much as forward; songs complicate the interpretation of scenes; the realistic and the nonrealistic conjoin; and men are addressed but never appear on stage. Alderson's manipulation of language and silence, however, provides her clearest comment on sexuality in *The Virgins' Revenge*. In scene 1, when Psyche discourses on women's prehistoric power and their subsequent loss of it, she makes language the main site of the battle. She pauses specifically over the word *virgin,* the meaning of which, she explains, men reduced from an "independent woman of strength and mystery" to "a woman who's never been fucked" (10). She explains how men, building up their vocabulary with *whore,* further succeeded in splitting "the same woman . . . in two" (10). Psyche's angry story about this linguistic transformation of women from subjects to subjected is paralleled by Phil's story of silencing, replayed in sometimes muted form in each of the four scenes. The mythological Phil, of course, has her tongue cut out by Tereus to prevent her from telling a tale of sexual abuse. The loss is presented more symbolically in the Victorian segment where Phil—playing out sexual fantasies for customers—is told by Psyche, "If you speak out but *one word* he will not pay" (25). Language is the main site of the women's subjugation; but the play suggests that the women's possibilities for power also begin there.

Although clearly comic, Alderson's play is angry, violent, and confrontational. Through its assaults, it offers an investigation of sexuality that does not retreat from the complex nature of the issue. Timberlake Wertenbaker, in *New Anatomies* (1981), likewise offers a sophisticated analysis of sexuality and its institutional and cultural contexts. In considering the play's structural qualities in chapter 9, I suggested that its cross-gender casting facilitated its main character Isabelle's pursuit of a genderless existence. Here I would like to suggest how Wertenbaker's analysis of sexuality is connected to that utopian impulse. To open this chapter, I pointed to Wertenbaker's consciousness of the complex nature of desire. At one moment she acknowledges that "eroticism is *very* liberating." At the next she qualifies herself remembering that the etymology of *eros* links it to both the erotic *and* to the asking of questions. For Wertenbaker, then, eros is necessarily and simultaneously sexual and political. This focus on a politically conditioned sexual knowledge is what distinguishes Wertenbaker's theater. She sadly notes the current division of left-wing political drama from "sexualized" plays, having found that discussions of sexuality are often seen as "anti-socialist." In her work, however, she strives to combine politics with the "enjoyment of life" (the combination is modeled on ideals she finds in socialism) (interview). *New Anatomies* portrays Wertenbaker's focus on the indivisibility of sexuality and a broader political realm.

With Isabelle's mumbled "I need a fuck" (299) in the opening speech, Wertenbaker establishes this play's hard-edged portrait of sex.

Moments later, when Isabelle addresses her chronicler, Severine, her imagery is equally startling: "Your face looks like a big hungry European cock" (300). In the third scene, when Isabelle's sister Natalie coolly says of marital sex, "You get used to it," Isabelle interprets the statement to mean "brutal pain and brutal pleasure, and after, languor" (308). The romance, warmth, and intimacy that informed the physical in *Time Gentlemen Please, Womberang,* and *Steaming* are absent. The toughness in Wertenbaker's play explains the breakdowns in love and desire in the play; these are most disturbingly present in the dissolution of Isabelle's family. But more important, the play's harsh portraits of sexuality make the connection of self and sexuality reflective of the complex psychological territory both grow out of. The difference in the play's portrait of selves and sexualities is first established in the intimacy Isabelle and her brother Antoine share as children. Their love includes lingering embraces, terms of endearment like "beloved" (303–4), and shared dreams of defying conventionality. Although there are suggestions of incest, theirs is an innocent connection, the one relationship in the play that succeeds—though only for a while—in denying societal restrictions on affection. Because she wants to reclaim this non-gendered utopia of childhood as her goal, Isabelle dedicates her adult life to recreating the conditions necessary to nurture such love. She realizes, however, that she must challenge social and political orders as well as gender conventions to allow for all the freedom she wants.

I want to pause over two specific moments during which Isabelle struggles to define the new sexuality that can allow her to love and to be herself. First, during their conversation in the Paris salon (the scene in which women dressed as men far outnumber women dressed as women), Isabelle and Severine consider unconventional blueprints for physical relations:

> *Severine:* We could travel together. I'd enjoy that.
> *Isabelle:* Do you really like women?
> *Severine:* *(Seductive)* Have you lived in the Orient and remained a prude?
> *Isabelle:* Me? Ha!
> *Severine:* There are thousands of women in this city who would do anything to be made love to by me. But I like women with character.
> *Isabelle:* I'm not a woman. I'm Si Mahmoud. I like men. They like me. As a boy, I mean. And I have a firm rule: no Europeans up my arse. (327)

As Severine opens Isabelle's eyes to the possibility of lesbian attachments, Isabelle dreams of a different unconventionality—attachments of men to men (her comment is complicated, of course, by her being female). The many layers of possibility in this exchange are indicative of the ways in which this play presents the self more as a collection of possibilities than as a unified whole. The self's sexuality is also diversified and plural. A second moment, this one near the end of the play, similarly points to the complexities of sexual desire. As she describes the challenges to and changes in her sexuality that occur while she is cloistered with men at the monastery, Isabelle refuses to interpret her actions in a single or predictable way:

> There were many young men of great beauty in those rooms, and
> we don't hate love. But I couldn't join. They would know I was
> not completely a man, and also, much of that was gone. Slowly,
> slowly, the torment of the senses opens to the modulation of the
> dunes. Only a ripple here and there betrays the passage of the storm.
> (337)

Instead of envisioning her physical connections to others in traditional or recognizable ways, Isabelle relies on metaphor to express the mutability of her desires. She is constrained, in the desert, by her disguise as a man. Yet ironically, within that constraint she finds her thinking about sexuality broadened, the urgency of desire reduced.

More than any other play considered in this chapter, Wertenbaker's *New Anatomies* presents a portrait of self that is both changing and multiple. The analysis of sexuality, similarly, suggests that women change and choose their desires, always conditioned by their knowledge of political and social contexts. A woman's possibilities for happiness depend on her abilities to analyze the forces that shape her. The play is less obviously comic than the others discussed in this chapter; nevertheless, Wertenbaker persists in the comic hopefulness of her worldview, noting, "If there is to be a reconciliation of some sort it will be through eroticism" (interview).

The connection between social and cultural contexts and the construction of female sexuality that both Alderson and Wertenbaker point to also undergirds Sarah Daniels's comprehensive portrait of female self and sexuality in *Byrthrite* (1986). In her foreword to the published version of the play, Jalna Hanmer glosses the play's combined attention to the

patriarchal construction of female bodies and the historically different
development of female subjectivity. She concludes: "The use of medicine
and science controlled by men to challenge the independence and subjectivity of women continues as does the challenge to it by women." As a
part of that challenge by women, Daniels's play suggests, as much as any
play considered in this chapter, that comedy serves well as the primary
mode for current theatrical analyses of woman's self and sexual identity.

*Byrthrite* takes place in seventeenth-century Essex where a group of
young women have created some less-than-sanctioned ways of organizing themselves. These range from support groups for lying-in and birth-
ing to nascent theater companies to female soldiering. Until her death
near the end of the play, seventy-year-old Grace is the spiritual guide of
the group, sustaining its forays into such dangerous behavior (especially
dangerous considering the prevalence, at this time, of witch hunts). In
action that moves the women to fuller realization of patriarchal power
as well as to a strengthened female subversion of such power, bodies are
of central concern. Daniels attends to anorexia, wet nurses, rape, men-
struation, mothering, bleeding (as a medical cure), birth (involving new
seventeenth-century technologies like forceps), and sex—heterosexual,
lesbian, and gay. Daniels balances a realization of the negative effect of
male control of women's bodies against her characters' mounting challenge to such power. Early in the play, the most central character, Rose,
voices the complete loss of self the patriarchy forces on women through
control of their bodies. As she complains to Grace about the unwanted
amorous attentions of a farmer, she concludes, "I hate my body. . . . I
hate mere thought of touching bodies never mind else" (13). But by late
in the play, Grace counteracts Rose's self-negation by declaring women's
bodies the source of their power:

> Our sex with its single power to give birth, pose a threat to men's
> power over whole order of villages, towns, counties and countries.
> That control depends on women cur-tailing to men's ideal of how
> they should behave. (39)

In the world of this play, so created to sensitize its audience to the
possibilities for self-identity and -growth in women's bodies, Daniels
maps a way to create female subjectivity where only male subjectivity
has before been known. This body-based movement from a male to a
female order is consonant with the other plays I have examined in this

chapter; but in *Byrthrite* the building of a new order is the most complete. In her early self-deprecatory fashion, Rose dismisses her way of thinking by noting that it "is connected but not in a straight-line way" (13); similarly, Daniels's creation of female subjectivity unfolds in anything but a "straight-line way." Daniels begins with a critique of men and their institutions. She is later able to detail the design of a "female way," with a woman-powered focus on both sexuality and language.

As reviewers of the play noted, Daniels's criticism of men and the world they have created is constant, tough, and bitter. Played by a single actor, the men who *do* appear act reprehensibly, attempting rape, murderous doctoring, and careless soldiering. As Jane and Rose (both posing as soldiers) ponder the behavior of men at the opening of part 2, Jane summarizes the conclusion about men that the play as a whole projects—men must claim their power negatively, ultimately through death:

> So then, and I've been thinking on this, maybe is compensation for their inabilities. Alarmed that they cannot give life they do find glory in death. Surely that serves as explanation enough as to why they oft set themselves dangerous tasks for no other purpose than to prove themselves—t'is envy of birth. (20–21)

To elaborate on the specific problems men have created for the world, Daniels has her characters expose what they see as the limitations of four crucial patriarchal institutions: the church, the class system, the military, and medicine.

The church is woefully represented by a parson who finds all women, including his wife Helen, evil, and who categorizes any irregular behavior in his wife "hysterical humour" (24). A misguided parishioner's mangling of the Lord's Prayer further suggests the shallowness of the church this person represents: "Our father witch chart in heaven / Hello to thy brain / Give us this day our daily bread / Forgive us our panes" (24). The class system and its monarchical roots are similarly demonized. The class privilege of Lady H has given her position, but little power and no knowledge; she gives up her money to claim a truer self among the community of peasant women. An anti-Royalist message is also present in what little Daniels offers about the war. For example, as Rose flees from her soldiering in the war, she succinctly sums up her commitment (and that of fellow volunteers) to the fight for social equality: "And do you imagine that this war with its blood and death and gore has meant nothing to me? For it is about no one being a servant to another. No more rich and idle by virtue of their birth but every person equal" (26). The women soldiers are staunchly on the anti-Royalist side.

The greatest share of the play's antipatriarchal energy is directed against the military and medicine, the two main sources of the men's death-power. The fact that three women pass as soldiers for part of the play mocks the bravado usually associated with the military. An even more direct critique of military war machines is voiced through the peace protests the women stage in London. And the one male soldier who appears attempts a rape for which two women soldiers kill him. The most intensive scrutiny of a patriarchal institution is reserved for professional medicine, a discipline just gaining its first foothold in the seventeenth century. While only one doctor appears in the course of the play, the shadow of the profession's quickly growing power unsettles the women in a most basic, most physical way. The specter of modern science and its threats to midwives and female control of birth are a main subject of four of the play's five songs. Each of the songs forces on the audience a Brechtian catapulting from a seventeenth-century dialect to a twentieth-century technical vocabulary. Rupture is also the topic of the songs. Two verses of "From a Dish to a Dish" suggest the alarms Daniels sounds against the scientific and medical moves that begin in the seventeenth century but continue in the twentieth:

> And hormonal manipulation is bombing women's ovaries
> And it's unethical not to experiment on spare embryos.
> We're in charge of the future, the future perfect nation.
> We're in charge of women's bodies, and isn't she a sensation.
>
> I look at her in the Petri dish
> And I fuck her with scientists' wish
> That I'll create a full-grown dish
> Who'll satisfy my every wish .
> And I'll father the perfect nation. (36)

One of the primary alternatives to the disturbing world these institutions delineate is the sexuality of the play's women. For most of these women, sexuality is defined through sex with other women. While heterosexual relations, ironically, empower women to bring forth life, they are not part of the play's resolution. Related to this female sexual alignment is Rose's discovery that while dressing as a man brings her new freedom, it distances her from her self. The play's resolution in a purely female sexual world is not, however, the main basis on which Daniels portrays a reclamation of the self. The power of language is the primary force of the feminist order Daniels proposes.

There are nearly as many references to language as to bodies in the play. Many of the early comments on "tongues" carry with them both positive connotations of female assertiveness and negative connotations that connect a talkative woman with shrewishness. Other comments provide direct indictments of male control of symbolic language. As the play's women begin to gain power, however, language becomes one of their primary tools. For example, just after Mary complains of the potential power men will gain with the printing press, Daniels signals that both Rose and Grace can claim the same power, since they read and write. The women's acuity in language is also clear in their own amateur etymology. Helen notes that for most men Eve is "but a misspelling of Evil" (29). Rose more materially deconstructs Lady H's use of the phrase "for love nor money," noting, "I was but musing on our language. Where the words 'for love' mean 'for nothing'" (34).

Two very public displays of this female command of language provide convincing evidence of the women's abilities to make political use of the linguistic powers they are acquiring. Helen's transformation from subservient wife to Quaker preacher provides the first example of the women's public control. Having made a central part of her new sermonizing agenda "the nature of women's accumbrements" (28), Helen preaches to crowds of women (for instance, those gathered in an inn in part 2, scene 2) with rousing feminist rhetoric:

> The battle of men against men is not the war of our time but the fight women have had for their lives. We have shaken their opinion of us as the weaker sex. . . . And they have responded with ways more forceful than ever before. Now is not the time for slowing down, for our lives swing more lightly in the balance than ever before. (37)

Second and even more central to the play is Rose's bold claim to the public sphere of playwrighting. From early in the play, a primary motivation for the women's gatherings has been to work out a performance of the play Rose is writing. Grace even expresses her dream of forming "a band of travelling players to go from county to country entertaining women" (19). A troupe is never formed, but Daniels's self-reflexive concentration on playwrighting (this even includes her self-parodic scene during which Grace and Rose discuss the relation of art to life [38–41]) intensifies the connection between this play and contemporary empowerment even more than the Brechtian songs do. The final action, which consists of the women burying Rose's play along with Grace, shows plainly that Rose's play and its language are for the twentieth century as much as for the seventeenth:

> Jane:    *(remembering)* That's why I brought this box for copied version
>          to be secured within and buried next to Grace.
> Rose:    But it's not had a life yet.
> Helen:   So if it doesn't cam to pass in your lifetime one day when you're
>          long gone it'll be uncovered.
> Rose:    But s'pose it never gets unearthed?
> Jane:    *(turning to face* Rose) You're not the only woman in the world,
>          Rose. (44)

The radical nature of Daniels's treatment of female self and sexuality lies in the reverberations of Rose's and Helen's language. The women in the play have learned how their world and even their selves have been conditioned by the male institutions operating all around them. Yet only in their increasingly assertive use of language can they begin to construct a lasting counterworld in which their values and concerns are operative. As Lacanian feminists point out, changes for women's selves and sexualities are predicated on their growing facility with linguistic constructions.

And Daniels, for one, never forgets the link between an empowering language and its physical connections. Deaf Ursula's signing, especially during the dumb show of part 2, scene 8, is a slick reminder of the inseparability of body and language. Similarly, the women's future plans to reclaim their "byrthrite" acknowledge both body and language: Lady H's goal is to set up schools for midwives (35, 43), while Rose's is "teaching girls to read and write" (43). Michael Billington, one of many reviewers who found more to criticize than to praise in *Byrthrite*, complained of Daniels's conjoining of a feminist critique of patriarchy and the successful recovery of selves: "The arguments about methods of childbirth are grafted arbitrarily onto an upbeat story about a female self-discovery" (review). Yet this play's power lies squarely in its blend of a forceful exposure of patriarchy with a coherent, joyous counterpoint. Daniels's acknowledgment of the complicated symbiosis of self, sexuality, and language makes her play representative of the more sophisticated stage presentations of women's identity and its sexual roots.

The authors of the plays I have considered here leave little doubt that they work from some connection between self-growth and sexuality. And there is clearly a growing awareness of the unique role language plays in such a psychological nexus. For some writers, a direct line between a feminist awareness of sexuality and the freedom to express the self must be privileged; yet as many more are grappling with the complexities of multiple selves and mutable sexualities. If identity is a "strategy," one understood as increasingly complex, then attention to the self demands consideration not only of sexuality, but also of language, gender, and society. As British women playwrights seek to change their world through comedy, their integrations of self and sexuality will continue to provide some significant readings of this unsteady realm.

## Chapter 11

# Redeeming Comedy's Core: Women and Community

Communities have traditionally been celebrated in comedy and relied on as the social glue by which divisions are healed, recreants reclaimed, and romances endorsed. Plays like *As You Like It, The Way of the World,* and *The Philanderer* are representative in using community as the onstage context for the marital couplings of the ending. These groups certify or coerce (if needed) such traditional connections. Other comic plays rely on community in less celebratory ways. In *Women in Mind,* for example, the community that gathers at the end marks Susan's exclusion from, not her inclusion in, the family groups. And in *The Constant Wife,* although John and Constance close out the play alone together onstage, it is their invisible social community that ensures the containment of Constance's rebellion. As I noted in each of the last three chapters, community remains a key element in the revisions of contemporary women's comedy. New models of female agency often grow out of group protagonists and group settings, and new endings posit communities that deny, simply through their existence, the status quo. The importance of community for women's rewriting of British comedy goes beyond the incorporation of plural heroines and reconstituted endings, however. Accordingly, in this chapter, I want to widen my consideration of how comedy's basis in community is being claimed by women. After a brief consideration of the range of manifestations community is currently taking, I turn to analysis of theater women's predilection for working in groups (both on the fringe and elsewhere) and then to several plays in which this predilection is an issue. Such study of both production and text will show that while community is basic to the conception and production of women's comedy, it proves to be an idea more complex and less universally positive than it at first promises to be.

Undeniably, community has been at the heart of women's recent ventures in British theater. Most prominently, theater groups and collectives have been responsible for the bulk of women's theater of the last two decades. Among the groups producing theater have been Monstrous Regiment, the Women's Theatre Group, Spare Tyre, Scarlet Harlets, Resisters, Mrs. Worthington's Daughters, Theatre of Black Women, Sadista Sisters, Parker and Klein, Hormone Imbalance, Beryl and the Perils, Hard Corps, Clean Break, Raving Beauties, and Siren Theatre Company. Organizations that have supported and encouraged the advancement of women in theater include the Conference of Women Theatre Directors and Administrators, Women in Entertainment, and the Feminist Theatre Study Group. Paines Plough, the Women's Playhouse Trust, and others have run workshops for women writers. Also building on this sense of group, the International Women in Experimental Theatre Conference, Magdalena (held in Cardiff in 1986), was organized around its participants' collaborative devising of a conference show. And even the publishing of plays has brought women together; several women's plays are frequently published together in single volumes, most notably in Methuen's now seven-part series, *Plays by Women* (1982–88), in Methuen's two-volume *Lesbian Plays* (1988–89), and also in collections like the Playwrights' Press's *Female Voices* (1987). One result of this omnipresence of communities is that even playwrights, who are traditionally used to the isolation of writing, judge their theater experiences in terms of groups. For Sue Townsend, collaboration with a group "is the only way to work" (interview). And for Bryony Lavery, group involvement ensures theatrical quality: "I am sure the best plays come from a dialogue or conversation between a lot of people" (interview).

As Townsend's and Lavery's comments suggest, an idealization of women's communities infuses present attitudes toward the pervasive communities of women's theater. To those within the groups and to those encouraging them critically, collections of theater women have come to represent both a vital support system and a base for subversive activity. Rachel Du Plessis amplifies the potential for subversion in suggesting that female community, contradicting the status quo through its very existence, defines a revolutionary fashioning of a new future (*Writing beyond the Ending*, 178–97).[1] In other words, the literary imagining of a group of women is inherently disruptive. Writing about theater from his anthropological perspective, Victor Turner corroborates this sense of the group as a threat to the status quo. Referring to the communities that theater creates during performance, he concludes that from them a natural subversion results. The collection of performers and audience gathered for each performance sets up "an alternative and more 'liberated' way of being socially human" (*From Ritual*, 51). With groups present both on- and offstage, theatrical comedy may be the most likely literary generator of the socially and ideologically powerful groups both Du Plessis and Turner valorize. And women playwrights indeed have explored options for transferring comedy's communally based, disruptive power beyond the boundaries of the theatrical space. Yet success has not always accompanied theatrical attempts to idealize women's groups and comic communities. In the analysis to follow, I will outline the range of communities, groups, and collectives that give shape to the contemporary theater while I also study the tensions that have accompanied the growing sophistication in women's theater communities both on- and offstage. The transition from my chapter 10 study of emerging selves to my present analysis of viable communities might seem reasonably direct. Women's theater has not moved as quickly as one might expect, however, from the agency of the individual woman to the valorization of the group.

I outlined in chapter 7 how the symbiotic development of theater groups (both male and female) and the British fringe theater affected men and women notably differently. The net result of the difference was that to accomplish the work they envisioned for themselves, women had to create their own groups committed to change in both theatrical production and in broader social and political realms. The men instrumental in establishing British alternative theater were as radical as the women in their theatrical practice and politics. But only the work of the women's groups has led to the development of a "women's theater" in the fringe and beyond; and only from the women's groups has come steady attention to the female communities of comedy.

## Women's Theater Groups

Women's theater collectives and groups can be usefully divided into two overlapping categories. First there are the groups that have been inspired by the anti-establishment spirit of the alternative theater: to study them is to outline the communal core from which the majority of women's plays and performances has sprung. Second, there are the groups that

have carried the agenda of fringe theater, with appropriate modifications, to venues beyond the fringe. To study them is to speculate
about future directions in women's theater communities.

## Women's Groups on the Fringe

For many who have been active in the theater, Joint Stock Theatre
Group has come to represent the best in collaborative, alternative theater. The group is widely credited with having defined collective theater
work on the fringe. Rob Ritchie's history of the company, *The Joint
Stock Book,* details how since 1974 the Joint Stock model has brought
people together in creating influential theater, including David Hare's
*Fanshen* (1975), Stephen Lowe's *The Ragged Trousered Philanthropists*
(1978), Caryl Churchill's *Cloud Nine* (1979), Howard Barker's *Victory*
(1983), and Sue Townsend's *The Great Celestial Cow* (1984). Joint
Stock's usual production method is a progression from group workshops
to author's writing to an extended rehearsal period. This roughly three-
step procedure for generating each play is guided by what have become
standard principles of most collective work: Joint Stock refuses to privilege the thoughts of writer and director, applauds the value of shared
experience, begins with a political commitment to its audience, and
revels in the extra work collective production requires. Additionally,
because its work is designed by and for the collection of individuals who
make up the group, Joint Stock's subject matter is community: "Typi-
cally, Joint Stock shows explore a particular community, caught at a
moment of disturbance or adjustment, and we are led to consider a
collective destiny, the shifting energies of a common life" (Ritchie, *Joint
Stock Book,* 11). As Turner describes "communitas," he suggests the
egalitarian goals of such group work. The more equal the members of a
group become, says Turner, the more their individuality is strengthened
and the more the group is cemented—"The more spontaneously 'equal'
people become, the more distinctively 'themselves' they become" (*From
Ritual,* 47).

Although Joint Stock's community has always included women and
has supported Caryl Churchill in particular, its pivotal place in championing egalitarian collaboration must be distinguished from its tangential
relationship to the work of predominantly or exclusively female groups.
Not only does the group continue to shun the label "feminist" (Dawson
interview), but Carole Hayman (one of the women who has been most

closely connected to the collective) also records the collective's history
of resistance to women's writing (Ritchie, *Joint Stock Book,* 110). In spite
of its tentative support of women, however, Joint Stock has set a high
standard for the theatrical quality of all collective work and for the close
scrutiny of the social and political status quo. The group's persistence
and its resistance to the conventions of theater have encouraged women's
groups by helping to establish an audience for fringe theater that is
receptive to the different kind of plays that collectively produced theater
can engender.

The energizing collective work that has fueled Joint Stock since
1974 has also powered collective theater predominantly by and for
women. While extending Joint Stock's antipathy to hierarchy and its
commitment to left-wing politics, the women's groups have also made
women the specific point of theatrical focus. The sizable presence of
these women's groups (many of which I listed earlier in this chapter) can
be gauged by the volume of work they have created; among the collectively written or produced plays I have already discussed in part 2 are
*Cloud Nine, Serious Money, The Great Celestial Cow, Pulp, Time Pieces,
Trafford Tanzi, Fixed Deal, Care and Control, Amid the Standing Corn,
Just Desserts, You've Gotta Be Kidding, Pax, Madonna in Slag City, New
Anatomies, Our Country's Good, Floorshow,* and *Time Gentlemen Please.*
Since Wandor *(Carry On)* and Itzin *(Stages in the Revolution)* have
mapped the general territory of such work, I would like to focus on two
particular aspects of the collective process that have had the greatest
impact on women's writing of comedy: the accommodation of specialization and the relationship between groups and writers. In creating their
communities and their comedy, women have constructed a collective
theater that has erased some old problems while creating some new
tensions.

In the most extreme experimentation with collective theater,
women's groups have dispensed with hierarchy altogether and have
made each production decision collectively—from the colors on publicity posters to salaries for collective members to semantic refinements of
dialogue. Although in their early days nearly every women's group
attempted to operate collectively, small groups such as the Scarlet Harlets and Parker and Klein have most successfully approached this ideal.
For the Scarlet Harlets, founded in 1982, a collective with a maximum
of four members has facilitated the intensive adaptation of the collective
model. Member Sue Long notes that for the three-month-long writing

and rehearsal period of their 1986 show *Toe on the Line,* the group's three members worked "totally together all the time" (Long and Neave interview). The result of their togetherness was a show in which the bonding of the three actors to one another was extended into an intimate relationship with the audience during production. For the two members of Parker and Klein, democracy has also come easily. Like the Scarlet Harlets, these two jointly hammered out each line of the dialogue for their first show, *Devilry* (1984). Yet in their next two years, they found the total rejection of specialization impractical. After sharing every task of their first show, Debby Klein has accepted the writing task, an outside director is hired, and both Klein and Parker continue to act. Parker and Klein have discovered relatively quickly a lesson most women's theater groups, and especially those of long standing, have now internalized, namely that specialization need not be equated with discriminatory hierarchies.

Thus, in the majority of women's theater collectives now operating, undifferentiated, vehemently antihierarchical collectives have gradually adopted a more flexible attitude about specialization and have acknowledged the efficiency of dividing responsibility. As with Parker and Klein, a common pattern has been for groups to find that their early commitment to the complete sharing of work naturally matured into a production process in which individual members could polish newly found specialized skills. Jane Boston, a founding member of Siren Theatre Company, is articulate in analyzing this recurring movement away from passionate, completely democratic collectives to a specialization not dependent on hierarchy. The process of putting together the group's first three shows closely resembled that of a woman's consciousness-raising group. As Boston explains, each of the three members worked on everything, including writing: "We thrashed every word out. . . . Every word was part of us. . . . It was very painfully collective" (interview). But the political clarification and personal confidence this relentlessly collective process brought to the group gave the women the professionalism, in subsequent shows, to divide and develop their individual skills. For Siren as for other women's groups, it was specifically the collaborative process that allowed the women to identify the theater skills they had not been able to practice or even test elsewhere. Individual members focused on music or writing or directing as suited their talents. And in the encouraging environment of the group, the women also found that it was not specialization of skills that had stood in their way in traditional theater,

but a competitive, nonsupportive environment, a hierarchy that devalued actors' opinions, and a drama (mostly male-authored) that over-
looked women's points of view. The new openness to specialization and
skills, which had originally been rejected by these groups as male preserves, has contributed to a growing maturity in women's theater work.
So while Boston mourns the loss of "that collective distinction," she
acknowledges that by trading the demanding time and energy commitment of the early collective work for the polished shows that resulted
from specialization, Siren has advanced (interview).

As my discussion of group-generated plays and shows in chapters 8 and
9 demonstrates, this increasingly sophisticated group production has engendered new priorities in writing. Referring to collective work by both
men and women, Ritchie generalizes that Joint Stock writers produce
"plays so strikingly different from their other work" when writing with
the collective (*Joint Stock Book,* 12). Writers Caryl Churchill and Lou
Wakefield identify this sense of difference when they both report that in
writing *for* a group, playwrights end up writing *about* a group. Churchill
pinpoints the difference in a new equality of actors' parts: "Because
everyone is involved it's taken for granted that everyone will have good
parts. So you can't write a couple of main characters and give everyone
else very little to do" (Betsko and Koenig, *Interviews,* 79). Similarly,
Wakefield connects the close working relationship between writer and
actors to the writer's new need to be skilled at group scenes: "Speaking
as a writer, it is ever so difficult to think about having two or more
people talking at a time. You inevitably forget them" (interview). Significantly, the changes Churchill and Wakefield agree on privilege the
community that comedy depends on. The literary experimentation that
collective work can be credited with promoting must, however, be balanced
against the loss in spontaneity that has accompanied the maturation of
such work. Once more, Turner provides useful terms for understanding
this change. As he traces a development from "spontaneous communitas" to a much more institutionalized "normative comunitas," he marks
the loss in subversive potential that must accompany such a transformation (*From Ritual,* 47–51). Steve Gooch *(All Together Now)* notes, similarly, that in the aging of alternative theater groups, the revolutionary
eventually accommodates itself to the system in some way. The specific
manifestations of such changes and growth, losses and gains, can be
noted in the work of the two oldest and most influential women's theater
groups—the Women's Theatre Group and Monstrous Regiment.

The Women's Theatre Group, founded in 1974, has played a prominent role in defining the possibilities of women's collective theater and
in doing so has left a record of the complexities of collaborative work.
*Time Pieces* (1982), for example, both suffered and gained from its several stages of collaboration and its loosely defined relationships between
director and actors. *Time Pieces* was originally written in part by actor
members who had researched the history of British women in the twentieth century. However, the final script was collated and shaped by
director (and nonmember) Lou Wakefield, in what had become a necessary deviation from group control. Unfortunately, the shifting roles of
director, writer, and actor and the resultant misunderstandings about the
sharing of decision-making power created tensions and resulted in a
production that Wakefield later voiced mixed responses to. Looking
back, she found it, variously, "simplistic," "naive," and "very, very
jolly" (interview). To compare *Time Pieces* with the Women's Theatre
Group's later collaboration with Deborah Levy, *Pax* (1985), is to focus
on a different set of rewards and tensions that grew from a still more
complicated joint effort. While *Time Pieces* collects a series of vignettes
around two characters' perusing of a family photo album, the four characters of *Pax* are only teasingly and mysteriously connected. The shadowy web of relationships and actions in the play stems in part from the
fact that *Pax* is less the result of workshop than of a commission from
the group to Levy "to write an 'anti-nuclear' play" (author's note following published play text, 112). The added maturity and obscurity of this
play are emblematic of the sort of collaborative effort that is now often
liberating the writer, challenging the company, and frustrating or de-
lighting the audience.

   *Pax* has four "archetypal" characters, each of whom has a crucial
role in the development of the play's political statements. The Keeper,
to whose "retreat" the others—the Mourner, HD (the Hidden Daughter), and the Domesticated Woman—come, is central in facilitating the
group's interaction by creating an atmosphere in which the characters
are emotionally and ethically challenged. The two scenes in which the
four characters recreate the funerals of the Mourner's mother and HD's
father show most directly how the interconnections of the play are designed to encourage growth both collectively and individually. In act 2,
scene 5, HD helps the Mourner accept her mother's death by playing the
role of the mother and explaining the mother's difficult life choices. This
moving interaction allows all four characters, in the second funeral of

act 2, scene 7, to come to personal realizations during the dramatization of HD's father's funeral. Levy and the Women's Theatre Group have created a play whose group genesis has infused all of its parts: it has an equal distribution of acting parts, it has individual and collective growth intertwined, and it offers celebration but only as muted by the strains of tension among characters. Levy's subsequent collaboration with the group the following year (*Our Lady* [1986]) reinforces my contention that this particular collaboration of group and writer has brought both to the forefront of a maturing community theater. One reviewer of *Our Lady*, for example, found that the "innovative" work of the Women's Theatre Group complemented Levy's "fiercely original" and daring work (Carne). For the Women's Theatre Group, then, collective work has resulted in a succession of shows that has moved the group toward both greater reliance on playwrights and a more complex feminism. In the process, the more comic scenes of *Time Pieces* have been replaced by the more encumbered joy of a play like *Pax*.

Monstrous Regiment, founded in 1975, one year after the Women's Theatre Group, has shared in the development of sophisticated collaborative work. This second group too has been conscious of and has profited from the need to accommodate the writer's special skills. As administrator Sandy Bailey notes, "We have moved much, much more to recognizing writing as the skill and craft that it is . . . a very particular skill" (interview). And recent production choices have been expressions of the group's interest in maintaining a fluidity among the many possibilities for joining collective work and playwrighting. In addition to the commissioning of a playwright to work with them in a series of workshops and rehearsals similar to Joint Stock's, the group has pursued other creative options. It has presented women's plays from French, Italian, and American theater; it has devised shows without an "outside" writer; and it has even produced plays by men (quite successfully in Jorge Diaz's *My Song is Free* [1986], a play about women political prisoners in Chile). Monstrous Regiment's long-lasting collaboration with writer Bryony Lavery constitutes something of a fifth option for the group, one that best illustrates how women's penchant for comedy has developed along with women's theater communities.

Lavery's writing for Monstrous Regiment includes *Time Gentlemen Please* (1978), *Gentlemen Prefer Blondes* (1979–80), *Calamity* (1983–84), and *Origin of the Species* (1984–85). The continued interdependence of group and writer has come in for the criticism that the collaboration has inhibited the advancement of both parties; in reviewing *Calamity,* for example, Michael Coveney linked a lack of animation in longtime Monstrous Regiment actors Gillian Hanna and Mary McCusker to Monstrous Regiment's inability to venture beyond Lavery and her writing. Ironically, however, praise for *Calamity* also linked its success to the cohesion of the group's and the writer's efforts. Lavery's own feelings about collaborative work reinforce this more positive focus on group work as she notes that writing within a community is the only reasonable way to work:

> My work is something that is part of a group of people which is actors, designers, administrators, and audience. So I can't imagine a situation in which I would write in a garret. . . . I like a lot of people. Actors, designers, directors have supplied ideas that are in my script and vice versa. I would hate to write plays which I would then send off and were done by people I didn't know. What a curious thing to do. (Interview)

Though Lavery disdains labels like "comic" or "tragic," her greatest skill is in writing comedy. And in her comedy the intersection of collaborative writing and community produces effective theater. In *The Origin of the Species,* for example, Lavery cements the developing relationship between the "old Lady" Molly and her million-year-old but youthful archeological find, Victoria, through laughter. The community of this play is an intimate one of two, but the two women's growth is interdependent. While this play shares with *Pax* a fluid movement from serious to tragic to comic to brooding, happy moods predominate in *The Origin.* Collaborative theater—and perhaps especially its comic products—cannot and should not always be removed from tension or trouble. And thus *The Origin* is not better than *Pax* for being brighter and less threatening. Yet those collaborations that move in the direction of comedy seem to profit most highly from group production. In such situations, in other words, the method of production reinforces the comic dependence on community. In reviewing Monstrous Regiment's 1987 show *Alarms* (by Susan Yankowitz), Lyn Gardner noted that "it is directed and performed with a conviction and vitality that we have come, over ten years, to expect from Monstrous Regiment." As part of the "establishment" of women's alternative collaborative theater, Monstrous Regiment, like the Women's Theatre Group, continues to work on the assumption that theater for women must grow out of a group of women. Its success with comedies suggests also how frequently comedy has become the vehicle for group production.

The variations on collaboration, community, and comedy that the Women's Theatre Group and Monstrous Regiment have most prominently put before London audiences have been repeated in the work of other groups. Before I consider the particular problems that now attach to the joining of writers and groups, I would like to finish my consideration of the various directions in group work with a brief consideration of two additional collaborative products, *Chiaroscuro* and *The Fence*, which raise additional issues about the products of collaboration.

*Chiaroscuro* (1986) focuses on racial issues. The fourth drama supported by the Theatre of Black Women, this play authored by Jackie Kay braids together the stories of four young women, each of whom has faced or is facing racism, sexism, and/or homophobia. The four are given roughly equal treatment; and each experiences extremes of hope and despair. The play ends, however, on a song, sung by all four, that stresses the progress they have all made toward strengthened identity. As in the plays of Monstrous Regiment and the Women's Theatre Group, the way the group develops is as important as the personal growth of the individual characters. As one reviewer neatly sums up, the message for all is that "only when we face our fears do we find our strengths" (Tudor). This play is the product of a black women's theater group committed to examining issues of racism as well as sexism. But recently women's theater groups that are not primarily black have joined such groups in searching for an ideal of community that is racially integrated. Once again the work of Joint Stock has been prominent as several of its productions have focused on racial matters and involved racially mixed casts: Townsend's *The Great Celestial Cow* had one white woman join seven Indian cast members, and in Churchill's *A Mouthful of Birds* (1986) the cast was racially integrated. Similarly, the Women's Theatre Group and Levy's *Our Lady* presents three would-be Madonnas, two of whom are black. The fact that reviewers of all three productions questioned the "purpose" of such integration (Jan McKenley complained of *Our Lady* that "the only mystery in this pretentious piece is why Levy poses two black women as potential Madonnas") only underlines the continuing necessity for groups committed to erasing all prejudice to continue creating racially mixed communities.

The Greenham Collective's *The Fence* (1984) is a final example of

collective work that suggests both how widespread the idea of egalitarian
production is and how difficult it can be to harness the energies of the
group. The play, written by all of its six participants, recalls the earlier,
more democratic models of collaboration. That communal composition
helps to account for the play's many presentations of and tributes to
groups. While none of these qualities sets the play apart, the published
documentation of its group birth does. Accompanying the nine pages
of the play text are nine more pages recording the six women's experiences of the production. All six credit the community effort for personal
as well as political transformations. Fiona Wood states this most directly:
"Women together are strong. And together through this journey I have
discovered strengths I never knew I had" (117). Carmel Caddell links the
model of collective writing to her hopes for women's political power:
"This play is based on trust. Half-way through its making I realised how
depressed I would feel if we didn't get it together—it would be very hard
for me to go on hoping for a peaceful world if we six women couldn't
find a way to make a whole out of our very different paths" (117). Yet
these women found, as do most who collaborate, that frustrations are a
built-in part of the process of community building. While Sally Wood
details the disagreements, misunderstandings, and dissatisfactions that
plagued the women, Max Holloway offers encouragement in her report
of ups and downs:

> But a few words of warning. You need at least four to five months
> to work together and for each person to have a commitment to the
> group. This is a very sensitive way of working and growing and it
> should be seriously acknowledged that collective work means ex-
> actly that. Collective therefore means supportive together, whilst
> each retaining one's own powerful individuality. These are the in-
> gredients for trust. Be prepared for extreme swings of energy and
> trust. This is essential to growth. (132).

Any group of women who have collaborated on a theatrical production
would report, similarly, a mixture of pride, achievement, and disappointment. This persistent mixture raises a central question, however:
What is the lasting importance of collaborative, collective theater to
women and their comedy?

Basically, the communities of women's fringe theater have left a
twofold legacy. First, the context of women's theater has irrevocably

been established as communal. In many play programs, "written by" has been replaced with "text by," "scripted by," or "devised with company by" to stress the joint creativity that has inspired the vision of the play. It is equally common now for women (whether they are writers, directors, or administrators) with ideas they want realized on stage to turn to women's groups. Theaters like the Oval House, Drill Hall, and the Soho Poly commit much of their resources, time, and space to women's work. And the recent formation of the Women's Comedy Workshop stands as but the latest proof that the bonds are strong between such continuing collective work and comedy. Two of this group's first shows, *Mummy* (1987) and *Puppet States* (1988) (both written by Bryony Lavery), are evidence of the sophistication that group work is bringing to women's comedy; one reviewer of *Mummy* speaks of a "complex style" situated in the "shadowy world" between drama and performance theater (Connor). Although the workshop's experimentations with myth, black humor, satire, and feminism have earned them mixed reviews, the fact that a women's theater group dedicated to comedy has formed so recently marks the persisting need for theater women to bring together community and celebration. In discussing the accommodation of specialization in women's collective theater in the last few pages, I have considered issues and plays whose connection to comedy may sometimes have seemed tangential. Yet my goal has not been to suggest that every play produced by a theater group is comic. Rather, my goal has been to note how the production communities of contemporary theater coincide with comedy's basis in community and how these communities intensify women's tendency to write plays grounded in joy. Most women's groups have not, like the Women's Comedy Workshop, made comedy their expressed goal. Yet most, by dedicating themselves to group work, have taken up residency in the community that comedy depends on and studies.

While women's theater groups have promoted the development of comedy and its communities, the second legacy of collective work has been growing tensions among women in the theater. I have already described several times the trade-offs that are involved in community-driven theater, noting, for example, that the commitment to egalitarian measures can be wildly inefficient. Lyn Gardner, Mary Remnant, Sue Dunderdale, and others keeping watch over women's theater find the problems of group work not incidental but pandemic, even suggesting that the usefulness of collective theater for women has been played out

(interviews). Dunderdale, in fact, argues that such theater has been unhealthy for a long time:

> I don't think they [women's theater groups] would have outlived
> their usefulness if they had been stringent about handing over, to
> constant generations of young people. What happened was that
> there was always a[n unchanging] group of women. . . . [The
> groups need] a constant changeover and flow to challenge them. If
> they stick they don't challenge their ideas, they find ways of ma-
> nipulating each other, they get stuck, they don't challenge them-
> selves as artists. They get weaker and weaker. (Interview)

As changing politics and diminishing resources have exacerbated the
stressful nature of the situation, the collaborative relationship between
theater groups and authors has been the most threatened. Women playwrights, many of whom owe their careers to women's groups and most
of whom are sympathetic with the groups' political goals, now often
find that what they consider their authorial territory overlaps with what
the group considers its prerogative. Consequently, writers have become
apprehensive about taking on group work. Even Deborah Levy, who
has found early backing for her work primarily from women's groups
(not an unusual case for a woman writer) admits to a "confusion about
collectives," which can be either "hell to work with" or "wonderful"
(interview). Playwrights Timberlake Wertenbaker and Michelene Wandor concur that nonstressful joint ventures are still possible when groups
clarify—before collaboration begins—exactly what they want from a
writer (interviews). Yet such prescribed conditions can often mean a
limited, unfulfilling role for the author. Not surprisingly then, when
playwrights are expected to bring their full talents and inspiration to
bear on a project (and this is most often the case), clashes invariably
develop between author and commissioning group. Wertenbaker describes one particularly bad experience early in her career: "I used to
have meetings with them [a women's group] in which I would walk out
in despair, and I almost didn't write the play. . . . A group will pull itself
together by attacking an outsider . . . and the writer is always the outsider" (interview). While Wandor, Pam Gems, and Louise Page have
voiced similar disappointment with joint ventures, the theater groups,
too, have their horror stories to tell. Because of disagreements between
author Melissa Murray and group members, Monstrous Regiment had

to cancel *The Execution* midway through its 1982 tour. And according to actor Hazel Maycock, the 1986 Women's Theatre Group production of *Fixed Deal* suffered from continuing interpretive disagreements between the group and its author/director team (interview). The fact that most of these groups survive on shoestring budgets and year-to-year luck with funding and audiences underscores the precarious financial situation that contributes to this unstable artistic combination of author and group.

As a result of this increasing tension, the two most powerful forces in women's theater today—the theater groups and the women playwrights—are often now pursuing divergent goals. The women's groups are struggling to maintain their politics, visibility, and status by supporting a succession of new women writers; and the best-known writers, who can choose where to produce their work, are frequently maturing in male-run theaters and companies. In these new connections between established theater communities (often outside of the fringe) and women writers, a second generation of uneasy relations is arising. The Royal Court theater, which operates between the opulent spaces of the West End and the cramped quarters of the fringe, has made a concerted effort to produce women's work, including plays by Caryl Churchill, Sue Townsend, Timberlake Wertenbaker, Sarah Daniels, Andrea Dunbar, Anne Devlin, and Louise Page. In 1986, the Court's literary manager, Philip Palmer, reported that approximately one quarter of the theater's plays were written by women and one quarter directed by women (interview). Yet Carole Hayman, who has been a part of the Court's formal hierarchies and informal networks for many years, predicts that women's involvement in the Royal Court will be limited as long as men run it (interview). In other words, despite the increased presence of women, the Court's community remains a hierarchical one.

At the two nationally subsidized theaters there has been, likewise, an increasing though undependable attention to women's work. The National Theatre has recently formed a women's company and has produced work by Michelene Wandor, Debbie Horsfield, and Sarah Daniels. The support of the Royal Shakespeare Company (RSC) for women has been of longer standing, which means, on the one hand, that it has produced major writers such as Churchill, Page, Gems, Wertenbaker, and Levy, and, on the other hand, that several women now connect their RSC work with the trouble that established theater signals for women. Several of these writers have expressed specific concerns about the company's support for women. Page, whose *Golden Girls* premiered at the RSC, says of the company that its message to women writers is "not to write about women" (interview). Gems, after seeing *Queen Christina* (1977), *Camille* (1984), and *The Danton Affair* (1986) done by the company, is still saddened that a woman often leaves behind her female network to gain the major exposure the RSC can offer (interview). Wertenbaker, who translated *Mephisto* (1985) for the company, turned down an offer to write for its women's group, having envisioned that the tensions of collaborative work in the subsidized theater would be magnified there (interview). And Levy, who did write for the RSC women's group, produced *Heresies* (1986), a play whose mixed critical reception sums up the way communally inspired and generated plays continue to clash with the established theater.

   *Heresies* resulted from over a year of formal and informal research, rehearsals, and workshops. The result is a play that binds together the stories of an architect whose inventive planning clashes with his vindictive response to his family, a Hungarian woman struggling to keep custody of her child, two elderly women whose wisdom and music delights and helps those younger, and a woman confused by her conflicting connections to her husband and her lover. As Levy's play developed around her sense of an architect as someone who creates "some part of the face of the future" (play program), she had the company visit architectural sites like Euston Station and the new Lloyd's building. The collective production models that Levy had known on the fringe were clearly the basis of this play's genesis. The production that resulted was greeted with a mixture of praise and support, ridicule and anger. Reviewers dissatisfied with the work tended to make some connection between collaboration and formal failure. For David Nathan, *Heresies* was dismissible as a play seemingly "written by a committee." Michael Billington criticized its lack of "any clear dramatic focus." And Michael Coveney criticized its narrative movement in concluding that it "emerges sideways." Ironically, reviewers with positive responses also linked the play's group genesis to its success. Lyn Gardner described a play "beautifully presented by a cast and production team who have total commitment to and faith in the material." For several reviewers, the play was effectively intense, aiming at a worthy goal of "plurality" (Warner). And to Michael Ratcliffe, the play's vibrant sense of community was its most sterling quality: "The Group will develop and do better work, but there is already a harmoniousness to it which is not solemn and a dignity which is not dull." These reviews document the uneasy marriage of established theater to female authorship and female community. Yet in the qualified positive response that the play generated lies the suggestion that the marriage will continue.

The difficulty of bringing women's groups and female authors together has had an effect on most of the drama women are now writing, replicating with a new cast of characters the theater's standard tension between the author and others. The specific effect on comedy, though not immediately evident, is basic. Implied in the material I have just offered is a general separation of women's theater groups (though not women playwrights) from the more prominent London stages. In a parallel fashion, women's comedies, which privilege groups—either the groups who have contributed to putting the plays together or the groups actually *in* the plays—have remained, by and large, off the larger stages. A few of the comedies I have considered in part 2 have been produced at the Royal Court (most, interestingly, have come from Joint Stock and not from all-women's groups), but only a handful have been connected to the National Theatre or the Royal Shakespeare Company. Levy's *Heresies* includes the comic among its many moods, but Levy's play did not fare particularly well with the theater establishment. As more women come to the main stages, their connection to comedy will make its way with them. Both the stages and the women's comedy seem likely to change in the process. It remains to be seen how the threat inherent in women's comic communities will affect broad-based theatrical communities.

Women's Groups beyond the Fringe

In considering the work of women at the National Theatre and the RSC, I have initiated my study of the second main category of women's theater communities, those that function primarily beyond the fringe. Out of the work nurtured by the alternative theater have grown several women's theater groups that aspire to a position in the theater establishment. As a consequence, their work is less politically extreme. Their communities, however, continue to be challenged by some of the same tensions and instabilities that have beset alternative theater groups. I will consider two such groups, the Women's Playhouse Trust, which has fought to make women's theater financially independent, and the

Colway Theatre Trust, which has spearheaded a substantial movement to redefine the broader theater community.

From its inception in 1980, the Women's Playhouse Trust has distinguished itself from alternative theater groups as its members have assumed that women no longer need to exist in what they consider—in every way other than aesthetically—the ghetto of fringe theater. Thus the group has set as a main goal the acquisition of a large, established theater building (none of the other women's theater groups has a theater building, though this is common for fringe companies), and has campaigned intensively for the "big money" such a purchase demands. Sue Parrish, one of the four founding members of the group, acknowledges that the Trust is conservative in its feminism, since it has developed toward capitalistic goals. But she stresses that the Trust credits the "extremists" of fringe, feminist theater with having made possible the Trust's grandiose goals. While the Trust pursues a "high profile," says Parrish, it is still a part of the larger community of women in theater— "We all give each other validity" (interview).

Even without its own theater, the group has brought most of its productions to high-profile theaters: Aphra Behn's *The Lucky Chance* at the Royal Court in 1984, Ntozake Shange's *Spell #7*, also at the Court in 1985, Louise Page's *Beauty and the Beast* at the Old Vic in December, 1985, Clare McIntyre's *Low Level Panic* at the Royal Court Upstairs in March, 1988, and Winsome Pinnock's *A Hero's Welcome,* also at the Royal Court Upstairs, in 1989. As these plays demonstrate, the Trust has set as its goal the production of plays by women: "We are there as a forum for women playwrights, contemporary women playwrights and dead ones as well (but there aren't so many of those)" (Parrish interview). In addition, the Trust has planned a series of commissions—of which *Beauty and the Beast* was the first—to women writers. Perhaps of greater significance, six of those plays are slated to be part of the Trust's unprecedented co-commissioning agreement with Methuen Publishing: Methuen has agreed to share commissioning costs with the Trust on its first six original shows, thereby gaining the option to publish the new work. This joint commissioning, the first of its kind in Great Britain, is an indication both of the support that does exist for women's work in traditional theater hierarchies and of the Trust's ability to earn such support.[2]

However, because it has obtained its successes through coalitions with publishers, corporate sponsors, and aristocratic board members, and because it has accepted much of the traditional theater hierarchy, the Women's Playhouse Trust has disappointed many of the fringe theater women who, with their own pioneering, made the Trust possible. Sandy Bailey of Monstrous Regiment voices the exclusion many feel: "They [The Women's Playhouse Trust] unfortunately have sold out. . . . They have had to tone the whole thing down. . . . It has moved beyond us" (interview). Sue Long of the Scarlet Harlets echoes the complaint, noting that the Trust has "made no attempt to contact women's groups" (Long and Neave interview). And Louise Page and Pam Gems, both formerly on the Trust's board, are no longer affiliated with its work. In addition to these symptoms of uneasiness, the Trust has been accused of adopting the hierarchies of male-operated theaters. It has also not, to date, turned to the collaborative devising so common in women's alternative theater. Thus, just as women working at the Royal Court, the National Theatre, and the RSC have had difficulty negotiating the maintenance of their politics and community in the established theater, so too has the Women's Playhouse Trust been limited by the theatrical context it has chosen for itself. Undeniably, the Trust has played an important role in putting women's work on the main stages of London. But the Trust's unique position is also likely to occasion a continuing debate about what changes come to women's work and communities when women move from the liberal fringe to the more conservative, more commercial West End. Although the Trust began with comedy in *The Lucky Chance,* most of its productions have not been identifiably comic. Page's *Beauty and the Beast* is an important example of excursions from realism, as I noted in chapter 8; and McIntyre's *Low Level Panic* is a significant study of sexuality that I will discuss in chapter 12. Joyful, comic plays, however, while so central to women's current theatrical enterprise, may not be the ticket to the Trust's success.

A second, more anomalous case of new directions in women's theater communities is the Colway Theatre Trust, until late 1985 under Ann Jellicoe's direction.[3] Although the Trust and its "community plays" owe nothing directly to the pioneering of the London fringe groups, its work, like that of the Women's Playhouse Trust, is connected to the new processes and arrangements to which women's groups have committed themselves.[4] Jellicoe founded the Colway Theatre Trust in 1978 in Lyme Regis, her home in Dorset. Although the aims of the group are not predominantly feminist, production protocol resembles that of the London women's groups in its emphasis on shared work and its sustained demands for time and energy. In her book *Community Plays,* Jellicoe describes in detail the production process of her community plays, stressing the extended time commitments (1–2 years), the huge number of participants (up to two hundred local, mostly amateur, actors and a total of three or four hundred participants), and the invigorating results: "a new form of theatre" (*Community Plays,* 8). Making the local community the subject, process, and product of her efforts, Jellicoe has produced a community-based theater that both expands and curtails the efforts of other women-led groups to connect theater and women.

From one perspective, feminists can applaud the way Jellicoe's community theater allows for transformative theater experiences. Referring to the plays' harnessing of multiple individual energies to create and alter large communities, Jellicoe finds these productions "the most exciting work I have ever done" (interview). Even Howard Barker, whose plays are usually brutal and pessimistic, has been altered by the communal process:

> Seeing that production [the 1981 production of his *The Poor Man's Friend*], I realized that the theatre is also a civilizing influence. I don't mean civilizing in the sense that a writer and producer are coming to town, offering education to the people, but of the civility of a community which is drawn together and develops its strength from sharing in an artistic experience. . . . it's an experience of celebration in a way that no professional production I have ever worked on before is a celebration. (*Community Plays,* 122)

Just as powerful are the transformations experienced by the amateur participants from towns like Lyme Regis, Bridport, Sherborne, and Axe Valley, who find not only that the play process alters the individual consciousness but also that it generates new social awareness in the community (see *Community Plays,* 257–61).

Not surprisingly, this transformative, communal atmosphere invites—almost prescribes—comedy. Jellicoe notes that Barker's *The Poor Man's Friend* (1981) was "extremely funny," uncharacteristically so for the playwright (interview). And David Edgar understandably finds "carnival" the best way of categorizing the work Jellicoe has promoted: "And increasingly I think that what Ann Jellicoe has created over the years are not plays or pageants, but kinds of carnival, and it is that reality which provides the sense of an event not just of commitment and energy but of moral force and artistic scale" (*Community Plays,* 120).[5]

While Trust productions have encouraged transformations through comic communities, Jellicoe's work departs from the feminism of the London community theater. Specifically, an ambiguous relationship exists between Trust productions and both women and politics. Jellicoe's own play, *The Western Women* (1984), which she describes as "a high point in our [the Trust's] work," is perhaps the most ostensibly feminist of the productions Jellicoe oversaw. Jellicoe herself connects the play with both women and comic joy: "I think that the whole play has something to do with the fact that it was a celebration of women" (interview). The play, which is about a group of seventeenth-century Lyme Regis women who protect their city from the Royalists during siege, in fact, puts onstage the women's communities that have been the backbone of the Trust's people-intensive operation. The central presence of women onstage in this play was replicated in all stages of production. For example, Jellicoe had originally commissioned another woman, Fay Weldon, to write the script. When the commission did not work out, Jellicoe took over from Weldon. And the fact that the play was focused on a group of women seems to have made it easier for Jellicoe to write. She credits the group of actors with offering instrumental help on the script itself, in basic collaborative fashion:

> With *The Western Women* we were able to improvise from strength. The atmosphere at rehearsal was so good and the cast so confident that if something was not working we felt no despair but simply looked for a better way. One of the finest scenes did not arrive until very late in the rehearsal period. . . . As we rehearsed the women began to find a voice and drawing together finally, with thrilling force, gathered the whole community to resist the enemy. The episode was shattering in its intensity of feeling. The sense of fulfillment amongst these women, both as characters in the play and as real people was deeply moving. (*Community Plays,* 33)

Sheila Yeger's work on *The Ballad of Tilly Hake* (1985) also marks the Trust's combination of women and community: Jellicoe notes that this woman writer taught the Trust the most "about how a writer may interact with a community" (*Community Plays,* 34). *The Western Women* and *The Ballad of Tilly Hake* are exceptions in their female base, however, for although women have provided the Trust's sustaining energy and camaraderie, Jellicoe has fought a constant battle to get her writers to provide sufficient parts for women. She has even gone so far as to recommend that the Trust's commissioned writers (still mostly male) provide for "baskets" of women to ensure parts for all women volunteers. And while her own efforts have both directly and indirectly supported women in the communities with whom she works, Jellicoe discourages any notion of politics—feminist, socialist, or otherwise—in her enterprise. She concludes bluntly, "Politics are divisive" (*Community Plays*, 122). Thus the Trust's community productions have avoided contemporary settings to avoid political viewpoints that might disrupt the community as a whole. More specifically, Jellicoe asks that the socialist writers who have worked with her put aside their own political agendas. While it is impossible to erase politics, the Trust seeks to distance them as much as is possible by making its priority community history, pride, and cooperation. Such prohibitions against political activism, though sometimes grudgingly accepted by authors, have had the effect Jellicoe is after. Her policies have fostered artistic growth as they have ensured more harmonious community involvement. Sheila Yeger first bristled on being instructed to mute her politics, but now endorses the exercise: "What happened was that a very, kind of, coarse play, one in which I made my usual statements in my usual way, had somehow been transmuted into a much more subtle and, I think, much more human play. I was somehow persuaded off my customary soapbox and it had been a good thing that I had been persuaded" (Jellicoe, *Community Plays*, 123).

Jellicoe's community theater is not designed for feminism or politics, although both have informed her decisions and prescriptions. But because Jellicoe's work is multiply based on communities—much more so than the Women's Playhouse Trust—its connections to comedy are more secured. Central to Jellicoe's work has been the kind of celebration that comes from cementing a community. Yet Jellicoe's experimenting with community theater suggests, as does the work sponsored by the Women's Playhouse Trust, that beyond the fringe, women's theater communities lose many of their distinctive qualities. As I will suggest further in chapter 12, the contexts of women's theater influence both the politics and the reception of that theater. And the appearance of and dependence on comedy varies with the context.

## Communities in Women's Plays

Although women's work in the theater has primarily taken place in the
alternative theater of London's fringe, both the Women's Playhouse
Trust and the Colway Theatre Trust are representative of women's communities in more established theater venues. Both the more radical and
the more conventional groups suggest that any constellation of women
in theater points not only to community concern, but also to changes in
traditional organization and hierarchy within the theater company. The
various groupings of women have also resulted in a corpus of plays
largely or in part comic. Invigorated by the power they have created for
themselves through their communities, women have often privileged
celebration and laughter in their productions.

The plays that the varied groups of women offstage have produced
are the most widely accessible evidence of the intertwined presence of
comedy and communities in British women's contemporary drama. In
the plays themselves, frequent subjects are the benefits in and the pressures of groups of women. As I have shown previously, many recent
plays focus thematically and structurally on groups of women, among
them *Bazaar and Rummage; Steaming; Golden Girls; Dusa, Fish, Stas, and
Vi; Madonna in Slag City; When I Was a Girl . . . ; Red Devils; Amid the
Standing Corn; The Great Celestial Cow; The Fence; Chiaroscuro; Basin;
Time Pieces; My Mother Said I Never Should;* and *Byrthrite.* While some
of these plays have resulted directly from group collaboration and workshop (both *Amid the Standing Corn* and *The Great Celestial Cow* are Joint
Stock productions, for example) the majority have been more indirectly
inspired by and toward groups. I am not claiming that women's theater
is more naturally communal than the norm. Theater is always a communal process dependent on both cooperation and division of duty. Yet the
British women playwrights who have begun and refined their trade in
the context of collaboration and group inspiration have produced plays
in which women characters especially are qualitatively different—they
are likely to connect to other women. I have written in previous chapters
about the most obvious results of this community influence—group protagonists, redefined and plural endings, and the shared maturation of
selves. I would like to close this chapter with a look at the expansive
consideration of female-to-female relationships that has also resulted in
contemporary plays.

Feminist considerations of British drama from Shakespeare to Stoppard invariably note the paucity of female friendship and relationship. In part 1, I noted this absence even in plays both comic and woman-centered. The plays women are now writing have become the first substantial body of works where women respond primarily to each other. Andrea Dunbar's experience in writing *Shirley* (1986) is instructive. In completing her play, Dunbar found that a planned concentration on male-female relationships gave way to an increasingly prominent female focus. Setting out to explore Shirley's teenage relationships with boys, Dunbar was compelled more often to attend to Shirley's relationship to her mother (Hayman interview). The play ends gently, with the two women—free for the first time in the play from troubled relationships with men—chatting comfortably about their own connection. Other plays provide similar evidence that, in many situations where women have traditionally been presented as adversaries, a group context and community consciousness have encouraged positive new representations of women and their relationships. And in plays like *Ripen Our Darkness* (1981), *Loving Women* (1984), and *The Great Celestial Cow* (1984), the writers actually portray the transition from patriarchal to female models of women's relationships. Such transformation often serves as the foundation for the play's upbeat and joyful comic endings. None of this is surprising.[6]

What is surprising is how the communities of women's theater have prompted playwrights to examine the negative as well as the positive shadings of women's interactions. In many of the earliest women's plays, woman-to-woman relationships were a panacea for personal and social dilemmas. Men were bad, women were good, and the more women the better. A group of women automatically meant feminism, solidarity, and celebration. In many plays still, women finding other women leads to happiness, positive change, and/or progress. I have discussed such variations in preceding chapters. But a growing maturity in women's theater has also freed playwrights to explore women's relationships, especially family relationships, with more range and complexity.[7] For example, in Catherine Hayes's *Not Waving* (1984), Page's *Real Estate* (1984), and Daniels's *Neaptide* (1986), the focus is on troubled mother-daughter relationships. While Daniels's Val and Joyce reach a hard-won reconciliation at the end of the play, Hayes's Jill and Miriam remain bitterly estranged, and Page's Gwen and Jenny struggle through a reconstruction of their shared past only to determine that their problems are irreconcilable. In Churchill's *Objections to Sex and Violence* (1975) as well as in her *Top Girls* (1982), the central relationship is between sisters. The bond is not an easy one in either play. Family ties are complicated not only by the crises of personal problems but also by the exchange of political and philosophical ideas that are not in harmony. Likewise, Anne Devlin's *Ourselves Alone* (1985) follows sisters Frieda and Josie through their intense though very difficult engagements with Irish politics. As these two and their longtime friend Donna cope with their passions for men and their commitment to their country, the choices they make continually suggest that women, not men, have priority in their lives. In Jacqueline Rudet's *Money to Live* (1984), such family relations remain important but make way for the priorities of friendship. Charlene's relations with sister, mother, and brother are important, but her renewed friendship with Judy guides and molds her actions. As Judy prepares Charlene for the financial and psychological independence her new career as a stripper promises, the two share themselves emotionally, intellectually, and bodily. The love, humor, and respect with which they treat each other sets a high standard for all the relationships in this play's black community.

The greater share of these plays that focus on family veer away from comedy as a guiding principle; this is in part because the examination of familial tensions results in stalemate and division as often as in reconciliation. These sophistications in characterization are still connected with women-authored comedy, however. As I can suggest through two final examples, women's comedy has led to comfort as well as distress for the families and communities women form on stage. I turn first to Charlotte Keatley's *My Mother Said I Never Should* (1987), which closely studies four generations of the women in one family. The play suggests that hope still often transcends difficulty for women collectively working on redefinitions of family. I close with Sarah Daniels's *The Gut Girls* (1988), a play in which the presence of female community means joy and the loss of it means defeat.

Keatley's play pieces together the lives of four women, from four generations of the Partington-Bradley-Metcalfe family. In act 1, Keatley scrambles chronology, offering scattered scenes from the intertwined lives of the four, scenes that range from 1940 to 1982. Having thwarted conventional expectations about chronology, she then concentrates the action of her last two acts: act 2 consists of one long scene set in 1982, and act 3 consists of six scenes, five set in the present—1987—followed by a final scene, chronologically the earliest in the play, set in 1923. This organization, with its defiance of time and its 1980s concentration, allows Keatley to highlight feminist interpretations of these women's life choices. Yet there is an additional feature of her organization that most clearly broadcasts Keatley's investment in community as a major factor in her play about family. Interspersed throughout the action (three times in act 1 and twice in act 3) are five scenes in which all four of the characters (separated in age by as much as seventy-one years) appear playing together as children aged five to nine. Keatley opens the play with one of these timeless playground scenes, establishing the women's community as central, but simultaneously raising doubts about how effectively that community incorporates generational ties and familial obligations. For as the children in scene 1 gather, they propose a game of killing "all our Mummys" (1). In their cruel innocence, then, the children establish the play's ambivalence about female familial attachments. The play goes on to show the four women alternately overwhelmed by family responsibilities (one nineteen-year-old gives up the raising of her daughter to her mother) and cemented by them (at the end the oldest and the youngest of the four—great-grandmother and great-granddaughter—are happily living together). In short, the play is anything but a romantic celebration of women's family connections. Along with the loving attachments the women share come misunderstandings, resentments, and divergent paths.

Yet Keatley ends the play by suggesting that her array of female-to-female family connections, while not uniformly sanguine, adds up to a happy world. The monologue of the final scene takes the audience back to 1923 when the oldest character, Doris (in her youth), is reporting to *her* mother news of her engagement. Doris ends her speech thus: "Oh Mother, I'm so happy, SO HAPPY! I suppose, really and truly, this is the beginning of my life!" (39). Her joy is genuine. Yet since viewers know the vicissitudes of Doris's whole life, her youthful claims for happiness are seen as misplaced and overstated; in a play so full of women, for example, it is both ironic and naive for her to connect her happiness to a man. In addition, her marriage does not prove to be particularly joyful. However, despite the reservations about female community implicit in Doris's speech and despite her misplaced faith in marriage, happiness remains her goal. And while Doris does not know this in 1923, connections with the other women in her family will be her path to obtaining such a goal. She will be happiest, for example, in 1987, when she settles in with her great-granddaughter. In other words, as the play ends, Doris dreams of a happiness that the preceding action can confirm, though not as she might predict. Keatley's comedy, then, is representative both of how female community is central to women's redefinition of family and of how that community, while it is women's main source of joy, is troubled.

Sarah Daniels's *The Gut Girls* does not end so happily. But although its bright moments fill only the first segments of the play, Daniels's play offers a final commentary on the interdependence of women's comedy and women's communities. Daniels focuses the action on Ellen, Maggie, Polly, Kate, and Annie, the "gut girls" who make their living by gutting animal carcasses. Those all around them are repulsed by the smell, gore, and unsightliness of such work, but these five young, turn-of-the-century women find independence, camaraderie, and good times in their trade. More than half of the play is devoted to the women as they inventively and joyfully finagle their way through the unprestigious routine of their lives. In developing Annie and Polly through the group action, Daniels displays the comedy that has been so central in all of her plays. Annie is the "new girl" in scene 1, and Daniels uses her for two kinds of orientation. First, Daniels alerts the audience to the gruesome life of the gutting girls by allowing them to rehearse it all for Annie. Second, Daniels uses Annie's growing perceptiveness to alert her audience to the gut girls' radical politics. Both men and social class come in for extensive condemnation. And when, in part 2, scene 4, Annie complains of the men who are in charge of her life, her vindictive words suggest that the group has transformed her from a helpless victim of men and hierarchy (she had been raped by a former employer and had borne his child out of wedlock) to an active participant in a communal campaign against injustice:

> You know what they should do, don't yer—pull their cocks off. They'd only have to do it to one. That would make all the others stop and think 'Now do I really want to rape this woman or do I want my cock pulled off.' (52)

Her movement toward autonomy replicates that of many women in other women's comic plays. As in those other plays, such growth is dependent on community support.

Polly even more clearly represents the spirit of comedy in Daniels's play. From her opening speech, Polly claims the spirited clown as her persona. For instance, when Annie wilts before the bloody reality of her new job in the first scene, Polly offers her the relief of puns—"That's right. Offal by name, awful by nature. *(Holds up a piece of liver.)* Feeling a bit liverish meself" (1). And throughout the early action, she buoys the women's spirits with her irreverent, gutsy responses to those in authority. Annie's growing assertiveness and Polly's comic boldness are two primary components of the female community on which the first part of *The Gut Girls* depends. Daniels connects both female autonomy and power to the group of women who have found a shared joy in their struggle to survive. In the bulk of this chapter and in preceding chapters, I have argued that such connections are central in women's plays. But Daniels's play does not end with such community or its joy, for the play is about what it means to lose such community. And in the dismantling of her group during part 2, she outlines the forces that can simultaneously destroy both community and comedy.

As part 2 develops, news filters down to the gut girls that their jobs are in danger. And almost immediately, Polly's laughter—so basic to the good times—proves inadequate relief. As Annie tells Polly, laughter has become superfluous: "Ellen's telling us that we ain't going to have no jobs and all you can think about is having a laugh" (54). The girls do all lose their jobs, and as their community disperses, they lose the independence and strength their grouping allowed them to acquire. Polly becomes a maid to the upper-middle-class household of Priscilla, eventually falls victim to class barriers, and is unfairly charged with the attempted murder of her master. Her final words record her powerlessness (81). Annie also takes a position as a maid and concludes that she must forget any dreams she has had (80). Maggie reluctantly marries. Kate becomes a nanny and learns to be grateful for the gentility the position requires of her. And Ellen, who has spent much of the play urging the working women to unionize, takes a factory job making buttons. Her final words—and they constitute the last speech in the play—suggest that even she has relinquished the rhetoric of community. As Daniels records her women's loss of community in the play's final scenes, she also records their loss of self and power. And predictably, her characters lose joy and hope as well as laughter. By connecting the dissipation of laughter to the disruption of her community, Daniels shows how dependent comedy and community are on one another. *The Gut Girls* does not end like a comedy: despair predominates. But through her bleak conclusion, Daniels argues backhandedly that comedy and community are interdependent. Thus, even in plays that cannot offer the final happiness of comedy, women playwrights are celebrating community as the heart of a feminist theatrical enterprise.

The community so central to comedy is acquiring many dimensions in contemporary women's theater. Theater collectives do not always attain their goals; community does not always triumph in the plays. But community, even with its blemishes and dangers, is integral. Just as it is the basis for women's power in comedy, however, community is also the source of the suspicion that continues to surround women's theater. In the mass mixed audiences most women would like to reach, a prejudice remains against the potentially radical values and priorities in a community of women. In short, the combination of women's groups and their radical rhetoric remains threatening. As I conclude my study in the next chapter, I will focus on the confrontation and confusion that continue to surround women's participation in the broader communities of contemporary British theater.

# The Contexts of Contemporary Women's Comedy: Men's Comedy, Audiences, Reviewers, and the Future

One of my main goals throughout this book has been to offer a text-based approach to women and comedy that is sensitive to the generic, social, and political contexts that condition theater. To conclude my study of contemporary women's comedy, I turn to the more significant extratextual factors that have formed and continue to influence women's comedy. I will consider first the relationship between the plays and their viewers—specifically how women's comedy has been affected both by women's definition of audience and by the plays' professional reception. I will then study how women's visions of their future in the theater incorporate the convergence of women, comedy, and change. Tension and confrontation as well as triumph mark women playwrights' accommodation to and modification of the contexts in which they operate.

As an introduction to these extratextual investigations, however, I return to two textual issues for a concluding overview. In my argument throughout part 2, I have undoubtedly raised two key questions for my readers: (1) Even with all of their differences, are women's comedies in fact formally and ideologically separate from men's? (2) Do the differences counsel that women's work be seen as something other than comedy? In answer to these two questions, in my "recapitulation" which follows, I summarize the claims I have made for women's comedy throughout part 2 before I concentrate on the contexts that are shaping the future of that comedy.

### Recapitulation: Women's and Men's Comedy in Contemporary Britain

By exploring various portraits of male and female comedians in chapter 7, I initiated my argument that contemporary comedy by women is marked by qualities rare in men's comedy. In chapters 8, 9, 10,and 11, I have developed this argument by detailing the structures, characters, techniques, and concerns that distinguish women's drama. Yet women's and men's comedy do not constitute completely discrete worlds.

Some comedy now being written by women, for example, cannot be seen in the revisionary tradition I have outlined. In the dramatic work of Fay Weldon and Mary O'Malley, connections to traditional comedy are often stronger than those to the transformative drama I have been discussing. Weldon attends to gender stereotypes in the couple-swapping adventures of *I Love My Love* (1984), yet her play settles into the status quo when it concludes with the two married couples reunited, wearier but wiser. Weldon's feminist anger colors the action, but the play bears out her character Derek's lament that women are so similar that the behavior of any one is predictable based on the action of the lot. In her earlier *Action Replay* (1980), Weldon's cubist construction of the action around the repetition and modulation of a few scenes opens up possibilities for unfamiliar interpretation. But the structural experimentation does not challenge standard expectations about comedy's conclusion. When the play's three women are brought together at the end—stripped of the three men they have been mated with in various ways—defeat, not community, dominates. For Weldon, comedy is a way to bear the unbearable rather than a conduit to change or a chance for joy. O'Malley's most successful play, *Once a Catholic* (1977), also shies away from a woman-supportive comedy, even though it adopts a group protagonist and relies on an episodic collection of short scenes. In a traditional manner, its joy accumulates not from its community of schoolgirls but in spite of their female backbiting. It is probable that the women-centered plays of both Weldon and O'Malley are feminist in intent. Yet each author adopts enough of the traditional comic structure that any gestures toward social or generic dissidence are muffled.

While the work of some women does not fit the pattern I have described in earlier chapters, the work of some men does. Both Stephen Lowe and Steve Gooch are often nominated as male playwrights who are advocates for women. Lowe's *Touched* (1977), though more lyric than comic, offers a portrait of a community of women facing the homefront deprivations of World War II. In both *Female Transport* (1973) and *The Women Pirates Ann Bonney and Mary Read* (1978), Gooch has recreated a segment of lost female history through an episodic syncopation similar to the structural organizations of several women writers. More specifically, *Female Transport* ends with a triumphant, communal celebration of female power that puts it in a league with *Steaming* and *Bazaar and Rummage*. Besides such obviously feminist plays, countless contemporary plays by men employ one or more of the formal transformations that have marked a new strain of comedy among women writers: episodic, splintered plots; group protagonists; cross-gender and multiple-role casting; nonrealistic staging; and indeterminant endings. Such similarities signal important continuities in the work of both women and men. But the work of writers like Weldon, O'Malley, Lowe, and Gooch are still exceptions; a difference in women's comedy persists. By turning my attention to Doug Lucie's *Progress* I can offer some final readings of that difference.

In chapter 5 I noted that traditional comic treatments of women had taken on bleak dimensions in the contemporary theater; with its darkness, Ayckbourn's *Woman in Mind* is representative of mainstream comic portraits of women. But even in the plays they have written for London's alternative stages, men have produced a comedy filtered through despair. Lucie's *Progress* (1984) offers an example of such alternative comedy; the play, while so similar to many women's comedies in its concerns, is notable, finally, for its difference from them. Instead of offering a comic world where hope or strength can be generated, Lucie has produced a comedy similar to Ayckbourn's in its desperation.

Like most of the women's comedies noted in preceding chapters (indeed, like most comedies), Lucie's *Progress* is about desire and human relationship. Like many of the women-authored plays, it also displaces a traditional concentration on male-female relationships with considerations of unorthodox relationships, including several that are gay or lesbian. Lucie's men's support group, his enlightened discussion of pornography, his analysis of wife-beating, and his attention to class distinctions are also familiar results of a preoccupation with feminist-leftist politics. Additionally, there accumulates in the play's protests against social protocol the possibility for a radical re-examination of self and relationship. Lucie ridicules the hypocrisies of the young-professional life in which such issues have taken trendy precedence, but he shares with many women writers a desire to make sense of the new relational and social options encouraged by feminism.

The differences between Lucie's comedy and the comedy written by women are subtle. In a moment I will focus on the crucial difference in Lucie's ending, but several other distinctions prepare for that major turn. To begin with, his play owes much to the linear intensity of its well-made plot. Where the play is finally headed carries more weight than any of its well-written and thoughtful moments. And even though the exploration of new relationships mandates reconsiderations of attitudes, the play begins and ends with a focus on the married couple Ronee and Will, and never deviates from a totally realistic stage presentation. A second foreshadowing of the convention that marks the ending slips in with the doubting and despair that shadow this play. Specifically, men are portrayed as incapable of reform or honesty. As the central agent of this darkened mood, Will not only sexually propositions the young Ange but also demonstrates what even he would call an unhealthy curiosity about pornography. It is the ending itself, however, that most unambiguously aligns Lucie's play with the comic tradition more than with those women's plays that are attempting to modify it.

The play concludes with most of its men drunk. In their stupor, they degenerate from egalitarians to sexist jokers. They even compile a list of women the men would like "to lay." As Ronee puts it to Ange, in describing her husband Will, "There's your 'nice' man. There's your open, honest, charming man who can't get his mind past your tits. Whose idea of maturity is to screw everything in sight" (40). Lucie forces his audience to register this degeneration by reintegrating Mark (Ronee and Will's boarder) back into the action of the play's ending. Since the opening scene, Mark has represented the unredeemed male chauvinist pig, a man proud of his sexist and coarse ways. When Mark joins the more liberated men in the final, drunken scene, viewers cannot help but notice that the other men have "sunk" to Mark's level. Throughout its action, Lucie's play has been about the pressing need for men to take on a responsible part in creating a nonsexist world. But Lucie meets that need with men who cannot, ultimately, transcend their sexism, however desperately they want to. Almost the opposite had happened; the play's world of changing gender roles and sex relationships has called up the men's worst fears, and brought out the worst in them. One of the greatest of the men's fears is realized in the play's events when Ronee leaves Will not for another man, but for a woman. The "progress" of the title is ironic, then. In his conclusion, Lucie appends to his title a question mark. Focusing on the hypocrisy that has accompanied such forays into the relational world beyond traditional marriage, Lucie suggests that progress may not have occurred at all.

Lucie shows the ugly emotions and fears that accompany anyone venturing into new paradigms of relationship. He is chillingly successful in making vivid his portrait of social degeneration. My point, however, is that his bleak conclusion puts this play within the parameters of comic tradition, separating it from those plays seeking to transform genre, characters, or society. When Lucie's characters admit to relational failure in the end (while they continue to yearn for relational change), they certify the retrograde position of characters like Mark, not the progressive world that has framed the play's action. One simple index of the conventionality of the ending is that the joy remaining in the intact lesbian and gay couples is discounted by the failure in the central heterosexual couple. The reviewers who applauded Lucie's confessions about the failures in contemporary life are an even more telling gauge of the play's investment in tradition. By and large, according to reviewers, Lucie's pessimism has qualified him to stand as the voice of his generation. Sheridan Morley called Lucie "our best war correspondent in the political battle of the sexes," while John Barber added that "Lucie is our best spokesman for the confusions and hang-ups of his generation." A third reviewer, Kenneth Hurren, concluded that Lucie offers "an affirmation of real values."

I could cite many other contemporary comedies anchored in this same despair, plays most often written by men. Lucie's play represents an attitude about comedy and the world that continues to prevail today. And it is the malaise Lucie finds himself forced to accept and that a large portion of the audience reads as "true" that sets this play and those like it apart from the contemporary plays by women that I have studied in part 2. Many women writing comedy have carved out a corner for joy on the contemporary stage. Not all of the women's plays have ended happily or served up their joy unalloyed. But the vast majority have found room for the belief in, if not the actuality of, happiness. Most have created a world where there is change for characters and their world. And it is such positive vision that distinguishes the women's work, even more basically than the formal innovations or the novel subject matter. In other words, the difference in women's comedy depends on optimism.

This optimism, which so centrally accounts for the difference between men's and women's contemporary comedy, also accounts for
my claim that British women's current theater work is comic even while
it ventures far outside of what is conventionally recognizable as comedy.
And in answer to my second question—do the differences between
men's and women's comedy demand that women's work be seen as
something other than comedy?—I answer no, that women's work remains comedy, even fiercely so. Let me specify the grounds of my
response. My study in part 2 has focused on the structure, characters,
and concerns of which women's comedy is now composed. These qualities indeed set the plays apart. But more essentially, it is the mood of the
women's plays—the brightness and hope that grow out of (or perhaps
account for) the structures, the characters, and the concerns—that constitutes their overriding difference. Thus, when I answer that this comedy
remains comedy, I am so responding because this comedy retains comedy's joy in an age of despair. I noted in chapter 1 that the increasingly
persistent issue that has dominated studies of twentieth-century comic
drama is whether *any* comedy is possible in this century. (Lucie's play is
but one more example of a play that asks this question centrally.) In
positing an alternative, countertradition of contemporary women-
authored comedy that privileges the joy absent in Lucie and discounted
by comic theoreticians like Iser, Blau, and Winston, I do not pretend to
dismiss their grim conclusions. I can explain, however, why such disparate visions of twentieth-century comedy—one so sanguine and one so
bleak—co-exist and why the differences correlate with gender.

   C. W. E. Bigsby, in his study of British playwrights with socialist
agendas ("The Language of Crisis"), suggests that contemporary writers
are currently finding themselves stalemated by opposing desires—to
convey, on the one hand, the disintegration of twentieth-century existence, and to urge, on the other, social reform. In most of the women's
plays I have examined in part 2, the authors investigate the possibilities
for such reform, but by minimalizing their attention to pessimistic
worldviews, they detach themselves from what many have concluded
is the only realistic way of viewing the world. Much in the minority, the
women insist that optimism and hope are essential for human persistence
in the late twentieth-century world. The women, thus, are approaching
their comic task with a combination of cultural and aesthetic assumptions that separate them from many men who share their general political

outlook. The most powerful explanations of such different assumptions seem to be historically based.

The confidence in happiness that women express in their plays is more than a naive, misguided protest against the powerful, philosophically dominant misgivings in current appraisals of comedy. It is the result of the very different experiences out of which women write, different experiences that have been exacerbated in this century. Feminist critics who have studied the connections of women to modernism have discovered that the generally accepted literary milestone of "modernism" is gender-specific and records basically male responses to the twentieth century. Sandra Gilbert's work on World War I is representative. Studying the contrasting effect of the war on men and on women, she argues that while for men the war represented an end to hope, freedom, and ambition, for women it provided the avenue to new skills, new outlooks, and new roles ("Soldier's Heart"). The result of the experiential difference Gilbert details has been that for men the literary tradition has (in this century) been dominated by a new sense of despair and disconnection, and that for women literature has become a novel way to examine new circumstances. Fiction and poetry, along with drama, have seen the divisive effect of this gender distinction. And countless investigations by feminist critics have begun to record the nuances of this basic difference. Thus a hopeful comedy that flies in the face of standard contemporary judgments of comedy—judgments that privilege black comedy as the only real possibility for this century—is but one piece of a literary landscape women are changing.

The writers I have considered in the last five chapters are in many ways indebted to the comic tradition of Shakespeare, Congreve, Shaw, and Ayckbourn. They have borrowed from such men as well as from Behn the belief in women's power; but following more closely in Behn's footsteps, they have wrestled with issues of women's agency by changing the basic formulas of comedy. In spite of their extensive reworking of the genre, the women's work remains comic, however, and it remains so primarily because of its foundation on hope. For all its innovations in narration and character and its novel specifications about production, the most distinctive feature of women's comedy is that it privileges joy in privileging women. The plays' optimism is so startling an addition to contemporary literature that the drama has been much too easily discounted.

## Defining an Audience on the Fringe and Elsewhere

This difference in men's and women's basic outlook is a significant factor
in the way women's comedies are offered to and accepted by contemporary London audiences. How women writers define and approach their
audiences is clearly related to their hopefulness as well as to their central
concern with gender issues. And as I study the relationship between
comic women playwrights and their audiences in the next paragraphs, I
will mark additional ways women continue to claim a different territory
for their work. After outlining women playwrights' preferred concepts
of audience, I will detail their accommodations to the actual audiences
they find in various venues. I begin with a representative example of the
efforts of two playwrights to exact active responses from their audiences.

Mavro and Coqino, the two characters in Maro Green and Caroline
Griffin's surreal, expressionistic, and generally comic *More* (1986), refuse
an audience its normal, passive response. At one of several moments
during which the house lights come up, Mavro talks directly with audience members, even demanding responses from them: "Now. Who's
been on holiday this year? Oh, a lot of you. Has anyone been to Spain?
Not Bad" (46). Later, near the end of the play when both Mavro and
Coqino discuss their debilitating conditions through puppets (Mavro is
an anorexic, Coqino an agoraphobiac), the audience is lured into clap-
ping for the puppets, only to be severely upbraided for what Mavro and
Coqino label an invalid response:

> *The puppets speak in concert, rising to a shriek.* ["More"
> is the name Mavro and Coqino give both of the pup-
> pets they "give birth" to.]

|             |                                                     |
| ----------- | --------------------------------------------------- |
| *More:*     | Let's put a good face on it. |
|             | Understanding will do. |
|             | Shout "More" if you want to, but more important perhaps |
|             | Put your hands together and give them [Mavro and Coqino] a clap! |

> *The puppets go on bowing until the audience clap. If there
> are lights, they dip. The audience must think it's the end.*

| *Mavro and Coqino:* | *(to the audience)* No, no. Don't clap. Can we have the lights please. Sorry, that's a real mistake. Take no notice. Oh dear, oh dear. |

*They pluck off the puppets and stuff them in their pockets.*
(57)

Such direct and abrupt contact with the audience has become common-place in recent comedies by women. In *More* the authors shock their viewers by forcing them into a "wrong" response. Green and Griffin can then expect even more focused audience attention on their actual conclusion. Other, less combative examples of playwrights engineering their audiences abound. The "narrator" in the Women's Theatre Group and Libby Mason's *Double Vision* (1982), for example, provides not only distanced, knowing voice-overs directed at the audience, but also guidance to the play's three "possible and plausible endings"(48). And in *Fixed Deal,* the Women's Theatre Group and Paulette Randall's 1986 show, actors similarly refused traditional divisions of audience and stage by singing directly to the audience and sitting in its midst. Such redefinitions of the relationship between those onstage and those in the audience have become integral to women's comic theater. The shattering of theatrical illusion and the encouragement of self-conscious response are reflections of the way women are envisioning their stages and their audiences. The experimental nature of such staging suggests that the women playwrights still expect to see their work staged outside the West End; less clear from these examples, but every bit as important, the writers also expect to see women as the key component of their audience.

In the smaller theaters of the London fringe, women have been most likely to find acceptance of their dramatic experimentations and their political commitments. The direct approach of *More* is obviously suited to the intimate theaters of the fringe and to the predictably leftist sympathies of the audience. Yet even while working in fringe theaters, women express various expectations about and ideals of their audiences. Hazel Maycock (of the Women's Theatre Group), Sue Long (of Scarlet Harlets), Karen Parker and Debby Klein (of Parker and Klein), and Jane Boston (of Siren Theatre Company) are among those who envision an audience with aims and ideals similar to their own (interviews). To them, this similarity means a predominantly female and often largely lesbian audience. As these performers well know, the fringe remains the theater venue most accommodating of what are still treated as minority tastes. Predictably, there are other women theater professionals who envision for their work a broader audience that welcomes not only women, but also men and a range of classes, races, and ages. Louise Page is among writers who want to avoid speaking "to the converted" (Betsko and Koenig, *Interviews,* 361). Many other theater practitioners join her in a call for a broad-based audience for women's work, including Sue Townsend, Jane Dawson (of Joint Stock), Bryony Lavery, and Katina Noble (of Spare Tyre) (interviews). Thus, even within the cramped universe of fringe theater, women's ideal conceptions of their audiences vary.

Despite such differences, however, women—whether they see themselves playing to a limited or a general audience—have been constructing an idea of audience that is making new sense of fringe venues. This idea of audience is distinguished by two main traits. First, there has been a new privileging of the audience as a "community." In addition to often erasing traditional divisions of actor and audience (as in *More*), playwrights have expressed a strong desire to conjoin the various groups that constitute theater. Ann Jellicoe explored some of the parameters of such audience community over twenty years ago, asserting that any one person's response to a play is inseparable from the response of the entire audience ("Some Unconscious Influences"). Jellicoe's move toward large-scale community theater suggests her continuing dedication to the audiences she defines as a series of communities. Similarly, the communities that I studied throughout chapter 11 are almost always viewed by writers and actors as vehicles for encouraging further interactions and connections in the audience. The presence of these audience groups is now widespread; they range from the self-help groups that form at the end of Spare Tyre performances to the audiences that share the catharsis of laughter Townsend encourages. Such communities are distinguished from the alliances of conventional audiences by degree more than kind; but for women in the theater, the group connections are a crucial reinforcement of the politics of change in their plays.

Second, and still more important, women's reformation of audience includes a recognition of women *in the audience* as subjects. In other words, the new subjectivity presented onstage in women's plays is complemented by a new attitude toward spectators. Feminist theorists in film studies have led the way in providing a semiotically based understanding of how audiences have traditionally been assumed to be male.[1] As theater critics are beginning to point out, such assumptions are similarly present in theater, and have traditionally molded every aspect of play production. But the contradictory assumption that an audience can be and often is female is now identifiable in many women's plays. There are dangers, of course, in essentializing the responses of audience members by gender; assuming that all women will respond to theater in a predictable—however radical—way overlooks the complexities of production. Thus, I am not suggesting that women playwrights' attitudes to their audience be interpreted in a monolithic way. However, I am suggesting that women's plays often operate from modified assumptions about the subject status of the spectator. And when the assumption is that the viewer is a woman, the play itself may be altered. Both Elin Diamond and Teresa de Lauretis have undertaken the difficult task of finding a theoretical basis for understanding how this female spectator may operate in the theater. In a feminist reading of Brecht's Gestus, Diamond suggests that the historicization of the spectator liberates her into subjectivity— "Looking at the character, the spectator is constantly intercepted by the actor/subject, and the latter, heeding no fourth wall, is theoretically free to look back" ("Brechtian Theory," 90). In other words, the interactive staging practices so common now in women's work not only encourage but also depend on the intense participation of the spectator. In her wider arena of film and theater, de Lauretis stresses the complications in looking for a female spectator; she notes that positing a lesbian audience may be the most radical and the most useful tactic for theoreticians ("Sexual Indifference," 168–73). For de Lauretis, the lesbian spectator provides the purest example of a female audience member unencumbered by the sexual and cultural baggage of male desire.

Such gestures to the female subjectivity of audience members has specific ramifications for comedy. Detailing how the female audience member experiences both male-generated and feminist-inspired comedy, Lisa Merrill argues that feminist humor offers women spectators expanded opportunities. The woman responding to a male comic, says Merrill, is forced to empathize with the male speaker: "Her identification with the joke teller, and the joke is somewhat schizophrenic. To be amused she must discount and devalue her own experience" ("Feminist Humor," 279). But, Merrill continues, the woman responding to feminist humor that posits a female spectator finds herself acknowledged, supported, and empowered:

A strong, rebellious humor empowers women to examine how we have been objectified and fetishized and to what extent we have been led to perpetuate this objectification.

In a feminist comedy, we are no longer cast as an omniscient audience laughing at a character "unknowingly betraying" herself, rather, the context and the character interact in such a way as to stir our empathy as much as our amusement. It is the situation which is ridiculed, rather than the characters struggling to negotiate their circumstances. Questioning one's circumstances is a rebellious posture. To refuse to see the "humor" in one's own victimization as the "butt" of the joke or the "object" of ridicule, while seizing and redefining the apparatus of comic perspective so that it is inclusive of women's experience is a necessary and powerful gesture of self-definition. (279–80)

Women playwrights claim they are writing for women. According to many of the writers, in fact, women have been posited as their primary or only auditors. And in the comic realm, as Merrill suggests, that may translate into a situation where the women in the audience stand to gain as much from comedy as do the characters themselves. Those in the audience can share in the power and independence of the comic women on stage. Yet as I suggested in chapter 10, issues of identity are encumbered by the possibilities of multiple, plural, or fractured selves. Thus, while the playwrights are attending to their audience members in new and significant ways, the spectators are only as altered as are the characters themselves.

Controlling the details of theatrical reception is extremely difficult, as I will argue again in my look at reviewing. Yet women playwrights are attending to the dynamics of production, as to other aspects of the comic process, and the result is a workable idea of audience both based on communities and designed for responsive women. However, the fringe theater that has allowed the writers to nurture such an audience is no longer their only venue. And as they venture into larger, more commercial theatrical spaces, women are seeing their work conditioned by additional forces. In the previous chapter, I investigated the varying ways in which women have brought their communities to a range of British stages. My goal, in part, was to note the differing demands of the varying venues on women's groups. The range of stages has also provided a variety of audiences for women's drama; and the different audiences—many of which do not fit the profile women playwrights have been developing in the fringe theater—have resulted in qualitatively different plays. I can make this point about different audiences and altered plays most expeditiously by showing how the same play has acquired different complexions on the fringe, in the West End, and in between. While women continue to develop their ideal audience on the fringe, on other stages they are experiencing and often suffering from the demands of less sympathetic audiences.

Recently, more and more women have seen their work done on prominent London stages. As I mentioned in chapter 11, the Royal Shakespeare Company (RSC) has for years welcomed women's work in its small theaters. But now even the main stages at the National Theatre (NT) and the RSC have showcased women-authored work. The RSC has produced both Timberlake Wertenbaker's translation of Ariane Mnouchkine's *Mephisto* (1985) and Pam Gems's *The Danton Affair* (1986) on the main Barbican stage. The NT has featured Michelene Wandor's collaboration with director Mike Alfred, *The Wandering Jew* (1987). Yet tellingly, none of these three plays is comic or woman-centered. Gems admits of *The Danton Affair,* in fact, that it marginalizes its few women characters. Caryl Churchill's *Serious Money* (1987) and Timberlake Wertenbaker's *Our Country's Good* (1988) (both of which came to the West End from the main stage of the Royal Court) are evidence, however, that women's comedy as well as their more serious drama can also "cross over." While Churchill's play is centered on the male-dominated, frenetic world of London's LIFFE (London International Financial Futures Exchange), Wertenbaker's play—to which I will turn in closing this chapter—locates in the West End's Garrick Theatre comedy unmistakably from a woman's point of view.

Such a small sampling of main-stage productions by women is not sufficient to warrant major conclusions about the viability of women's comedy on main stages. (Plays like Gems's *Dusa, Fish, Stas, and Vi* and Dunn's *Steaming,* for example, have brought both all-female casts *and* comedy to the West End.) To work toward such conclusions, however, I will look in some detail at the transfer of two women-authored plays from the fringe to the West End. An investigation of both Olwen Wymark's *Nana* (1987) and Sharman Macdonald's *When I Was a Girl, I Used to Scream and Shout . . .* (1984) offers insight into the issues involved in the main-stage production of women's work developed on the fringe. In each case, when prominent fringe productions transferred to the West End, changes in venue involved not only changes in audience, but also changes in theatrical effectiveness and politics.

After playing at the fringe Almeida late in 1987, to reviews that raved about Wymark's adaptation of Zola's *Nana* as "a model of clarity and compression" (Spencer), the play *Nana* transferred to the Mermaid in early 1988. What had been previously judged to be a fluid, experimental production was found to be marred by misplaced effects and clumsy, even pretentious staging. Lyn Gardner noted of the transfer production that the play had "not traveled well"; and Neil Bartlett more specifically identified a dilution in the original production's flashiness and guts. Their responses are indicative of the mixed reviews that greeted the transfer. The intimacy, stylization, sexuality, and decadent pace that combined to make the original production exciting and provocative did not integrate easily with the expanded scope of the Mermaid production. Similarly, Pam Gems's *Camille* (1984) also made a transfer to the West End during which Gems's revisions of an originally male story of female sexuality were co-opted by proscenium staging.[2] In Gems's play as in Wymark's, what had originally seemed a disruptive and troubling revision of historical myth became a predictable, titillating love story that punished women.

Unlike these two transfers, Sharman Macdonald's *When I Was A Girl, I Used to Scream and Shout . . .* is a comedy. Such a denomination may be a distinction without much difference, however, as this play too found the West End less than hospitable. Once more the audience expectations that are encouraged by large stages led many reviewers to notice cracks in what had seemed originally a tight, successful play. David Nathan suggested, for example, that the play could be seen, on transfer, to be lacking in substance sufficient for an expanded stage—"A play that looked good in the intimate surroundings of a London pub theatre, needs more substance to fill the wide-open spaces of a West End stage." Claire Armistead noted with more sympathy, "Part of the problem . . . is the flattening out of a play which began life in an intimate theatre and finds itself suddenly straddled in a proscenium arch." In general, reviewers treated the transfer production quite generously. However, the variance of opinion about this play's success as a transfer can stand as a final indication of the strained connection between women's work on the fringe and their involvement in West End production. At the optimistic end of the spectrum, reviewer Michael Billington used the example of *When I Was a Girl . . .* to argue for the aesthetic vitality of the fringe–West End conduit: "[This play] reminds us that the commercial theatre depends on the subsidised sector for much of its energy. Starve subsidised companies and you will eventually kill the West End." More

depressing for those who would like to take women's West End exposure as a measure of a maturing women's theater, reviewer Carole Woddis found that the West End smothered the good in Macdonald's play:
"Flung onto the wide open spaces of the Whitehall, Simon Stokes (the
Bush's director) has succumbed to West End dictums, and within its
smart external shell Macdonald's sharply observant and delicately complex emotions disappear almost without trace."

The mixed success of women's work on London's main stages suggests the quandary women remain in when speculating about their goals
for audience and exposure. Because both the fringe and the West End
carry their own very different production limitations, women have continued to look elsewhere in search of appropriate production venues.
Julia Pascal, for example, has consciously avoided both the smallest
stages of the fringe and the biggest of the West End. Troubled by both
the "ghetto" of women's fringe theater and the token gestures to women
from major subsidized companies, she has formed her own theater company, produced plays that are politically "dangerous" (on Northern Ire-
land, anti-Semitism, and South Africa, for example). Many women have
set TV as their goal, or settled for what has been the more receptive
(though less prestigious) medium of radio. Women are not alone in
feeling both loyalty to and disappointment in the fringe theater. After
more than twenty years of existence, the whole fringe is facing the
question of its future with some urgency. However, it is hard not to
imagine the fringe as a major venue for women's drama. As the transfer
productions of *Nana* and *When I Was a Girl . . .* suggest, the fringe is still
the most likely home for the new vision of audience developing out of
women's comedy. But women undoubtedly will continue to press for
broader exposure. For women with maturing visions of their own theater, the fringe may not continue as the primary location in which they
can build their own audiences.

## Appreciating and Depreciating Women's Comedy:
## Reviewers and Gender

Women retain some choice in securing theaters and audiences for their
plays despite the obstacles they face. They have no freedom of choice,
however, when it comes to reviewers. And unfortunately for them,
women have not fared well with London's theater reviewers. I opened
chapter 8 with a survey of reviewers' dismay at women's comic struc-

tures. Those reviews and others I have turned to throughout part 2 make it obvious that the mostly male community of reviewers has found its relationship to women's work troubled.[3] The extent of the problem can be seen in the work of Sarah Daniels, who has served as a lightning rod for some of the most vicious attacks on women. As Remnant shows in her introduction to volume 6 of *Plays by Women,* the reception of Daniels's *Masterpieces* divided the critical community, demonstrating how women's work has been viewed with suspicion and fear:

> Condemning Daniels' work as polemic and propagandist, many critics made little attempt to approach her ideas rationally, but instead insisted petulantly that they just weren't true. . . . Amidst a growing awareness of the part played by anti-black, anti-Irish and anti-Semitic jokes in perpetuating racism, the critics dug in their heels and insisted that the very idea that misogynist jokes had anything to do with misogyny was patently ridiculous. Daniels' anger was merely a "cascade of bile" (Shulman) and her "scream of outrage" (Wardle) was drowned out by their own. While, with a few exceptions, female reviewers reacted to Daniels' work with warmth and shocked recognition, much of criticdom had taken up arms against her: conceding that she could, at times, muster a certain surreal humour, many dozens of column inches were dedicated to her annihilation as a playwright. (8)

Happily, in the last few years the atmosphere has improved; with the growing number of women finding stages for their work, antipathy to women's work has diminished and female points of view are commonly both understood and welcomed. The relationship between playwrights and their journalistic judges remains complicated, however. The relationship also remains critical, since reviewers first shape the expectations of the general theater-going audience. And since comedy so basically depends on its outreach to audience, the unpredictable connections of reviews and women's theater have had an exaggerated effect on work in the genre.

While a critical study of reviews can discover evidence about the theater not available elsewhere, such study also has its limitations. Reviews, essentially, are meant both to report and to evaluate; and for purposes like mine, both functions are useful. The reporting about the production—its appearance, its feel, its energy—create a record of the onstage interpretation of a play. The evaluative, however, is clearly the more important function of reviews. For the typical newspaper or magazine reader, of course, reviews help answer the question, is this play, this production, worth my money? For my purposes, the reviews can offer additional evaluative information about a play and its production: a review can recreate details about the reception of a play by an actual audience, and can judge the quality of both play and production and thus suggest what the production reveals about the play. In sum, a review recreates and evaluates the context of production to judge the onstage effectiveness of dramatic literature. But reviews also have their limitations. A review, cannot, for example, neatly separate out an author's intentions from her producers' decisions. Responsibility for triumphs or failures is often indeterminable. Additionally, reviews must be recognized as responses in which opinion is encouraged; and unsubstantiated judgments are often both necessary and welcome. Reviews, like any kind of interpretation, have their own bias. Such bias is, however, immensely revealing. And the way such bias may be affected by both the playwright's and the reviewer's sex is my major study in the pages to come. In earlier chapters, I have made extensive use of reviews to suggest how the dimensions of production have played their role in the development of contemporary women's comedy. I have relied on both the reporting and the evaluating of reviews. In studying the gender-related bias that may attach to such reviews, I want to expand on an issue raised by my use of reviews throughout the book: how the sex of the reviewer and the playwright factor into reviewers' response to women's comedy. In my following discussion, as in earlier segments of the book that rely on reviews, I am not using reviews to judge the quality of plays or productions so much as I am using them as signs of the sexually charged atmosphere that women's drama demands.

Because of their increasing presence in the theater, women have intruded on the formerly male-determined relationship between theater professionals and theater reviewers. As a result, the dominance of men in the reviewing profession has come in for close scrutiny. In her 1986 survey of the gender of London theater reviewers, for example, Lyn Gardner (herself a reviewer) details what she terms a "ridiculous imbalance" between men and women ("The Naked Critic," 7). In a parallel fashion, the predominance of male reviewers has raised suspicions among women playwrights. Pam Gems, scrutinizing the motivations of male reviewers, concludes, "Men fear and hate women more than

women fear and hate men. . . . There is a spiteful revenge in some criticism of women's work" (Betsko and Koenig, *Interviews,* 202). Similarly,
Wertenbaker has noted that the male fraternity of critics is threatened
by women's still-novel appearance as writers: "Go to a play on opening
night, and the critics invariably look like a group of people with a bad
case of fear of flying; when they discover that the pilot is a woman, sheer
panic breaks out" (quoted in Gardner, "The Naked Critic," 6). The fear
and paranoia that many women suspect is rarely discoverable in unambiguous terms in the reviews themselves. But what is observable in even
the male reviewers most supportive of women's work is the men's self-
consciousness of themselves as men.

    Not many years ago, it was common for reviewers to confess to
feeling personally attacked by women's dramas. Michael Coveney's
1982 response to Sue Townsend's *Bazaar and Rummage* is representative:
"The resounding shuffle of women closing ranks against the chauvinist
blast of a male-dominated society has become a theatrical hazard for the
male-dominated critical fraternity." Recently such indignation has given
way to less sensitive self-reference. Coveney's 1987 response to a
woman's play *about* women's theater, for example, is good-humored:
"This is a fresh and illuminating look at the self-professed women's
theatre movement, and one that mercifully deprives male critics of the
jokes at its expense" (review of *Dreams of San Francisco*). Other reviewers
also remain strongly male-identified and express reservations about the
various results of plays told from a woman's point of view. Nicholas de
Jongh, for example, identifies the shocks he received from Wymark's
*Nana* as attributable to his sex—"Olwen Wymark's adaptation of the
huge novel retains a vestigial power to shock male members of the
audience." Michael Billington, in voicing a desire for stronger male
characters from women writers, repeats a common appeal from male
reviewers: "Dare she [Jacqueline Holborough] write a play next time in
which men are not simply incredible, off-stage nasties but credible onstage characters?" (review of *Dreams of San Francisco*). And Martin
Hoyle, a bit more bitterly, faces the accusing feminism of Jude Alderson's *The Virgins' Revenge* (1985) by defensively aligning himself with
eight thousand years of men: "If those members of the male sex who
inflicted pain on women over the past 8,000 years had had any inkling
of the expiation their posterity would undergo in the twentieth century
fringe theatre, they might have desisted. On second thoughts, they
might have redoubled their efforts." These reviewers are, of course,

men; and in displaying how their gender plays into their reviews, I do not mean to suggest that there should be no male reviewers or that they should attempt to erase their conditioning as men. However, the theater community must recognize the severe handicap the prevalence of male reviewers places on women playwrights. Men looking for a male point of view in women-authored plays (this is usually an unconscious search, of course) will consistently find such plays lacking. Concomitantly, women looking for the recognition and praise they need from reviewers will find themselves disappointed.

Ironically, the solution to the predominance of male reviewers is not simply to add more women to the reviewing ranks. There are now many more women reviewing drama than there were just a few years ago. But for women, analyzing women's plays is not automatically easier than it is for men. In fact, Gardner found that most female reviewers felt themselves to be more tightly straightjacketed than men in responding to women's work. If the women reviewers were too supportive of women, their critical authority and objectivity were questioned. If they were too critical, they were marked as traitors ("The Naked Critic"). Although it has not been easy for women to make a space for themselves in the critical hierarchy, women's responses to women's drama are now commonly put before the public. And as men self-consciously speak from their position as men in reviewing, so too must the women often speak as women. In reviewing Marcella Evaristi's *Commedia* (1982), for example, Victoria Radin welcomes the play's ability to reach the women in its audience: "Though the essentially Oedipal subject is universal and one that every woman in the audience will recognize with a sinking heart, the author presents it to us wrapped in the extravaganzas of a family of second and third generation Glaswegian Italians." Carole Woddis more aggressively celebrates the female point of view in *The Virgins' Revenge:* "Its catalogue of (s)exploitation against women will have any self-respecting woman in the audience ready to mow down the next man who steps into view."

Both reviews are representative in displaying the tendency of women reviewers to be supportive of the often feminist agenda of women's plays. But along with such support has often come a detailed scrutiny of the women writers' politics, a scrutiny rare in reviews written by men. Drawing from her own experience with female reviewers, Louise Page has concluded of this tendency that "women critics tend to be looking for feminism as they know it" (interview). The reviews clearly bear her out when, for example, Victoria Radin asks of Page's *Real Estate* (1984), "Is the play, like Caryl Churchill's 'Top Girls,' a comment on the post-feminist woman as bitch?" Two other examples suggest the intensity that accompanies such close ideological examination by women reviewers. Lyn Gardner demands to know of Holborough's *Dreams of San Francisco* "where, if anywhere, the author's sympathies lie. Is she [Holborough] really suggesting that female solidarity is impossible and that 20 years of feminism have been more enslaving than liberating?"[4] And Julia Pascal spares no words in attacking what she judges to be the confused feminism of Anne Devlin's *Ourselves Alone* (1985): "This play is an insidious attack on Republicanism through the respectable guise of Feminism. But is it feminist? The three women continually define themselves through their men."

The established presence of women reviewers has standardized some new questions and new views of contemporary theater and is contributing to the changing contours of women's theater. Yet reviewing remains painfully gender-conscious, for both men and women. In further detailing the way gender factors into reviewing, I will suggest finally that while women's work is getting treated much more fairly now, audiences and their reviewers continue to approach woman-authored drama with an eye—however feminist—to gender.[5] This maturing consciousness of gender does not have the power to transform the contemporary theater into a women's haven. Nor does it (or should it) mean that every woman-authored play is to be applauded. But it makes it less likely that women's plays will be automatically discounted.

While there are occasional reviews—still—in which it is assumed that women can't manage a plot and that men are but targets in women's plays, attention to gender is usually expressed more subtly. For instance, the woman's play under review is commonly studied alongside other women's plays and rarely compared to men's work. Comparisons of women's work only to women's work enables some reviewers to diminish the importance of the new play under review. John Barber opens his review of Louise Page's *Golden Girls* (1984), for example, by contrasting it with other women's plays. While he intends to praise Page's work, he actually pigeonholes it as women's work: "I have often enjoyed plays written by women, but I do not recall when one had me so excited—and breathless—as I became during Louise Page's 'Golden Girls' at The Pit." Billington's consideration of Julia Kearsley's *Under the Web* (1987) is more generous; but in his meditation on TV and theater writing, he too diminishes women's work by judging it only in relation to other women's work:

> New writing for the theatre has many advantages over television. It can tackle explosive subjects, employ a richer poetic language, exploit the medium's imaginative freedom. That doesn't automatically make for good drama; but even plays I didn't greatly warm to, such as Deborah Levy's *Heresies* and Heidi Thomas's *Indigo,* at least tested the peculiar license of theatre.

Finally, at least four different reviewers of Andrea Dunbar's *Shirley* (1986) compared it to Shelagh Delaney's *A Taste of Honey,* each intending a compliment.[6]

The dismissal that attaches to such comparisons is clearest when examinations of women in the context of other women's work are compared to examinations of women in the context of men's work. It must be noted, first, that such comparisons of women's work to men's are rare. And when they are made, the play under review is commonly seen as exceptional. Reviewers of Caryl Churchill's hit comedy *Serious Money* (1987), for example, frequently applauded the play by comparing it to men's writing. Churchill is mentioned in the same sentences with David Hare, Howard Brenton, Ben Jonson, Philip Massinger, William Congreve, Clive James, John Betjeman, and Hilaire Belloc.[7] Most women's work is analyzed in the context of other women's work; that the rare play such as Churchill's *isn't* suggests that many reviewers still take male models as the true measure of success.

Beyond the occasional complimentary comparison to men's work, women's work is praised in several other ways that also reveal a continuing difference in the treatment of women's plays. Those plays that shield audiences from feminist politics, for example, are likely to garner critical support. While Daniels's *Byrthrite* offended the larger share of its reviewers with its separatist feminism (Mark Lawson is representative in finding the play "a lecture rather than a play"), plays less aggressively feminist can earn praise, sometimes just for being politically tempered. Of *Top Girls,* for instance, John Barber happily notes that "the theme is not crudely feminist." Similarly, Susie MacKenzie recommends the controlled feminism of Wertenbaker's *The Grace of Mary Traverse* (1985): "You won't find any clotted feminist cant in Timberlake Wertenbaker's new play, which charts a woman's progress through male dominated

territories, but you will find a sharp wit and close eye focused on men."
Responses to Churchill's *Serious Money,* too, show that the less woman-
centered a work is, the more likely it is to be rewarded with critical
praise. Michael Ratcliffe is comforted by the play's nonselective and
wide-ranging indictments: "This is not a feminist critique of a male
world. Men, women, blacks, Latin Americans and Jews are all on the
money game, and join in the chilling rap of mindless obscenities. . . ."
Giles Gordon takes his praise one step further in placing good art above
politics: "She [Churchill] is formidable not because her politics is of the
Left but because she is an artist who can transmute her thoughts about
society into superbly organized and orchestrated plays." Women-
authored plays that devote a sizable portion of their attention to men also
seem more likely to please the reviewing community. For example,
Lucy Gannon's *Raping the Gold* (1988), which centers on a troubled,
redundant foundry worker and offers one woman in a cast of seven,
received strong reviews. Not only is Gannon's work often described as
"impressive," but reviewers tag her an important upcoming writer.[8] I
do not mean to imply that this play or others I have cited are not worthy
of such praise, only to note that male-oriented plays are more likely than
female-oriented plays to attract reviewers' sympathies. The qualities that
have come to mark women's comedy—groups of women, growing female autonomy, and sexuality in particular—are exactly the qualities
that are least likely to elicit positive responses from the reviewing community.

Indeed, the differences with which women's work is treated remain
most prominent in plays that include explicit treatments of sex and sexuality. As I detailed in chapter 10, theatrical attention to the issues surrounding women's sexuality and subjectivity has resulted in some unstable theater. Women's attention to their physical lives has also forced
reviewers to respond to the complicated issues involved. Reviews of
Clare McIntyre's *Low Level Panic* and Julia Schofield's *Love on the Plastic*
demonstrate the discomfort that continues to attach to the volatile issue
of women's sexuality, a discomfort present despite the upbeat comedy
also central to so many of these plays. *Low Level Panic* (1988) takes place
in a bathroom that the play's three women share, and here the women
are casual and open about their bodies, sexuality, and fantasies. The
majority of reviews from both men and women were levelheaded, but
two particular responses demonstrate the difficulties some reviewers had
in interpreting such direct portraits of women's sexuality. Charles

Spencer's view is the more traditional. Finding himself startled by the female nudity, he complains first that a male playwright wouldn't be allowed to offer it and second that this particular woman's offering erases the possibilities of fun that might ordinarily attach to such a physical display:

> At the start of *Low Level Panic* at the *Royal Court Theatre Upstairs,* an attractive young woman climbs naked out of her bath and, after drying herself and donning a dressing gown, proceeds to enlarge—at length and in considerable detail—on her sexual fantasies.
>
> If a man had written the scene it would doubtless provoke outraged charges of gratuitous sexism but since the play has been written by a woman, Clare McIntyre, and is presented by the Womens Playhouse Trust, the audience can relax in the knowledge that the drama will be ideologically sound. And so it disappointingly proves to be.

Nicholas de Jongh works through his discomfort quite differently. He suggests that it is feminist women, not men, who will be most dismayed by the show of bodies:

> Clare McIntyre's extraordinary new play at the Theatre Upstairs for the Women's Playhouse Trust is liable to dismay and confound some feminists. *Low Level Panic* depicts three unattached young women, sharing their lives and a home somewhere, and views the trio almost exclusively as erotic beings, dressing themselves up at party time.

Working from the assumption that female nudity and eroticism can only be bad for women, he objects to the display and thereby hopes to align himself with feminists. However, de Jongh has not appreciated that women's bodies can exist onstage as something other than objects for men.

The difficulties both reviewers feel forced to express are apparent also in reviews of Julia Schofield's *Love on the Plastic* (1987), a play that studies the women involved in a Mayfair prostitution club. The majority of reviewers recognized one of the play's main points—that "it is money rather than sex which is the aphrodisiac" (Gardner review). Yet the glaring exception was Eric Shorter, who left the exposé feeling both cheated and aroused. He complained not so much that the play was bad as that it was a sexual tease:

> We are robbed of much theatrical satisfaction because the author has not bothered to confect a proper plot beyond the invisible boss's threat to impose a £10 polltax on his staff, and because no character provokes our sympathy for long. The girls are shapely. Some of the acting is good, and the author conveys her disgust with such places. There is nothing for voyeurs, and there isn't much for anyone who ever read or heard about sexual clip joints. . . . Let us hope it won't provoke in other spectators, as it provoked in me, a disconcerting urge afterwards to head straight for the West End to test the validity of Miss Schofield's observations, in the hope of finding if not more humanity, a touch more humour.

The issue of women's sexuality continues to be explosive; this will continue to leave women writers vulnerable to the misunderstandings of reviewers, especially when the reviewers confront this issue at the heart of women's comedies.

While these changing responses to women's plays bear on the composition and success of women's comedy, direct responses to the idea of women's comedy itself have changed little in recent years. I detailed in chapter 7 how women's comedy has been doubly discredited because it is comedy and because it is women's. Reviewers' repeated references to Townsend's *Bazaar and Rummage* (1982) as a "little comedy" are but one example of the lightness with which women's comedy is approached. In his review of the play, Michael Billington even suggests that Townsend lacks an understanding of the operation of serious comedy:

> But I think Ms. Townsend needs to be taught by someone that laughter can be a very effective counterpoint to the unendurable (as in *Joe Egg*) but that it can't be used simply to decorate it; and that plays that tackle complex subjects like agoraphobia have a responsibility to show that there are no facile, easy cures.

Paradoxically, while women are accused of misappropriating comedy, they also remain open to the charge of being humorless, though scores of women's comedies have graced the London stages in recent years. Milton Shulman begins his 1987 review of *Dreams of San Francisco,* for example, by recalling the uncomplimentary stereotype of the humorless feminist: "It is conventional wisdom that feminists have a limited sense of humour. Most plays concerned with women's rights rarely concede that the struggle could be a laughing matter." For women playwrights, so centrally committed to comic communities and comic outreach, the gender-consciousness of reviewing reflects a public still less than eager to accept their work.

Setting their work before the community of reviewers remains hazardous for women. It is only fair to conclude this overview, however, with two samples of the fairness and support that now can be found with increasing regularity in reviews of women's plays. Andrew Rissik's study of the context for *Low Level Panic* displays both an acceptance of women's work as mainstream and an acknowledgment that women are playing a major role in reshaping contemporary drama:

> In work such as Anne Devlin's *Ourselves Alone,* or Robert Holman's *The Overgrown Path,* or Nick Ward's recent *Apart From George,* there has been a discreet but unmistakable insistence that life is fickle, random and subjective; that we can make sense of it not by doing anything but by feeling and reacting, by scrutinising the emotionally-charged thoughts which external action inevitably prompts in us. Drama of this kind may seem loose, inconsequential and disorganised, but it has lent the conventional stage play a new vantage point. It has retrieved the soliloquy, and diminished the importance of that staple of melodrama, the grand confrontation scene where everything is finally said.
>
> Clare McIntyre's *Low Level Panic* at the Theatre Upstairs is a Royal Court play *par excellence;* low-key and conversational, full of quiet, incidental angst, and wary of the well-planned climax. Its focal point is the communal bathroom of a shared flat, where three single women are preparing for a night out, and the possibility of romance.

Rissik begins by placing McIntyre in a context that includes and values work by both women and men; this allows him to begin his specific look at her play by accepting her premises. When such acceptance of women's ideological premises do appear, it provides a reasonable basis for enthusiastic responses to a play's feminism. Reviews like Rissik's ensure that Claire Armistead is no longer alone when she so comfortably opens her

review of *When I Was a Girl, I Used to Scream and Shout . . . (1984)* this
way—

> The forbidden apple of female sexuality can seldom have been
> served up so raw and ripe to a West End audience as in this comedy
> by Sharman Macdonald plucked from the ever lengthening list of
> past successes at the Bush. That in itself can only be a good thing:
> it is high time someone wrested the issue from the sweaty palm of
> male fantasy and presented it as something with a life and a growth
> of its own.

Women can still criticize their treatment by reviewers with just
cause, but reviewers are showing signs of learning to understand and
appreciate the differences of women's work. For a woman's comedy
particularly committed to change on generic, personal, and social levels,
such accommodations are encouraging.

## The Future for Women's Comedy: The Challenge of
## Politics and Change

An assessment of the future seems necessarily to follow from my description of a woman's comedy so forward-looking: a comedy that has
declared its independence from the male tradition, that has shaped its
own audience, and that has brought new gender-consciousness to the
ranks of reviewing. In its various contexts, this comedy has proved
sensitive though resilient. I close by speculating about the obstacles and
achievements that may lie ahead for a comedy so committed to change.

Vera Gottlieb ("Thatcher's Theatre") sets a challenge for all contemporary theater practitioners as she outlines how the Thatcher years have
brought the British theater to a crisis point. After noting the widening
gap between the politics onstage and those offstage, she warns that the
theater "cannot do what its society is not doing"; indeed, she adds, there
is a strategic problem in attempting to exist outside of "the prevalent
ideological climate" (104). Yet in spite of this unsupportive situation, she
counsels the maintenance of a continued theatrical protest. She speaks
to the special situation of women writing comedy in the last decade of
the century by urging that protestive drama *must* go on, even against the
prevailing current:

But so long as the theatre fails to fulfill its function of "a good night out" (John McGrath) *and* of simultaneously providing illumination, intervention, and opposition, then it will remain not only unsatisfying and seriously inadequate, but effectively in collusion with today's ideological climate. (104)

Gottlieb published her evaluation of the contemporary theater in May of 1988. At the same time, she and Simon Trussler organized a meeting of theater practitioners and academics to discuss the state of theater that she had described, with such concern, in her essay. In the abbreviated transcript of the meeting (published in *New Theatre Quarterly*, "Theatre in Thatcher's Britain," May 1989), many of Gottlieb's colleagues go on record as sharing her concerns.[9] The bleakest sentiment about the state of the theater came from *New Theatre Quarterly* editor Trussler, who noted, "In England—and I might as well express it in as defeatist a way as I can—there seems to have been a breaking of the will" (115). While all of those present did not come to such dark conclusions, the discussion established, with a consensus of opinion, that alternative, socialist theater is threatened: funding is scarce, enthusiasm is rare, and energies are scattered.

Neither Gottlieb in her essay nor the group in its discussion directly addresses women's comedy as a part of the present theatrical landscape. The general role of women in the alternative theater is, however, considered briefly by Juliet Stevenson and Pam Brighton as they participate in the discussion. Stevenson objects to the notion that there is currently little energy and optimism in the theater (this notion is an assumption for most of those who engage in the discussion), and for her counterexample points to the creative energy women have brought to theater. In her response to Stevenson, Brighton discounts the importance of women's work, noting, "I think the women's movement *is* very important in terms of how women see themselves. But I don't think it's terribly important in terms of that real political battle. Women's theatre and a lot of ethnic companies have been—politically and culturally—red herrings in the last ten years" (119). These divergent responses—the one locating in women's theater a much-needed optimism, the other dismissing women's work as incidental—offer extreme ways of evaluating both women's recent contributions to the theater and their chances of contributing to the future of that theater. This exchange also suggests how undefined the rule of women's theater remains in the broader realm of contemporary theater. Besides exposing such uncertain evaluations of women's theater, the overall discussion also suggested that most theater practitioners continue to overlook women's efforts. Even with five women among the fourteen participants, women's actual and potential contributions to the theater were rarely brought up. To the majority of those concerned about the state of British theater, women's work still does not present itself as a major component of the future.

While women's work was not a specific consideration of either Gottlieb or those who joined her and Trussler for the communal discussion, all participants in the debate agreed on the necessity of reshaping the face of British theater for the future. Gottlieb cited Caryl Churchill as one model of a playwright whose anti-establishment voice has remained strong and whose work may survive into the future. Those gathered for the group discussion recommended, additionally, that a wide range of options be developed for approaching that future. In closing my study of women and comedy, I would like to add to this discussion of the contemporary theater by focusing on women's work. For the theater work women are doing—and particularly their comic work— makes its own distinctive propositions about the future. The debate I have summarized in the last two paragraphs suggests that women will most likely make their contributions to British theater as outsiders; that they will continue to need inventive strategies to make themselves visible. Women working through comedy do, however, share with their colleagues Gottlieb, Trussler, and others a sense of urgency. Women have created a comedy with a unique optimism and audience, a comedy that is changing the nature of reviewing. It remains to be seen how much this comedy can change its world.

Women are increasingly visible in the theater. But as the Gottlieb-Trussler discussion once more demonstrates, women's situation remains tenuous. Signals from both left and right continue to cloud the reception of women's offerings. For example, in his "Joint Manifesto for the Left on Cultural Politics in the Post-Thatcher Era" (co-written with playwright Howard Barker), Tony Dunn counsels the left to take the road leading toward "high culture" and implies that community theater, women's theater, and the efforts to encourage female subjectivity have not only been overplayed by the left but are now *out*played. The literary, cultural future he envisions is premised on a classically based and (therefore) mostly male tradition. Response from the right is chillingly similar in its retreat from the inclusive impulses that have motivated much women's theater. The 1988 regulation that prohibits the public funding of any group supporting or encouraging gays or lesbians (clause 28 of the Local Government Act) is a direct blow to many women's theater groups. Understandably, many women are discouraged not only by such cultural and legal developments, but also by similar events in recent theatrical history. In the late 1980s, many women still active in the theater find themselves troubled by colleagues who have chosen to abandon the difficult life of bringing feminism to the theater. Louise Page sums up the forces that are pushing some women out: "It was easy ten years ago because the battles were up front and they were big and you could get all that energy. But the persistent push, push, push is just very, very tiring" (interview). Pam Gems keeps a watch over the casting lists in *Radio Times* and *TV Times* to note that men are still offered about twice as many parts as women are (interview). And both the report on women in the British theater by the Conference of Women Theatre Directors and Administrators (it covered 1982–83) and the 1987 follow-up "What Share of the Cake? The Employment of Women in the English Theatre" (by Caroline Gardiner; published by the Women's Playhouse Trust) are comprehensive reminders of the limited number of women administrators, directors, and writers in theater. The ever-diminishing public funding for women's theater only adds to the bleak picture some women see when they generalize now about women in theater.[10]

Within this grim atmosphere, some women, understandably, see that very little gain has come from women's efforts in the theater. Lou Wakefield says bluntly, "No I don't think it has changed at all for the better" (interview). Wandor specifies the nature of this stasis:

> What I am saying is that nothing really has changed yet. Yes, there are a few more women playwrights. . . . There are more women directors visibly working. . . . There is a much higher consciousness, energy in the way women approach their work as performers. But in terms of theatre overall and what plays are being done in the theatre and how they are being done, I don't think anything has really been dented. And I think that is just a measure of how difficult it is. I couldn't even begin to imagine a situation in which it might really, really change. . . . I think it is a very, very long haul. (Interview)

Sue Dunderdale extends this analysis by stressing that the problem is societywide. As long as men run the world, their ethic will rule the theater; and more often than not, she asserts, women will be "absorbed into reflecting [men's] cultural values anyway" (interview). Louise Page provides a metaphoric summary of the despair that runs deep: "You are swimming against the tide all the time, and yet the sea doesn't look that way to you. The sea to you looks quite easy, but there is this endless male tide coming at you" (interview). Very few women working in the British theater today are ignorant of their short and still-threatened history, and those I have quoted look ahead to little change. Such dark assessments do not tell the whole story, however. In spite of all the institutional, cultural, and theatrical discouragements, this dark view is not shared by all women in the theater. Even the discouraged women have been persistent in their efforts to effect the change they have defined as so slow and unlikely. So it should not, finally, be surprising that in a women's theater guided by the hope and joy of comedy, a brighter outlook has also survived.

For those who have maintained optimism about the possibilities for women in theater, ideas about the present and future of the theater collect around two central questions: How should women be treated in the theater? And how will theater change the world? The first question has concerned men as much as women. In the RSC and the Royal Court, for example, recent artistic directors have pondered the issue of how to include women in their operation. The two theaters have found themselves attempting both to support women and to protect an abstraction they label "quality." Colin Chambers documents the divisive response within the RSC:

> We have discussed and do discuss quite often how should the company overcome its clear bias. And you then get caught up in this argument to do with positive discrimination as against something supposedly called quality.... There are roughly two positions inside the company.... One is that we must in some way encourage women to be represented, but that they must go through exactly the same process of selection or competition or whatever as everybody else, i.e., the men. The other is that the very process is precisely the process that excludes them. And that you have got to do something much more radical and actually interventionist, and that is a much bigger risk. (Interview)

Philip Palmer echoes Chambers's concern in reporting similarly of the Royal Court's wish to bring women to full equality:

> There is a very strong sense that there has to be change. But you have to do it in such a way that you are not actually undermining the objectives of theatre itself, which you would do if you took on a woman writer who really wasn't good enough. You would destroy actors and you would undermine the theatre's reputation. . . . It would be nice if we were actually among the first to do something about it [the imbalance of men and women]. (Interview)

For those like Chambers and Palmer who exert some power over the shape of the most prominent alternative theater, the drive to produce "quality" theater is complicated by their sensitivity to issues of class, age, and politics as well as of gender. Yet as long as the differences of women's work are held up to standards of quality derived primarily from men's plays, the division between women's writing and "quality" work will likely remain.

Many of the women addressing the issue of women's future in the theater bypass the conundrum Chambers and Palmer report by assuming—to begin—that women *will* create quality theater just as men may. The burden of proving this has fallen mostly to the women. As my preceding chapters have suggested, female "quality" work has a novel appearance that extends to structure, character, presentation, content, tone, and politics. Several women have suggested strategies for establishing such women's work as a normal order of theatrical business. Some, for instance, have called for the theater community—theaters, reviewers, and audiences—to "allow" women to fail, to establish a system that would ensure the availability of failure for women as it now does for men. Wandor has even called for a program of affirmative action. In her introduction to volume 4 of *Plays by Women,* she proposes that all subsidies be contingent upon theaters adopting a "graduated quota system" whereby over a set period of years (perhaps three to seven), the proportion of women writers in a theater would increase to 50 percent (10). She argues that this policy would force the theaters to open up to, even welcome, women's points of view and imaginations.

It is when women consider the second question about their future in the theater that they most freely exercise their hopes, their imaginations, and their fledgling power. Asked how theater will change the world, they respond with tales of transformations—both witnessed and projected. Like many others steeped in comedy, Sue Townsend is proud to relate stories of the individual women she has seen her plays affect directly. Seeing their lives not only sympathetically portrayed but also celebrated in *Bazaar and Rummage,* many of the agoraphobiacs who bravely ventured out to see the play (some hadn't left home in years) earned self-esteem. Townsend reports more specifically on the influence of *The Great Celestial Cow* (1984): an Asian friend, on hearing one of the play's Asian women characters boast about opening her own account at the Building Society, defied her own family protocol to open a similar account (Townsend interview). Writers, actors, and directors associated with Spare Tyre, Siren Theatre Company, and the Scarlet Harlets note that their efforts to interact directly with audiences also have resulted in transformations in their audience members' life-styles and politics.

Yet many women have been especially careful to downplay the long-term results of such individual change; they realize that theater has a potent but limited power to change and that expectations of change must account for this limitation. While the theater may change individuals, it changes institutions too rarely. For example, Jane Boston is unwilling to conclude that Siren Theatre could effect direct political action; she does, however, assert that theater practitioners move toward change by adding to the "range of ideas" in the theater and that such change means the audience may shift "our perceptions of how we see ourselves culturally" (interview). Deborah Levy also speaks of perceptions in noting that theater "moves the spirit. And I think that the spirit is a revolutionary thing" (interview). It is the spirit that theater moves to resistance, she claims. Yet Timberlake Wertenbaker comes closest to articulating this common combination of a belief in change and an acknowledgment of the oblique change theater encourages; she also suggests that the changes urged by women's theater are identifiably female:

It [women's theater] seeps in. I think it has a very, very slow influence. . . . And I think we are finding out more and more that in any case it is a political action which is very worthwhile and it may be a sort of feminine political action . . . as well. Women's work irritates and that is a good thing. (Interview)

Women caution that it is naive and reductive to draw a direct line from theater and its individual change to political or social change. They believe concurrently, however, that the theater does change people's lives and that this change will slowly change the world. If the past provides any prediction of the future, the change will be slow.

Through a final example, I can best convey my image of the future of women's comedy on the British stage. Timberlake Wertenbaker's *Our Country's Good* (1988) is an optimistic play premised on the belief in change she expresses in the statements I have just quoted. The play also indicates how the distinguishing features of contemporary women's comedy continue to be replayed and reshaped as part of a maturing women's theater. Wertenbaker's play may, in fact, signal the coming of age of women's comedy. While drawing on the last twenty years of women's theater, it proudly and daringly points to the future.

The most amazing aspect of Wertenbaker's play is its incisive portrait of theater's transformative power. I will end my discussion with a full account of this play's transformative power, but I begin with an overview of the play's rich comedy. As much as any other single play I have discussed in part 2, *Our Country's Good* is built out of the features I have identified as characteristic of British women's contemporary comedy. After opening with a "stunning series of tableaux" (Conway review) that depict the horrors of an eighteenth-century sea-crossing from England to Australia, the play is concerned with a new convicts' colony in Australia in 1787. The three-part cast of characters—female convicts, male convicts, and their military supervisors—come uneasily together when the colony's governor, Arthur Phillip, arranges for the convicts to put on George Farquhar's *The Recruiting Officer* under the supervision of Lieutenant Ralph Clark. The bulk of the play records the debates and efforts surrounding the production of Farquhar's play in this unlikely location with an even unlikelier crew of actors. And the bulk of the play is delivered in a range of dramatic modes that have become common in women's comedy.

Reviewer Dominic Gray's description of the staging during the original Royal Court production records Wertenbaker's use of many compositional strategies I reviewed in chapters 8 and 9:

> Timberlake Wertenbaker's play is episodic, fragmentary, and occasionally scrappy. But this disjointedness gives room for a rich variety of styles and rapid changes of focus and texture. A breathtaking

tableaux illustrating the horrors of the journey from England opens the play, before giving way to a naturalistic scene in Australia. Later we have Brechtian scene-titles and costume changes, and other scenes of almost surrealist nightmare. The audience's sympathies and perspectives are thus constantly questioned and made to contradict themselves.

As Gray notes, the play departs not only from conventional linear narrative, but also from realism. In his reference to the surreal, Gray seems to be referring specifically to act 2, scene 3, in which midshipman Harry Brewer speaks to the dead who haunt him, or act 2, scene 4, in which the brutal treatment of the convicts is foregrounded. Still more important excursions from realism are the act 2 appearances of a character Wertenbaker calls "the Aborigine." The figure appears three times (and apparently only in dialogue with the audience) during the convicts' play rehearsals, making plaintive and poetic pleas about Australia as a newly invaded country. Wertenbaker's departures from realism are clearly laden with criticisms of British claims to the Australian continent and of the physical brutality with which the convicts were treated. And as in many other women's plays, this politically motivated presentational plurality is coupled with cross-gender casting and the actors' assumption of multiple roles. The characters themselves talk about such substitutions by sex and number, at once interested in and repulsed by the possibilities. And reviewers' responses to both the 1988 Royal Court original and the 1989 Royal Court revival suggest that women playing soldiers' roles (while still dressed in decolleté) provided some unforgettable scrambling of conventional character-actor lines. While such departures from conventional narrative and presentation do not in and of themselves reflect the play's comic nature, Wertenbaker's attention to community and to issues of self and sexuality clearly do.

Original director Max Stafford-Clark notes in the published version of the play how he, Wertenbaker, and a Royal Court acting company "workshopped" the play, creating the context out of which Wertenbaker produced the script. As at least one reviewer—Martin Hoyle of the *Financial Times*—noted, this communal generation contributed to the cohesion of the original production. The workshopping has also, clearly, resulted in a comedy built around groups. While each of the play's three main communities operates from internal loyalties, the group of women convicts is representative in showing the individual characters' ties to the others in their group. Dabby and Mary, for example, plead to Ralph Clark to cast them as friends in Farquhar's play—they want to replicate onstage their offstage friendship. However, this is by no means a play about separatist communities: and in the play's conclusion, the three motley collections of characters find themselves conjoined in the spectacle of theater. The bonding that the convict groups, especially, undergo is paralleled by transformations on the individual level. And for the women characters, the transformation is a development of self that takes into account their compromised sexuality.

The sexual is a major dimension of the women convicts' lives as they work toward autonomy through the course of the play. Both on the sea journey and in their early days in Australia, the women must either succumb to the men's sexual demands or pay the price of ridicule, exclusion, or torture. But as in Sarah Daniels's *Byrthrite,* the women find ways of counteracting their relative lack of sexual power not so much by physical assertiveness as by claiming a linguistic power ordinarily denied them. For example, as three of the women rehearse their lines in act 1, scene 8, they begin to learn that by claiming the genteel language of Farquhar's play, they can claim a dignified self unavailable to them in the limited vocabulary of their sexual prostitution. Such empowering realizations accelerate as the play goes on. While in act 1 Mary claims that she can act a part only by becoming it—by losing her self—in act 2 Dabby has come so far as to deny the temporary power of theatrical roles. She demands a real power: "I want to play myself" (46). And in much different circumstances still later, Liz, within hours of hanging for a crime she did not commit, realizes that her voice does count. When she finally speaks up to deny the charge against her, she finds her words because Farquhar has expanded the possibilities of language for her (50). Liz's pregnant silences before her accusers are transformed into a language she draws from Farquhar but that expresses her own new sense of self-worth: "Your excellency, I will endeavour to speak Mr. Farquhar's lines with the elegance and clarity their own worth commands" (50). As Billington notes, hers is an especially powerful moment of "self-realisation" (review).

In detailing Wertenbaker's reliance on the various components of women's contemporary comedy, I have not stressed the way in which such qualities come together to make a funny and joyful play. Almost without exception, the reviews that greeted the original production marked the genuine good feelings to be found in *Our Country's Good.*

The words "joyous," "comic," "funny," "entertaining," "celebration," "hope," "merry," "rousing," and "optimistic" fill the reviews. But besides being a comedy in such recognizable fashion, besides serving as a catalogue of the methods by which women now make comedy, Wertenbaker's is also a play self-consciously *about* comedy. I noted in chapter 9 that Wertenbaker's characters find laughter a crucial tool for claiming power. But her commentary on comedy also extends to more abstract aspects of the genre. She deals in particular with the two qualities by which I outlined the genre in part 1—inversion and ending. In her revision of both, Wertenbaker articulates the transformative power women are now commanding in their theater.

As soon as the officers running the Australian colony are introduced to the idea of staging a play, debate about the nature of theater begins. And as *The Recruiting Officer,* a comedy, is the specific play at issue, that debate centers on comedy's explosive middle. Ralph talks about his production's potential to "change the nature of our little society" (24) and details how in even initial readings of the play, the convicts seemed to "lose some of their corruption" (25). Major Ross agrees on the revolutionary potential of the play, but can only see such results negatively: he reads the connotations of such change as "insubordination, disobedience, revolution" (26). Later, Governor Phillip adds his approval to these reports of comedy's rebellious possibilities, telling Ralph: "If you break conventions, it's inevitable you make enemies, Lieutenant" (40). As these three representative moments suggest, everyone concurs in finding dangerous the inverted, irregular action comedy allows. And this danger exists doubly, on the level of Wertenbaker's play as well as Farquhar's— in other words, just as Farquhar's play is threatening to the status quo of the convict colony, so is Wertenbaker's disruptive of the status quo in Britain in 1988. More specifically, with its highlighting of comedy's potential revolution, Wertenbaker's play allows for two conclusions about the place of inversion in contemporary women's comedy. First, as if it were an example of Turner's liminoid, her play suggests that inversion remains a potentially radical move. By allowing for a true testing of new orders, new roles, new selves, and new languages, Wertenbaker's own inversion opens up possibilities for essential change. And second, because Wertenbaker's action is shaped by a cleverly crafted diversity in narrative, characterization, and presentation, such inversion is not contained, as it might be by a traditional ending. As I have argued many times before, the comic play's ending is the most crucial factor in the effectiveness of the play's change. Wertenbaker's own ending, as well as her commentary on comic endings and their transformative potential, suggests, finally, the power women can harness in their comedy.

Several times throughout the play, the idea of the happy ending in Farquhar's comedy is discussed. Both the convicts and the suspicious authorities seem to be comforted by the closure such an ending has traditionally signaled. Wertenbaker never allows Farquhar's play to end, however (*Our Country's Good* ends with the opening of *The Recruiting Officer*), and her own ending belies any predictable return to order. For what happens in the end of Wertenbaker's play is that the radical changes promised by the play's inversions come to fruition. In short, Wertenbaker actualizes the comic theater's greatest promise—transformation. While transformation is indeed the play's ending point, such transformation and its ties to theater develop gradually and are not confined to the end. Halfway through the play, for example, Ketch, one of the male convicts, sees acting in Farquhar's play as his chance to change his life. He pleads to Ralph:

> Some players came into our village once, they were loved like the angels, Lieutenant, like the angels. And the way the women watched them—the light of spring dawn in their eyes.
> Lieutenant.
> I want to be an actor. (32)

Similarly, as act 2 begins with four of the player-convicts in chains, another convict, Mary, calls up the power of theater in urging the encumbered players to rehearse despite their situation: "This is the theatre. We will believe you" (39). The contrast between the convicts' disenfranchised lives and the liberation promised by the theater is great. But the theater's transformative power is real when, as Major Ross interrupts a rehearsal by physically humiliating the convicts, they turn to Farquhar's lines to see them through the brutalizing (43). Such signs of the personal power the convicts find in their theater accumulate and reach critical mass as the play reaches its end. (Liz's transcendence of silence, which I noted above, draws on her confidence in theater; and Wisehammer's proposed new prologue to Farquhar's play is likewise a sign of his emerging identity.) All of the signs of both individual and group transformation allow the ending to be a certification that change is possible, that the theater promotes not only individual growth but also communal liberty.

The play ends, seemingly so simply, with the convicts beginning their performance. What makes the moment so powerful is that the transformation of the convicts into Farquhar's genteel characters, in itself magical, combines with Wertenbaker's playlong focus on other transformations to carry the final moments beyond Farquhar or eighteenth-century Australia. The accumulation of transformations means that the final moments belong more outside of Wertenbaker's play than in it; the challenge of the play's politics is left with its audience. The power of this ending may best be gleaned through the response of reviewers who experienced the play's accumulation of changes. Charles Spencer writes of the play as a "celebration of the theatre" and speaks of at least one character change as a redemption. Billington's exuberance is even more representative. He finds the play's comic brightness convincing and refreshingly welcome: "But what makes this play work is its very assumption that drama has the capacity to change lives and liberate imaginations: in these crass times it is heartening to find someone standing up for theatre's antique spiritual power." But finally, the responses of both Kate Kellaway and Lydia Conway indicate how the transformation at the heart of Wertenbaker's play offers radical possibilities for change that reach far beyond the confines of the theater. Kellaway notes, "'Our Country's Good' is about theatre's power to spill over into life and overtake circumstance." And Conway finds this a play about life beyond the theater: "By design and by example it is a civilizing experience that burst out of the confines of the auditorium and rings in the ears for days afterwards."

In a theater now so full of despair, Wertenbaker's play stands as evidence that women's comedy makes a crucial contribution to the contemporary theater. The superlative reviews of the play (and the awards that came later) suggest two conclusions about women's future in the theater. First, the reviews suggest the full acceptance that can now greet women's comedy, a comedy built on departures from traditional comedy. Second, the reviews suggest how welcome the optimism of a play like *Our Country's Good* is. Billington's last comment in the preceding paragraph is representative of the rare, liberated feeling this play brought to the contemporary stage. As I noted in chapter 9, Wertenbaker's play has more male than female characters and makes no claim for separatist theater. But its women remain key players in the transformations it effects. And the play indicates the vast possibilities open to the women who will continue to express themselves through comedy. As Wertenbaker shows, to bring women and comedy together is to demand change.

Wertenbaker's play makes a hopeful statement about the future role of women in the theater. Optimism about women's roles in the theater may also be drawn from the number of women who continue to put their own energy and investments into a theater increasingly defined by their own lives, beliefs, successes, failures—and plays. And for women, to channel their lives into a theater triply dangerous—dangerous as theater, as comedy, and as women's—is to strive for a theater with potential, above all, to change the world, a world these women see as having rested too long in the exclusive care of men. As Julia Pascal asserts,

> I think art is dangerous. I think theatre is very dangerous. And I think that's why we [women] are put in the ghetto. I think women in comedy are a very dangerous cause because there is something anachronistic and uncontrollably endemic in the position of being a woman. . . . It is no accident that women are ghettoized. (Interview)

No one can predict women's future role in the British theater. I can show with certainty that more and more women are writing, directing, and assuming significant new roles in the theater; yet Wandor's ideal of a theater half female is unlikely to be implemented any time soon. The present situation points back to discrimination and forward to equality: while women's groups have lost ground through funding, women have gained stature in the established theater; while black women's theater has been privileged in recent years, lesbian theater has become a new target for cutbacks. And it must be stressed that the current endangered status of lesbian theater is a threat to all women's theater, for the lesbian theater has most frequently provided the radical basis on which the reformations of all women's theater have been stacked.[11] Yet against the grain, across the grain, and with the grain, British women's theater goes on. It grows. As the heart of this theater, women's comedy will remain the primary site for the maturing years of women's theater. While women's theater is not and will not be any more monolithic than men's, it will build on a tradition that privileges female subjectivity, community, joy, and laughter. As American humorist Nicole Hollander reminds us, she who laughs, lasts.

# Notes

## Chapter 1

1. Torrance's attitude is particularly puzzling because the strategies most comic heroines employ to assure their power would seem to fit in so nicely with his theory of comic heroism.

2. Among those in agreement with Feibelman are L. C. Knights ("Notes on Comedy") and Benjamin Lehmann ("Comedy and Laughter").

3. See *The Myth of Deliverance*, 56 especially, where Frye points to William Morris as the example of an artist combining a commitment to social change with a drive to preserve tradition. Nicholas Grene *(Shakespeare, Jonson, Molière)*, Robert Heilman *(Ways of the World)*, William McCollom *(Divine Average)*, and Malcolm Kiniry ("Jacobean Comedy") deal directly with what they also see as contradictory social impulses in comedy.

4. While Frye is up-front with his assumption that comedy is an identifiable convention and structure *(A Natural Perspective,* 46), most who study comic types and patterns simply assume that there is comedy and that it has an identifiable, reproducible form. McFadden *(Discovering the Comic)* directly asks, "Does the comic exist?," finding that the answer is yes. For more general study of genre theory see Hernadi *(Beyond Genre)* and Strelka *(Theories of Literary Genre)*. The authors represented in the "On Convention: I" issue of *New Literary History* 13 (Autumn 1981) chart a parallel course, studying literary convention through the lens of structuralism, semiotics, and deconstruction. I will return to the issue of changing conventions later in the chapter.

5. Even from feminists, direct consideration of women in comedy is still rare. Important early work has been done by Little *(Comedy and the Woman Writer)*, Wilt ("Laughter of Maidens"), Park ("As We Like It"), Bamber *(Comic Women, Tragic Men)*, French *(Shakespeare's Division of Experience)*, and Zeitlin ("Travesties of Gender and Genre"). More recently, the work collected in Barreca's *Last Laughs* generally celebrates the power women can find in comedy. In her introduction, Barreca herself makes the most cogent case for the radical possibilities women can find in comedy. Others who have touched on the issue of women and comedy include Trilling ("Liberated Heroine"), Berggren

("Woman's Part"), Garner *("A Midsummer Night's Dream"),* Toth ("Female Wits"), and Wandor *(Carry On).*

6. In an early book, *Process, Performance, and Pilgrimage,* Turner finds women "quintessentially liminal" (105). However, in this study both his belief in the power of the carnival and his locating of change in women grow out of the still single idea of the liminal. And it is the liminal, when later contrasted to the liminoid, that Turner will find inherently reactionary. Thus, because Turner has not yet offered his theory on the limitations of liminal inversion, his early conclusions on women and carnival have a limited application. It is only with the concept of liminoid in hand that Turner acknowledges the problematic route to social change that inversion provides.

7. Bamber *(Comic Women, Tragic Men)* is the most convincing in arguing that comedy's ending and marriage do not have to mean curtailment of power and loss of freedom for women. Separating the failure of feminist "shrews" from the more subtle victories of comic heroines as "other," she concludes that comedy offers women an unmatchable playground for real status (30–43). Yet she still does not account for the structural power of the comic ending. She says comedy is only sexist when it is a battle of the sexes (35); I contend that for the comic heroine that battle never ends. For a very different account of the role of marriage in drama, see Sue-Ellen Case ("Classic Drag"), who notes that marriage has been imposed as a penalty on women since *The Oresteia.*

8. Bamber makes this point in the context of Shakespearean comedy *(Comic Women, Tragic Men,* 35).

9. See Cavell *(Pursuits of Happiness)* for a study of what he finds a genre of remarriage in Hollywood film. He pays particular attention to the growth of a female consciousness in the films. While he finds marriage problematic, what he calls "remarriage" offers a significant revision of the institution.

10. See my earlier study, "Comic Textures and Female Communities," which outlines the destruction such heterosexual endings bring to female friendships in comedy.

11. More feminist critics than I can name have located the heroine's subversive tactics in literature written by both men and women. Early work in this area—that by Gilbert and Gubar *(Madwoman),* Kolodny ("Dancing" and "A Map"), Edwards *(Psyche as Hero),* Miller *(The Heroine's Text),* and Pratt et al. *(Archetypal Patterns)*—has established the recognition of such strategies as central to feminist literary criticism. For studies of these subversive strategies as they appear in comedy (primarily fiction) see Barreca's collection, *Last Laughs.*

12. The terms on which Constance takes off with Bernard are never entirely clear. Maugham appears to have intended the ambiguity. Responding to an American woman's query about what happens, Maugham replied: "I think Constance went off with Bernard and did not think much of it when she did. But I may be wrong. The author does not always know" (10 September 1935; Morgan, *Maugham,* 298).

13. While feminist work in reader response criticism has offered strategies in which the positing of a female and or feminist reader can effect some such new interventions, Neely and Jardine are pointing more to the establishment of a

critical context through which the literature, its women, and its relation to women can be judged. For current work in feminist reader response criticism, see Flynn and Schweickart's *Gender and Reading*.

## Chapter 2

1. Not *As You Like It*, however, but *Love's Labor's Lost* offers the most substantial evidence of Shakespeare's inclination to center on women in an attempt to disrupt comic form. The collision of women and comedy in that play is highlighted by Berowne as he bemoans his still unmarried state at the play's end:

> Our wooing doth not end like an old play;
> Jack hath not Jill. These ladies' courtesy
> Might well have made our sport a comedy.
>
> (5.2.864–66)

While a study of *Love's Labor's Lost* would allow for a fruitful investigation of that play's renegade women, I turn to *As You Like It* instead, and to a collection of women both disruptive and accommodating. *As You Like It*, in the range of rebellion to be found in its women, offers a more complete portrait than *Love's Labor's Lost* of the paradoxes that attach to women in comedy.

2. See also Jardine, who concurs that the gender swapping does not necessarily benefit women (*Still Harping*, 19–20). Kimbrough ("Androgyny") is among those who do find the play's androgyny a sign of sexual equality.

3. See Montrose ("'The Place of a Brother'") for a similar view that the reversals of comedy operate as a "structure for her [Rosalind's] containment."

4. See Rutter *(Clamorous Voices)* for a perceptive reading of the friendship between Rosalind and Celia. In Rutter's interview with actor Juliet Stevenson, they discuss the great feminist possibilities of the connection as well as the persistent difficulties the two cousins face in a patriarchal world.

5. In their playing of the cousins in the 1985–86 RSC production, actors Fiona Shaw and Juliet Stevenson attempted to transmit Celia's ascendancy in the early portions of the play (Rutter, *Clamorous Voices*, 103).

6. Marjorie Garber (*Coming of Age*, 140–70) and George Gordon (*Shakespearian Comedy*, 31–32) read the movement of women away from each other in the play positively, each finding a psychic gain in such separation. Marilyn French (*Shakespeare's Division of Experience*, 79) and Carole McKewin ("Counsels of Gall") are even more optimistic: French refers to plays such as *As You Like It* as rare literary sites where female bondage is transformed to female bonding. Most recently, however, both Janet Adelman ("Male Bonding," 82–84) and Carol Neely *(Broken Nuptials)* have advanced the view that, like mine, finds the play's female friendships ultimately sacrificed by the women. In her book, Neely returns again and again to the conclusion that Shakespeare's plays consistently separate women. Thomas MacCary *(Friends and Lovers)* provides a

complementary study of male friendship, finding that marriage is also often a deathblow to male bonds.

7. Antonia Fraser offers an encyclopedia of specific examples on marriage and Renaissance women. Her study of women in all classes (*The Weaker Vessel*) suggests how the portrait of marriage varied from class to class and decade to decade.

8. I am responding to the production that transferred from Stratford-upon-Avon to London. For a thorough description and feminist analysis of the original Stratford production, see Rutter, *Clamorous Voices*, 97–121.

9. Stevenson's analysis of the production (and its feminist possibilities) is somewhat more optimistic than mine. See Rutter, *Clamorous Voices*, 95–121.

## Chapter 3

1. David Roberts and Harold Weber both summarize the general conditions for women in this half-century by matching advances with retreats. Weber, for example, notes that the increase in women's sexual freedom remained linked to a sexual double standard (*Restoration Rake-Hero*, 147). The two critics note that the transfer of commerce and business out of the home both removed women from monetary power and encouraged a new valuation of women against the ideal of leisure (which, of course, ended in their devaluation [Roberts, *The Ladies*, 6]). Both also note that the radical political and social ideas inspired by the civil war and revived in the bill of rights passed at the end of the century were more clearly applicable to men than women, but still responsible for a climate of change affecting women.

2. Roberts convincingly refutes John Harrington Smith's 1948 argument ("Shadwell, the Ladies, and the Change in Comedy") that the women in the late Restoration audience were responsible for the shift to sentimental comedy.

3. Such determinations are frequently accompanied by conclusions that Congreve "overturned" the "traditions of comedy" (Holland, *The Ornament of Action*, 243) and that he "had no model for the kind of social drama he had conceived" (Powell, *Restoration Theatre Production*, 197). Such aesthetic advances, I would counter, are qualified by Congreve's conventional comic heritage.

4. With *As You Like It*, I marked in detail the way language both accommodated women's freedom and restricted it. Language is crucial in the developments of *The Way of the World* also, but not in a way that grants women power. Commentators on the play have analyzed at length the sophisticated wit that drives the play's dialogue; what makes the play unusual, they note, is that all of the characters—even Witwoud and Petulant—have highly developed linguistic skills. Thus the command that Millamant demonstrates through her language is not unique. She rails about the insipid language of others; she recites poetry to suit her needs; but even after all the linguistic sensitivity she displays, she is without words as the play ends. Congreve awarded the epilogue to the actor playing Millamant. But while this address on critical taste may free an actor from the confines of her stage role, it does not significantly mitigate against Millamant's own forecast of her dwindling into a wife.

5. Weber notes that Congreve regularly uses song to contradict the narrative move toward marriage (*Restoration Rake-Hero*, 129).

## Chapter 4

1. A fuller account of the versions of *Pygmalion* is found in Dukore ("Middleaged Bully").

2. Act 2 originally consisted of two separate acts. In his final version of the play, Shaw joined the two with the curiously unstageable stage direction, "The library remains unoccupied for ten minutes" (186).

3. From *Ellen Terry and Bernard Shaw: A Correspondence*, ed. Christopher St. John (New York: Putnam, 1932), 101. As quoted in Turco (*"The Philanderer,"* 48). Both Peters (*Bernard Shaw*, 116) and Turco (55–58) extend Terry's tragic reading.

## Chapter 5

1. My generalizations about contemporary British comedy in this chapter are based on the still dominant comic tradition of mostly male playwrights. I will qualify the conclusions I offer here when, in part 2 of this book, I turn to the still marginalized women writers offering alternative comic vistas.

2. In analyzing Shakespeare, Congreve, and Shaw, I began with a study of the status quo in their comic worlds. Given the nature of Ayckbourn's inversions in *Woman in Mind*, I have collapsed such considerations in my analysis of reversals.

## Chapter 6

1. See Diamond ("Brechtian Theory / Feminist Theory") for a study of how this prologue demonstrates Behn's consciousness of the sex-gender system she inhabits.

2. See Langdell ("Aphra Behn and Sexual Politics") for a study of the various feminist messages Behn conveys in her prologues, epilogues, dedicatory letters, etc.

3. Burns writes in detail of Behn's use of "exotic forms" (*Restoration Comedy*, 126–29).

4. There is another bedchamber in the play: Sir Feeble's. Here he is foiled from his pursuit of Leticia twice, in act 3, scene 2, and act five, scene 2. But as the action indicates, this is a space he controls and one in which Leticia is as powerless as anywhere else in the play.

5. In chapter 10, I will discuss at length the ways in which contemporary women playwrights are negotiating the complicated intersection of self and sexuality. Behn's work prefigures some of the most sophisticated recent work as she shows a woman's quest for autonomy based in an acknowledgment of the constructed nature of her sexuality and affected by the multiple selves she adopts to meet her world.

6. Pert and Bearjest are also married, although this marriage is more an indication of the bountiful happiness of the ending than of the resolution of any preceding plot. More interestingly, the marrying-off of Pert, Julia's maid, may connect Julia to conventional marriage in an oblique way.

## Chapter 7

1. See Forte for an analysis of differences that may attach to female authorship in the contemporary theater. She argues that the sex of the author (as well as the viewer) *does* make a difference in the reception of a play. Yet she also raises perplexing questions about what may happen when the sex of the author is unknown ("Realism, Narrative, and the Feminist Playwright").

2. In general, she finds the tradition of comedy to be male. More specifically, she notes that it is a valid and necessary enterprise to study women's comedy apart from that of men; that only the twentieth century has seen a major change in the women of comedy; that women-authored comic constructions are different from those of men and thus easily misinterpreted; and that the comic conclusion has been the main site of women's radical revisions of comedy. Finally, she sums up existing criticism of women and comedy by saying, "It is the inability of the critical tradition to deal with comedy by women rather than the inability of women to produce comedy that accounts for the absense of critical material on the subject" (introduction to *Last Laughs,* 20).

3. See my review of the book in *Theatre Journal.* For an account of women and comedy in general studies of the contemporary British theater, see Roger Wilmut's two books, *From Fringe to Flying Circus* and *Didn't You Kill My Mother-in-Law?* In *From Fringe* Wilmut almost completely excludes women from his history of contemporary comedy. That he begins with tales of men in drag at Cambridge University's "Footlights Club" is indicative of the way he allows men, throughout his study, to usurp any position women might claim. In his more recent *Didn't You Kill my Mother-in-Law?,* however, he attempts to study alternative comedy with attention to work both nonsexist and nonracist, and he details the work of several women comics.

## Chapter 8

1. Judith Stephens ("Compatibility") presents a very different view of the relationship between women playwrights and traditional structures, arguing that women have found and will continue to find room for their concerns in traditional dramatic structures.

2. Regina Gagnier associates women's humor with anarchy, pointing to the "prolonged disruption" frequently occasioned by women's humor ("Between Women," 145).

3. Zeitlin extends this argument in "Playing the Other," where she asserts that Greek tragedy is powered by the need to contain women and the feminine. In a brief reference to Greek Old Comedy, she also implies that it is limited by its consistent choice of "the idealized past" (83).

4. I must also note that Michelene Wandor has provided me with a critical model to follow. While she currently claims that the search for particular male or female forms is misguided (*Carry On,* 183; interview), she has previously provided a list of "features which have appeared in various plays" by women, a list that my work in part 2 reflects. Her list includes (1) the breaking of sexual and body taboos, (2) the insistence on female friendship, and (3) the reassessment of history from a female point of view (*Understudies,* 71). Wandor cautions that form can only be considered along with content and that any form is potentially revolutionary. Many others, however, are writing about the difference form makes. John McGrath finds not only that form determines content, but also that an old form can cancel out a new meaning (*A Good Night Out,* 20).

5. For a full account of the comic structure of this play, see my "Revisionary Endings."

6. Structurally, the efforts of Gems, Wandor, and Dunbar are not remarkably different from the plays I considered in part 1. Other factors that I will cover in the next few chapters do distinguish these women's plays. But most important, as I will argue in chapter 12, women's optimism generally separates their work from that of men.

7. There are several useful studies of Churchill and her work to which I refer the reader in search of a more general appraisal of Churchill. See Randall, *Caryl Churchill*; Keyssar, *Feminist Theatre* and "The Dramas of Caryl Churchill"; Diamond, "(In)visible Bodies" and "Refusing the Romanticism"; Thurman, "Caryl Churchill"; Truss, "Fair Cop"; Solomon, "Witches"; and Wandor, *Carry On.*

8. The issue of female subjectivity is clearly related to these purposeful comic heroines. I study the connections between women-authored comedy and subjectivity at length in chapter 10.

## Chapter 9

1. Eugenio Barba claims that "the actor's sex is of little import" and cites Oriental theater, especially, as an important example of the asexuality of acting ("Actor's Energy," 238–39). His discounting of the actor's sex, however, overlooks the gender imbalance of traditional theater.

2. Another recent development in intrusive casting has been casting against racial type. As I have intimated, *Cloud Nine, The Great Celestial Cow,* and *New Anatomies* all make racial stereotyping an issue by calling for actors to take on parts outside of their own race or culture. Such casting accompanies a growing presence of blacks in London's theater and an increasing number of plays about race. While only some of the recent works by and/or about blacks make use of cross-racial casting, the focus on racial stereotypes is becoming a significant part of the drama all women are writing. Drawing attention to racial typing, as to gender typing, allows women writers to broaden their social indictments.

3. In her study of Churchill, Elin Diamond deals with similar dichotomies and conflations between representational theater and the potential subversions of production ("[In]visible Bodies").

4. In analyzing *Floorshow* and *Time Gentlemen Please* I am working from scrambled and probably partial scripts that I acquired from the Monstrous Regiment archives.

5. Emily Toth ("Female Wits") notes similarly that the endings of women's comedies are often communal.

## Chapter 10

1. On the related notion of whether or not critics can still reasonably talk of "subjects" and "selves" in a critical world influenced by deconstruction, see Nancy Miller, who argues that "because the female subject has juridically been excluded from the polis . . . her relation to integrity and textuality, desire and authority, is structurally different" ("Changing the Subject," 106).

2. For an extended analysis of Lacanian readings of the female self as they relate to theatrical performance, see Freedman, who specifically investigates the possibilities for the theater to effect and reflect change through different constructions of the subject ("Frame-Up," 377).

3. Féral quotes Annie Leclerc, *Parole de Femme* (Paris, 1974), 53.

4. The term *sexuality* will take on a range of meanings in this chapter. In tracing the etymology of the word, Pat Caplan notes that its initial appearance in 1800 makes it coterminous with the birth of the splintering world of modern society. She adds that in the 1980s people have generally come to see sexual orientation and behavior as the "core of the self" (2). Her stress on the inseparability of modern self and sexuality aligns her work with that of Rose, Irigaray, and others. Jeffrey Weeks's thorough analysis of the term *sexuality* and its use is also based on a modern equation of self and sexuality; yet with gestures to both Foucault and Lacan he specifies two complications in the connection. First he finds that sexuality is as much about "word, images, ritual and fantasy" as about bodies (*Sexuality,* 3). And second, he notes that as a cultural construct, sexuality has been and will continue to be appropriated in various ways. He notes this cultural relativism, for example, by detailing how early twentieth-century sexologists defined sexuality by dividing men from women. And he notes a similar, though slightly less essentialist, conflation of self and sexuality in the sexual "liberationists" of the 1960s who proclaimed "sexual freedom" for all. By demonstrating how in the last two hundred years sexuality has been the site of combat for political, social, and cultural issues, Weeks argues that when individuals are knowledgeable about the linguistic complications and cultural relativity of sexuality and its ties to self, choice can then *be* a factor in the formation of both individual and collective sexualities (13, 14). Thus change in the understanding of sexuality is possible (208).

5. According to Dunn, the amount of nudity depends on the individual production (interview). I refer to her own suggestions in stage directions in noting that two-thirds of the characters appear nude.

6. The play was replaced by *The Last of the Red Hot Lovers*. See "Note" in the *International Herald Tribune,* 10 April 1986, 16.

7. The movie version of the play, with Vanessa Redgrave and Sarah Miles, provides further evidence of the possible distortions of Dunn's feminist intent.

**Chapter 11**

1. See Sandra Zagarell ("Narrative of Community: The Identification of a Genre") who identifies a tradition of such disruptive community in fiction by women.

2. It is not clear how the recent changes at Methuen will affect this agreement.

3. In protest against cuts in funding, Jellicoe resigned her leadership post in the Trust in December 1985. She regrets handing over her position to a man, perhaps because she realizes that women have made the Trust work (interview).

4. Jellicoe's community theater, especially since the publication of *Community Plays,* may be the most well-known organization of its kind, but is not unique. Jellicoe's former assistant Elizabeth Katis is now directing urban community plays in London (Jellicoe, *Community Plays,* 20). "Clerkenwell: A Play on Wheels" toured the city of London in August of 1988. The Living Archive Project in Milton Keynes is being run by Roy Nevitt and Roger Kitchen (see Nevitt's "Community Spirit"). And John McGrath, in *A Good Night Out,* argues for a working-class base to a slightly different conception of community theater. See Woodruff ("Community") for an analysis of Jellicoe's community theater that finds her definition of community naive and her avoidance of politics dangerous.

5. The 1987 transfer of David Edgar's Trust piece, *Entertaining Strangers,* to the Cottesloe stage of the National Theatre reinforces the difference in concept, form, and outreach that Trust community plays employ. While London reviewers found acting and technical production values to applaud in the London production, reviews were generally tepid. The clear message was that a transfer from such "community theater" can't work for "professional theater"; as Martin Hoyle said, "deprived of the element of local involvement, the play leaves one wondering what this gallumphing *ersatz* village pageant is doing at this address." Not coincidentally, there is a parallel here between women's comic drama and the Trust's community plays; both are recognized as being outside of conventional dramatic patterns.

6. Keyssar *(Feminist Theatre)* provides a useful analysis of the woman-to-woman relationships in many British and American plays.

7. Feminist researchers in both psychology and sociology have recently been expanding investigations of female friendship, which until now focused largely on pathology or demographics. For example, Glenace Edwall ("Women's Friendship") is working on the intriguing hypothesis that women may most easily and naturally test their assertiveness in friendships with other women. Just as researchers in these fields are, for the first time, studying women's expectations of rewards from and emotions in friendships, so too are women playwrights exploring onstage the many ways women relate to one another.

## Chapter 12

1. Kaplan *(Women and Film)*, de Lauretis *(Alice Doesn't)*, and Silverman *(The Acoustic Mirror)* have offered some of the most significant studies of the standard assumption that the spectator is male. Case summarizes the correlations between film audiences and theater audiences *(Feminism and Theatre*, 118–24), suggesting the formal changes that will accompany the infusion of woman as spectator in the theater. On the issue of the "subjective" response of theater spectators, see also de Marinis ("Dramaturgy"), who urges the valuation of audience as "subjects" (101), though he suggests that the "closed" performances of women's theater reduce the subjective freedom of an audience.

2. See my essay "Revisionary Endings: Pam Gems's *Aunt Mary* and *Camille*."

3. In the first two chapters of *The Feminist Spectator as Critic*, Jill Dolan argues similarly that both reviewing standards and traditional notions of the canon are male-determined. Through the example of Marsha Norman's *'night, Mother*, she shows how male reviewers relentlessly attempt to make women's drama into male drama (see especially 19–40).

4. It should be noted that male reviewers have on occasion also questioned women playwrights' feminism. On Holborough's *Dreams of San Francisco*, for example, Gardner is joined by Jim Hiley, who also expresses his difficulty in categorizing the politics of the play.

5. See Dale Spender *(Mothers of the Novel)* for an analysis of the work of women reviewers before the twentieth century.

6. For reviews of Dunbar's play see *London Theatre Record*, 23 April–6 May 1986, 464–66.

7. For reviews of *Serious Money* see *London Theatre Record*, 26 March–22 April 1987, 369–75.

8. For reviews of Gannon's play see *London Theatre Record*, 25 March–7 April 1988, 397–400.

9. Those joining Gottlieb and Trussler for the discussion were Clive Barker, Pam Brighton, Colin Chambers, Trevor Griffiths, Peter Holland, Kate Harwood, Albert Hunt, Nesta Jones, John McGrath, Paul Moriarty, Rob Ritchie, and Juliet Stevenson. The follow-up article in *New Theatre Quarterly* reports on a later, larger conference in which these theater professionals and others continued the discussion of a crisis in contemporary theater. The later conference resulted in a manifesto calling for a renewed commitment to a democratic and subsidized theater (see Lavender, "Theatre in Crisis").

10. See Gillian Hanna's interview ("Waiting for Spring") for further insight into the state of women's theater today. After comparing the theater of 1989 to that of 1978, she comes to grim conclusions, suggesting that in the late 1970s, "none of us, even in our worst nightmares, saw what was coming in the next ten years" (56).

11. De Lauretis articulates the importance of lesbian representation in "Sexual Indifference."

# Works Cited

**Primary Works**

Unless otherwise indicated, I have cited published or manuscript copies of plays below. For plays not available to me in print or manuscript, I have cited performance date, place, and/or company. All dates that appear in parenthesis in part 2 of my text are dates of initial production.

Alderson, Jude. *Madonna in Slag City*. Performance at Oval House, 1986.
———. *Rachel and the Roarettes*. Author's manuscript copy, 1985.
———. *The Virgins' Revenge*. Author's manuscript copy, 1985.
Ayckbourn, Alan. *Henceforward. . . .* London: Faber and Faber, 1988.
———. *Sisterly Feelings: A Related Comedy*. London: Samuel French, 1981.
———. *Woman in Mind: December Bee*. London: Faber and Faber, 1986.
Barker, Howard. *The Poor Man's Friend*. Colway Theatre Trust performance at Bridport, 1981.
Barnes, Peter. *Red Noses*. London: Faber and Faber, 1985.
Behn, Aphra. *The Works of Aphra Behn*. Ed. Montague Summers. 6 vols. 1915. Reprint, New York: Benjamin Blom, 1967.
Caulfield, Anne. *The Ungrateful Dead*. In *Female Voices*, 85–114.
Churchill, Caryl. *Cloud Nine*. New York: Methuen, 1984.
———. *Fen*. London: Methuen, 1983.
———. *Light Shining in Buckinghamshire*. London: Pluto Press, 1978.
———. *Objections to Sex and Violence*. In *Plays by Women*, ed. Wandor, 4:11–53.
———. *Serious Money*. London: Methuen, 1987.
———. *Soft Cops*. London: Methuen, 1984.
———. *Top Girls*. London: Methuen, 1984.
———. *Traps*. London: Pluto Press, 1978.
———. *Vinegar Tom*. In *Plays by Women*, ed. Wandor, 1:15–43.
Churchill, Caryl, and David Lan. *A Mouthful of Birds*. London: Methuen, 1986.
Churchill, Caryl, Bryony Lavery, Michelene Wandor, and David Bradford. *Floorshow*. Monstrous Regiment company manuscript, 1977.
Congreve, William. *The Way of the World*. Ed. Kathleen Lynch. Lincoln: University of Nebraska Press, 1965.

Daniels, Sarah. *Byrthrite*. London: Methuen, 1987.

———. *The Gut Girls*. London: Methuen, 1989.

———. *Masterpieces*. London: Methuen, 1984.

———. *Neaptide*. London: Methuen, 1986.

———. *Ripen Our Darkness* and *The Devil's Gateway*. London: Methuen, 1986.

Davis, Jill, ed. *Lesbian Plays*. London: Methuen, 1987.

Dayley, Grace. *Rose's Story*. In *Plays by Women*, ed. Wandor, 4:55–80.

Devlin, Anne. *Ourselves Alone*. London: Faber and Faber, 1986.

Diaz, Jorge. *My Song Is Free*. Monstrous Regiment performance at Drill Hall, 1986.

Dunbar, Andrea. *Shirley*. With *Rita, Sue, and Bob Too*, 75–103. London: Methuen, 1988.

Dunn, Nell. *Steaming*. London: Amber Lane, 1981.

Evaristi, Marcella. *Commedia*. Edinburgh: Salamander Press, 1983.

Fairbanks, Tasha. *Pulp*. Siren Theatre Company performance, 1985.

*Female Voices*. London: Playwrights' Press, 1987.

Fleming, Jill. *The Rug of Identity*. In *Lesbian Plays*, ed. Davis, 85–112.

Gannon, Lucy. *Raping the Gold*. Performance at the Bush Theatre, 1988.

Gems, Jonathan. *Susan's Breasts*. Performance at Royal Court Upstairs, 1985.

Gems, Pam. *Aunt Mary*. In *Plays by Women*, ed. Wandor, 3:13–48.

———. *Camille*. In *Three Plays*, by Pam Gems, 73–153. Harmondsworth: Penguin, 1985.

———. *The Danton Affair*. RSC performance at the Barbican, 1986.

———. *Dusa, Fish, Stas, and Vi*. In *Plays by Women*, ed. Wandor, 1:45–73.

———. *Loving Women*. In *Three Plays*, by Pam Gems, 155–217. Harmondsworth: Penguin, 1985.

———. *Queen Christina*. In *Plays by Women*, ed. Remnant, 5:13–49.

Gooch, Steven. *Female Transport*. London: Pluto Press, 1974.

———. *The Women Pirates Ann Bonney and Mary Read*. London: Pluto Press, 1978.

Green, Maro, and Caroline Griffin. *More*. In *Plays by Women*, ed. Remnant, 6:39–61.

Greenham Collective. *The Fence*. In *Peace Plays*, ed. Stephen Lowe, 116–35. London: Methuen, 1985.

Griffiths, Trevor. *Comedians*. New York: Grove, 1976.

Hayes, Catherine. *Not Waving*. London: Faber and Faber, 1984.

———. *Skirmishes*. London: Faber and Faber, 1982.

Holborough, Jacqueline. *Dreams of San Francisco*. Performance at the Bush Theatre, 1987.

Horsfield, Debbie. *Red Devils*. In *Plays by Women*, ed. Wandor, 3:51–90.

Jellicoe, Ann. *The Knack* and *The Sport of My Mad Mother*. London: Faber and Faber, 1985.

———. *The Western Women*. Colway Theatre Trust performance at Lyme Regis, 1984.

Johnson, Terry. *Unsuitable for Adults*. London: Faber and Faber, 1985.

Kay, Jackie. *Chiaroscuro*. In *Lesbian Plays*, ed. Davis, 57–84.

Kearsley, Julia. *Under the Web.* Performance at the Soho Poly Theatre, 1987.

Keatley, Charlotte. *My Mother Said I Never Should.* London: Methuen, 1988.

Lavery, Bryony. *Calamity.* Monstrous Regiment performance, 1983–84.

———. *Gentlemen Prefer Blondes.* Monstrous Regiment performance, 1979–80.

———. *Mummy.* Women's Comedy Workshop performance at Drill Hall, 1987.

———. *The Origin of the Species.* In *Plays by Women,* ed. Remnant, 6:63–84.

———. *Puppet States.* Women's Comedy Workshop performance at Riverside Studios, 1988.

Lavery, Bryony, with Monstrous Regiment. *Time Gentlemen Please.* Company manuscript copy, 1978.

Levy, Deborah. *Heresies.* London: Methuen, 1987.

———. *Naked Cake.* Oval House performance, 1986.

———. *Our Lady.* Women's Theatre Group performance, 1986.

———. *Pax.* In *Plays by Women,* ed. Remnant, 6:85–113.

Lowe, Stephen. *Touched.* London: Methuen, 1979.

Lucie, Doug. *Progress* and *Hard Feelings.* London: Methuen, 1985.

Luckham, Claire. *Trafford Tanzi.* London: Quartet Books, 1983.

Macdonald, Sharman. *When I Was a Girl, I Used to Scream and Shout.* . . . London: Faber and Faber, 1985.

McIntyre, Clare. *Low Level Panic.* Women's Playhouse Trust performance at Royal Court Upstairs, 1988.

Maugham, W. Somerset. *Collected Plays of W. Somerset Maugham,* vol. 2. London: Heinemann, 1931.

Munro, Rona. *Piper's Cave.* In *Plays by Women,* ed. Remnant, 5:109–44.

Murray, Melissa. *The Execution.* Monstrous Regiment performance, 1982.

O'Malley, Mary. *Once a Catholic.* London: Amber Lane, 1978.

Page, Louise. *Beauty and the Beast.* London: Methuen, 1986.

———. *Golden Girls.* London: Methuen, 1985.

———. *Real Estate.* London: Methuen, 1985.

———. *Salonika.* London: Methuen, 1983.

Parker, Karen, and Debby Klein. *Devilry.* Authors' manuscript copy, 1984.

Pinnock, Winsome. *A Hero's Welcome.* Women's Playhouse Trust performance, 1989.

Red Ladder. *Strike While the Iron Is Hot.* In *Strike While the Iron Is Hot,* ed. Wandor, 17–62.

Remnant, Mary, ed. *Plays by Women,* vols. 5–7. London: Methuen, 1986–88.

Rudet, Jacqueline. *Basin.* In *Black Plays,* ed. Yvonne Brewster, 113–39. London: Methuen, 1987.

———. *Money to Live.* In *Plays by Women,* ed. Remnant, 5:145–81.

Scarlet Harlets. *Toe on the Line.* Performance at Oval House, 1986.

Schofield, Julia. *Love on the Plastic.* Performance at the Half Moon Theatre, 1987.

Shakespeare, William. *William Shakespeare: The Complete Works.* Ed. Alfred Harbage. New York: Viking, 1969.

Shange, Ntozake. *spell #7.* In *Three Pieces,* by Ntozake Shange, 1–52. Harmondsworth: Penguin, 1981.

Shaw, Bernard. *The Philanderer*. In *The Bodley Head Bernard Shaw,* vol. 1. London: Max Reinhardt, 1931.

Siren Theatre. *From the Divide*. 1982.

Spare Tyre. *Just Desserts*. 1984.

———. *You've Gotta Be Kidding*. London performance, 1986.

Théâtre de l'Aquarium. *Shakespeare's Sister*. Monstrous Regiment performance, 1982.

Thornton, Jane. *Amid the Standing Corn*. Director's manuscript copy, 1985.

Townsend, Sue. *Bazaar and Rummage, Groping for Words* [later titled *Are you Sitting Comfortably?*] and *Womberang*. London: Methuen, 1984.

———. *The Great Celestial Cow*. London: Methuen, 1984.

Wakefield, Lou, and Women's Theatre Group. *Time Pieces*. In *Plays by Women,* ed. Wandor, 3:125–62.

Wandor, Michelene. *Aid Thy Neighbor*. In *Five Plays,* by Michelene Wandor, 115–64. London: Journeyman Press, 1984.

———. *Aurora Leigh*. In *Plays by Women,* ed. Wandor, 1:105–37.

———. *To Die among Friends*. In *Five Plays,* by Michelene Wandor, 1–44. London: Journeyman Press, 1984.

———. *Wanted*. London: Playbooks, 1988.

———. *Whores d'oeuvres*. In *Five Plays,* by Michelene Wandor, 67–89. London: Journeyman Press, 1984.

———, ed. *Plays by Women,* vols. 1–4. London: Methuen, 1982–85.

———, ed. *Strike While the Iron Is Hot*. London: Journeyman Press, 1980.

Wandor, Michelene, and Mike Alfreds. *The Wandering Jew*. London: Methuen, 1987.

Wandor, Michelene, and Gay Sweatshop. *Care and Control*. In *Strike While the Iron Is Hot,* ed. Wandor, 63–113.

Weldon, Fay. *Action Replay*. London: Samuel French, 1980.

———. *I Love My Love*. London: Samuel French, 1984.

Wertenbaker, Timberlake. *The Grace of Mary Traverse*. London: Faber and Faber, 1985.

———. *New Anatomies*. In *Plays Introduction: Plays by New Writers,* 297–339. London: Faber and Faber, 1984.

———. *Our Country's Good*. London: Methuen, 1988.

———, trans. *Mephisto,* by Ariane Mnouchkine. RSC performance at the Barbican, 1985.

Women's Theatre Group. *My Mother Says I Never Should*. In *Strike While the Iron Is Hot,* ed. Wandor, 115–41.

Women's Theatre Group with Libby Mason. *Double Vision*. In *Lesbian Plays,* ed. Davis, 29–55.

Women's Theatre Group, and Paulette Randall. *Fixed Deal*. Oval House performance, 1986.

Wymark, Olwen. *Best Friends*. London: John Calder, 1984.

———. *Nana*. Performance at the Almeida Theatre, 1987. Performance at the Mermaid Theatre, 1988.

Yankowitz, Susan. *Alarms*. In *Female Voices,* 115–50.

Yeger, Shiela. *The Ballad of Tilly Hake.* Colway Theatre Trust performance at Ottery St. Mary, 1985.

## Interviews

My interviews and discussions with the following people inform my study throughout part 2. Quotations from these interviews appear in the text without page references.

Alderson, Jude. 13 April 1986.
Bailey, Sandy. 30 April 1986.
Boston, Jane. 3 March 1986.
Chambers, Colin. 6 May 1986.
Dawson, Jane. 10 February 1986.
Dunderdale, Sue. 13 May 1986.
Dunn, Nell. 26 February 1986.
Gardner, Lyn. 18 February 1986.
Gems, Pam. 22 April 1986.
Hayes, Catherine. 1 March 1986.
Hayman, Carole. 13 May 1986.
Jellicoe, Ann. 17 March 1986.
Lavery, Bryony. 12 May 1986.
Levy, Deborah. 5 May 1986.
Long, Sue, and Jacqui Neave. 23 April 1986.
Maycock, Hazel. 18 April 1986.
Noble, Katina. 19 May 1986.
Page, Louise. 16 April 1986.
Palmer, Philip. 15 May 1986.
Parker, Karen, and Debby Klein. 11 April 1986.
Parrish, Sue. 25 February 1986.
Pascal, Julia. 25 April 1986.
Remnant, Mary. 5 March 1986.
Townsend, Sue. 16 May 1986.
Wakefield, Lou. 13 February 1986.
Wandor, Michelene. 1 May 1986.
Wertenbaker, Timberlake. 3 May 1986.

## Secondary Works

Adelman, Janet. "Male Bonding in Shakespeare's Comedies." In *Shakespeare's "Rough Magic": Renaissance Essays in Honor of C. L. Barber,* ed. Peter Erickson and Coppélia Kahn, 75–103. Newark: University of Delaware Press, 1985.
Andresen-Thom, Martha. "Shrew-Taming and Other Rituals of Aggression: Baiting and Bonding on the Stage and in the World." *Women's Studies* 9 (1982): 121–43.

Armstrong, Nancy. "Introduction: Literature as Women's History I." *Genre* 19 (Winter 1986): 347–69.

———. "Introduction: Literature as Women's History II." *Genre* 20 (Summer 1987): 101–10.

Bakhtin, Mikhail. *Rabelais and His World,* trans. Helene Iswolsky. Cambridge, Mass.: MIT Press, 1968.

Bamber, Linda. *Comic Women, Tragic Men: A Study of Gender and Genre in Shakespeare.* Stanford: Stanford University Press, 1982.

Banks, Morwenna, and Amanda Swift. *The Joke's on Us.* London: Pandora, 1987.

Barba, Eugenio. "The Actor's Energy: Male/Female versus Animus/Anima." *New Theatre Quarterly* 11 (August 1987): 237–40.

Barratt, Michele. "Rethinking Women's Oppression: A Reply to Brenner and Ramas." *New Left Review* 146 (July/August 1984): 123–28.

———. *Women's Oppression Today: Problems in Marxist Feminist Analysis.* London: Verso, 1980.

Barreca, Regina, ed. *Last Laughs: Perspectives on Women and Comedy.* New York: Gordon and Breach, 1988.

Basnett, Susan. "Women Experiment with Theatre: Magdalena '86." *New Theatre Quarterly* 3 (August 1987): 224–34.

Basnett-McGuire, Susan E. "Towards a Theory of Women's Theatre." In *Semiotics of Drama and Theatre: New Perspectives in the Theory of Drama and Theatre,* ed. Herta Schmid and Aloysius Van Kesteren, 445–66. Amsterdam: John Benjamin, 1984.

Belsey, Catherine. "Constructing the Subject: Deconstructing the Text." In *Feminist Criticism and Social Change,* ed. Newton and Rosenfelt, 45–64.

———. "Disrupting Sexual Difference: Meaning and Gender in the Comedies." In *Alternative Shakespeares,* ed. John Drakakis, 166–90. London: Methuen, 1985.

Bentley, Eric. *The Life of the Drama.* New York: Atheneum, 1964.

———. *Thinking about the Playwright: Comments from Four Decades.* Evanston, Ill.: Northwestern University Press, 1987.

Berggren, Paula. "The Woman's Part: Female Sexuality as Power in Shakespeare's Plays." In *The Woman's Part,* ed. Lenz et al., 17–34.

Bergson, Henri. "Laughter." In *Comedy,* ed. Sypher, 61–190.

Betsko, Kathleen, and Rachel Koenig. *Interviews with Contemporary Women Playwrights.* New York: Beech Tree Books, 1987.

Bigsby, C. W. E. "The Language of Crisis in British Theatre: The Drama of Cultural Pathology." In *Contemporary English Theatre,* ed. C. W. E. Bigsby, 11–51. Stratford-upon-Avon Studies, no. 19. London: E. Arnold, 1981.

Birdsall, Virginia. *Wild Civility: The English Comic Spirit on the Restoration Stage.* Bloomington: Indiana University Press, 1970.

Blau, Herbert. "Comedy since the Absurd." *Modern Drama* 25 (December 1982): 545–67.

———. *Take up the Bodies.* Urbana: University of Illinois Press, 1982.

Booth, Wayne C. "Freedom of Interpretation: Bakhtin and the Challenge of Feminist Criticism." *Critical Inquiry* 9 (September 1982): 45–76.

Braverman, Richard. "Capital Relations and *The Way of the World.*" *ELH* 52 (Spring 1985): 133–58.

Brenner, Johanna, and Maria Ramas. "Rethinking Women's Oppression." *New Left Review* 144 (March/April 1984): 33–71.

Bristol, Michael E. *Carnival and Theatre: Plebeian Culture and the Structure of Authority in Renaissance England.* New York: Methuen, 1985.

Bull, John. *New British Political Drama.* New York: Grove, 1983.

Burns, Edward. *Restoration Comedy: Crises of Desire and Identity.* London: Macmillan, 1987.

Caplan, Pat, ed. *The Cultural Construction of Sexuality.* London: Tavistock Publications, 1987.

Carlson, Susan. "Comic Collisions: Convention, Rage, and Order." *New Theatre Quarterly* 3 (November 1987): 303–16.

———. "Comic Textures and Female Communities 1937 and 1977: Clare Boothe and Wendy Wasserstein." *Modern Drama* 27 (December 1984): 564–73.

———. Review of *The Joke's on Us,* by Morwenna Banks and Amanda Swift. *Theatre Journal* 40 (December 1988): 574–75.

———. "Revisionary Endings: Pam Gems's *Aunt Mary* and *Camille.*" In *Making a Spectacle: Feminist Essays on Contemporary Women's Theatre,* ed. Lynda Hart, 103–17. Ann Arbor: University of Michigan Press, 1988.

Case, Sue-Ellen. "Classic Drag: The Greek Creation of Female Parts." *Theater Journal* 37 (October 1985): 317–28.

———. *Feminism and Theatre.* New York: Methuen, 1988.

Case, Sue-Ellen, and Jeanie K. Forte. "From Formalism to Feminism." *Theatre* 16 (Spring 1985): 62–65.

Cave, Richard Allen. *New British Drama in Performance on the London Stage: 1970–1985.* New York: St. Martins, 1988.

Cavell, Stanley. *Pursuits of Happiness: The Hollywood Comedy of Remarriage.* Cambridge, Mass.: Harvard University Press, 1981.

Charlton, H. B. *Shakespearian Comedy.* New York: Barnes and Noble, 1938.

Charney, Maurice. *Comedy High and Low: An Introduction to the Experience of Comedy.* New York: Oxford University Press, 1978.

Cixous, Hélène. "Aller à la mer," trans. Barbara Kerslake. *Modern Drama* 27 (December 1984): 546–48.

Cixous, Hélène, and Catherine Clément. *The Newly Born Woman,* trans. Betsy Wing, intro. Sandra Gilbert. Minneapolis: University of Minnesota Press, 1986.

Colie, Rosalie. *The Resources of Kind: Genre Theory in the Renaissance,* ed. Barbara K. Lewalski. Berkeley: University of California Press, 1973.

Conference of Women Theatre Directors and Administrators. *The Status of Women in the British Theatre,* 1982–83. London: 1984.

Congreve, William. *Letters and Documents,* collected and ed. John C. Hodges. New York: Harcourt Brace and World, 1964.

Cook, Albert. *The Dark Voyage and the Golden Mean: A Philosophy of Comedy.* New York: Norton, 1949.

Cornford, Francis MacDonald. *The Origin of Attic Comedy.* Cambridge: Cambridge University Press, 1934.

Corrigan, Robert W., ed. *Comedy: Meaning and Form.* San Francisco: Chandler, 1965.

Coss, Clare, Roberta Sklar, and Sondra Segal. "Notes on the Women's Experimental Theatre." In *Women in Theatre: Compassion and Hope,* ed. Karen Malpede, 235–44. New York: Drama Book Publishers, 1983.

Curb, Rosemary K. "Re/cognition, Re/presentation, Re/creation in Woman-Conscious Drama: The Seer, the Seen, the Scene, the Obscene." *Theatre Journal* 37 (October 1985): 302–16.

Davies, Andrew. *Other Theatres: The Development of Alternative and Experimental Theatre in Britain.* London: Macmillan, 1987.

Davis, Natalie Zemon. *Society and Culture in Early Modern France.* Stanford: Stanford University Press, 1975.

de Lauretis, Teresa. *Alice Doesn't: Feminism, Semiotics, Cinema.* Bloomington: Indiana University Press, 1981.

———. "Sexual Indifference and Lesbian Representation." *Theatre Journal* 40 (May 1988): 155–77.

———. *Technologies of Gender: Essays on Theory, Film, and Fiction.* Bloomington: Indiana University Press, 1987.

———, ed. *Feminist Studies / Critical Studies.* Bloomington: Indiana University Press, 1986.

DeMarinis, Marco. "Dramaturgy of the Spectator." *TDR* 31, no. 2 (Summer 1987): 100–114.

DeRitter, Jones. "The Gypsy, *The Rover,* and the Wanderer: Aphra Behn's Revision of Thomas Killigrew." *Restoration* 10 (Fall 1986): 82–92.

Diamond, Elin. "Brechtian Theory / Feminist Theory: Toward a Gestic Feminist Criticism." *TDR* 32, no. 1 (Spring 1988): 82–94.

———. "(In)visible Bodies in Churchill's Theatre." *Theatre Journal* 40 (May 1988): 188–204.

———. "Mimesis, Mimicry, and the 'True-Real.'" *Modern Drama* 32 (March 1989): 58–72.

———. "Refusing the Romanticism of Identity: Narrative Interventions in Churchill, Benmussa, Duras." *Theatre Journal* 37 (October 1985): 273–86.

Dolan, Jill. "The Dynamics of Desire: Sexuality and Gender in Pornography and Performance." *Theatre Journal* 39 (May 1987): 156–74.

———. *The Feminist Spectator as Critic.* Ann Arbor: UMI Research Press, 1988.

Donaldson, Ian. *The World Upside-Down: Comedy from Jonson to Fielding.* Oxford: Clarendon Press, 1970.

Dover, K. J. *Aristophanic Comedy.* Berkeley: University of California Press, 1972.

Dubrow, Heather, *Genre.* London: Methuen, 1982.

Duffy, Maureen. *The Passionate Shepherdess: Aphra Behn, 1640–89.* London: Jonathan Cape, 1977.

Dukore, Bernard R. "The Middleaged Bully and the Girl of Eighteen: The Ending They *Didn't* Film." *Shaw Review* 14 (September 1971): 102–6.

Dunn, Tony, and Howard Barker. "Take a Walk on the Wilde Side: Joint Manifesto for the Left on Cultural Politics in the Post-Thatcher Era." *Guardian*, 10 February 1986.

Du Plessis, Rachel Blau. *Writing beyond the Ending: Narrative Strategies of Twentieth-Century Women Writers.* Bloomington: Indiana University Press, 1985.

Edwall, Glenace. "Women's Friendship: Theory, Data, and Implications for the Social Sciences." Paper presented at the National Women's Studies Association Annual Conference, Minneapolis, June 1988.

Edwards, Lee R. *Psyche as Hero: Female Heroism and Fictional Form.* Middlebury, Conn.: Wesleyan University Press, 1984.

Ellenberger, Harriett. "The Dream Is the Bridge: In Search of Lesbian Theatre." *Trivia* (Fall 1984): 17–59.

Elson, John. *Post-War British Theatre.* London: Routledge and Kegan Paul, 1976.

Erickson, Peter. "Sexual Politics and Social Structure in *As You Like It.*" *Massachusetts Review* 23 (Spring 1982): 65–83.

Feibelman, James. *In Praise of Comedy: A Study in Its Theory and Practice.* New York: Macmillan, 1939.

Féral, Josette. "Writing and Displacement: Women in Theatre," trans. Barbara Kerslake. *Modern Drama* 27 (December 1984): 549–63.

Flynn, Elizabeth A., and Patrocinio P. Schweickart, eds. *Gender and Reading: Essays on Readers, Texts, and Contexts.* Baltimore: Johns Hopkins University Press, 1986.

Forte, Jeanie. "Realism, Narrative, and the Feminist Playwright—A Problem of Reception." *Modern Drama* 32 (March 1989): 115–27.

———. "Women's Performance Art: Construction of the Social Subject." Presentation at "New Languages for the Stage" Conference, Lawrence, Kans., 28 October 1988.

———. "Women's Performance Art: Feminism and Postmodernism." *Theatre Journal* 40 (May 1988): 217–35.

Fraser, Antonia. *The Weaker Vessel.* New York: Knopf, 1984.

Freedman, Barbara. "Frame-Up: Feminism, Psychoanalysis, Theatre." *Theatre Journal* 40 (October 1988): 375–97.

French, Marilyn. *Shakespeare's Division of Experience.* New York: Summit Books, 1981.

Frye, Northrop. *Anatomy of Criticism.* Princeton: Princeton University Press, 1957.

———. *The Myth of Deliverance: Reflections on Shakespeare's Problem Comedies.* Toronto: University of Toronto Press, 1983.

———. *A Natural Perspective: The Development of Shakespearian Comedy and Romance.* New York: Columbia University Press, 1965.

Fujimura, Thomas. *The Restoration Comedy of Wit.* New York: Barnes and Noble, 1952.

Gagnier, Reginia. "Between Women: A Cross-Class Analysis of Status and Anarchic Humor." In *Last Laughs*, ed. Barreca, 135–48.

Gallagher, Catherine. "Who Was That Masked Woman? The Prostitute and the Playwright in the Comedies of Aphra Behn." In *Last Laughs,* ed. Barreca, 23–42.

Garber, Marjorie. *Coming of Age in Shakespeare.* London: Methuen, 1981.

Gardiner, Judith Kegan. "Aphra Behn: Sexuality and Self-Respect." *Women's Studies* 7 (1980): 67–78.

Gardner, Helen. "Happy Endings: Literature, Misery, and Joy." *Encounter* 57, no. 2 (August 1981): 39–51.

Gardner, Lyn. "The Naked Critic." *Plays and Players,* April 1986, 6–7.

Garner, Shirley Nelson. *"A Midsummer Night's Dream:* 'Jack shall have Jill; / Nought shall go ill.'" *Women's Studies* 9 (1981): 47–63.

Gilbert, Sandra M. "Soldier's Heart: Literary Men, Literary Women, and the Great War." *Signs* 8 (Spring 1983): 422–50.

Gilbert, Sandra M., and Susan Gubar. *The Madwoman in the Attic.* New Haven: Yale University Press, 1979.

Gohlke, Madelon. "'All that is spoke is marred': Language and Consciousness in *Othello.*" *Women's Studies* 9 (1982): 157–75.

Gooch, Steve. *All Together Now: An Alternative View of Theatre and the Community.* London: Methuen, 1984.

Gordon, George. *Shakespearian Comedy and Other Studies.* London: Oxford University Press, 1944.

Gottlieb, Vera. "Thatcher's Theatre—or, After 'Equus.'" *New Theatre Quarterly* 14 (May 1988): 99–104.

Grene, Nicholas. *Shakespeare, Jonson, Molière: The Comic Contract.* London: Macmillan, 1980.

Griffiths, Trevor. "Transforming the Husk of Capitalism." *Theatre Quarterly* 22 (Summer 1976): 25–46.

Gruber, William. "The Polarization of Tragedy and Comedy." *Genre* 13 (Fall 1980): 259–74.

Hanna, Gillian. "Waiting for Spring to Come Again: Feminist Theatre, 1978 and 1989." Interview by Lizbeth Goodman. *New Theatre Quarterly* 6 (February 1990): 43–56.

Hayes, Catherine. "Up to Now." In *Women and Theatre,* ed. Todd, 75–81.

Hayman, Carole. *City Limits,* 30 April–6 May 1982.

Heilman, Robert. *The Ways of the World: Comedy and Society.* Seattle: University of Washington Press, 1978.

Henriques, Julian, Wendy Hollway, Cathy Irwin, Couze Venn, and Valerie Walkerdine. *Changing the Subject: Psychology, Social Regulations, and Subjectivity.* London: Methuen, 1984.

Hernadi, Paul. *Beyond Genre: New Directions in Literary Classification.* Ithaca: Cornell University Press, 1972.

Holland, Norman. *The First Modern Comedies: The Significance of Etherege, Wycherley, and Congreve.* Cambridge, Mass.: Harvard University Press, 1959.

Holland, Peter. *The Ornament of Action: Text and Performance in Restoration Comedy.* Cambridge: Cambridge University Press, 1979.

Hollway, Wendy. "Gender Difference and the Production of Subjectivity." In *Changing the Subject,* Henriques et al., 227–63.

Holroyd, Michael, ed. *The Genius of Shaw: A Symposium.* New York: Holt, Rinehart, and Winston, 1979.

Hume, Robert D. *The Development of English Drama in the Late Seventeenth Century.* Oxford: Clarendon Press, 1976.

Irigaray, Luce. "Cose Fan Tutti." In *This Sex Which Is Not One,* trans. Catherine Porter and Carolyn Burke, 86–105. Ithaca: Cornell University Press, 1985.

Iser, Wolfgang. "The Art of Failure: The Stifled Laugh in Beckett's Theatre." In *Bucknell Review: Theories of Reading, Looking, Listening,* ed. Harry R. Garvin. Lewisburg, Pa.: Bucknell University Press, 1981.

Itzin, Catherine. *Stages in the Revolution: Political Theatre in Britain since 1968.* London: Methuen, 1980.

Jardine, Lisa. Paper presented at the MLA Convention, San Francisco, December 1987.

———. "'The Moor, I know his trumpet': Problems with Some New Historicist Readings of Shakespearean Female Figures." Paper presented at the World Shakespeare Congress, West Berlin, April 1986.

———. *Still Harping on Daughters: Women and Drama in the Age of Shakespeare.* Sussex: Harvester Press, 1983.

Jellicoe, Ann. *Community Plays: How to Put Them On.* London: Methuen, 1987.

———. *Some Unconscious Influences in the Theatre.* Judith Wilson Lecture, 1967. Cambridge: Cambridge University Press, 1967.

Kahn, Coppélia. *Man's Estate: Masculine Identity in Shakespeare.* Berkeley: University of California Press, 1981.

Kaplan, E. Ann. *Women and Film: Both Sides of the Camera.* New York: Methuen, 1983.

Kaul, A. N. *The Action of English Comedy: Studies in the Encounter of Abstraction and Experience from Shakespeare to Shaw.* New Haven: Yale University Press, 1970.

Kennard, Jean. "Convention Coverage; or, How to Read Your Own Life." *New Literary History* 13 (Autumn 1981): 69–88.

Kern, Edith. *The Absolute Comic.* New York: Columbia University Press, 1980.

Kerr, Walter. *Tragedy and Comedy.* New York: Simon and Schuster, 1967.

Keyssar, Helene. "The Dramas of Caryl Churchill: The Politics of Possibility." *Massachusetts Review* 24 (Spring 1983): 198–216.

———. *Feminist Theatre.* New York: Grove, 1985.

Kimbrough, Robert. "Androgyny Seen through Shakespeare's Plays." *Shakespeare Quarterly* 33 (Spring 1982): 17–33.

Kiniry, Malcolm. "Jacobean Comedy and the Inquisitive Grasp." In *Comedy: New Perspectives,* ed. Maurice Charney, 45–57. New York: New York Literary Forum, 1978.

Knights, L. C. "Notes on Comedy." In *Comedy: Meaning and Form,* ed. Corrigan, 181–91.

Kolodny, Annette. "Dancing through the Minefield: Some Observations on the

Theory, Practice, and Politics of a Feminist Literary Criticism." *Feminist Studies* 6 (Spring 1980): 1–25.

———. "A Map for Rereading; or, Gender and the Interpretation of Literary Texts." *New Literary History* 11 (Spring 1980): 451–67.

Langdell, Cheri Davis. "Aphra Behn and Sexual Politics: A Dramatist's Discourse with Her Audience." In *Drama, Sex, and Politics,* ed. James Redmond, 109–28. Vol. 7 in *Themes in Drama.* Cambridge: Cambridge University Press, 1985.

Langer, Susanne. "The Comic Rhythm." In *Comedy: Meaning and Form,* ed. Corrigan, 119–40.

Lavender, Andy. "Theatre in Crisis: Conference Report, December 1988." *New Theatre Quarterly* 5 (August 1989): 210–16.

Lavery, Bryony. "But Will Men Like It? or, Living as a Feminist Writer without Committing Murder." In *Women and Theatre,* ed. Todd, 24–32.

Lehmann, Benjamin. "Comedy and Laughter." In *Comedy: Meaning and Form,* ed. Corrigan, 163–78.

Lenz, Carolyn Ruth Swift, Gayle Greene, and Carol Thomas Neely, eds. *The Woman's Part: Feminist Criticism of Shakespeare.* Urbana: University of Illinois Press, 1980.

Levin, Harry. *Playboys and Killjoys: An Essay on the Theory and Practice of Comedy.* New York: Oxford University Press, 1987.

Lewis, Jane. "The Debate on Sex and Class." *New Left Review* 149 (January/ February 1985): 108–20.

Link, Frederick. *Aphra Behn.* New York: Twayne, 1968.

Little, Judy. *Comedy and the Woman Writer: Woolf, Spark, and Feminism.* Lincoln: University of Nebraska Press, 1983.

Lynch, Kathleen. Introduction to *The Way of the World,* by William Congreve. Lincoln: University of Nebraska Press, 1965.

MacCary, W. Thomas. *Friends and Lovers: The Phenomenology of Desire in Shakespearean Comedy.* New York: Columbia University Press, 1985.

McCollom, William G. *The Divine Average.* Cleveland: Case Western Reserve University Press, 1971.

McDonald, Margaret Lamb. *The Independent Woman in the Restoration Comedy of Manners.* Salzburg: Institut für Englische Sprache und Literatur, 1976.

McFadden, George. *Discovering the Comic.* Princeton: Princeton University Press, 1982.

McGrath, John. *A Good Night Out.* London: Methuen, 1981.

McKewin, Carole. "Counsels of Gall and Grace: Intimate Conversations between Women in Shakespeare's Plays." In *The Woman's Part,* ed. Lenz et al., 117–32.

Maitland, Sara. *Vesta Tilley.* London: Virago, 1986.

Mander, Raymond, and Joe Mitchenson. *Theatrical Companion to Maugham.* New York: Macmillan, 1955.

———. *Theatrical Companion to Shaw: A Pictorial Record of the First Performances of the Plays of George Bernard Shaw.* London: Rockliff, 1951. Reprint, Folcroft Library Editions, 1971.

Markley, Robert. *Two-Edg'd Weapons: Style and Ideology in the Comedies of Etherege, Wycherley, and Congreve*. Oxford: Clarendon Press, 1985.

Mendelson, Sara Heller. *The Mental World of Stuart Women: Three Studies*. Brighton: Harvester Press, 1987.

Meredith, George. "An Essay on Comedy." In *Comedy*, ed. Sypher, 3–57.

Merrill, Lisa. "Feminist Humor: Rebellious and Self-Affirming." In *Last Laughs*, ed. Barreca, 271–80.

Miller, Nancy K. "Changing the Subject: Authorship, Writing, and the Reader." In *Feminist Studies / Critical Studies*, ed. de Lauretis, 102–20.

———. "Emphasis Added: Plots and Plausibilities in Women's Fiction." *PMLA* 96 (January 1981): 36–48.

———. *The Heroine's Text: Readings in the French and the English Novel, 1722–1782*. New York: Columbia University Press, 1980.

Moi, Toril. *Sexual / Textual Politics*. London: Methuen, 1985.

Montrose, Louis. "'The Place of a Brother' in *As You Like It*: Social Process and Comic Form." *Shakespeare Quarterly* 32 (Spring 1981): 28–54.

Morgan, Fidelis. *The Female Wits: Women Playwrights of the Restoration*. London: Virago, 1981.

Morgan, Ted. *Maugham*. New York: Simon and Schuster, 1980.

Morley, Sheridan. *"Steaming."* Broadway playbill, n.d.

Muir, Kenneth. "Congreve on the Modern Stage." In *William Congreve: Mermaid Critical Commentaries*, ed. Brian Morris, 133–54. London: Ernest Benn, 1972.

Musser, Joseph F., Jr. "'Imposing Naught But Constancy in Love': Aphra Behn Snares *The Rover*." *Restoration* 3 (Spring 1979): 17–25.

Neely, Carol Thomas. *Broken Nuptials in Shakespeare's Plays*. New Haven: Yale University Press, 1985.

———. "Constructing the Subject: Feminist Practice and the New Renaissance Discourses." *English Literary Renaissance* 18 (Winter 1988): 5–18.

Neufeld, James. "Indigestion of Widdow-hood: Blood, Jonson, and *The Way of the World*." *Modern Philology* 81 (February 1984): 233–43.

Nevitt, Roy. "Community Spirit." *Drama* 4 (1986): 11–14.

Nevo, Ruth. *Comic Transformations in Shakespeare*. London: Methuen, 1980.

Newman, Karen. "Portia's Ring: Unruly Women and Structures of Exchange in *The Merchant of Venice*." *Shakespeare Quarterly* 38 (Spring 1987): 19–33.

Newton, Judith, and Deborah Rosenfelt, eds. *Feminist Criticism and Social Change: Sex, Class, and Race in Literature and Culture*. New York: Methuen, 1985.

Nicoll, Allardyce. *The Theory of Drama*. New York: Benjamin Blom, 1966.

Note on *Steaming*. *International Herald Tribune*, 10 April 1986.

Novy, Marianne. *Love's Argument: Gender Relations in Shakespeare*. Chapel Hill: University of North Carolina Press, 1984.

Page, Malcolm. "The Serious Side of Alan Ayckbourn." *Modern Drama* 26 (March 1983): 36–46.

Palmer, John. *The Comedy of Manners*. London: G. Bell and Sons, 1913.

Park, Clara Claiborne. "As We Like It: How a Girl Can Be Smart and Still Popular." In *The Woman's Part*, ed. Lenz et al., 100–116.

Parten, Ann. "Re-establishing Sexual Order: The Ring Episode in *The Merchant of Venice.*" *Women's Studies* 9 (1982): 145–55.

Peters, Margot. *Bernard Shaw and the Actresses.* Garden City, N.Y.: Doubleday, 1980.

Playfair, Nigel. Selections from *The Story of the Lyric Theatre, Hammersmith.* London: 1925. Reprinted in *Congreve Comedies: A Casebook,* ed. Patrick Lyons, 229–31. London: Macmillan, 1982.

Polhemus, Robert. *Comic Faith: The Great Tradition from Austen to Joyce.* Chicago: University of Chicago Press, 1980.

Potts, L. J. *Comedy.* London: Hutchinson's University Library, 1948.

Powell, Jocelyn. *Restoration Theatre Production.* London: Routledge and Kegan Paul, 1984.

Pratt, Annis, with Barbara White, Andrea Loewenstein, and Mary Wyer. *Archetypal Patterns in Women's Fiction.* Bloomington: Indiana University Press, 1981.

Randall, Phyllis R., ed. *Caryl Churchill: A Case Book.* New York: Garland, 1988.

Rayner, Alice. *Comic Persuasion: Moral Structure in British Comedy from Shakespeare to Stoppard.* Berkeley: University of California Press, 1987.

Reinelt, Janelle. "Beyond Brecht: Britain's New Feminist Drama." *Theatre Journal* 38 (May 1986): 154–63.

———. "Feminist Theory and the Problem of Performance." *Modern Drama* 32 (March 1989): 48–57.

Remnant, Mary. Introduction to *Plays by Women,* ed. Remnant, vol. 6. London: Methuen, 1987.

———. Introduction to *Plays by Women,* ed. Remnant, vol. 7. London: Methuen, 1988.

Ritchie, Rob. *The Joint Stock Book: The Making of a Theatre Collective.* London: Methuen, 1987.

Roberts, David. *The Ladies: Female Patronage of Restoration Drama, 1660–1700.* Oxford: Clarendon Press, 1989.

Root, Robert L., Jr. "Aphra Behn, Arranged Marriage, and Restoration Comedy." *Women and Literature* 5 (Spring 1977): 3–14.

Rose, Jacqueline. "Introduction—II." In *Feminine Sexuality: Jacques Lacan and the école freudienne,* ed. Juliet Mitchell and Jacqueline Rose, trans. Jacqueline Rose. London: Macmillan, 1982.

Rowbotham, Sheila. *Woman's Consciousness, Man's World.* Harmondsworth: Penguin, 1973.

Rowbotham, Sheila, Lynne Segal, and Hilary Wainwright. *Beyond the Fragments: Feminism and the Making of Socialism.* London: Merlin Press, 1979.

Russo, Mary. "Female Grotesques: Carnival and Theory." In *Feminist Studies / Critical Studies,* ed. de Lauretis, 213–29.

Rutter, Carol. *Clamorous Voices: Shakespeare's Women Today,* ed. Faith Evans. London: Women's Press, 1988.

Sackville-West, Vita. *Aphra Behn: The Incomparable Aphra.* New York: Viking, 1928.

Salingar, Leo. *Shakespeare and the Traditions of Comedy*. Cambridge: Cambridge University Press, 1974.

Scouten, Arthur H., and Robert D. Hume. "'Restoration Comedy' and Its Audiences, 1660–1776." In *The Rakish Stage: Studies in English Drama, 1660–1800*, ed. Robert D. Hume. Carbondale: Southern Illinois University Press, 1983.

Shaw, Bernard. "Preface Mainly about Myself." In *Plays Unpleasant*, vol. 1 of *The Bodley Head Bernard Shaw*, 11–34. London: Max Reinhardt, 1931.

———. Preface to *The Theatrical "World" of 1894*, by William Archer. London: Walter Scott, 1895. Reprinted in *Shaw on Theatre*, ed. West, 41–53.

———. "The Problem Play—A Symposium." *The Humanitarian* 6 (May 1895). Reprinted in *Shaw on Theatre*, ed. West, 58–66.

———. *The Quintessence of Ibsenism*. 1913. Reprint. New York: Hill and Wang, 1957.

———. "Woman—Man in Petticoats." *New York Times Magazine*, 19 June 1927. Reprinted in *Platform and Pulpit*, ed. Dan H. Laurence, 172–78. New York: Hill and Wang, 1961.

Shershow, Scott Cutler. *Laughing Matters: The Paradox of Comedy*. Amherst: University of Massachusetts Press, 1986.

Silverman, Kaja. *The Acoustic Mirror: The Female Voice in Psychoanalysis and Cinema*. Bloomington: Indiana University Press, 1988.

———. "Histoire d'O: The Construction of a Female Subject." In *Pleasure and Danger: Exploring Female Sexuality*, ed. Carole S. Vance, 320–49. London: Routledge and Kegan Paul, 1984.

Smith, John Harrington. "Shadwell, the Ladies, and the Change in Comedy." *Modern Philology* 46 (August 1948): 22–33.

Soloman, Alisa. "Witches, Ranters, and the Middle Class: The Plays of Caryl Churchill." *Theater* 12 (Spring 1981): 49–55.

Spender, Dale. *Mothers of the Novel: One Hundred Good Women Writers before Jane Austen*. London: Pandora, 1986.

Stedman, Jane W. "From Dame to Woman: W. S. Gilbert and Theatrical Transvestism." In *Suffer and Be Still: Women in the Victorian Age*, ed. Martha Vicinus, 20–44. Bloomington: Indiana University Press, 1972.

Stephens, Judith. "The Compatibility of Traditional Dramatic Form and Feminist Expression." *The Theatre Annual* 40 (1985): 7–23.

Stevenson, Juliet. Letter to author, 20 July 1986.

Strelka, Joseph P., ed. *Theories of Literary Genre*. University Park: Pennsylvania State University Press, 1978.

Styan, J. L. *The Dark Comedy: The Development of Modern Comic Tragedy*. Cambridge: Cambridge University Press, 1968.

Sypher, Wylie, ed. *Comedy*. Garden City, N.Y.: Doubleday, 1956.

Taylor, John Russell. *The Second Wave: British Drama of the Sixties*. London: Eyre Methuen, 1978.

"Theatre in Thatcher's Britain: Organizing the Opposition." *New Theatre Quarterly* 5 (May 1989): 113–23.

Thurman, Judith. "Caryl Churchill: The Playwright Who Makes You Laugh about Orgasm, Racism, Class Struggle, Homophobia, Woman-hating, the British Empire, and the Irrepressible Strangeness of the Human Heart." *Ms.*, May 1982, 52–57.

Todd, Susan, ed. *Women and Theatre: Calling the Shots.* London: Faber and Faber, 1984.

Torrance, Robert M. *The Comic Hero.* Cambridge, Mass.: Harvard University Press, 1978.

Toth, Emily. "Female Wits." *The Massachusetts Review* 22 (Winter 1981): 783–93.

Trilling, Diana. "The Liberated Heroine." *The Partisan Review* 45 (1978): 501–22.

Truss, Lynne. "A Fair Cop." *Plays and Players,* January 1984, 8–10.

Turco, Alfred, Jr. *"The Philanderer:* Shaw's Poignant Romp." In *Shaw: The Neglected Plays,* ed. Alfred Turco, Jr., 47–62. University Park: Pennsylvania State University Press, 1987.

Turner, Victor. *From Ritual to Theatre: The Human Seriousness of Play.* New York: Performing Arts Journal Publishers, 1982.

———. *Process, Performance, and Pilgrimage: A Study in Comparative Symbology.* New Delhi: Concept Publishing Co., 1979.

Vance, Carole S., and Ann Barr Snitow. "Toward a Conversation about Sex in Feminism: A Modest Proposal." From "The Sexuality Debates." Special issue of *Signs* 10 (Autumn 1984): 126–35.

Vogt, Sally Peters. "Ann and Superman: Type and Archetype." In *Fabian Feminist,* ed. Weintraub, 46–65.

Walker, Nancy. "Do Feminists Ever Laugh? Women's Humor and Women's Rights." *International Journal of Women's Studies* 4 (January/February 1981): 1–9.

———. *A Very Serious Thing: Women's Humor and American Culture.* Minneapolis: University of Minnesota Press, 1988.

Wandor, Michelene. *Carry on, Understudies: Theatre and Sexual Politics.* London: Routledge and Kegan Paul, 1986.

———. Introduction to *Plays by Women,* ed. Wandor, vol. 1. London: Methuen, 1982.

———. Introduction to *Plays by Women,* ed. Wandor, vol. 4. London: Methuen, 1985.

———. *Understudies: Theatre and Sexual Politics.* London: Methuen, 1981.

Watson, Barbara Bellow. "The New Woman and the New Comedy." *Shaw Review* 17 (January 1974): 2–16.

———. *A Shavian Guide to the Intelligent Woman.* London: Chatto and Windus, 1964.

Weber, Harold. *The Restoration Rake-Hero: Transformations in Sexual Understanding in Seventeenth-Century England.* Madison: University of Wisconsin Press, 1986.

Weeks, Jeffrey. *Sexuality and Its Discontents: Meanings, Myths, and Modern Sexualities.* London: Routledge and Kegan Paul, 1985.

Weintraub, Rodelle, ed. *Fabian Feminist: Bernard Shaw and Women*. University Park: Pennsylvania State University Press, 1977.

Weir, Angela, and Elizabeth Wilson. "The British Women's Movement." *New Left Review* 148 (November/December 1984): 74–103.

Weisstein, Naomi, "Why We Aren't Laughing Anymore." *Ms.*, November 1973, 49–51, 88–90.

West, E. J., ed. *Shaw on Theatre*. New York: Hill and Wang, 1958.

Willis, Sharon. "Hélène Cixous's *Portrait de Dora:* The Unseen and the Unscene." *Theatre Journal* 37 (October 1985): 287–301.

Wilmut, Roger. *Didn't You Kill My Mother-in-Law? The Story of Alternative Comedy in Britain from the Comedy Store to Saturday Live*. London: Methuen, 1989.

———. *From Fringe to Flying Circus*. London: Methuen, 1980.

Wilt, Judith. "The Laughter of Maidens, the Cackle of Matriarchs: Notes on the Collision between Comedy and Feminism." *Women and Literature* 1 (1980): 173–96.

Winston, Mathew. "The Incoherent Self in Contemporary Comedy." *Modern Drama* 29 (September 1986): 388–402.

Woodcock, George. *The Incomparable Aphra*. London: TV Boardman and Co., 1948.

Woodruff, Graham. "Community, Class, and Control: A View of Community Plays." *New Theatre Quarterly* 5 (November 1989): 370–73.

Zagarell, Sandra A. "Narrative of Community: The Identification of a Genre." *Signs* 13 (Spring 1988): 498–527.

Zeitlin, Froma. "Playing the Other: Theater, Theatricality, and the Feminine in Greek Drama." *Representations* 11 (Summer 1985): 63–94.

———. "Travesties of Gender and Genre in Aristophanes' *Thesmophoriasouzae*." *Critical Inquiry* 8 (Winter 1981): 301–28.

Zelenak, Michael. "Philandering with Shaw: GBS 'Made in America.'" *Theater* 14, no. 3 (Summer/Fall 1983): 72–76.

Zimbardo, Rose. *A Mirror to Nature: Transformations in Drama and Aesthetics, 1660–1732*. Lexington: University of Kentucky Press, 1986.

**Reviews**

Armistead, Claire. Review of Aphra Behn's *The Rover* at the RSC. *Financial Times*, 9 November 1987. In *London Theatre Record*, 5–18 November 1987, 1443.

———. Review of Sharmon MacDonald's *When I Was a Girl, I Used to Scream and Shout . . .* at the Whitehall. *Financial Times*, 10 December 1986. In *London Theatre Record*, 3–31 December 1986, 1366.

Asquith, Ros. Review of Pam Gems's *Loving Women*. *City Limits*, 10 February 1984. In *London Theatre Record*, 30 January–12 February 1984, 68.

Barber, John. Review of Caryl Churchill's *Top Girls*. *Daily Telegraph*. In *London Theatre Record*, 29 January–11 February 1983, 82.

———. "But is Porn to Blame?" Review of Sarah Daniels's *Masterpieces*. *Daily*

*Telegraph*, 12 October 1983. In *London Theatre Record*, 8–21 October 1983, 878.

———. Review of Doug Lucie's *Progress. Daily Telegraph*, 14 February 1986. In *London Theatre Record*, 12–25 February 1986, 149.

———. Review of Louise Page's *Golden Girls. Daily Telegraph*, 30 April 1985. In *London Theatre Record*, 24 April–7 May 1985, 154.

———. Review of Shakespeare's *As You Like It* at the RSC. *Daily Telegraph*, 25 April 1985.

———. Review of Sue Townsend's *Are You Sitting Comfortably? Daily Telegraph*, 13 February 1986. In *London Theatre Record*, 29 January–11 February 1986, 137.

Bartlett, Neil. Review of Olwen Wymark's *Nana* at the Mermaid. *Time Out*, 17 February 1988. In *London Theatre Record*, 29 January–11 February 1988, 154.

Billington, Michael. Review of Alan Ayckbourn's *Woman in Mind. Guardian*, 5 September 1986. In *London Theatre Record*, 27 August–9 September 1986, 954.

———. Review of Aphra Behn's *The Lucky Chance. Guardian*, 12 July 1984. In *London Theatre Record*, 2–29 July 1984, 589–90.

———. Review of Sarah Daniels's *Byrthrite. Guardian*, 26 November 1986. In *London Theatre Record*, 19 November–2 December 1986, 1312.

———. Review of Sarah Daniels's *Masterpieces. Guardian*, 12 October 1983. In *London Theatre Record*, 8–21 October 1983, 879.

———. Review of Jacqueline Holborough's *Dreams of San Francisco. Guardian*, 2 December 1987. In *London Theatre Record*, 19 November–2 December 1987, 1541–42.

———. Review of Julia Kearsley's *Under the Web. Guardian*, 24 November 1987. In *London Theatre Record*, 19 November–2 December 1987, 1513–14.

———. Review of Deborah Levy's *Heresies. Guardian*, 18 December 1986. In *London Theatre Record*, 3–31 December 1986, 1390–91.

———. Review of Sharman Macdonald's *When I Was a Girl, I Used to Scream and Shout . . .* at the Whitehall. *Guardian*, 11 December 1986. In *London Theatre Record*, 3–31 December 1986, 1364.

———. Review of Sue Townsend's *Bazaar and Rummage. Guardian*. In *London Theatre Record*, 6–19 May 1982, 239.

———. Review of Sue Townsend's *The Great Celestial Cow. Guardian*, 4 April 1984. In *London Theatre Record*, 26 March–8 April 1984, 246.

———. Review of Timberlake Wertenbaker's *Our Country's Good. Guardian*, 19 September 1988. In *London Theatre Record*, 9–22 September 1988, 1267.

Carne, Rosalind. Review of Deborah Levy's *Our Lady. Guardian*, 30 September 1986. In *London Theatre Record*, 10–23 September 1986, 1047.

———. Review of Louise Page's *Salonika. Financial Times.* In *London Theatre Record*, 15 July–11 August 1982, 420.

Chaillet, Ned. Review of Aphra Behn's *The Lucky Chance. Wall Street Journal*, 27 July 1984. In *London Theatre Record*, 2–29 July 1984, 588.

———. Review of Pam Gems's *Up in Sweden. Times*, 29 October 1980.

———. Review of Sue Townsend's *Womberang. Times*, 29 October 1980.

Christopher, James. Review of William Congreve's *The Way of the World* at the Young Vic. *Time Out*, 29 March 1989. In *London Theatre Record*, 12–25 March 1989, 357.

Connor, John. Review of Bryony Lavery's *Mummy*. *City Limits*, 26 March 1987. In *London Theatre Record*, 12–25 March 1987, 321.

Conway, Lydia. Review of Timberlake Wertenbaker's *Our Country's Good*. *What's On*, 16 August 1989. In *London Theatre Record*, 30 July–12 August 1989, 1048–49.

Cooke, Alistair. Review of Cambridge University Footlights Club's *The Last Laugh*. *Manchester Guardian*, 19 June 1959. As quoted in Wilmut, *From Fringe to Flying Circus*, 7.

Coveney, Michael. Review of Aphra Behn's *The Lucky Chance* and *The Rover*. *Financial Times*, 11 July 1984. In *London Theatre Record*, 2–29 July 1984, 587–88.

———. Review of William Congreve's *The Way of the World* at the Chichester Festival. *Financial Times*, 2 August 1984. In *London Theatre Record*, 30 July–12 August 1984, 677.

———. Review of Jacqueline Holborough's *Dreams of San Francisco*. *Financial Times*, 12 January 1987. In *London Theatre Record*, 19 November–2 December 1987, 1540–41.

———. Review of Bryony Lavery's *Calamity*. *Financial Times*, 26 January 1984. In *London Theatre Record*, 1–30 January 1984, 39.

———. Review of Deborah Levy's *Heresies*. *Financial Times*, 17 December 1986. In *London Theatre Record*, 3–31 December 1986, 1390.

———. Review of Shakespeare's *As You Like It* at the Manchester Royal Exchange. *Financial Times*, 13 January 1986. In *London Theatre Record*, 1–14 January 1986, 37.

———. Review of Sue Townsend's *Bazaar and Rummage*. *Financial Times*. In *London Theatre Record*, 6–19 May 1982, 239.

Cushman, Robert. Review of Sarah Daniels's *Masterpieces*. *Observer*. In *London Theatre Record*, 8–21 October 1983, 880—81.

Darvell, Michael. Review of William Congreve's *The Way of the World* at the Young Vic. *What's On*, 29 March 1989. In *London Theatre Record*, 12–25 March 1989, 358.

de Jongh, Nicholas. Review of Alan Ayckbourn's *Relatively Speaking*. *Guardian*, 11 April 1986. In *London Theatre Record*, 26 March–8 April 1986, 327.

———. Review of William Congreve's *The Way of the World* at the Young Vic. *Guardian*, 3 March 1989. In *London Theatre Record*, 12–25 March 1989, 359.

———. Review of Sarah Daniels's *Masterpieces*. *Guardian*, 10 January 1984. In *London Theatre Record*, 1–30 January 1984, 10.

———. Review of Clare McIntyre's *Low Level Panic*. *Guardian*, 17 February 1988. In *London Theatre Record*, 12–25 February 1988, 196.

———. Review of Olwen Wymark's *Nana* at the Almeida. *Guardian*, 20 November 1987. In *London Theatre Record*, 5–18 November 1987, 1481–82.

Duffy, Maureen. "Of Loyalty, Money, and Power." Review of Aphra Behn's *The Lucky Chance*. In *Times Literary Supplement*, 27 July 1984, 843.

Farrell, Joseph. "Tron Theatre, Glasgow: Celestial Cow." Review of Sue Townsend's *The Great Celestial Cow*. *Scotsman*, 16 March 1984.

Gardner, Lyn. Review of Jacqueline Holborough's *Dreams of San Francisco*. *City Limits*, 10 December 1987. In *London Theatre Record*, 19 November–2 December 1987, 1539.

———. Review of Deborah Levy's *Heresies*. *City Limits*, 1 January 1987. In *London Theatre Record*, 3–13 December 1986, 1389.

———. Review of Julia Schofield's *Love on the Plastic*. *City Limits*, 7 July 1987. In *London Theatre Record*, 18 June–1 July 1987, 791.

———. Review of Olwen Wymark's *Nana* at the Mermaid. *City Limits*, 18 February 1988. In *London Theatre Record*, 29 January–11 February 1988, 154.

———. Review of Susan Yankowitz's *Alarms*. *City Limits*, 12 February 1987. In *London Theatre Record*, 29 January–11 February 1987, 126.

Gold, Sylviane. "Theater: Exploring the Malaise Anglais." Review of Alan Ayckbourn's *Woman in Mind* in New York City. *Wall Street Journal*, 15 March 1988. In *New York Theater Critics' Reviews* 1988 49 (16 May 1988): 263.

Gordon, Giles. Review of Alan Ayckbourn's *Woman in Mind*. *Punch*, 10 September 1986. In *London Theatre Record*, 27 August–9 September 1986, 954–55.

———. Review of Aphra Behn's *The Lucky Chance*. *Spectator*, 21 July 1984. In *London Theatre Record*, 2–29 July 1984, 588.

———. Review of Caryl Churchill's *Serious Money*. *London Daily News*, 30 March 1987. In *London Theatre Record*, 26 March–22 April 1987, 371–72.

Grant, Steve. Review of Alan Ayckbourn's *Woman in Mind*. *Time Out*, 10 September 1986. In *London Theatre Record*, 27 August–9 September 1986, 955.

Gray, Dominic. Review of Timberlake Wertenbaker's *Our Country's Good*. *What's On*, 5 October 1988. In *London Theatre Record*, 10 September–12 November 1988, 1266.

Grove, Valerie. Review of Louise Page's *Beauty and the Beast*. *London Standard*, 20 December 1985. In *London Theatre Record*, 4–31 December 1985, 1255.

Hewison, Robert. "Speaking the Unspeakable." Review of William Congreve's *The Way of the World* at the Greenwich Theatre. *Sunday Times*, 18 March 1984, 35.

Hiley, Jim. Review of Jacqueline Holborough's *Dreams of San Francisco*. *Listener*, 10 December 1987. In *London Theatre Record*, 19 November–2 December 1987, 1540.

Hoyle, Martin. Review of Jude Alderson's *The Virgins' Revenge*. *Financial Times*, 1 March 1985. In *London Theatre Record*, 27 February–12 March 1985, 194.

———. Review of William Congreve's *The Way of the World* at the Young Vic. *Financial Times*, 23 March 1989. In *London Theatre Record*, 12–25 March 1989, 356–57.

———. Review of David Edgar's *Entertaining Strangers*. *Financial Times*, 17 October 1987. In *London Theatre Record*, 8–21 October 1987, 1319.

———. Review of Louise Pages's *Golden Girls*. *Financial Times*, 30 April 1985. In *London Theatre Record*, 24 April–7 May 1985, 400.

————. Review of Timberlake Wertenbaker's *Our Country's Good*. *Financial Times*, 12 August 1989. In *London Theatre Record*, 30 July–12 August 1989, 1046.

Hurren, Kenneth. "Home and Colonial." Review of Caryl Churchill's *Cloud Nine*. *What's on in London*, 6 April 1979, 34.

————. Review of William Congreve's *The Way of the World* at the Chichester Festival. *Mail on Sunday*, 5 August 1984. In *London Theatre Record*, 30 July–2 August 1984, 679.

————. Review of Jonathan Gems's *Susan's Breasts*. *Mail on Sunday*, 26 May 1985. In *London Theatre Record*, 8–21 May 1985, 474.

————. Review of Doug Lucie's *Progress*. *Mail on Sunday*, 23 February 1986. In *London Theatre Record*, 12–25 February 1986, 151.

Jenkins, Peter. "Sex Puzzle." Review of Caryl Churchill's *Cloud Nine*. *Spectator*, 7 April 1979.

Kellaway, Kate. Review of Timberlake Wertenbaker's *Our Country's Good*. *Observer*, 18 September 1988. In *London Theatre Record*, 9–22 September 1988, 1265.

Kemp, Peter. Review of Alan Ayckbourn's *A Small Family Business*. *Independent*, 8 June 1987. In *London Theatre Record*, 4–17 June 1987, 714.

————. Review of William Congreve's *The Way of the World* at the Young Vic. *Independent*, 24 March 1989. In *London Theatre Record*, 12–25 March 1989, 359–60.

Khan, Naseem. Review of Aphra Behn's *The Lucky Chance*. *New Statesman*, 20 July 1984. In *London Theatre Record*, 2–29 July 1984, 589.

King, Francis. Review of Aphra Behn's *The Lucky Chance*. *New Statesman*, 20 July 1984. In *London Theatre Record*, 2–29 July 1984, 590–91.

————. Review of William Congreve's *The Way of the World* at the Chichester Festival. *Sunday Telegraph*, 5 August 1984. In *London Theatre Record*, 30 July–12 August 1984, 680.

————. Review of Jonathan Gems's *Susan's Breasts*. *Sunday Telegraph*, 26 May 1985. In *London Theatre Record*, 8–21 May 1985, 474.

————. "Characters Next Door." Review of Sue Townsend's *The Great Celestial Cow*. *Sunday Telegraph*, 8 April 1984. In *London Theatre Record*, 26 March–8 April 1984, 247.

Lawson, Mark. Review of Sarah Daniels's *Byrthrite*. *Independent*, 11 November 1986. In *London Theatre Record*, 19 November–2 December 1986, 1311.

McGarry, Peter. "Finding a New Sense to Love." Review of Caryl Churchill's *Cloud Nine*. *Coventry Evening Telegraph*, 3 March 1979.

McKenley, Jan. Review of Deborah Levy's *Our Lady*. *City Limits*, 2 October 1986. In *London Theatre Record*, 10–23 September 1986, 1047.

McKenzie, Susie. Review of Louise Page's *Salonika*. *Time Out*. In *London Theatre Record*, 15 July–11 August 1982, 419.

————. Review of Timberlake Wertenbaker's *The Grace of Mary Traverse*. *Time Out*, 31 October 1985. In *London Theatre Record*, 9–22 October 1985, 1055.

Masters, Anthony. "Congreve's World Is an Actor's Joy." *Times,* 28 July 1984, 20.

Merriott, John. Review of Aphra Behn's *The Rover* at the RSC. *Today,* 11 July 1987. In *London Theatre Record,* 5–18 November 1987, 1442.

Morley, Sheridan. Review of Aphra Behn's *The Lucky Chance. Punch,* 18 July 1984. In *London Theatre Record,* 2–29 July 1984, 589.

———. Review of Pam Gems's *Loving Women. Punch,* 22 February 1984. In *London Theatre Record,* 30 January–12 February 1984, 68.

———. Review of Doug Lucie's *Progress. Punch,* 26 February 1986. In *London Theatre Record,* 12–25 February 1986, 152.

Nathan, David. Review of Deborah Levy's *Heresies. Jewish Chronicle,* 26 December 1986. In *London Theatre Record,* 3–31 December 1986, 1390.

———. Review of Sharman Macdonald's *When I Was a Girl, I Used to Scream and Shout . . .* at the Whitehall. *Daily Mirror,* 11 December 1986. In *London Theatre Record,* 3–31 December 1986, 1363.

Nightingale, Benedict. Review of Alan Ayckbourn's *Way Upstream. New Statesman.* In *London Theatre Record,* 23 September–6 October 1982, 548.

O'Neill, Patrick. Review of Shakespeare's *As You Like It* at the Manchester Royal Exchange. *Daily Mail,* 10 January 1986. In *London Theatre Record,* 1–14 January 1986, 36.

Osborne, Charles. Review of William Congreve's *The Way of the World* at the Young Vic. *Daily Telegraph,* 23 March 1989. In *London Theatre Record,* 12–25 March 1989, 358.

Pascal, Julia. Review of Anne Devlin's *Ourselves Alone. City Limits,* 4 September 1986. In *London Theatre Record,* 27 August–9 September 1986, 933.

Radin, Victoria. Review of Alan Ayckbourn's *Woman in Mind. New Statesman,* 12 September 1986. In *London Theatre Record,* 27 August–9 September 1986, 953.

———. Review of Aphra Behn's *The Rover* at the RSC. *New Statesman,* 13 November 1987. In *London Theatre Record,* 5–18 November 1987, 1443.

———. Review of Marcella Evaristi's *Commedia. Observer.* In *London Theatre Record,* 26 March–8 April 1983, 238.

———. Review of Louise Page's *Real Estate. Observer,* 13 May 1984. In *London Theatre Record,* 7–20 May 1984, 382.

Ratcliffe, Michael. Review of Aphra Behn's *The Lucky Chance* and *The Rover. Observer,* 15 July 1984. In *London Theatre Record,* 2–29 July 1984, 588.

———. Review of William Congreve's *The Way of the World* at the Greenwich Theatre. *Observer,* 18 March 1984. In *London Theatre Record,* 12–25 March 1984, 214.

———. Review of Caryl Churchill's *Serious Money. Observer,* 29 March 1987. In *London Theatre Record,* 26 March–22 April 1987, 370–71.

———. Review of Deborah Levy's *Heresies. Observer,* 21 December 1986. In *London Theatre Record,* 3–31 December 1986, 1393.

———. "The Land of Hatchett Faces." Review of Shakespeare's *As You Like It* at the RSC. *Observer,* 28 April 1985.

Review of Spare Tyre's *You've Gotta Be Kidding*. *Portsmouth News*. Quoted in Spare Tyre publicity flier, n.d.

Rich, Frank. Review of Alan Ayckbourn's *Woman in Mind* in New York City. *New York Times*, 18 February 1988. In *New York Theater Critics' Reviews 1988* 49 (16 May 1988): 259–60.

Rissik, Andrew. Review of Clare McIntyre's *Low Level Panic*. *Independent*, 17 February 1988. In *London Theatre Record*, 12–25 February 1988, 198.

Shorter, Eric. Review of Louise Page's *Salonika*. *Daily Telegraph*. In *London Theatre Record*, 15 July–11 August 1982, 419–21.

———. Review of Julia Schofield's *Love on the Plastic*. *Daily Telegraph*, 6 July 1987. In *London Theatre Record*, 18 June–1 July 1987, 791.

Shulman, Milton. Review of Aphra Behn's *The Lucky Chance*. *Standard*, 11 July 1984. In *London Theatre Record*, 2–29 July 1984, 590.

———. Review of William Congreve's *The Way of the World* at the Young Vic. *Evening Standard*, 22 March 1989. In *London Theatre Record* 12–25 March 1989, 357–58.

———. Review of Jacqueline Holborough's *Dreams of San Francisco*. *Evening Standard*, 1 December 1987. In *London Theatre Record*, 19 November–2 December 1987, 1540.

———. "Cowed by Life in Leicester—And Guess Whose Fault It Is." Review of Sue Townsend's *The Great Celestial Cow*. *Standard*, 4 April 1984, 26.

Smith, Joan. Review of Alan Ayckbourn's *Woman in Mind*. *Sunday Telegraph*, 21 September 1986. In *London Theatre Record*, 27 August–9 September 1986, 962.

Spencer, Charles. Review of Pam Gems's *Aunt Mary*. *Plays and Players*, August 1982, 35.

———. Review of Clare McIntyre's *Low Level Panic*. *Daily Telegraph*, 17 February 1988. In *London Theatre Record*, 12–25 February 1988, 197.

———. Review of Timberlake Wertenbaker's *Our Country's Good*. *Daily Telegraph*, 12 September 1988. In *London Theatre Record*, 9–22 September 1988, 1265.

———. Review of Olwen Wymark's *Nana* at the Almeida. *Daily Telegraph*, 20 November 1987. In *London Theatre Record*, 5–18 November 1987, 1480–81.

Sutcliffe, Tom. Review of Louise Page's *Beauty and the Beast*. *Guardian*, 23 December 1985. In *London Theatre Record*, 4–31 December 1985, 1256–57.

Tinker, Jack. Review of William Congreve's *The Way of the World* at the Chichester Festival. *Daily Mail*, 2 August 1984. In *London Theatre Record*, 30 July–12 August 1984, 678.

———. "Good Chaotic Unclean Fun—Whatever It All Meant." Review of Caryl Churchill's *Cloud Nine*. *Daily Mail*, 30 March 1979, 3.

Tudor, Carol. Review of Jackie Kay's *Chiaroscuro*. *Spare Rib*, no. 165 (April 1986): 33.

Wandor, Michelene. Review of Sarah Daniels's *Masterpieces*. *Plays* 1 (March 1984): 33–34.

Wardle, Irving. Review of William Congreve's *The Way of the World* at the Chichester Festival. *Times*, 2 August 1984, 6.

————. Review of William Congreve's *The Way of the World* at the Greenwich Theatre. *Times,* 17 March 1984, 6.

————. "Four Drop-Outs from the Cat Race." Review of Pam Gems's *Dusa, Fish, Stas, and Vi. Times,* 2 February 1977.

————. Review of Shakespeare's *As You Like It* at the RSC. *Times,* 25 April 1985.

Warner, Marina. Review of Deborah Levy's *Heresies. Independent,* 18 December 1986. In *London Theatre Record,* 3–31 December 1986, 1391–92.

Warren, Roger. ".Odious Endeavours." Review of William Congreve's *The Way of the World* at the Chichester Festival. *Times Literary Supplement,* 17 August 1984, 918.

Woddis, Carole. Review of Jude Alderson's *The Virgins' Revenge. City Limits,* 8 March 1985. In *London Theatre Record,* 27 February–12 March 1985, 194.

————. Review of Aphra Behn's *The Rover* at the RSC. *City Limits,* 19 November 1987. In *London Theatre Record,* 5–18 November 1987, 1443.

————. Review of Sharmon Macdonald's *When I Was a Girl, I Used to Scream and Shout . . .* at the Whitehall. *City Limits,* 12 December 1986. In *London Theatre Record,* 3–31 December 1986, 1366.

# Index